U0017596

Ethnography
in China Today

A Critical Assessment
of Methods and Results

Ethnography in China Today:

A Critical Assessment of Methods and Results

Edited by

DANIEL L. OVERMYER

with the assistance of

SHIN-YI CHAO

❧ Yuan-Liou Publishing Co., Ltd.

Taipei, Taiwan, Republic of China, 2002

Ethnography in China Today : A Critical Assessment of Methods and Results

Editor — Daniel L. Overmyer
Assistant editor — Shin-Yi Chao

Copyright © 2002 by Yuan-Liou Publishing Co., Ltd.
All rights reserved.

ISBN 957-32-4604-X

Publisher — Yuan-Liou Publishing Co., Ltd.
Address — 7F-5, No.184, Sec. 3, Ding Chou Rd.,
          Taipei, Taiwan, R. O. C.
Tel — 886-2-23651212
Fax — 886-2-23657979
http://www.ylib.com
E-mail: ylib@ylib.com

Distributor — Lexis Book Co., Ltd.
Address — 10F-1, No.138, Sec. 2, Chin-Shan South Rd.,
          Taipei, Taiwan, R. O. C.
Tel — 886-2-23219033
Fax — 886-2-23568068
E-mail: Lexis@ms6.hinet.net

NT$700   US$25

This book is dedicated to Piet van der Loon,

a pioneer in the study of Chinese ritual theatre

CONTENTS

Contributors

DANIEL L. OVERMYER, Introduction..3

1. WANG CH'IU-KUEI, Chinese Ritual and Ritual Theatre 11

2. HOU JIE, Mulian Drama: A Commentary on Current Research and Source Materials .23

Studies in Chinese Ritual, Theatre and Folklore Series
A. Southwest China

3. CHEN YI-YUAN, The Drama of Redemption of Vows of the Living
   (Yangxi) in Sichuan: A Critical Review of Current Research...53

4. HSU LI-LING, Three Books on the Duangong Ritual of Jiangbei County,
   Sichuan by Wang Yue...67

5. JOHN LAGERWEY,
   a. The Altar of Celebration Ritual in Lushan County, Sichuan 75
   b. Duangong Ritual and Ritual Theatre in the Chongqing Area:
      A Survey of the Work of Hu Tiancheng 81

6. DAVID HOLM,
   a. A Review of the Celebration of the Bodhisattva Ritual of the Vernacular
      Priests of the Zou Lineage in Poji Township, Zhenxiong County, Zhaotong
      Region, Yunnan by Guo Sijiu and Wang Yong 109
   b. A Review of the Yangxi of Guizhou: The Theatrical Troupe of the Deng Lineage
      in Dashang Village, Limu Township, Luodian County by Huangfu Chongqing 117
   c. A Review of the Celebration of the Bodhisattva Ritual of the Han Chinese in
      Poji Township, Zhenxiong County, Yunnan by Ma Chaokai 129

B. Southwest China: Minorities

7. HO TS'UI-P'ING, Ritual Literalized: A Critical Review of Ritual Studies on the
   National Minorities in Guangxi, Guizhou, Hunan and Sichuan..................................135

8. LIU TIK-SANG, Ritual, Context, and Identity: The Lingmu Ritual of the
   Liangshan Yi People in Sichuan..157

9. DAVID HOLM, A Review of Pleasing the Nuo Gods in Cengong County,
   Guizhou 171

C. Eastern China

10. KENNETH DEAN, The Masked Exorcistic Theatre of Anhui and Jiangxi 183
11. PAUL R. KATZ, Recent Developments in the Study of Chinese Ritual Dramas:
    An Assessment of Xu Hongtu's Research on Zhejiang 199
12. ZHU QIUHUA, Achievements in the Study of the Tongzi Ritual Drama in Jiangsu.....231
13. BRIGITTE BAPTANDIER, Lüshan Puppet Theatre in Fujian...................................243
14. LI FENG-MAO, A Review of Ye Mingsheng's Study of the Lüshan Sect
    in Longyan, Fujian, and Its Rituals 257
15 POUL ANDERSEN, Taoist Ritual in the Shanghai Area 263

D. North China

16. DAVID JOHNSON, A "Lantern Festival" Ritual in Southwest Shanxi...........................287
17. FAN LIZHU, A Review of Minxiang: Civil Incense Worship in Liaoning,
    China by Ren Guangwei...297

Traditional Hakka Society Series

18. DANIEL L. OVERMYER, Comments on the Foundations of Chinese Culture in
    Late Traditional Times 313
19. DONG XIAOPING, The Dual Character of Chinese Folk Ideas about Resources:
    On Three Western Fujian Volumes in the Traditional Hakka Society Series..............343
20. TAM WAI-LUN, Local Religion in Southern Jiangxi Province: A Review of
    the Gannan Volumes in the Traditional Hakka Society Series....................................369

Contributors

POUL ANDERSEN, Seminar für Sinologie, Humboldt-Universität zu Berlin, Germany

BRIGITTE BAPTANDIER, Laboratoire d'Ethnologie et de Sociologie Comparative, Université de Paris X (CNRS), France

CHAO SHIN-YI 趙昕毅, Department of Asian Studies, University of British Columbia, Canada

CHEN YI-YUAN 陳益源, Department of Chinese Literature, National Chung-cheng University, Taiwan

KENNETH DEAN, Department of East Asian Studies, McGill University, Canada

DONG XIAOPING 董曉萍, Department of Chinese, Beijing Normal University, China

FAN LIZHU 范麗珠, Department of Sociology, Fudan University, China

HO TS'UI-P'ING 何翠萍, Institute of Ethnology, Academia Sinica, Taiwan

DAVID HOLM, Institute of Asian Languages and Societies, University of Melbourne, Australia

HOU JIE 侯杰, Department of History, Nankai University, China

HSU LI-LING 許麗玲, Section des Sciences Religieuses, École Pratique des Hautes Études, Paris, France

DAVID JOHNSON, Department of History, University of California at Berkeley, USA

PAUL R. KATZ, Institute of Modern History, Academia Sinica, Taiwan

JOHN LAGERWEY, École Pratique des Hautes Études, France

LI FENG-MAO 李豐楙, Institute of Chinese Literature and Philosophy, Academia Sinica, Taiwan

LIU TIK-SANG 廖迪生, Division of Humanities, Hong Kong University of Science and Technology, China

DANIEL L. OVERMYER, Department of Asian Studies, University of British University, Canada

TAM WAI-LUN 譚偉倫, Department of Religion, The Chinese University of Hong Kong, China

WANG CH'IU-KUEI 王秋桂, Institute of Anthropology, Tsing Hua University, Taiwan

ZHU QIUHUA 朱秋華, The Bureau of Culture, Lianyun Port, Jiangsu, China

The local customs here favor *nuo* 儺 [a form of exorcistic drama with masked performers]; the natives like to go barefoot with their hair loosened. Most often, *nuo* is a kind of incense burning, but during group worship, it is called *ma pi* 馬披. At the time of *ma pi*, the sound of gongs and drums is very loud. The first to arrive will receive blessings, or the so-called *kai shan* 開山 (mountain opening) gong. Chickens are killed for their blood in a ceremony called *jian sheng* 剪生 (cutting living things). Afterwards, a dance performance is staged where one can see ghosts and demons here and there like apparitions. Day and night the entire city basks in unreserved exhilaration.

. . .

From what we have discussed so far, we can see that almost every dramatic genre in the Jiangsu and Huai River region has its roots in *nuo* ritual.

> Zhu Qiuhua 朱秋華, "Achievements in the Study of the Tongzi Ritual Drama in Jiangsu."
> (See Ch. 12 below. The first quote is from a Qing author named Li Dou 李斗 (1764-1795); see note 4 of Ch. 12)

INTRODUCTION

Daniel L. Overmyer

The chapters of this book began as reports given at a conference held at the Chinese University of Hong Kong in May 1998, titled "Ethnography in China Today: A Critical Assessment of Methods and Results." This conference was organized by Professor Tam Wai Lun 譚偉倫 of Department of Religion and the Centre for the Study of Religion and Chinese Society of Chung Chi College at the Chinese University, John Lagerwey of the École Française d'Extrême-Orient (EFEO), and by the South China Research Centre of the Hong Kong University of Science and Technology, the Department of Religion (CUHK), and the Department of Anthropology (CUHK).[1] The thirty-two scholars who

---

1 The sponsors of this conference were: Chung Chi College, The Chinese University of Hong Kong; Institute of Chinese Studies (CUHK); Faculty of Arts (CUHK); South China Research Centre, The Hong Kong University of Science and Technology; Shih Ho-cheng Folk Culture Foundation, Taipei; and the Cultural and Scientific Service of the French Consulate, Hong Kong. Discussants of papers at the conference were Chuang Ying-chang 莊英章 of the Academia Sinica in Taipei, Myron Cohen of Columbia University, David Faure of Oxford University, David Holm of the University of Melbourne, David Johnson of the University of California, Berkeley, and Susan Naquin of Princeton University.

3

presented papers were from the China mainland, Hong Kong, Taiwan, the United States, France, Australia, Denmark and Canada. Their reports were critical reviews of books recently published in two series; the first, edited by Wang Ch'iu-kuei 王秋桂, of the National Tsing Hua University 清華大學 in Taiwan, is titled monograph series of "Studies in Chinese Ritual, Theatre and Folklore" (*Min-su ch'ü-i ts'ung-shu* 民俗曲藝叢書, Taipei: Shih Ho-cheng Folk Culture Foundation 施合鄭民俗文化基金會, 1993-). The sixty volumes of this series published by the time of the 1998 conference are based on texts and reports concerning local ritual and drama collected through fieldwork in thirteen provinces of China from Liaoning in the north to Guangdong in the south and Fujian in the southeast to Yunnan in the southwest. The researchers involved were local Chinese scholars guided by Professor Wang. This research has been supported by the Chiang Ching-kuo Foundation for International Scholarly Exchange (CCK Foundation) 蔣經國國際學術交流基金會 and the National Science Council 國家科學委員會, both of Taiwan. English abstracts of the first sixty volumes were published as a booklet by the Shih Ho-cheng Foundation in 1997, entitled "Studies in Chinese Ritual, Theatre and Folklore Series." The English translations of the titles of these volumes in the present book are taken from these abstracts.

The second series of books reviewed at the 1998 conference was the first five volumes of the Traditional Hakka Society Series, under the general editorship of John Lagerwey of the École Française d'Éxtrême-Orient (EFEO) in Paris, published in 1997. The many chapters of these books were written by local scholars about the history and customs of their home villages, with an emphasis on temple festivals and rituals of marriage and burial. These chapters began as reports given at prefecture-level conferences organized by Professor Lagerwey and such Chinese colleagues as Fang Xuejia 房學嘉 of Jiaying University 嘉應大學 in Guangdong, and Yang Yanjie 楊彥杰 of the Fujian Academy of Social Sciences 福建社會科學院. The editing of these reports emphasized clarity and completeness. The Hakka Society Series is co-sponsored by the EFEO and the International Society for Hakka Studies. Publication of its reports has also been supported by the Chiang Ching-kuo Foundation, together with the EFEO.

The present book includes twenty chapters selected from the conference reports, revised and edited for publication, together with this introduction and an introduction by Wang Ch'iu-kuei to the books in his series and the process that led to them. These chapters include reports on fifty-six volumes of the "Studies in Chinese Ritual Theatre and Folklore Series" and on the first seven volumes of the Hakka Society series. In addition, there is a review by Li Feng-mao 李豐楙 of a book in a new series edited by Wang Ch'iu-kuei, the "Collection of Traditional Chinese Ritual Texts" (Zhongguo chuantong keyiben huibian 中國傳統科儀本彙編) published in Taipei by the Hsin Wen-feng Publishing House 新文豐出版公司. There will be fourteen volumes in this series, all of which deal with texts and rituals of Daoist origin. The volume reviewed here is by Ye Mingsheng 葉明生 on the rituals and dramas of Lüshan 閭山 Daoism in Fujian province. It brings the total number of books reviewed here to sixty-four.

An important supplementary source for several of these reviews is articles in the journal Min-su ch'ü-i 民俗曲藝 (Studies in Chinese Ritual, Theatre and Folklore), also edited by Wang Ch'iu-kuei and published by the Shih Ho-cheng Folk Culture Foundation. Most of the reviews include references to other studies as well.

The present book is intended to inform the wider world of scholarship of this new Chinese research, which provides the most detailed information ever available about Chinese local culture, drama and religion. Together with the excellent studies of this dimension of culture by scholars in Taiwan,[2] and with a revived interest in this area by other China mainland scholars,[3] it represents a resumption of the folklore studies movement of the 1920s and 1930s that was interrupted by the war with Japan. These new reports may also be seen as a complement to the work of anthropologists, who until recently have not been able to conduct many field studies in China. As such, this research provides

---

2 For a detailed bibliography of studies by Taiwan scholars, see Lin Mei-rong 林美容, *Taiwan minjian xinyang yanjiu shumu* 臺灣民間信仰研究書目 (A Bibliography of Taiwanese Folk Religion, expanded edition, Taipei: Institute of Ethnology, Academia Sinica, 1997).

3 For a survey and bibliography of recent studies by China mainland scholars, see Daniel L. Overmyer, "From 'Feudal Superstition' to 'Popular Beliefs': New Directions in Chinese Studies of Popular Religion," paper presented at the International Conference on Religion and Chinese Society: The Transformation of a Field and Its Implications for the Study of Chinese Culture, the Chinese University of Hong Kong, May 29-June 2, 2000. To be published in *Cahiers d'Éxtrême-Asie*, 12 (2001).

fresh information for an understanding of the culture of the majority of the Chinese people.

In his introduction to the first volume of the Hakka Society Series, John Lagerwey writes:

> We too decided to concentrate our attention on Hakka rural society, and that for several reasons: first, inasmuch as at least 95% of the Chinese population traditionally lived in villages — the figures now cited, after 15 years of frenetic urbanization, still hover around 70% — it seemed to us evident that our search for the "real China" could only lead us to the countryside. Second, while massive social change has occurred in rural China since 1949, that change has not wiped out the "old China" to the extent it has in the cities: few are the functioning temples in urban China and even fewer the religious festivals. In the cities, therefore, there is literally nothing left of traditional society to observe.
>
> A third motive might be called the "antiquarian urge." Chinese rural society is now also beginning to undergo decisive change: a village cannot export a third of its population to coastal factories without being radically altered.
>
> . . .
>
> Now is, therefore, our "last chance" to interview the old men and women of China and learn what life was like "before." The reader will soon discover that much of what is described in the pages that follow belongs to the irrevocable past.[4]

This emphasis on the urgency of research in Chinese local culture is echoed in a statement by David Holm of the University of Melbourne cited in Chapter One of this volume written by Wang Ch'iu-kuei, under the category of "Timeliness." In this perspective what we have here is nothing less than a cultural salvage project that should be extended as quickly as possible to other areas of China before it is too late. The precious memories of those who still remember the old ways are fast disap-

---

4   In Fang Xuejia, ed., *Meizhou diqu de miaohui yu zongzu* 梅州地區的廟會與宗族 (Temple Festivals and Lineages in Meizhou), International Hakka Studies Association and École Française d'Extrême-Orient, 1996, pp. 2-3 of the English preface.

pearing. Traditional anthropological fieldwork based on long-term residence in local areas of course remains important, but in the meantime we must record what we can, because a whole cultural ecosystem is rapidly changing or disappearing before our eyes. The study of such change is also important, but first its baseline should be understood in as much detail as possible. As John Lagerwey comments,

> Academics may be better at supporting library work, and they may be more systematic and sophisticated in their fieldwork, but no "participant observer" can ever find his way in the halls of memory as precisely or as intimately as the "native sons" to whom it has been our privilege to listen each time we gather in conferences to report our findings.[5]

A basic theme in the books edited by Wang Ch'iu-kuei is the intimate relationship of ritual and drama, or better, drama as an aspect of ritual, dramatic performances offered to the gods to seek blessings and drive away harm, including many whose basic function is exorcism. In the West the pioneering study of this theme was "Les origines rituelles du théâtre chinois," by Piet van der Loon, published in 1977 in Volume CCLXV of the *Journal Asiatique*. A more recent study is *Ritual Opera, Operatic Ritual: "Mu-lien Rescues His Mother" in Chinese Popular Culture*, edited by David Johnson in 1989, and published by the Berkeley Chinese Popular Culture Project. In Japan excellent and detailed work in this area has long been done by Tanaka Issei 田仲一成, particularly in his *Chūgoku fukei engeki kenkyū* 中國巫系演劇研究 (Research on Chinese Shamanistic Theatre), (Tokyo: Tokyo Daigaku bunka kenkyūjo hōkoku, 1993). In 1997 Kristofer Schipper published an article based on No.13 in the *Min-su ch'ü-i ts'ung-shu* series edited by Wang Ch'iu-kuei, concerning the ordination of local Daoist priests in Guizhou province. The article is entitled "A Play about Ritual: The 'Rites of Transmission of Office' of the Taoist Masters of Guizhou (Southwest China)" in Dick van der Meij, ed., *India and Beyond: Aspects of Literature, Meaning, Ritual and Thought, Essays in Honour of Frits Staal* (London and New York: Kegan Paul International, in asso-

---

5   Fang Xuejia, ed., *Meizhou diqu*, pp. 3-4 of the English preface.

ciation with the International Institute for Asian Studies, Leiden and Amsterdam, 1997). In what follows this interrelationship of drama and ritual is explored first in the most widespread such tradition of all, that of the pious monk Mulian 目連 rescuing his sinful mother from purgatory. To do so he must vanquish many hostile forces with special powers granted him by the Buddha, so Mulian plays were easily incorporated into exorcistic rituals. A review of eleven volumes primarily concerned with Mulian begins the first section of this book, which deals with the volumes in the "Chinese Ritual, Theatre and Folklore Series." Reviews of these volumes then proceed by geographical areas, first "vernacular priest" ritual traditions in Southwest China,[6] the provinces of Sichuan, Yunnan, Guizhou and Guangxi. Next are studies of traditions of minority peoples in that same area, but also including Hunan.[7] There follow studies of evidence from Eastern China, here including Jiangxi, Anhui, Fujian, Zhejiang, Jiangsu and Shanghai with its surrounding area. Northern China is represented by studies based on fieldwork and materials from Shanxi and Liaoning.

The latter part of this book is devoted to reviews of volumes in the Hakka Society series, based on reports from Guangdong, Fujian and Jiangxi. Hence, it is a survey of recent ethnographic reports from every area of China except the far west. Almost all of these reports are based on a combination of field observation with studies of texts collected from the local areas investigated. In many of the studies edited by Wang Ch'iu-kuei entire texts of dramas are included, along with discussions of local geography, history and society, detailed descriptions of rituals, and in some cases musical scores. The reviewers note and summarize this material, and add their own comments and evaluations. Books in the Hakka Society series in general provide more detail about local geography, history and society, and add some information about economic activities as well. They also provide detailed descriptions of rituals, and

---

6 "Vernacular Priests" (*duangong* 端公) are local performers of rituals of petition and exorcism.

7 For the construction and history of distinctions between the Han Chinese and "minority peoples" or "nationalities," see Stevan Harrell, ed., *Cultural Encounters on China's Ethnic Frontiers* (Seattle and London: University of Washington Press, 1995). The evidence reviewed in the present book does not support clear distinctions between the Han and other peoples; there was much mutual influence.

excerpts from local written materials such as lineage genealogies and stone inscriptions, but do not include texts of ritual dramas.

The overwhelming impression one gains from reading this material is that local ritual traditions throughout China were or are very lively and dynamic, based on the principle of "praying for blessings and driving away harm" by a wide variety of actions, invocations and dramatic performances. This can be seen in *nuo* exorcism plays by masked performers representing gods and demons, in dramatic gestures and blood sacrifices by vernacular priests (*duangong*) to purify homes and communities, and the "leaping plays" performed by some minority peoples in the Southwest. David Johnson's report on Huang Zhusan 黃竹三 and Wang Fucai's 王福才 study of a Lantern Festival in Shanxi notes drumming, dancing, and invocations to over 500 gods (see Ch. 16 below). Books in the Hakka Society series repeatedly note rituals performed by spirit-mediums to heal illness and drive away harmful forces, and provide detailed descriptions of temple festivals that mobilized entire communities, even networks of communities, to honor their gods, renew the forces of life, and dispel harm. For me, all of this confirms in detail the argument of my 1980 article "Dualism and Conflict in Chinese Popular Religion" concerning the pervasive theme of struggle with hostile forces, and the implicit semi-dualistic world view that underlies it.[8]

There is also much interesting material in the volumes here reviewed concerning rituals to make and repay vows to the gods, funeral rituals and retrospective ceremonies to aid the dead, *feng shui* 風水, ancestor worship, and weddings, as well as other topics. At the social level we learn much about lineages, temple organization, village alliances and temple festivals as the "social glue" of an area because they regularly bring people together (see Tam Wai Lun's report, Ch. 20). We also learn of interactions between local traditions and those of the Daoist priests and Buddhist monks who are brought into communities for their ritual expertise. In this context, while the priests perform their own rituals, for the people they are potent aids in the perpetual struggle to "summon blessings and expel the crooked and perverse," as well as to placate the homeless dead.

---

8 This article was published as a chapter in *Transitions and Transformations in the History of Religions*, edited by Frank E. Reynolds and Theodore Ludwig, Leiden: E.J. Brill, 1980.

The comprehensive reports surveyed in this volume remind us anew, with more detail than ever before, of the actual worldview and values of the ordinary people of China, which are both dynamic and practical. We have here the basic values and symbolic culture of the great majority of the population; this is indeed, as I say in my own report below, "the foundations of Chinese culture in late traditional times." These values and activities of those at the demographic base of that culture are what has defined it and kept it together for many centuries; they provide the underlying identity of its people. This identity is first and foremost of those who maintain local ritual traditions, worship gods and ancestors, celebrate annual festivals, divine their fortunes from the space, time and phenomena around them, and struggle against harmful forces. These local traditions interacted with those of state approved versions of Daoism, Confucianism and Buddhism, but they remained the common base shared by all.

In sum, the materials discussed in this book provide an opportunity for a fresh understanding of Chinese culture, an understanding based on the lived experiences and values of its people. Next steps in such local research could include reports from north China provinces such as Hebei, Henan and Shangdong that are not dealt with here, ritual traditions in larger cities and their environs, and longer-term fieldwork in clusters of villages at the *xiang* 鄉 (township) level; what Dong Xiaoping 董曉萍 in Ch. 19 below calls "mid-level" research. We also need to know more about how ritual traditions are affected by the rapid economic and social changes that are taking place across China. Beyond all this is the need for systematic synthesis and analysis of all the new primary materials made available in the books reviewed here. Only with such analysis can the contributions of this material to an understanding of China be made clear.

Because of the different backgrounds and disciplines of the authors of these reviews, in this volume we have followed their preferences in style, annotation and romanization.

I

CHINESE RITUAL AND RITUAL THEATRE

Wang Ch'iu-kuei

From July 1991 until July 1996 I directed a research project entitled "Chinese Regional Theatre in Its Social and Ritual Context" funded by the CCK Foundation which supplied NT$21 million. This was supplemented by annual grants from the National Science Council of the Republic of China for two related projects: "Mulian Drama" and "Chinese Ritual and Ritual Theatre." The total NSC grants amounted to seven and a half million N.T. dollars. All in all, I spent well over one million U.S. dollars over a period of five years on three research projects which were actually treated as one. In all three projects, our main concern was theatre in which the performance serves a ritual function. Our basic idea was to treat theatre as an integral part of ritual and ritual as theatre. Together they form what might be called the "ritual performance."

My co-directors initially included P. van der Loon of Oxford, Jacques Pimpaneau of Paris, David Johnson of U.C. Berkeley, Chan Sau-yan 陳守仁 of the Chinese University of Hong Kong, and in Taiwan, Li Feng-mao 李豐楙 of the Academia Sinica, and Ch'iu K'un-liang 邱坤良 of the National Institute of Arts. John Lagerwey of the

EFEO in Paris, David Holm of Melbourne (formerly of Macquarie), Ken Dean of McGill and Yung Sai-hing 容世誠 of Singapore joined the project in 1992. The original plan was to organize several international research teams to conduct field work in as many sites as possible in mainland China. We soon found that it was not feasible. In the first place, team members were usually not free at the same time. Even when a team was finally organized and reached a field-site, it aroused so much suspicion that little could be done. I changed the strategy and started recruiting local researchers from Liaoning, Shanxi, Anhui, Hunan, Jiangsu, Jianxi, Zhejiang, Fujian, Guangdong, Guangxi, Sichuan, Guizhou and Yunnan. I spent more than one year training them. It took me an even longer time negotiating with officials of the Ministry of Culture to obtain an official letter of approval for a joint project to be undertaken by myself and the Association for the Study of Nuo Theatre 中國儺戲學研究會 of which all the local researchers were members. By the fall of 1992 I was able to build up a network of researchers in the thirteen provinces mentioned above. Whenever any of the co-directors went to any of the places to do field work they were assisted by competent local researchers. In January 1993 I called an international conference in Hong Kong to present the initial results of our project. Another international conference was held in May 1994 in Taipei. In it more and better papers were presented.

In December 1993, we published the first ten books in the monograph series "Studies in Chinese Ritual, Theatre and Folklore" 民俗曲藝叢書 as partial results of the project. Another ten followed in May 1994 and still another ten in November of the same year. In October 1995 we published another ten volumes. Ten more were added in July 1996 and another ten were published in November 1997. There are twenty more to be published. Of the sixty volumes already published, sixteen are the joint results of two other projects also funded by the CCK Foundation, namely "The Structure and Dynamics of Chinese Rural Society" directed by John Lagerwey, and "Ritual Theatre in China" directed by David Holm. It may be remarked in passing that printing costs (eventually it will amount to more than NT$12 million for the eighty books) were not included in our original budget. Funding for publication has had to come from other sources. The publisher, Shih Ho-cheng Folk Culture Foundation, of which I have been executive director since 1989, will have paid for one-third of the expenses. The proceeds from the sale of the books plus a supplementary grant from CCK Foundation will be enough to meet another third. I have been soliciting donations to cover the remaining one-third. As of now I'm still short of one and a half million N.T. dollars.

The eighty books in the monograph series "Studies in Chinese Ritual, Theatre and Folklore" can be divided into five categories: (1) field reports, (2) collections of primary sources, (3) play scripts or ritual texts or collections of the same, (4) monographs and (5) collections of research papers. I'll quote David Holm's description of the first category in which lies the main value of the series:

> For the fieldwork reports in the series, researchers concentrated on describing one particular kind of ritual in its original context. The emphasis in each study is on the description of an entire ritual sequence as actually performed in a genuine village setting, and no part of the proceedings is omitted as "unseemly." In presentation, the typical format of a monograph is a main text followed by various appendices. The main texts describe the locality, the performers and other participants, the deities worshipped, the ritual sequence, and other aspects of the performance. The appendices are often as lengthy as the main text, and present materials such as texts of ritual plays, ritual manuscripts, photographic illustrations, plans of the village and ritual area, and photographs of the *mudrās* used by the priests. In all respects, the aim is to provide the reader with ample and reliable information that is adequately contextualised. (Interim Review of the series submitted to the CCK Foundation in 1995, p. 4.)

Each of the rituals receives for the first time such detailed ethnographic study. Most of the rituals described were previously unknown to scholars.

So far Western studies of Chinese ritual have been limited to Taoist rituals. In Taiwan, Hong Kong or Southeast Asia where most Western scholars do their field work, rituals are accompanied by theatrical performances, but there rituals are performed in what is called the *neitan* 內 壇 or inner altar, which is usually indoors, while a theatrical troupe unrelated to the ritual troupe performs plays in what is called the *waitan* 外壇 or outer altar, which lies outdoors. By contrast, in most of the ritual theatre we have investigated, ritual and theatrical performances are done by the same ritual masters and their assistants in the same ritual area. Thus ritual and theatre are truly inseparable from each other. In the rituals under study we have also found that there are varying degrees of combinations of Taoism, Buddhism, Confucianism and shamanism. We also see interesting cases of the diffusion of Taoism or popular religion. For example, ritual texts originating in Jiangxi are used by priests of the Tujia 土家 minority in Guizhou, and deities originating in Fujian such as Chen Jinggu 陳靖姑 enter the pantheon of the Zhuang 壯 minority in Guangxi.

Another discovery is the regional variations of the same type of ritual theatre. Take *yangxi* 陽戲, for example. There are four variations in Sichuan alone and one in Guizhou. Again there are at least three variations of *qingtan* 慶壇 in Sichuan and one in Guizhou. The *yangxi* is performed to redeem vows formerly made to the deities, and *qingtan* has a celebrating nature. However, these are over-simplifications, and each performance of ritual is unique in its own way.

Scholars of oral and performing literature should be interested in the material preserved in the ritual tradition, which has been so tenacious that even the Cultural Revolution failed to disrupt it. One of my local researchers, Wang Zhaoqian 王兆乾 of Anhui, collected surviving manuscripts of Guichi *nuoxi* 貴池儺戲 plays. One of the plays, entitled *Chenzhou tiaomi* 陳州糶米 (a Baokong 包公 story), copied during the Guangxu period (1875-1908), is almost identical to a chantefable (*shuochang cihua* 說唱詞話) text of the same title printed during the Ming Chenghua 成化 reign (1465-1487). This chantefable is among the sixteen *cihua* uncovered from a tomb in Shanghai in 1976. Nothing similar has ever been found elsewhere. Several other Guichi *nuo* plays, notably *Xue Rengui zhengdong ji* 薛仁貴征東記 and *Hua Guan Suo* 花關索, also share general features and a number of identical lines with their *shuochang cihua* counterparts. For at least four hundred years, there has been a continuation of tradition unnoticed by all other people than the villagers who have carried it on. This is something worth looking into.

It is also interesting to note that some of the play scripts of Guichi *nuoxi* take the form of chantefable. The use of chantefable texts as play scripts can also be found in Anshun *dixi* 安順地戲 from Guizhou, *Guan Suo xi* 關索戲 from Yunnan and festival plays (*sai xi* 賽戲) from Shanxi.

So far, historians of Chinese theatre have based their studies mainly on printed texts edited by men of letters before publication. The ritual theatre has something much richer, more genuine and more diverse to offer. Moreover, the number of play scripts preserved in ritual theatre far exceeds that of all the printed texts available to us. There are over 250 different schools of regional theatre in China. In the fifties, the Institute of Theatre in each province collected manuscripts of all kinds of plays. Some of them were edited and published, as in Shanxi, Shenxi, Hunan, Guangdong, Guangxi and Fujian. But most were set to fire during the Cultural Revolution. Fortunately, those collected by the Institutes of Theatre represent only a small part of the whole theatrical tradition. A fairly good number of manuscripts has survived in each of the villages investigated by us. Many of the playscripts in each ritual theatre have been preserved. Where manuscripts are lost, reconstructions could sometimes be made from the memories of the ritual masters/actors. For example, so far we have collected eighteen manuscripts and reconstructed two oral texts (*kou-tu ben* 口吐本) of the Mulian drama from seven provinces. Eight have already been edited and included in the series. Several more will be published. These texts will make possible for the first time an adequate study of the Mulian drama, which is the most important and widespread of all Chinese ritual dramas. The results of our project also contribute to minorities studies (so far we have studied rituals of the Tujia, Miao 苗, Yi 彝, Zhuang, Gelao 仡佬, Maonan 毛南 and Zang 藏 minorities) as well as to the study of popular traditions such as Meng Jiangnü 孟姜女, Guan Yu 關羽, Guan Suo, Xue Rengui, Miao Shan 妙善, Huangshi nü 黃氏女 and others.

Our results include yet another series, namely the "Collection of Traditional Chinese Ritual Texts" 中國傳統科儀本彙編, of which one volume was published in 1996, nine are ready for publication, and four more are in preparation. Each volume is devoted to a particular *tan* 壇 or altar troupe and is divided into two parts. Part one describes the origins of a given *tan*, the group of priests associated with it, its rituals and their related manuscripts, the structure of the ritual arena, liturgical instruments, vestments and music. Part two consists of facsimile reprints of the liturgical manuscripts (in some cases printed texts) arranged according to the order in which they are used in actual performance. All the other materials used in the performance such as announcements (*biao* 表), statements (*wen* 文), talismans (*fu* 符), registers (*lu* 籙), memorials (*shu* 疏) and dispatches (*die* 牒) are reproduced in an appendix, and each book will be amply illustrated with photographs. This collection does not limit itself to Taoism but also includes studies of various troupes of popular Buddhism and shamanism. The whole series, when completed, will make possible for the first time a detailed comparison and evaluation of the diffusion and impact of Taoist and other ritual traditions across much of China.

Another series to be published is the "Compendium of Traditional Chinese Secret Manuals of Hand Gestures and Ritual Steps" 中國傳統訣罡秘譜彙編. Like the "Collection of Traditional Chinese Ritual Texts," it is the result of the three projects directed respectively by David Holm, John Lagerwey and myself. The SMC Publishing Inc. 南天書局 in Taipei has agreed to publish it. The first volume will be available soon.

Other publications resulting from the project include proceedings of two international conferences, four issues of a Newsletter reporting the state of the field, and several special issues in the journal *Min-su ch'ü-i* 民俗曲藝. Among them are five collections of research papers, one collection of field reports and one collection of Mulian plays.

The reasons we have been able to achieve such results are as follows:

1. Timeliness:

I'll quote again from David Holm's remarks in the "Interim Review" of the series "Studies in Chinese Ritual, Theatre and Folklore" and elaborate:

> China, like many other parts of the world, is currently undergoing a cultural mass extinction episode. Another important feature of the Ritual Theatre project therefore is its timeliness. China was of course closed to foreign researchers for many years, and even in the 1980's the kind of international collaboration between PRC, Taiwan

and Western scholars exemplified in this project would have been impossible. The inception in 1991 was almost perfectly timed to coincide with the end of the Ministry of Culture surveys [The "Eight Great Compendia (*ba da jicheng* 八大集成) of the indigenous performing arts], when many scholars who had participated in that project in the PRC were looking around for new opportunities to get their material published. For many genres of ritual theatre the project has come along at the last possible moment, as more and more of the older generation of 'old artists' are dying off every year, in many cases taking their relatively complete knowledge of ritual and performance traditions with them to the grave. With the new wave in China's modernization since 1990 or so, more and more indigenous genres are dying out as traditional communities are disrupted by the unbridled ferocity of 'market forces.' Were another project of this kind to be mounted in ten years' time, the results would be much poorer, and the historical continuities much harder to trace. Even as things are, many of the volumes in this series state explicitly that they are documenting a tradition that has already become fragmented. (p. 4.)

Since the early eighties, there has been an especially strong interest in the study of *nuo* 儺 drama and Mulian drama in the PRC. International conferences are held almost every year, each in a different locality. Most of our researchers had taken part in the drama survey and some in the music and dance surveys. The establishment of the Association for the Study of Nuo Theatre in November 1988 symbolized the government's full endorsement of ritual theatre studies, and central and local leaders of cultural and minority affairs were among the advisors to the Association. It was through Mr. Qu Liuyi 曲六乙, the president of the Association, that I eventually obtained the approval of the Ministry of Culture to carry on my project in the PRC.

2. Sufficient Funding

This enabled me to recruit at the same time researchers in the thirteen provinces mentioned above and in Singapore, as well as to hire editors and assistants in Taiwan. There was a period when we had forty local researchers and a twelve-member editorial team working together so that the results were reviewed, revised, edited and published with due speed. This encouraged the researchers to compete with each other in producing more and better results. Adequately supported, some of my co-directors and assistants were able to undertake fieldwork with local researchers in many sites, and to attend conferences held in various provinces in the PRC where special sessions were arranged for the discussion of important issues in current research. Sufficient funding also made it possible for me to call two international conferences so that local researchers could profit from comments and suggestions by other scholars. Invitation to such conferences was considered an honor for which local researchers would strive.

3. Good Communication:

Because the pilot project was funded by the CCK Foundation and the subject of study was at first interpreted as research on the "superstitions" of the people, we encountered a great deal of resistance in the PRC in the beginning. In July 1991, all my co-directors, Professor Li Yih-yuan 李亦園 and I went to Guangzhou to meet with Xue Ruolin 薛若琳, deputy director of the National Institute of Arts 中國藝術研究院, Huang Ying 黃穎, former vice minister of Minority Affairs, Qu Liuyi, president of the Association for the Study of *Nuo* Theatre and some local researchers including Tuo Xiuming 庹修明, from Guizhou, Gu Jianguo 顧建國 from Guangxi, Yu Yi 于一 from Sichuan, Zhu Jianming 朱建明 from Shanghai and Huang Jingming 黃鏡明 from Guangdong. At the two-day conference, though most local researchers expressed eagerness to join the project, the attitude of the leaders from Beijing was cordial but reserved. Nearly all my co-directors were pessimistic about the prospects of the project. They felt that without the blessing of the central government the project would go nowhere.

Mr. Huang Ying, however, told me in private that he would give me his support. I therefore decided then to start the project in Guizhou with the cooperation of Tuo Xiuming of the Guizhou Institute of Ethnography 貴州民族學院, which is beyond the control of the Ministry of Culture. Later all other local researchers except Huang Jingming also agreed to work for the project. However, at an international conference on *nuo* theatre held in October 1991 in Jishou 吉首, Hunan, they were forced to return the payments I offered them through one of my assistants who attended the conference. I went to Beijing in November of the same year to negotiate with officials from the Taiwan office of the Ministry of Culture and that of the State Department. I explained to them the scientific nature of the project, its significance and its goal. However, my request for official approval was denied. I had to make another trip to Beijing in March 1992. By that time the project in Guizhou had gone so well that it won the support of Mr. Wang Hengfu 王恒富, head of the Department of Culture of Guizhou province. Under pressure from the members of the Association for the Study of Nuo Theatre, Mr. Qu Liuyi submitted a petition to the Ministry of Culture for approval to work with me. Though formal approval was not forthcoming until February 1993, all my local researchers were free from harassment, and more people, including Xue Ruolin joined the project. At the same time, I have always kept direct communication with local researchers. I pay them and receive material from them directly so that there is neither exploitation nor censorship.

4. Correct Methodology

(1) Recruitment: Since the late eighties I have been collecting articles, monographs and collections of papers on Chinese ritual theatre published in the PRC. And, since 1989, when I took over from Ch'iu K'un-liang the editorship-in-chief of the journal *Min-su ch'ü-i*, I have been publishing contributions submitted by PRC scholars. With the help of Tuo Xiuming I published a double special issue entitled "Chinese Nuo Theatre and Nuo Culture" 中國儺戲儺文化專輯 (*Min-su ch'ü-i* 69/70) in January/March 1991. Before the project started I had either known by reputation or corresponded with nearly all major researchers of ritual theatre in the PRC. Of them I recruited only those who were experienced in fieldwork and had at their disposal first-hand material. I chose the thirteen provinces because I happened to find local researchers whom I believed I could work with there.

(2) Training: Before I started the project, I had asked two anthropologists, Lu Li-cheng 呂理政 and Wang Sung-shan 王嵩山, to design for me a "memorandum for field research" in which detailed instruction is given regarding the writing of a field report. It was my idea that context was of paramount importance

and that whatever was reported had to be specific. After much discussion the memorandum was written by Wang Sung-shan and revised by Lu Li-cheng and myself. Together with a Chinese translation of P. van der Loon's "Les origines rituelle du théâtre chinois" (*Journal Asiatique* 265 [1977], 141-168) and other reading material, the memorandum was distributed to all local researchers.

Afterwards, to work with them, David Johnson was sent to Shanxi, Jacques Pimpaneau to Jiangxi, Wang T'ien-lin 王天麟 (one of my senior assistants) to Hunan, Anhui and Guangxi, Chan Sau-yan to Guangdong, Piet van der Loon to Fujian, Li Feng-mao to Sichuan and Ch'iu K'un-liang to Yunnan. Guizhou remained my main "territory" though I also made occasional trips to Yunnan, Sichuan, Guangxi, Guangdong, Fujian, Zhejiang and Jiangsu to check on the progress of the project. Some of my co-directors and I also tried to attend every relevant international conference held in the PRC, where we gathered project members for special sessions. Drafts of field reports started to come in a year after the project started. My two senior assistants and I read them carefully, offered detailed comments and sent them back for revision. This process was often repeated more than once. It took us a long time to rid local researchers of their intellectual arrogance (that they are superior to the old artists and ritual masters) and their ideological prejudice (that rituals are superstitious). Style sheets for field reports and critical editions of play scripts and ritual texts as well as detailed instruction regarding videotaping, photographing and music transcription were provided. But it took much practice before local researchers gradually learnt to meet my requirements. After I was satisfied with a revised draft, it was given to a copy editor who would make further corrections or ask for more information. Often another revision was required. While asking local researchers to revise their reports I would send them relevant articles or books so that they had examples to follow. All researchers wrote me letters asking various questions. Besides answering such questions, I also sent them regularly form letters pointing out common defects in their reports.

(3) Requirements: What I require of each researcher is that he or she write an objective and detailed report on a particular ritual performed on a particular occasion by a particular troupe in a particular time at a particular place, providing as much as possible the historical, geographical, cultural and social context. Such a report should be supported by a videotape of the actual performance where possible or at least by ample photographic illustrations, and photocopies of all ritual texts and play scripts used in the performance. To win full collaboration of the local researchers, I have offered them adequate financial aid, information and material otherwise unavailable to them and full credit for their work, which I publish as soon as possible once it meets my requirements. On their part, they have to win the full cooperation of their subjects, especially the ritual masters.

(4) Cultivation of a trusting relationship: This is the key to successful fieldwork. The nature of the relationship determines the nature of information and material obtained. During the Cultural Revolution, many ritual masters were persecuted. As a result, they were suspicious of any outsiders. One of my Sichuan researchers, Mr. Hu Tiancheng 胡天成, told me at the beginning of his fieldwork that the vernacular priest (*duangong* 端公) he wished to interview refused to talk to him. I told him that he had to either find a way or give up his project. Mr. Hu first befriended the priest's assistant, who would then tell him when and where the priest was to perform a ritual. Mr. Hu would be there every time socializing with the patron even before the priest arrived. He would then attend the whole ritual. For half a year Mr. Hu refrained from asking any questions. Then it happened that the priest was giving a party for his son's wedding. Though uninvited, Mr. Hu went to it with a generous gift (bought with project funding). Greetings were exchanged. The next time the priest saw Mr. Hu at a ritual he nodded to him. After the ritual, Mr. Hu offered to help carry home the basket in which musical instruments were placed. By then the priest was convinced that Mr. Hu meant no harm. He would admit Mr. Hu to his living room and chat with him. But it was only after another half year that the priest would show Mr. Hu his altar and his collection of ritual

texts. In this way Mr. Hu got to know all the priests in the Jielong 接龍 area of Ba county 巴縣 in Chongqing. When two priests quarrelled, Mr. Hu would be asked to serve as a mediator. All the priests have now confided in him the utmost secrets of their trade. That is how Mr. Hu was able to compile the first volume of the "Compendium of Traditional Chinese Secret Manuals of Hand Gestures and Ritual Steps." To make cultivation of such trusting relationships possible, the researcher has to be a native or at least a resident of the area where fieldwork is being done. Therefore my arrangement has been to let particular local researchers investigate their own local rituals.

So far I have deliberately stopped short at "archiving." However, now that we have accumulated a great amount of evidence, perhaps some kind of comparative study is in order. In my form letter dated 29/2/1996 to project members, I encouraged them to attempt analysis and interpretation of the material presented in their reports. Unfortunately, now when there are well-trained researchers who know better than ever before what to do and how to go about doing it, we have run out of funding. John Lagerwey and David Holm were kind enough to help keep my network going till 1997. Now they are as hard up as I am. In February, 1997, I revisited Anshun, Guizhou. In one village, Toupu 頭鋪, I witnessed parts of two ten-day *jiao* 醮 held respectively in two adjacent temples by Taoist priests (*daoshi* 道士, as they call themselves) from a Buddhist Linji 臨濟 tradition as shown on a genealogical tablet. This certainly deserves investigation. Then I went to Wu'an 武安 in southern Hebei to attend an international conference. In one of the villages there, Guyi 固義, we watched the highlight of the "Catching the Yellow Ghost" (*zhuo huanggui* 捉黃鬼) ritual. It was very impressive. I started to train a local researcher there, Mr. Du Xuede 杜學德, who had already completed a report. From the conference papers, which are rather inferior in quality, we can also see there are rituals we have never heard of going on in various places. But we can only sigh at the sight of the vast sea. The journal *Min-su ch'ü-i* can support some small projects with the honoraria it offers. This is not enough. But there is little else I can do.

2

MULIAN DRAMA:

A COMMENTARY ON CURRENT RESEARCH AND SOURCE MATERIALS

Hou Jie

Mulian drama 目連戲, an important form of popular drama in China, is also a kind of ritual drama that integrates theatrical art and religious themes and practices. Precisely because Mulian drama has been a popular dramatic form for centuries and is highly diversified in content, it reflects and influences the religious life of the Chinese people. The following list of titles bear witness to the complexity of this genre: *Mulian benzhuan* 目連本傳 (the original story of Mulian), which includes *Mulian qianzhuan* 目連前傳 (the first or former part), *Mulian houzhuan* 目連後傳 (the second or latter part) and *Mulian waizhuan* 目連外傳 (the "unofficial" story), and *Hua Mulian* 花目連, etc. In some regions it is divided into da Mulian 大目連 (bigger Mulian), xiao Mulian 小目連 (smaller Mulian) and ya Mulian 啞目連 (silent Mulian). As popular drama, it is widespread among cities and rural areas in many parts of China, with huge numbers of performers and audience in local communities. Mulian drama has aroused the interests of scholars as an important area of research because it is intimately connected with social, political, intellectual, cultural, ethical, religious and ethnographical issues in China.

From 1984 onwards, there has been a number of international conferences devoted to Mulian drama held in Hunan, Anhui, Fujian and
Sichuan provinces. In 1987, the University of California in Berkeley
hosted an International Conference on Mulian Drama and published the
proceedings two years later. Especially noteworthy is the Zheng
Zhizhen 鄭之珍 Academic Conference on Mulian Drama held in Qimen
祁門, Anhui Province, where Mulian drama was staged for the first time
in forty years. In the past decade, Mulian drama has continued to
inspire researchers from around the world.

I. The *Min-su ch'ü-i* and Mulian Drama

A note-worthy development in Mulian drama studies is the success of
the *Min-su ch'ü-i ts'ung-shu* 民俗曲藝叢書 (Studies in Chinese Ritual,
Theatre and Folklore Series), the combined efforts of its chief editor,
Professor Wang Ch'iu-kuei 王秋桂 and scholars in the PRC and
Taiwan. The *Min-su ch'ü-i ts'ung-shu* has published a series of case
studies and special issues on Mulian drama together with collections of
rare texts, research papers and source materials.

Among the sixty volumes (published in six series) are: Mao
Gengru 茆耕如 ed, *An Outline Catalogue of Materials on Mulian Plays*
目連資料編目概略 (No. 2, 371 pages), Huang Wenhu 黃文虎 ed., *The
Chaolun Text of the Mulian Play* 超輪本目連 (No. 16, 272 pages), Liu
Zhen 劉禎 ed., *The Pu Xian Theatre Version of Mulian Rescues His
Mother* 莆仙戲目連救母 (No. 17, 490 pages), Xu Hongtu 徐宏圖 and
Wang Ch'iu-kuei eds., *Mulian Plays from Zhejiang: A Collection of
Materials* 浙江省目連戲資料匯編 (No. 21, 620 pages), Xu Hongtu ed.,
Mulian's Mother Rescued: A Mulian Play from Shaoxing 紹興救母記
(No. 22, 293 pages), Xu Hongtu, *The Mulian Drama of the Han People
in Kong Village, Dongyang Municipality, Zhejiang Province* 浙江省東
陽市馬宅鎮孔村漢人的目連戲 (No. 23, 203 pages), Li Ping 李平 and
Li Ang 李昂 eds., *The Complete Festival Mulian Plays* 目連全會 (No.
39, 146 pages), Mao Gengru and Wang Ch'iu-kuei eds., *A Collection of
Materials on the Mulian Drama in Anhui* 安徽目連戲資料集 (No. 54,
352 pages), and *The "Red at Both Ends" Performance Text of the
Mulian Play from Gaochun, Jiangsu* 江蘇高淳目連戲兩頭紅臺本 (No.

57, 174 pages), Zhao Ming 肇明 ed., *A Xianfeng Period (1851-1861) Manuscript of the Mulian Play in Diaoqiang Style* 調腔目連戲咸豐庚申年抄本 (No. 58, 489 pages), and Xu Hongtu ed., *The Old Shaoxing Manuscript of The Story of How Mulian Saved His Mother* 紹興舊抄救母記 (No. 59, 149 pages). All these books were published between 1993-1997. In addition, Nos. 77 and 78 of the journal *Min-su ch'ü-i* are special issues devoted to Mulian drama. Other published articles include: Li Huaisun 李懷蓀 "The Mulian of Chenhe Drama: A Preliminary Study" 辰河戲目連初探 (No. 62), Li Ping, "A Brief Study of the Origins of Mulian Drama and Qingyang Style" 目連戲與青陽腔淵源淺說 (No. 81), Cai Fengming 蔡豐明, "The Mulian Drama of Shaoxing and Popular Beliefs in Ghosts and Gods" 紹興目連戲與民間鬼神信仰 (No. 82), Wu Hsiu-ling 吳秀玲, "A Survey of the International Conference on Mulian Drama in Sichuan, 1993" 九三年四川目連戲國際學術研討會簡介 (No. 86), Yang Mengheng 楊孟衡, "A Study of a Mulian Drama in Three Parts and the Historical Status of Mulian in Ancient 'Sai' " 目連三段論：兼談古賽目連之歷史地位 (No. 86), Wang T'ien-lin 王天麟, "The Mulian Drama in a Salvation Ritual at the Xianrui Altar, Yangmei Township, Taoyuan County" 桃園縣楊梅鎮顯瑞壇拔度齋儀中的目連戲 (No. 86), Yung Saihing 容世誠 and Zhang Xuequan 張學權, "The Mulian Drama of Xinghua and the 'Release of Souls' Ritual in Southeast Asia" 南洋的興化目連戲與超度儀式 (No. 92), Li Feng-mao 李豐楙, "Integration and Transformation: the Mulian Drama in the Daoist Salvation Ritual in Taiwan" 複合與變革：臺灣道教拔度儀中的目連戲 (No. 94, 95), Xu Shuofang 徐朔方, "Three Topics on Mulian Drama" 目連戲三題 (No. 99), Zhao Ming, "The Mulian Drama of the White God: Religious Thought and Performance" 目連戲白神(燿無常)的思想與表演特色 (No. 100), Liu Zhen 劉禎," 'Nanny Wang Cursing the Rooster' and Chinese Popular Culture" 王婆罵雞與中國民間文化 and a number of related articles (No. 101). No. 87 is a special collection of texts and No. 93 is a collection of essays on Mulian drama.

The editors and authors of the *Min-su ch'ü-i ts'ung-shu* are aware of the significance of Mulian drama in the study of Chinese culture and local customs and have put in great effort in this direction. In preparing materials for publication, they consulted a wide variety of sources such as Buddhist texts, transformation texts or *bianwen* 變文, sūtra lectures,

texts for story-telling, fictional texts, and Sanskrit texts. Other related
source materials include: precious volumes or *baojuan* 寶卷, *zidi shu* 子
弟書, *xilian* 戲聯 (stage couplets), local historical records, historical
anecdotes, and abstracts, miscellaneous collections, records of meetings
and collections of essays. Sources directly derived from Mulian drama
performances include critical introductions and epilogues, surveys of
troupes, dramatic conventions, religious texts for rituals, musical scores
and tunes, and play scripts and titles, together with visual illustrations,
photographs and appendices. Besides the collection and publication of
rare and unique copies, such in-depth research makes valuable contributions to the recovery of rare and important sources concerning Mulian
drama.

The texts collected in *Min-su ch'ü-i ts'ung-shu* are invaluable cultural treasures since many of them are the only existing copies. In
selecting the better copies for publication, the editors widely consulted
major play texts to verify the originality and accuracy of the final work.
Synopses, summaries of plot and comparisons of styles are also included to reflect the local character of each play.

The performance texts collected in the *Min-su ch'ü-i ts'ung-shu* are
very often the only existing copies. For instance, *Saving the Mother in
Shaoxing* is a hand-written text by a group of performers in Shaoxing
County in Zhejiang. The existing copy is printed; the identity of the
recorder and the date of recording are unknown, and the original script
has been lost. In Gaochun 高淳 County, Jiangsu Province, a huge flood
in 1954 destroyed all the Mulian play scripts, and the existing *Mulian:
The Chaolun Version* was recorded by the actor Chaolun 超輪 (1890-
1960) during a stage performance. *As* for *"The Red at Both Ends"
Performance Text of the Mulian Play from Gaochun, Jiangsu*, the play
originally belonged to a Zhao family in Dingbu 定埠. It did not have a
title; the existing copy was recorded by Chen Zhongmei 陳忠美 of
Dingbu in 1935. According to Chen, the script was in a local collection,
and he had consulted an oral transcription of the play from an old
Mulian performer when preparing the existing copy. *An Old Shaoxing
Manuscript of "The Story of How Mulian Saved His Mother"* was
recorded by Yang Xing 楊杏 of the Jingyi Tang 敬義堂, Shaoxing in
1883 (the ninth year of Emperor Guangxu 光緒 in the Qing dynasty)
and was circulated locally. *Tiaoqiang Mulian Drama: The Hand-written*

Script of the Gengshen Year of the Xianfeng Period 調腔目連戲咸豐庚
申年抄本 [date unclear; the Xianfeng reign period was 1851-1861, but
the nearest gengshen date corresponds to 1864), was discovered in
Qianliang Village 前良村, Xinchang 新昌 County, Zhejiang in 1992.
This antique and damaged script is probably the oldest surviving copy
of *tiaoqiang* Mulian drama.

The collections of Mulian performance texts published in the *Min-
su ch'ü-i ts'ung-shu* are an invaluable contribution to international
scholarship. They help preserve the numerous rare documents and oral
literature recently recovered, and in turn enhance our understanding of
the rich cultural meaning of these extant texts. The *Min-su ch'ü-i
ts'ung-shu* represents the combined efforts of international scholars in
promoting research in this field and therefore lays a solid foundation for
the future.

It has been widely acknowledged that *Mulian Rescues His Mother
and Preaches Goodness* 目連救母勸善戲文, edited by Zheng Zhizhen
in the Ming dynasty, is closely connected to the Mulian dramatic tradition in popular culture. Although Zheng's work represents a landmark
in the study of Mulian drama and to some extent defines the genre as it
appeared from antiquity up to the pre-Ming period, it did not pose any
limits on the development of Mulian drama as a popular cultural art
form. From the numerous texts published in the *Min-su ch'ü-i ts'ung-
shu*, it is obvious that due to its wide popular appeal across the country,
Mulian drama has developed over time and space, and therefore exhibits
a distinctive "regional" character.

"Although the hand-written script originated from Zheng's copy, it
gradually merged with popular song versions and developed a unique
character of its own. ... The hand-written copy is not a direct replica of
Zheng's, but has its own identity and value."[1] To take another example,
the play *Mulian Rescues His Mother in Pu Xian*, a popular Mulian
drama in the Putian 莆田 and Xianyou 仙游 regions of Fujian Province,
has a distinctive Buddhist character which differs from the combination
of Confucian, Buddhist and Daoist themes in a typical Mulian play. In
this Pu Xian drama, the usual theme of Buddhist monks and nuns suffering from retribution for their disobedience is not prominent. Moreover,

---

1 Li Ping and Li Ang eds., *The Complete Festival Mulian Plays*, p. 12.

since Mulian drama is always performed in the local dialect using a lot of colloquial expressions, it always has a strong local character. The Mulian performance texts published in the *Min-su ch'ü-i ts'ung-shu* aptly reflect this aspect of the popular tradition and so make comparative studies more fruitful.

Every text published in the *Min-su ch'ü-i ts'ung-shu* has a brief introduction to the different versions of the text in question. This, I think, is the greatest contribution of the *Min-su ch'ü-i ts'ung-shu*. In his introduction to *Mulian: The Chaolun Version*, Huang Wenhu compares the similarities and differences between Chaolun's text and Zheng Zhizhen's *Mulian Rescues His Mother and Preaches Goodness*. He points out their similarity in plot structure, but notes that in *Chaolun*, the lyrics and dialogues are more colloquial. He also notes that three acts in *Chaolun*, namely "Praying for a Son" 求子, "Sending out the Spirit" 出神 and "Redemption of Vows" 還陽, are absent in Zheng's script. There are also many details depicting mundane life in *Chaolun* that are absent in Zheng's script, for example "Exhorting the Father" 訓父, "Cursing the Rooster" 罵雞, and "Seeing off the Rooster" 送雞. Scenes reminiscent of miscellaneous acrobatics performances, e.g. the "fighting scene," and those that carry a distinctive "local color," e.g. "Zhaofang" 招方, "The Nine Palaces" 九殿, "Beating the Dogs" 打狗, and "Expelling the Prostitute" 趕妓, further distinguish the Chaolun's version from Zheng's. In some scenes, the same story is rendered in different ways. For example, Zheng's play includes the act "Generous Donations to the Masses" 博施濟眾 with scenes such as "Which Family?" 何家, "Beaten Paralysed" 打癱, "A Plum Branch" 一枝梅, "A Pious Woman Offering Herself for Sale" 孝婦賣身 and "Falling Over" 倒事. The lyrics, dialogue and dramatic presentation are also different in the two texts.[2]

Compared with Zheng's text, the Mulian Drama of Pu Xian has a unique character of its own. For example, a more vivid portrayal of daily life is achieved through an added emphasis on the character of Liu Jia 劉賈. The lyrics, moreover, go beyond Zheng's version in favor of a crisp and condensed style that nonetheless retains a lot of uncommon expressions in the Xinghua dialect that often intrigue the outsider.[3] In

2 Huang Wenhu, pp. 9-11.

3 *Ibid*, pp.6-9.

The Old Shaoxing Manuscript of "The Story of How Mulian Saved His Mother", the plot is similar to Zheng's but its lyrics and spoken parts are unique in style. The spoken parts are in the Shaoxing dialect, and many of its linking scenes are absent in Zheng's script, for example, "A Big Gathering" 大會, "Four Scenes" 四景, "Fake Lord" 假霸, "Stealing the Rooster," "Cursing the Rooster," "Cursing Back" 回罵, "Out Mourning" 出吊, "Exhorting the Father," and "Thunder Strike" 雷擊. These scenes can be performed individually in the form of popular skits.

II. The Editing of Mulian Play Texts and Anthropological Research

Most of the texts and research materials published in the *Min-su ch'ü-i ts'ung-shu* are the result of meticulous editorial efforts from which researchers and readers can greatly benefit. For example, the editors of *Chaolun's Text* (Huang Wenfu), the Pu Xian *Mulian Rescues His Mother in Pu Xian* (Liu Zhen), *Mulian's Mother Rescued* (Xu Hongtu), *The Complete Festival Mulian Plays* (Li Ping and Li Ang), *The Red at Both Ends* (Mao Gengru), *The Xianfeng Period Manuscript of the Mulian Play* (Zhao Ming), and *The Old Shaoxing Manuscript* (Xu Hongtu) have carefully cross-referenced different versions to ensure that the final work resembles the original as far as possible.

The Complete Festival Mulian Plays is based on a hand-written copy from Shanghai. Other sources consulted include Zheng Zhizhen's script, a hand-written copy from Southern Anhui, and a hand-written copy from Zhejiang, from the Fudan University collection. Discrepancies in the lyrics and spoken dialogue are carefully delineated in the editorial notes at the end of each play. Numerous errors were detected in the preparation of *Mulian Rescues His Mother in Shaoxing* since the performer who wrote the play was not well-educated and, unavoidably, more errors resulted from the making of a printed "replica." Based on the printed replica, Xu Hongtu's edition strives to preserve its original appearance and at the same time eliminate the mistakes by consulting the text used in Shao drama 紹劇 and some other versions.[4] Explanatory notes on the content and colloquialisms are added at

---

4 *A Collection of Traditional Opera in Zhejiang: Shaoju* 浙江戲曲傳統劇目彙編, 1962,

the end of the play. Other noteworthy research studies include *Mulian Plays from Zhejiang: A Collection of Materials* (edited by Xu Hongtu and Wang Ch'iu-kuei), *A Collection of Materials on the Mulian Plays of Anhui* (edited by Mao Gengru), and *The Mulian Drama of the Han People of Kong Village, Dongyang Municipality, Zhejiang* (edited by Xu Hongtu).

No doubt the *Min-su ch'ü-i ts'ung-shu* presents a vast collection of source materials; however, anthropological discoveries are at best a dormant potential in this exciting collection of first-hand materials. As a religious art form that combines musical, dramatic and ritual elements, any research that limits itself to the recovery of written documents such as play texts will find it hard to capture the true meaning of Mulian drama. In addition to play scripts, researchers have to pay more attention to other important details such as the music, singing technique, dancing and musical instruments used that form part of the artistic whole. Unfortunately, this aspect of Mulian drama is absent in the *Ts'ung-shu*, which has hitherto concentrated on the collection and editing of play texts.

Professor Wang Ch'iu-kuei has provided a clue to more comprehensive research in this area, such as peripheral cultural studies, ethnographical research, anthropological research and studies of operatic art.[5] Obviously, anthropological approaches to Mulian drama will bring new insights to extant scholarship in the field.

The Mulian Drama of the Han People in Kong Village is a report on Xu Hongtu's field study in Kong village. He recorded in situ the Han people's "New Year Worship of *Guanyin* (goddess of mercy) in the Luoqie Temple," and the ritual drama *Mulian Saving His Mother*. This book gives a detailed account of the general background of Kong village and its religious practices. There are also details concerning the ritual performance, its process and structure, details about the performing troupe and its acting techniques as well as local dramatic convention. The appendix includes the stage text according to Zhu Fuyu 朱福雨, the master of the Zhu family Mulian Troupe. In addition, it goes to great lengths to describe the organization of the troupe, the religious drawings of the deities, and the ritual implements used, the outlook and setup of

---

5 "Preface," *Min-su ch'ü-i*, No. 77(1992): 1-30.

the stage, the performers involved, their singing technique, and also the songs and stage-props. Xu's book, in essence, contains a rich source of information on popular religion and rituals.

A Collection of Materials on Mulian Drama in Anhui is another example in the *Min-su ch'ü-i ts'ung-shu* series that goes beyond materials collection. Its content is diverse, including critical introductions to previous studies of Mulian drama, anecdotes in local historical records, details about Mulian troupes, local dramatic conventions, religious texts for rituals and holy invocations, songs and tonal variations, stage plays, and field reports on live performances. These details give an overall picture of the development of Mulian drama, especially the recent revival of Mulian theatre and troupes in many regions. For example, in 1988, the Zheng Zhizhen Academic Conference on Mulian Drama was held in Qimen, Anhui Province, to commemorate the 470th birthday of Zheng Zhizhen; highlights were performed by a Limu troupe 栗木班. Later on in 1990, the Limu crew organized a training class for the village youths in order to reinvigorate this popular tradition.

Mao Gengru's essays on the performance of Mulian drama are rich in details, such as the special masks customarily used on stage, stage setup and stage couplets, different kinds of charms, tunes and names of tunes, the accompanying gongs and drums used (together with selections of musical scores), the deployment of percussion instruments, and the rhythmic patterns of gongs and drums. This collection gives a panoramic view of the the entire process of the performance and the unique characteristics of the ritual itself. At the same time, there is a special collection of the couplets used on stage, which are further divided into couplets for the deity altar, couplets in the play, couplets for the stage, and couplets about funny episodes, etc. in different regions such as Fujian, Hunan, Sichuan and Anhui. These details bring us closer to the reality of Mulian stage performances in various parts of the country and also the local people's understanding of Mulian drama, as in these passages:

> ...her husband is a Mr. Liu... upright and crooked, sincere and false, making a myriad of faces; Mulian is born, Guanyin comes forth. He purifies the King Yama of the Underworld, and snubs the little devils. Pious, kind and righteous, all of the same nature.

Those who do evil things perish. If they do not, it is not that they will not be destroyed, but it is because their ancestors' goodness remains; when this goodness is exhausted, they will indeed perish. Those who do good things prosper; if they do not, it is not that they will not prosper, but that their ancestors' evil remains; when this evil influence is exhausted, they will certainly prosper.[6]

Among the collections published in the *Min-su ch'ü-i ts'ung-shu*, obvious differences exist among Mao's *A Collection of Materials on Mulian Drama in Anhui,* and *An Outline Catalogue of Materials on Mulian Plays*, Xu Hongtu's *The Mulian Drama of the Han People in Kong Village*, and *A Collection of Materials on Mulian Drama in Zhejiang.* In *A Collection of Materials on Mulian Drama in Zhejiang* a comprehensive table comparing the important play scripts of Mulian drama in different regions is included, such as in Hunan, Anhui, Jiangxi and Fujian. This method is not used in Mao's two books. In this respect, Xu and Wang have completed a task that was not taken up by Mao.

The division of topics and categories in *An Outline Catalogue* seems to be quite arbitrary in some cases. In fact, it would be much better if its scope could be expanded to a nation-wide level, rather than limiting itself to the Southern Anhui region. Moreover, some sections like "Excerpts of Documents from Past to Present," "Lu Xun's Writings on Mulian drama," "Special Topics," and "A Miscellany of Commentaries" very often overlap one another in content and therefore need reorganizing in a more systematic way. The lack of a coherent structure is also apparent in the overall arrangement of topics and their respective content. For instance, indexes and excerpts are put together in one section, while lengthy paragraphs appear in the middle of a special topic index.

Mao's volume has accounted for the efforts made by the public to revive Mulian drama; however, the Mulian rituals practiced in local communities are left out. As far as I know, in Jiangsu, Zhejiang and Anhui, different kinds of Mulian drama can be found in rural communities, and the rituals related to Mulian drama are an indispensable part of funeral activities. To the extent that Mulian drama continues to be a living tradition among the local people, anthropological studies play an

---

6   Mao Gengru, *A Collection of Materials on Mulian Drama in Anhui*, pp. 171-172.

important role in understanding it apart from the collection of extant
play texts and documents, for its meaning runs deeper than a general
understanding of popular and lost cultures.

III. Mulian Drama and Popular Religion

The materials collected in the *Min-su ch'ü-i ts'ung-shu* go beyond the
realm of ethnic drama studies toward an understanding of the social
function of Mulian drama as a kind of religious drama. For centuries,
Mulian drama has been intimately connected with the religious life of
local people; this is why in the *Min-su ch'ü-i ts'ung-shu* there is a strong
emphasis on the religious characteristics of Mulian drama.

Mulian drama is popular in so many different regions because it
has a special meaning to its audience. As local theatre, Mulian drama
differs from other dramatic forms because it derives its energy from religious beliefs. Sometimes Mulian drama is regarded as a ritual in itself
and becomes part of the religious life of the local people. In China,
ancestor worship is very common, so Mulian drama is mainly performed as a ritual to release souls from purgatory. As a result, in
Buddhist and Daoist ceremonies such as "Yulanpen hui" 盂蘭盆會 and
"Luotian dajiao" 羅天大醮, Mulian drama is frequently staged. The
purpose is to release the souls of one's ancestors in the past seven generations so that they can be free from suffering as "hungry ghosts." [7] In
the eyes of the living, this ritual not only provides food for the dead but
can also protect them from being disturbed, by pacifying the homeless
and wandering ghosts in the other world. In many places, Mulian drama
is staged every year on the fifteenth day of the seventh month in the
lunar calendar, when the Mid-year Festival and Yulanpen hui are celebrated together. Sometimes a family in mourning will invite a Mulian
troupe to perform a ritual for the departed.

To many people, Guanyin 觀音, the goddess of mercy, is the pioneer in every ritual who opens up purgatory to release the souls of the
dead; her role, therefore, closely resembles that of Mulian, who is

---

7 Xu Hongtu, *The Mulian Drama of the Han People in Kong Village, Dongyang Municipality,
Zhejiang*, p. 65.

famous for his piety. In some areas Mulian drama is staged four times in every lunar year to commemorate the goddess, i.e. on the nineteenth day of the second month (the birth of Guanyin), the twentieth day of the third month (the transformation of Guanyin), the nineteenth day of the sixth month (the death of Guanyin) and the nineteenth day of the nineteenth month (Guanyin's attainment of realization 正果). Also, every ten years on the nineteenth day of the first lunar month, Mulian drama is staged as part of the grand dedication ceremony of Guanyin images.

The Chinese people believe in the unity of Heaven (*tian* 天) and humans, and so look to Heaven, a symbol of the sacred realm, for help and protection. Since in Mulian drama the gods of all directions are gathered together, its performance is believed to possess a divine power to endow good fortune and dispel calamities. There is also the general belief that Mulian drama has the power to forestall and relieve disasters and epidemics. In an agricultural society, people have little means to confront the elements; very often they resort to staging Mulian drama as a plea for deliverance.

According to an historical anecdote, during the reign of the Tongzhi 同治 Emperor in the Qing Dynasty (1862-1874), the Pu Xian region of Fujian Province was ravaged by both human and natural disasters: "When the battles and the epidemics were gone, performers were gathered to perform Mulian drama. The locals believed that it could deliver them from destruction and violence."[8] Some areas were under locust attacks and Mulian drama was staged to drive away the locusts. "It is the customs of the South (Jiangnan 江南) to believe in shamanism and prayers; in order to dispel the locusts, they set up a stage and invited actors to perform the play *The Legend of Mulian Saving His Mother* 目連救母傳奇. They made paper horses and offered vegetable meals to them. After a while, the locusts did no more damage."[9] Moreover, the power of Mulian drama to drive away evil can be extended to the treatment of the human body. In the Ningpo 寧波 region, when performing

---

8   Guo Jianling 郭箴齡, *Random Notes about Mountain People* 山民隨筆.

9   Zhang Lingying 章寧楹, *Miscellaneous Thoughts on the Cliff of Righteous Words* 諤崖脞説 in Wang Liqi 王利器, *Historical Sources of Censored and Destroyed Fictional and Dramatic Works of the Yuan, Ming and Qing Dynasties* 元明清三代禁毀小説戲曲史料 (Shanghai: Shanghai guzhi chupan she, 1981, second ed.), p. 127.

Mulian drama, the Wang Lingguan 王靈官 (the master of spirits of the underworld), Pan guan 判官 (the prosecutor of the underworld), and little demons are the first to appear on-stage. When the Wang Lingguan has given orders to the Pan guan and little demons, they will jump off the stage and run into the families of the sick or the insane and drag them back to the stage. The little devils will smear chicken blood on the faces of the affected, lead them to go round the stadium and back in front of the stage, wrap them up in a fishing net and take them to the temple. The sick and the mad will stay there until the performance is over the next day. When all this is done, it is believed that the evil spirits inside these people are dispelled.[10]

From the existing sources of Mulian drama we learn that it has its roots in real life experiences that go beyond human control. This aspect of Mulian drama well explains its religious meaning and social function. The popularity of Mulian drama in local communities has not only enriched the religious life of the people, but also reveals a symbiotic relationship between the ordinary and the divine worlds in popular religion. Mulian drama is different from other institutionalized religions because it is not a religious sect, nor is it under the control of a clergy. However, we cannot overlook the traditional pattern integral to Mulian drama that is deeply rooted in the religious life of the common people in China. As a popular art form, Mulian drama is a manifestation of ordinary people's perception of the unknown or mysterious world. Those who participate in the performance of Mulian drama include professional actors as well as local farmers and artisans, who organize themselves to participate in the ritual to express their religious sentiment. "The group now performing yagui drama 啞鬼戲 (i.e. mime performance) is called the 'Taiping (peace) Society.' It is funded by local donations. With the exception of a memorial tablet stating the principles of the performance, yagui drama does not have a written text. It is either orally transmitted or taught by example from generation to generation... Participants are all local farmers, artisans or small proprietors in groups of forty to fifty."[11] During the performance, the following taboos must

---

10 See Jiang Bin 姜彬, ed., *The Popular Religions and Customs of the Wu and Yue Regions* 吳越民間信仰民俗 (Shanghai: Shanghai wenyi chubanshe, 1992), pp. 380-381.

11 Xu Hongtu and Wang Ch'iu-kui, p. 116.

be observed: one must cleanse the body and abstain from sex three days before the performance; speaking and walking in open spaces are forbidden once make-up is finished; and all paper caps and stage props have to be burnt downstage when the performance is over. These rules have to be strictly followed because Mulian drama is not only a theatrical performance, but a manifestation of the divine realm.

The most important reason why Mulian drama is endowed with such divine powers (i.e. to relieve suffering souls, dispel disasters and give protection and peace) is that in China people have a general belief in the divine realm represented in popular art forms. They also make use of different kinds of rituals in the performance to reinforce the sense of mystery in Mulian drama. For example, "Raising a Flag to Summon Souls" 豎招魂幡 is for gathering and giving out supplements to the wandering or homeless ghosts of the night so that peace can be maintained in a place; in "Sacrifices to the Gods" the magic charm "Under the Protection of The Gods of Five Directions" 五方五位鎮臺符 is posted on the four pillars and the "three-star wall" 三星壁 of the stage to invoke the five gods as patron saints, namely the Green Emperor 青帝 in the East, the Red Emperor 赤帝 in the South, the White Emperor 白帝 in the West, the Black Emperor 黑帝 in the North, and the Yellow Emperor 黃帝 at the Center. A painting of all the gods is posted on the backstage wall and worshipped at an incense altar. The ritual to invoke the gods begins with the incantation *qingshen zhou* 請神咒 (invoking the gods) so that the various gods will descend to the altar, and the wandering and homeless ghosts will come together. Afterwards, such Buddhist figures as Luohan 羅漢 (Arhats), Jingang 金剛 (guardian spirits), Wenshu 文殊 (Mañjušri), Puxian 普賢 (Samantabhadra), Guanyin (goddess of mercy) and the Buddha himself, and all the deities will be invited to come down from heaven. When all this is done, the prayer for peace is delivered by an actor prior to the performance. Holding the sticks of incense (in three *zhu*, 炷, or bunches of three), the actor comes forward to the stage and kneels down to pray: "The local community is holding a Yulanpen *hui*, and is carrying out a ritual for peace to relieve suffering souls and give them aid. We now cordially invite the Great Emperors of Taiqing 太清 (Grand purity), Shangqing 上清 (Supreme purity) and Yuqing 玉清 (Jade purity) to assume their holy thrones. We also ask the wicked ghosts, wandering souls and all other ghosts and goblins to come here and to receive their aid. If we speak vulgar or foul words during our play, please conceal our shame. Do not let yourselves be angry with your apprentices. Bless all country folk old and young, and all members of the troupe, and keep us in peace."

In Shitai County 石臺縣 in Anhui, an "Altar in Honor of the Chang Gods" 祭猖臺 has to be set up in every performance of Mulian drama to welcome the [five] Chang gods 猖神. Five people will play the role of the gods. The lineage or village head will hold up lanterns to lead the procession. The lead actor will carry peachwood tablets representing the five phases metal, wood, water, fire and earth, while the other actors carry metal forks. The five actors, now known as the "five Changs" will be accompanied by the masses and march from the lineage hall to a "*fengshui* spot" chanting incantations all the way. The village or lineage head will kneel down to welcome them with fireworks, chanting blessings of good fortune to the beating of gongs and drums. All this is done to drive away devils and disasters so that peace will come to the whole village. When all this is done, the performance can formally begin. After the performance, the leading actor will quietly proceed to the sacred altar to burn incense and recite incantations. Then he will lift up the five wooden tablets as a gesture of "seeing off the Changs."[12]

From all of this we can see that the common people are very serious about Mulian drama and the religious meaning it represents. The combination of religious drama with ritual further enriches the meaning of the drama. At the same time, the audience of Mulian drama is far more than a passive group of onlookers; rather, they are active participants deeply immersed in the religious atmosphere of the ritual. In the rural areas of Anhui, country folk have to go on a vegetarian diet for ten days or even one month before the Mulian troupe arrives. They will abstain from eating meat until the troupe has left the village.[13]

IV. The Future of Mulian Drama Studies

This essay is mainly a review of the recent publications in the *Min-su*

---

12 Mao Gengru, *A Collection of Materials on the Mulian Plays in Anhui*, pp. 67-68.

13 *Ibid*, pp. 99-100.

ch'ü-i ts'ung-shu concerning Mulian drama. This is by no means an easy task because the play texts and source materials in question are extremely diverse and huge in number.

To be as objective as possible, contributors to the *Min-su ch'ü-i* series have put in great efforts in tracking the development of Mulian drama in different parts of China. Many unique copies thought to have been lost have now been recovered and carefully differentiated, be they an index of titles or actual play scripts. The numerous musical texts and visual illustrations of historical stage settings, play scripts, plot structures, actors and the temples and monasteries where Mulian drama was staged included in this series have greatly enhanced our knowledge of this popular dramatic form. Even the incantations and religious drawings, which have hitherto been kept secret, are now made available to the public. These are invaluable sources for an in-depth study of the ritualistic practices connected to Mulian drama. About sixty percent of the materials on Mulian drama in these collections are here published for the first time.[14]

By comparison, research studies on Mulian drama by overseas Chinese scholars are under-represented in the *Min-su ch'ü-i* series. So far only a few such essays have been published, for instance "Transformation Mulian Plays in the Daoist Salvation Ritual in Taiwan" and "A Preliminary Study of Mulian Drama in the Daoist Badu Ritual in Central and Southern Taiwan" by Li Feng-mao, "The Mulian Drama in the Salvation Ritual of the Xianrui Altar Troupe, Yangmei Township, Taoyuan County" by Wang T'ien-lin, "A Preliminary Study of the Mulian Play in the Pu Xian Association Fengjia Salvation Ritual in Singapore" by Tanaka Issei 田仲一成, and "The Mulian Drama of Xinghua and the 'Release of Souls' Ritual in Southeast Asia" by Yung Saihing and Zhang Xuequan. A more comprehensive understanding of Mulian drama would result if the editors of the *Min-su ch'ü-i* could pay more attention to current research in other countries such as Singapore.

In central and southern Taiwan, Mulian drama takes on a wide variety of forms in funeral activities such as the famous *gezai* plays 歌仔戲, the mini-drama performed by Daoist priests, and popular songs (or *xiao diao* 小調) accompanied by stringed instruments. A more representa-

---

14 *Ibid*, p. 3

tive form is the mini-drama performed by the so-called "black head" Daoist priests 烏頭道士 during Daoist rituals. It originates in the regions of Zhangzhou 漳州 and Quanzhou 泉州 in Fujian. Usually the Daoist priests in charge have to be natives of these regions. In northern and central Taiwan, however, the "immigrant" communities use the so-called "fulao" and Hakka dialects as the medium of performance. Sometimes, *gezai* plays may form part of Daoist mini-drama. As an integral part of the "Mulian Rescues His Mother" story, *gezai* plays first emerged in Fujian Province. First introduced to Taiwan by immigrants in the Ming and Qing dynasties, Mulian drama has remained an important part of funeral ceremonies. In the popular *badu* salvation ritual 拔度儀, "Mulian drama is differentiated from ordinary outdoor performances (or *yetai* drama 野台戲) because it is ritualized and takes on a special religious meaning. As such, Mulian drama can be regarded as ritual drama."[15] In the Hakka region in the north, the redemptive ritual *da xue pen* 打血盆 (breaking the pan of blood) is still very much in practice. The origin of this ritual is the popular belief that women have sinned because the blood of childbirth contaminates the earth. *Da xue pen* is usually carried out by the Mulian character and the woman's family members when she dies, a traditional practice originating from the story of Mulian itself.[16]

In countries like Singapore and Malaysia, the Wooden Body Mulian drama (mushen Mulian xi 木身目連戲) of Pu Xian is part of a rarely seen ritual to release the souls of the dead from suffering. In the Sanjiao (Three teachings) Monastery 三教堂 near Kuala Lumpur, Mulian drama has been part of the annual Yulan Pudu Ceremony 盂蘭普度會 for over half a century. Similarly, in Selangor and Sembilan, troupes are invited to perform Mulian drama for one or two days. In Singapore, Mulian drama is also staged by the Qiongyao Sect 瓊瑤仙教 during the Gongjian Salvation Gathering 公建普度會 of the Xing'an Palace of the Empress of Heaven 興安天后宮.[17] Mulian drama, there-

---

15 Li Feng-mao, p. 84

16 Wang T'ien-lin, "The Mulian drama in the Salvation Ritual of the Xianrui Altar Troupe, Yangmei Township, Taoyuan County."

17 Yung Saihing and Chang Xuequan, "The 'Xinghua' Mulian Drama and the 'Release of Souls from Suffering' Ritual in Southeast Asia." *Min-su ch'ü-i*, 92(1994): 819-852.

fore, is "the integration of dramatic performance and religious ceremony; as a result, the two become an undifferented whole."[18]

So far we have noticed that the major focus of the *Min-su ch'ü-i* series is on the development of Mulian drama in Mainland China, particularly Jiangsu, Zhejiang, Fujian and Anhui provinces. Contributors to this series have put much emphasis on the discovery and collation of source materials and play texts in the target areas (especially Hunan and the southern provinces mentioned above) where Mulian drama is performed. Their pioneering efforts have led to a major breakthrough in the study of Mulian drama. Nonetheless, a question remains to be answered once we consider the overall picture of the development of such drama: what about Mulian drama in other regions? In this respect, the *Min-su ch'ü-i* seems to have overlooked the development of Mulian drama in areas other than those we have noted above. While researchers who publish in the *Min-su ch'ü-i* continue their exploration in these target areas and draw conclusions from this initial phase of research, we are looking forward to new discoveries in areas such as Sichuan, Hubei, Guangxi, Jiangxi and Shanghai.

As far as I know, in Sichuan, where Mulian drama is extremely popular, the performance of Mulian 搬目連 has a long history and is still a living tradition in local communities: "Every year at the spring festival there will be a performance called "Chasing Ms. Liu" 捉劉氏. The play is very different in form from those in other areas, ... The actors are actively engaged in the social activities of the audience. For instance, banquets are held to celebrate Liu's wedding and child birth, and the performers' costumes are the same as the current fashion. This kind of live performance has a very touching effect on the audience."[19] The Mulian drama of Sichuan is extremely diverse and the plot structure of each play is usually rather complex. There are a large number of outstanding performers, and the performances, along different rivers have their own distinctive local colors. Mulian performances are often com-

---

18 Yung Saihing, *The Anthropology of Operatic Art: A Preliminary Study of Ritual, Drama and Social Groups* 戲曲人類學初探 (Taipei: Rye Field Publishing Co., 1997), p. 16.

19 Chen Fang-ying 陳芳英, "Mulian Rescues His Mother: the Evolution of the Story and Related Literature" 目連救母故事之演進及其有關文學之研究. Unpublished master's thesis, Research Institute of Chinese Literature, National Taiwan University, p. 166.

bined with religious activities practiced by the performing groups. These are integrated into rituals like *fang wu chang* 放五猖 (exiling the five Chang gods) and *zhuo hanlin* 捉寒林 (chasing after the hanlin devils). In Sichuan, there is even a Liu's Tomb to commemorate an actress who played the role of Ms. Liu in a Mulian drama performance in Qingti Crossing, Taihe Township, Shehong County sometime during the reign of the Qianlong Emperor in the Qing Dynasty. The actress was accidentally killed by a pitch fork during a "Rolling Fork" 滾叉 scene. The audience held a large funeral for the actress, and on her tombstone was inscribed the honorary title "The tomb of Qingti née Liu, Mother of Mulian the Sacred Monk of Tang" 唐聖僧目連之母劉氏青堤之墓. From then on, the local people composed new texts for the Liu and Fu families following the slogan "Four generations of ancestors, double perfection in faithfulness and filial piety." This was done to eliminate the scenes depicting the immoral conduct of Ms. Liu and the Fu family. In these new versions, even the hometown of Mulian was moved to Qingti, and any troupe that did not conform to the new versions would be expelled. Some audiences would even voice their grievances for Liu, as in the following antithetical couplet:

> Falling into the River of Blood and the Sea of Suffering,
> For the sake of cold meat and rotten fish:
> Oh! Liu is so wronged!
> Calling forth the Sleep Demon and the Emperor of the Underworld,
> Her case to be vindicated.
> Roaming about in hell and in heaven,
> Suddenly, the merciful cloud and the precious moon appear:
> Oh! The Buddha is so powerful!
> Thus I inquire, kind gentlemen and pious sons:
> From where comes all this?[20]

In Sichuan, the staging of a comprehensive forty-eight part Mulian drama is not uncommon. The longest one on record is a performance in

---

20 Wen Yubo 溫餘波, "The Ziyang River Branch of Sichuan Drama: Records of Performing a Mulian Play" 川劇資陽河流派 "扮目連" 實況憶述, *A Collection of Literary and Historical Sources of the Inner River Region* 內江文史資料選輯, Vol. 1.

the Chenghuang Temple 城隍廟 at the East Gate of Xu Prefecture 敍府 東門 which lasted for one year, from 1929 to 1930. Given the unique character of Mulian drama in Sichuan, researchers should go beyond the publication of texts and conference proceedings toward more in-depth analysis of this popular dramatic form. On the other hand, in Sichuan, especially Chongqing City, vast resources of play titles and texts are waiting to be recovered. in the future researchers can therefore better utilize these local resources in this part of the country and organize their research in a more systematic manner.

The Mulian drama of Hubei is another area that has not received much attention. However, according to *The "High Tune" Repertoire* 高 腔劇目 of the Sun Tian Fu Tai 孫天福泰 troupe of Ma Township, a great number of plays have stood the test of time; e.g. *Three Masons Scrambling for a Seat* 三匠爭席, *Urging Sister to Eat Meat* 勸姓(姐)開 葷, *Selling Oneself to Bury Mother* 賣身葬母, *Sending the Son out to Do Business* 遣子經商, *Liu Jia Asking for Money* 劉賈借錢, *Zhao Jia Hitting His Father* 趙甲打父, *The Goddess of Mercy Converting Bu (Mulian)* 觀音渡卜, *Mulian (Goddess of Mercy) Teasing Luo Bu* 目連 (觀音)戲羅卜, *Granny Wang Cursing the Chicken* 王婆罵雞, and *The Complete Legend of Mulian* 目連全傳, etc.[21] In addition, the scene "Longing for the Human World" 思凡 (also known as "Longing for Spring" 思春, and "The Little Nun Descending the Mountain" 小尼姑 下山) in Mulian drama is also present in other theatrical forms, such as Qing drama 清戲, Chu drama 楚劇, the *hua gu* (flower drums) drama of Jingzhou 荊州花鼓戲 and that of Donglu 東路, etc.

The Mulian drama of Guangxi is even less known. During the reigns of Emperors Tongzhi and Guangxu in the Qing Dynasty (1862-1907), a *Gui* drama 桂劇 actor named Jiang Qingchuan 蔣晴川 of the Ruixiang 瑞祥 troupe went to Yongzhou 永州, Hunan to learn the complete text of *Mulian Rescues His Mother*. Afterwards, Jiang signed a contract in Guangxi to perform this play in the form of *Guihua* 桂花 (cassia flower) drama for half a month; as a result, Mulian drama became more popular in the region. In Guangxi , Mulian drama is very rich in content. Famous scenes like "The Dumb Carrying the

---

21 Liu Zhen, *Mulian Culture in China* 中國民間目連文化 (Chengdu: Bashu shushe, 1997), p. 195.

Demented" 啞背瘋 and "Pitching Big Forks at Lady Liu" 大叉劉氏娘 have won the applause of many. Pitching forks 打叉 is a very demanding task. Usually, three metal forks, each weighing 2.5 kilograms, are used. These forks have sharp edges in the shape of a curling goat horn that can easily cut into the stage floor and the pillars. The action can be performed in three ways, namely thirty-six forks, seventy-two forks and one hundred and eight forks. Needless to say, all performers have to be well-trained and highly skilled in order to perform the multitude of actions using forks; examples are: "hanging the tablet" 掛牌叉, "four doors" 四門叉, "head-burying" 埋頭叉, "rising three levels" 連昇三級, "the Goddess of Mercy on her lotus seat" 觀音坐蓮, "a beauty freshening up" 美女梳妝, "hitting one's son from across the mountain" 隔山打子, "yellow dragon coming out of the cave" 黃龍出洞 and "lion rolling a ball 獅子滾球. During the "big fork pitching," 打大叉, body actions like somersaults, rolling, flinging and falling are part of the throwing and catching of forks. Sometimes, up to three forks are used in one single action. In "hitting one's son from across the mountain," for example, the King of Demons 鬼王 will throw, and Lady Liu will catch the forks. The two actors usually stand back to back in a hide-and-seek manner until they eventually discover each other. Liu will then perform a "forward wheeling" or *gulu mao* 估轆毛, while the King of Demons will throw his fork backwards. When Liu's wheeling is done, the fork will land precisely on the spot between her legs. In "yellow dragon," Liu is seen running away when the King of Demons throws three forks at her simultaneously. Liu, noticing the motion of the forks from behind her, swiftly avoids the deadly weapons. The forks will then make their way into the big wooden pillar on one side of the stage. Such exquisite technique can only be seen where Mulian drama is still a living tradition.[22]

Judging from the extracts from the "General Index of Traditional Opera in Beijing" concerning the story of *Mulian Rescues His Mother* and the published scripts used in the Yu drama 豫劇 in Henan Province, it is perhaps not unfair to say that the editors of the *Minsu quyi* have a

---

22 Zhou Minzhen 周民震, ed., *A History of Chinese Opera: Guangxi Region* 中國戲曲志・廣西卷 (Beijing: ISBN, 1995), pp. 363-365.

general preference for Mulian drama in the southern parts of China. It is therefore important to recognize the potential for further research in areas like Shanxi, Tianjin, Shanxi, Shandong, Beijing and Henan. This will not only fill a gap in existing scholarship but also facilitate a comparative study of Mulian drama in the north and the south. This is especially important if we consider the presence of Mulian drama titles across a wide spectrum of popular theatres; e.g., Yu drama in the north, the *daoqing* 道情 of Henan and Shanxi, the Shangdang clapper musical 上黨梆子 and Yuan 宛 clapper opera, Pu drama 蒲劇, *taiping diao* 太平調 (tune of peace), *huai diao* 懷調, Qin tunes 秦腔, the *donglu* clapper opera 東路梆子 and the Shangdong clapper opera 山東梆子, and especially the incorporation of Mulian drama in Beijing Opera.

In Shanxi, Mulian drama has long been a popular form of minidrama. For example, *A White Chimpanzee Clearing the Way*, a tambourine miscellaneous play of Southern Shanxi 晉南鐃鼓雜戲, is a Mulian drama dating back to the Song 宋 and Jin 金 periods. In Nanshe Village 南舍村, Lucheng County 潞城縣, researchers discovered a hand-written handbook dating from 1594 in the Ming dynasty entitled *Forty Modes and Tunes for the Occasion of Welcoming the Gods* 迎神賽社禮節傳簿四十曲宮調, which contains a title "Beating Qingti" 打青堤. This play begins with Mulian embarking on a career in business, and gradually reveals the sins of Ms. Liu and her punishment for them. The plot resembles that in transformation texts (*bianwen*), and it is identical to the script of the same title in the *yuan-ben* version of the Jin dynasty 金院本. This discovery throws light on the historical development of Mulian drama during the transitional period between "miscellaneous plays" 雜劇 and Yuan drama. Mulian drama is performed only once a year during the religious festivals of the lunar new year in local communities. All actors are local farmers, and the performance is handed down from one generation to the next. Any slight alteration in the story is considered as an offence against the spirits, who will no longer protect the people as a result. "This type of drama has all along preserved its original character because it has never made its way to the cities, nor has it come into contact with other dramatic forms."[23]

---

23 Zhu Hengfu 朱恒夫, *Studies in Mulian Drama* 目連戲研究 (Nanjing: Nanjing University Press, 1993), p. 35.

According to another historical anecdote, during the late Ming dynasty, a rich merchant surnamed Su 蘇 in Nangan Village 南杆村, Yi Township 翼鎮, was an amateur performer of Mulian drama. When he returned to his home town from Nanjing, he also introduced Mulian drama to the country folk. Soon afterwards, Mulian drama was staged in Dongshi Bridge 東石橋, Gu Town 故城 and other neighbouring communities. Up to the early Qing Dynasty, there were altogether seven troupes specializing in Mulian drama, each having a crew of thirty to fifty. Mulian drama then gradually spread to other areas such as Foushan 浮山, Qinshui 泌水, Jiang County 絳縣, Wenxi 聞喜, Quwo 曲沃 and Houma 侯馬, until the founding of the PRC. Plays performed throughout this period included *Mulian Saving His Mother* and *A Tour of the Underworld* 游地獄, of which two long versions and a few individual scenes could last for as long as seven days. *Mulian Rescues His Mother* consists of stories about the human world and is performed during the day, as reflected by these titles: "Dusting the Hall of the Buddha" 掃佛堂, "Liu Baoshun Visiting the Grave" 劉保順上墳, "Mulian Returns Home" 目連還家, "Ms. Liu Takes an Oath" 劉氏發誓, "Liu Dies in the Garden" 花園劉死, "Divination" 算卦, "Inviting the Famous Physician" 請名醫, "Jupiter's Gift of the Nine-hoop Chain" 太白金星贈九連鐶, etc. A clear boundary is drawn between day and night performances. *A Tour in the Underworld*, as the title suggests, is set entirely in the underworld and the performance is staged at night to reinforce the sense of horror. Special effects such as mutilated body parts, bleeding, and creepy masquerades of demons and goblins abound in this nocturnal drama.[24] Day and night performances must not be confused.

One significant difference between Zheng Zhizhen's *Mulian Rescues His Mother and Preaches Goodness* and the Shanxi version of *Mulian Saving His Mother* is that the latter has a tragic ending. In this play, the hero Fu Luobu 傅羅卜 (i.e. the Mulian character) is a devoted Buddhist. After his father's death, he journeys to the Western Heaven (*xi tian* 西天) to obtain scriptures from the Buddha. His mother, nee Liu, breaks her vegetarian diet on her birthday. When the heavenly

24 Guo Shixing 郭士星, *A History of Chinese Opera: Shanxi Region* 中國戲曲志·山西卷 (Beijing: Wenhua yishu chubanshe, 1990), p. 168.

beings learn of her conduct, they order King Yama 閻王 to bring her down to hell. Mulian, knowing what has happened, brings along the Buddhist scriptures and break open the gate of hell to "redeem" his mother. He searches from Court One to Court Ten of Hell, but Liu cannot be found, for by this time his mother has been reborn as a white dog of a gentleman's family in Wang's estate in Pingyang East Prefecture 平陽東府. Mulian then goes to Wang's estate to ask for the white dog. His request being granted, Mulian carries his mother and the scriptures all the way back home. On his way, he passes by Jupiter's melon field. To relieve her son from the heat, Liu (the white dog) steals two melons from the field, but this angers Mulian all the more, for he thinks his mother is unrepenting. Mulian then throws the two melons half way up the mountain, carries his shoulder pole of scriptures and goes to the Western Heaven to seek scriptures for the second time. Meanwhile, Jupiter reports Liu's crime to King Yama, who immediately dispatches two demon attendants to cut off the white dog's (Liu's) head, throw it into a gully and take the headless dog back to hell.

The Mulian drama of Shanxi exhibits a unique artistic character. Originating from singing, its body language is less elaborate than other major dramatic genres. In terms of costume, all heavenly beings wear gold face paint, and the attendant goblins and demons all wear masks. The most exciting part is the ten scenes in the Underworld, where all oil lamps are extinguished and the only illumination comes from the pale blue lighted from three bowls of wine to create a spooky atmosphere.[25] During the Ming dynasty, plays such as *Mulian Saving His Mother* and *Ms. Liu Qingti* 劉青提 *Touring the Underworld* were staged in the Shangdang region. Such performances came to be known as *gong zhan* group theatre 供盞隊戲 and mime group theatre 啞隊戲.

During the Tongzhi-Guangxu period (1862-1908), famous actors in Tianjin like Wang Hongshou and Lu Yuechao specialized in performing *Mulian Saving His Mother*. In the early years of the Republic of China, Xiao Lanfen, an actress famous for her exquisite handling of the high tune voice, won the hearts of many theatre audiences by her annual New Year performance of this play.[26]

---

25 See Lu Keyi 魯克義, et al., *A Brief Introduction to Dramatic Forms in Shanxi* 山西劇種概說 (Taiyuan: Shanxi renmin chubanshe, 1984), p. 629.

In Beijing, the story of Mulian is incorporated into many traditional genres such as the octagonal drum 八角鼓, short drum lyrics 鼓詞小段, *lianhua luo* 蓮花落, and popular songs 時調小曲. Its popularity was widespread in local communities as well as in the imperial court. During the mid-Qing period, the longest play script in Chinese history was written by Zhang Zhao for court performances. Entitled "The Golden Rules of Goodness," this Mulian drama consists of two hundred and forty scenes in ten volumes. Nowadays, highlights from Mulian drama are among the favorites of Beijing Opera audiences; examples are: "Luo Bu's Path" 羅卜路, "Setting a Plan for Begging Alms"定計化緣, "Preaching Goodness" 勸善, "Going Home" 回家, "Sweeping the Floor" 掃地, "Oath" 盟誓, "Keeping a Deathwatch" 守靈回煞, "Thinking of My Home Town" 望鄉, "Slippery Oil"滑油, "Six Palaces" 六殿, "Eight Palaces"八殿, etc. Especially worth noting is that Mulian dramas have been important performances for Beijing opera. In the late Qing, for example, opera troupes performed such plays as "Performing Mulian" 演目連, "Oath" 盟誓 "Madame Liu Thinks of Home" 劉氏望鄉, "Luo Bu's Path" 羅卜路, "Longing for the World" 思凡, "Yulanpen (Ullambana) Festival"盂蘭盆會, "Making Plans to Beg for Alms" 定計化緣, "Slippery Mountain" 滑油山, and "Six Halls" 六殿. Many actors and actresses are well known for performing Mulian drama. For example, Hao Lantian 郝藍田, one of the famous "top thirteen" actors in the capital, is best known for his rendering of *Mulian Saving His Mother*. The others like Jiang Miaoxiang 姜妙香, Wang Yaoxing 王瑤卿, Wang Guifen 汪桂芬, Wang Xiaonong 汪笑儂 and Gai Jiaotian 蓋叫天 are all well known for their exquisite techniques. The texts of *Monk Mulian Saving His Mother* 目連僧救母 and *Demonic Hindrances* 魔障 are still used today.

From the very beginning, Mulian drama has been part of the popular cultural and religious tradition of different social groups in China and therefore has a strong regional character. In this respect, it is not surprising to find variations even within one province or one county in terms of origin, plot structure, characters and presentation. For example, in the Pu Xian version of *Mulian Rescues His Mother* in Fujian, the

---

26 Gao Jieyun 高介雲, *A History of Chinese Opera: Tianjin Region* 中國戲曲志‧天津卷 (Beijing: Wenhua yishu chubanshe, 1990), p. 71, 404.

character of Liu Jia is given much more emphasis and becomes a complex, outstanding personality. In Jiangsu and Shaoxing, Mulian drama is further distinguished by its several branches, i.e. Shaoxing 紹興, Kaihua 開化, Gaochun and Shangyu 上虞, which differ in origin, content and form.[27]

To conclude, in order to further our understanding of Mulian drama, researchers have to broaden their scope to explore the valuable resources in different regions; that is to say, detailed analysis of particular sources has to go hand in hand with a macro-perspective that takes into account the overall pattern in which Mulian drama develops in different areas. Meanwhile, we anticipate more fruitful research on Mulian drama not only in China but other countries as well. We also expect that a broadening academic horizon will bring out the true implications of Mulian drama as an influential cultural phenomenon.

---

27 Jiang Bin, *Popular Religions*, p. 373.

Studies in Chinese
Ritual, Theatre and
Folklore Series

A.
SOUTHWEST CHINA

3

THE DRAMA OF REDEMPTION OF VOWS OF THE LIVING (YANGXI) IN SICHUAN

A CRITICAL REVIEW OF CURRENT RESEARCH

Chen Yi-yuan

I. Books Reviewed

1. Duan Ming 段明, *Yangxi Performed with Masks: The Ritual Theatre of Xinglong Village, Xiaogang Township, Shuanghe District, Youyang County, Sichuan* 四川省酉陽縣土家族苗族自治縣雙河區小崗鄉興隆村面具陽戲. *Min-su ch'ü-i ts'ung-shu* 民俗曲藝叢書(Studies in Chinese Ritual, Theatre and Folklore Series), No. 4, 1993. 310 pages. Abbreviate below as *Yangxi Performed with Mask.*

2. Hu Tian-cheng 胡天成, *Vernacular Priest Plays of Jielong in Sichuan, Vol. 1* 四川省重慶市巴縣接龍區漢族的接龍陽戲——接龍端公戲之一. *Min-su ch'ü-i ts'ung-shu*, No. 18, 1994. 490 pages. Abbreviated below as *Plays of Jielong.*

3. Yu Yi 于一, Wang Kang 王康, and Chen Wenhan 陳文漢, *The Yangxi of Zitong: A Report from Hongzhai Village, Maming Township, Zitong County, Sichuan* 四川省梓潼縣馬鳴鄉紅寨村一帶的梓潼陽戲. *Min-su Ch'ü-i ts'ung-shu*, No. 19, 1994. 215 pages.

Abbreviated below as *The Yangxi of Zitong*.

4. Wang Yue 王躍, *The Redemption of Vows to the Gods: The Huanyang Play as Performed for the Liu Household in Longgang Village, Shujia Township, Jiangbei County, Sichuan* 四川省江北縣舒家鄉龍崗村劉宅的還陽戲. *Min-su ch'ü-i ts'ung-shu*, No. 49, 1996. 322 pages. Abbreviated below as *Huanyang Plays*.

I have elsewhere pointed out the contribution of *Min-su ch'ü-i ts'ung-shu* in my initial commentaries on its first four series, all of which are "rich in content and valuable source materials," "full of vivid presentations of historical documents with high academic value" and "revealing and provocative." All this makes the *Min-su ch'ü-i ts'ung-shu* an "excellent example in the conservation of cultural treasures."[1]

It is encouraging indeed to see the publication of another two series with twenty more volumes on the list. This essay is a continuation of my previous work and concentrates on the four volumes on the *yangxi* in Sichuan cited above. A comparison is also made between these four volumes and studies on *yangxi* 陽戲 in other areas, i.e. *The Yangxi play of Guizhou: A Case Study of the Deng Family Troupe in Dashang Village, Limu Township, Luodian County* 貴州陽戲——以羅甸縣栗木鄉達上村鄧氏戲班爲例 (No. 38), and the *yangxi* in Yunan and Hunan which are not yet covered by the *Min-su ch'ü-i ts'ung-shu*. My aim is to give a more comprehensive view of the tradition and characteristics of *yangxi* in different regions.

II. Background

1. Since the four books under review are about *yangxi* in Sichuan, it is imperative that we have a basic understanding of the current state of research in this area in order to evaluate the present volumes.

2. Since we have four volumes on the same subject, it is necessary to summarize and comment on each volume before giving an overall evaluation.

1　See my essay "Qiangjiu wenhua yichan de chenggong dianfan 搶救文化遺產的成功典範," in *Zhongguo wenhua* 中國文化, 14 (1996): 259-261.

What follows is an overview of current research on *yangxi* in Sichuan.

Yangxi, a form of ritual drama to redeem vows, dispel harmful forces and acquire good fortune, has been widely practiced in many provinces on the mainland such as Sichuan, Guizhou, Yunnan and Hunan in the last 100-200 years. However, there has been a general lack of in-depth research on this subject. Studies on *yangxi* in Sichuan began only in the mid-1980's, when researchers took the initiative to compile collections of local dances, operatic music and the history of local opera in different regions of the country.

In 1987, a volume titled *The Lantern Drama and Nuo Drama of Sichuan* 四川燈戲與四川儺戲 was published by the editorial board of *A History of Chinese Opera: Sichuan Region* 中國戲曲志・四川卷. In this volume, a number of articles on this subject are included in the section "The *Nuo* Drama in Sichuan," for example "A Brief Introduction to the *Nuo* Drama in Sichuan" 四川儺戲簡述 (Yu Yi), "*Yangxi*" (Jiang Ying 蔣瑩), and "*Ti Yangxi* in Shejian" 射箭提陽戲 (Xiong Beide 熊北德). This volume represents the initial efforts in the study of *yangxi* in Sichuan. In April, 1989, the Conference on the *Nuo* Drama in Sichuan was held in Guangyuan City. The proceedings were subsequently published in *Nuo Drama: A Collection of Essays*, which also included other essays such as "The *Yangxi* of Jiange" 劍閣陽戲 (Wang Yansheng 王炎生, and Wang Xingzhi 王興志), and "The Ancient *Yangxi* of Zitong" 古老的梓潼陽戲 (Hao Gang 郝剛).

Research papers on *yangxi* have increased in number since 1990; for instance, Yu Yi ("The Art of Masks in Sichuan" 四川面具藝術概述) and Duan Ming ("A Kaleidoscope of Plastic Arts: the Use of Masks in Sichuan" 豐富多彩的造形藝術)[2] emphasize the use of masks in the *yangxi* of Youyang 酉陽 and Zitong. However, it is only in Wang Yue's essay "The Characteristics of *Yangxi* in Sichuan: A Preliminary Study" 試論四川陽戲的特色 that a more comprehensive study of this popular dramatic genre is attempted.[3] In his essay, Wang delineates the four main characteristics common to the *yangxi* in different regions, such as Zitong, Hechuan 合川, Jiangbei, Ba County and Youyang: (1) *yangxi* is

---

2 Yu's essay was published in *Yuzhou yi tan* 渝州藝譚, 1992.2: 96-99; Duan's essay was published in *Yuzhou yi tan*, 1992.3: 102-105.

3 *Yuzhou yi tan*, 1994.1: 68-72.

usually performed for the gods to ask for blessings; (2) the scale of the ritual is usually very large; (3) the dramatic form is versatile and uses a wide variety of stage devices such as puppets, masks and facial make-up; and (4) all these rituals honor the same gods, namely, the Master of Sichuan 川主, the Earth Master 土主 and the Medicine King 藥王. Wang's analysis is very reliable because it is made on the solid foundation of academic research in Sichuan.

Regional studies on *yangxi* in Sichuan after 1990 have increased both in number and in variety. For example, for *yangxi* in Youyang there is Duan Ming's "The Origins of the Masked *Yangxi* in Youyang" 酉陽面具陽戲的源流初探.[4] For *yangxi* in Jielong, we have Hu Tiancheng's 胡天成 "A Brief Introduction to *Yangxi* in Jielong" 接龍陽戲略述, while an in-depth account of the music of *yangxi* in Jielong is provided in Zhang Yongan's 張永安 "Nine Rhythms and Thirteen Tunes: Local Ritual Music in Jielong" 接龍民間祭祀音樂中的九板十三腔.[5] Studies in *yangxi* in Jiangbei include several essays by Wang Yue, namely "*Yangxi* in Jiangbei: An Introduction" 江北陽戲初探, "The 'Mulian' Character in Yin Drama: the Hand-written Copy of the Yin Play of Liu Jieyin and Its Performing Style" 陰戲中的目連——劉潔銀「陰戲」抄本及演出特色, and "The Four 'Plum Flower' Segments of Mulian Plays in *Huanyin* Drama: A Study of *Yangxi* in Jiangbei" 江北陽戲還陰戲中的目連戲 "梅花" 四壇.[6] Shejian *yangxi* is the subject of Luo Hong's 羅虹, "Shejian Ti *Yangxi* in Guangyuan" 廣元射箭提陽戲, and Yu Yi's "Nuo Drama: An Investigation of the Shejian Ti *Yangxi* in Guangyuan."[7] The *Yangxi* of Zitong 梓潼陽戲 is another noteworthy attempt. Edited by Huang Daode 黄道德 and Yu Yi, this collection of essays covers a wide range of interesting subjects, including: "Explorations in the *Yangxi* of Zitong" 梓潼陽戲的發掘 (Huang Daode), "The *Yangxi* of Zitong: A Unique Art Form" 藝術獨

---

4 *Yuzhou yi tan*, 1993.2: 72-77.

5 See Hu's essay in *Yuzhou yi tan*, 1992.3: 110-116, and Zhang's essay in *Yuzhou yi tan*, 1994.1: 73-84.

6 Respectively, in *Yuzhou yi tan*, 1992.2: 105-113; 1993.2: 62-71, and *Mulian xi yu Ba Shu wenhua* 目連戲與巴蜀文化 (special edition of *Sichuan xiju* 1993), August 1993: 83-86.

7 Luo, in *Minjian wenxue luntan* 民間文學論壇 1991.1: 57-58, and Yu, in *Bianguji* 邊鼓集 (Beijing: Wenhua yishu chubanshe), 1991, pp. 169-174.

特，表現手段別具一格的梓潼陽戲 (Yu Yi), "The *Yangxi* of Zitong" 梓潼陽戲 (Yao Guangpu 姚光譜 & Hao Gang), "The Hand-written Copies of *Yangxi* in Zitong" 梓潼陽戲的手抄本 (He Nong 何農), "Monk Mulian Touring the Six Grand Halls: A Preliminary Study of a *Yangxi* Script" 梓潼陽戲 "目連僧遊六殿" 劇本初探 (Chen Dezhong 陳德忠), "The *Yangxi* and the Local Drama of Zitong" 梓潼陽戲與梓潼戲 (Tang Yongxiao 唐永嘯), "On the Music of *Yangxi* in Zitong" 關於梓潼陽戲的音樂 (Yi Yu 一愚). The book also includes descriptions of local rituals such as "Opening Speech at the Stage Gate in Front of the Altar" 戲門啓白壇前儀, "Performance Devoted to Heaven" 天戲, and "Performance Devoted to the Earth" 地戲, all which are valuable academic sources.[8] Yu Yi further elaborates on the "earth performance" in the *yangxi* of Zitong.in another article "A Living Fossil of Ancient *Nuo* Ritual: Er lang Purging and Wenchang Purging" 古代驅儺的 "活化石" ──二郎掃蕩與文昌掃蕩.[9]

In general, there is still a discrepancy between research publications on *yangxi* and the huge popularity of *yangxi* in Sichuan. Moreover, these publications seem lacking in depth, probably due to regulations on published materials.

A very encouraging fact is that researchers in this field are very devoted to their subject. Due to their persistence, they have accumulated enough research materials for publication whenever the opportunity arises. No doubt Professor Wang Ch'iu-kuei has recruited the right people, who are all experts in *yangxi* in Sichuan, to work on his project, "Chinese Regional Theatre in Its Social and Ritual Context" 中國地方戲與儀式之研究.

It is only through these four volumes published in the *Min-su ch'ü-i ts'ung-shu* that academics in the field can have a better understanding of *yangxi* in Sichuan, and also the individual characteristics of its many regional forms, i.e. the *yangxi* in Youyang, Jielong, Zitong and Jiangbei, as will be explained later.

---

8 This volume was jointly published by the Cultural Bureau of Mianyang City , the editorial board of *A History of Chinese Opera: Sichuan Region* and the Cultural Bureau of Zitong County. Yao and He later co-authored another essay, "The Cultural Background of Yangxi in Zitong" 梓潼陽戲的文化淺識, published in *Min-su ch'ü-i*, 83 (1993): 149-159.

9 *Yuzhou yi tan*, 1993.4: 77-79.

III. Youyang *Yangxi* Performed with Masks

As Wang Yue has said in "The Characteristics of *Yangxi* in Sichuan: A Preliminary Study" (quoted above), *yangxi* in Sichuan performs the function of paying tribute to the gods for the redemption of vows; the ritual is very comprehensive in scale with a versatile dramatic form. These ritual activities honor the same deities, namely the Master of Sichuan, the Master of the Earth and the King of Medicine. Despite such similiarities, *yangxi* is also very localized in outlook and has developed many regional forms. The *yangxi* in Youyang, for example, has a greater emphasis on the use of masks compared with other regions, and is therefore called "masked *yangxi*."

Duan Ming's *Yangxi Performed with Masks* was published in December, 1993. In Youyang, masked *yangxi* is also known as *tiao xi* 跳戲 (or dance drama). Duan's book is based on his own observation of two such performances in February 1993 in Xinglong Village, one of which was performed in the home of Wu Changxin 吳長新 (*yuan zhu* 願主, the vow maker) for the redemption of vows; the other in the home of Wu Changfu 吳長富 (*tan zhu* 壇主, the altar master) to give thanks to the gods and worship the ancestors. The details of the rituals and the dramatic performances recorded by Duan were based on the oral descriptions of Wu Changfu. Duan also gives comprehensive accounts of the historical backgrounds of Xinglong Village and masked *yangxi*, the *tiao xi* ritual and its procedures, the *yangxi* troupes as well as the attitudes of the locals and the performers toward *tiao xi*. The appendix consists of details of the masked performances and, more importantly, original scripts of masked *yangxi* including *Lan Ji Zi* 藍繼子, *Giving a Belt [as a token]*; *[Promising] Appointment as an Official* 解帶封官, *Old Du Sending off the Son* [*of Liu Gao* 劉高] 老杜送子, *Winter Plum Flowers* 冬梅花 and *Big Laughter* 大笑記.

According to Duan, "performances by the troupe are all about the human world, for *yangxi* troupes never get involved in funeral ceremonies. All the characters are human beings and all except the heroine put on masks." (p. 15) "Although the masked performances in Xinglong Village have a typical structure (i.e. inviting the gods, giving thanks to

the gods, praying to the gods and sending off the gods), the actual procedure is less elaborate."(p. 84) Thus, the *yangxi* in Youyang is characterized by its extensive use of masks (around twenty to thirty in each
troupe) and a less refined ritual.

Unfortunately, this local form of *yangxi* is dying out due to the lack
of new performers. In Shuanghe District, Wu Changfu is the only
remaining mask maker, while the local public, even some troupe members themselves, are showing less and less interest in *tiao xi*. This is the
stark reality of this fading local tradition that Duan's book has brought
to our attention.

IV. Plays of Jielong

The situation of *yangxi* in Jielong is even worse than that in Youyang.
Ever since the government prohibition of all religious activities in the
1950's, local *yangxi* performances have almost completely died out.
This explains why Hu Tiancheng had to "conduct his research through
in-depth interviews and scrape through the intricate webs of source
materials in order to reconstruct a complete picture of *yangxi* performances in the old days." (p. 82)

In the past, *yangxi*, altar of congratulation, and prolongation of life
were the three major parts of *duangong xi* 端公戲 (the drama of the ver-
nacalar priest). Hu has done extensive field research and interviews
with performers on these subjects and the results are given in his
reports. His studies on the altar of congratulation and prolongation of
life have been published in the *Min-su ch'ü-i ts'ung-shu* (No. 34, 35).
Hu's study is primarily based on interviews with family troupe performers (Yang Zhongli 楊中立 of Baiyang Village 白楊村, Jiang Weilin 江
維林 of Yaotan Village 么灘村, and You Zemin 猶澤民 of Xinwan
Village 新灣村). In his attempt to reconstruct the operatic performances
of both the inside altar 內壇 and the outside altar 外壇, Hu has consulted a large number of *yangxi* play scripts, including the *Yangxi quanji* 陽
戲全集, a four volume collection from the Daoguang (1821-1850),
Xianfeng (1851-1861), Guangxu (1875-1908) and Republican periods
(1911-1949), and a total of some eighty versions of ten "gongtang"
plays 公堂劇本. The samples chosen for interviews come from a broad

spectrum of *yangxi* practitioners. Among the three family-run troupes, one specialized in inside altar worship, one in outside altar worship, and the other in both. These troupes no longer perform *yangxi* and have taken up funeral ceremonies and funeral music as a profession. From these sample interviews, Hu was able to recapture the details of *yangxi* performance in Jielong, especially the twenty-four plays (i.e. the twenty-four altars), even when recording a live performance became impossible.

Indeed, there are certain obstacles that remain when the author tries to discriminate between the various song scripts and play scripts used in the inside and outside altar respectively to reconstruct the entire process of *yangxi* performance. For example, the four volumes of *The yangxi quanji* are far from complete in their original form, for the titles, the texts, or even the contents page may be missing. Furthermore, the various altars are not arranged in the proper order, and some song scripts are either too brief or only used on special occasions. This is typical of this kind of written documents, which are rather spontaneous because local *yangxi* performances are highly flexible in form, and there is no rule against improvisation. Hu's "integrative analysis" seems too contrived in methodology. First, it attempts a rather rigid comparison between the order and titles of the different altars based on *The yangxi quanji* and the views of the performers (p. 58 -59); second, it seeks to supplement the existing sources with other *yangxi* song scripts outside of Jielong, and even with the religious texts used in the prolongation of life ritual, something very different from *yangxi* itself (p. 88-89). Hu's method in this respect, I think, should be carefully reconsidered.

As we shall see, Hu's treatment of the *gongtang* play script *Plum Flowers: Fortune telling* 梅花・算命 and the Daoguang period script *Weeping over the Tomb, Sitting in the Hall* 哭墳・坐殿 has overlooked the possibility that they may be used as transitions from *yangxi* to *yinxi* 陰戲(the redemption of vows for the dead), as in the *yangxi* of Jiangbei.

A minor discrepancy should be noted: the thirty footnotes in the first part of this book are missing in the present edition, probably due to an editorial oversight.

V. The *Yangxi* of Zitong

The performing style of *yangxi* in Sichuan differs regionally. As I mentioned, the *yangxi* in Youyang uses a lot of masks. In Jielong, "according to Jiang Weilin and others, only the Earth Deity 土地 wears the 'stage face cover' during the performance; all actors will have their faces painted."[10] How about the *yangxi* of Zitong? "According to the altar master Liu Yingfu, there were about twenty to thirty masks used in the *yangxi* of Zitong, but they have been either lost or damaged. At present, only three of them, the Earth Deity, the Underworld Magistrate 判官, and the deity Er-lang 二郎, are preserved in Dengjia Bay."[11] Today, *yangxi* in Zitong mainly uses string puppets to play the central roles, accompanied by masked and painted-face performances. According to "Jiang Guangjin 江廣金, Yu Wansheng 余萬盛 and other veteran performers of *duangong* plays [in Jiangbei], string puppet shows were part of *yangxi* performances in the past. Their masters have all seen these puppet shows. Going back in time, it was before the late Qing"[12] but they are now lost. Thus, we see that the string puppets in Zitong come from a very long tradition.

The *Yangxi of Zitong* was published in May, 1994. As part of their research, the authors carried out a covert investigation of the only secret *yangxi* gathering in 1987 and arranged a special performance. The result was a detailed description of the entire process of the *yangxi* ritual in Zitong, including the organization, the troupes, the performances as well as the dramatic form. We come to know that *yangxi* is also called "carrying the deities" (*ti lao ye* 提老爺). This nickname comes from *tian xi* 天戲 (a play for Heaven), a ritual for the redemption of vows, where thirty-two puppet deities are invited to go on-stage. *Tian xi* (also

---

10 Quotation from Hu Tiancheng, *Vernacular Priest Plays of Jielong in Sichuan*, Vol. 1, p. 69.

11 Quotation from Yu Yi et al., *The Yangxi of Zitong: A Report from Hongzhai Village, Maming Township, Zitong County, Sichuan*, p. 58.

12 Quotation from Wang Yue, *The Redemption of Vows to the Gods: The Huanyang Playas Performed for the Liu Household in Gang Village, Shujia Township, Jiangbei County, Sichuan*, p. 9.

called *yin yi tang* 陰一堂) and *di xi* 地戲 (a play for the Earth or *yang yi tang* 陽一堂) are held together to form the so-called *zheng xi* 正戲 (the play proper). The play proper consists of three successive parts, namely: "burning incense, setting off firecrackers, and hanging [scrolls of the] deities" 燒香放炮掛老爺, "opening address at the altar" 開壇啓白, and finally "seating the gods" 安神歸位. In order to please the audience, *qing xi* 清戲, a non-ritual drama featuring both Sichuan drama (*Chuan ju* 川劇) and popular lantern plays, are performed. Even Mulian plays such as *Monk Mulian Touring the Six Halls of the Purgatory* 目連僧遊六殿 have been used. The influence of Sichuan drama can be seen from the fact that *di xi* has adapted the singing tunes of Sichuan drama.

Also note-worthy is the religious coloring of *yangxi* in Zitong that differentiates it from the *yangxi* in other regions. In the past, *yangxi* was also known as "*yangxi jiao* (teaching)," from which women were prohibited. In addition to the "three saints" (The Master of Sichuan, the Master of the Earth, and the King of Medicine), they also worshiped the deity *Hua zhu* 化主 (the Emperor Wenchang of Zitong 梓潼文昌帝君). *Hua zhu* is honored as one of the *zheng shen* 正神 (central deities). This has to do with the long Daoist tradition in Zitong ever since the Zhang Daoling 張道陵 founded Heavenly Master Daoism 天師道 back in the Eastern Han Dynasty. From then on, Zitong has been a major Daoist center. As the authors say in the book, "the relations [between *yangxi* in Zitong and Daoism] are yet to be explored."(p. 108) For further discussion on this subject, see Wang Chunwu 王純五, "The Influence of Heavenly Master Daoism on *Nuo* Drama in Sichuan" 天師道對四川儺戲的影響.[13]

VI. *Huanyang* Plays of Jiangbei

Instead of the deity *Hua zhu* in Zitong, in the *yangxi* of Jiangbei the "six great uncles and aunts" 六位公婆 (i.e. three great uncles and three great aunts, or the three Feng brothers and their wives) are the preeminent deities besides the three saints. No performers can say for sure how

---

13 *Min-su ch'ü-i*, 96 (1995): 3-126.

exactly the Feng couples were deified, and in what way they are related to *yangxi*. They only know that in every ritual a special altar is provided to invite the six deities to enjoy sacred offerings. This altar is called "hui shu" 回熟 or "*hui bo gong shu*" 回伯公熟. It is not seen in *duangong* rituals elsewhere, not even the more complex *yangxi* in Jielong.

According to Wang Yue, *yangxi* in Jiangbei in general consists of twenty-four segments called the "twenty-four altars of *yangxi*" (*The Yangxi in Jiangbei*, 1996). Wang conducted a survey of a *huanyang* 還陽 (redemption of vows) ritual in the household of Liu Lunru 劉倫如 in Longgang Village in December 1992. The purpose of this ritual was to give thanks to the gods for the vows made by his parents who had passed away. Two altars were added at the beginning and end of the ritual, namely "Invitation" and "Serving Food", making a total of twenty-six altars. Compared to Hu Tiancheng's study of *yangxi* in Jielong, which also consists of twenty-four altars, Wang Yue's findings are very different in terms of the altar sequence and altar titles. Most interestingly, from the vernacular priests (*duangong* 端公) the author came to know that *yinxi* 陰戲, a special form of ritual drama, was derived from *yangxi*:

> "*Yinxi* is staged when someone has died before he or she could redeem his or her vows to the gods in the form of *yangxi*...The structure of *yinxi* is slightly different from that of *yangxi*. First, Daoist and Buddhist rituals such as "Calling Forth" 召請 and "offering Food" 獻食 are added...Second, in *huanyin xi* 還陰戲, four 'Plum' segments are added. Originally, the "Plum Flower" 梅花 and "Fortune Telling" 算命 segments were formal procedures in *yangxi*, but somehow they are no longer practiced in *huanyang xi* 還陽戲 but only in *huanyin xi*. Furthermore, during an actual performance, they are usually divided into four segments, namely "Plum Flower," "Fortune Telling," "Crying Over the Tomb" 哭墳 and "Sitting in the Palace" 坐殿.

Wang also observes that "*Yinxi* sometimes refers to only the four segments mentioned above. They are stories about Mulian, but the plot is different from that in Sichuan drama; thus, it is a very special kind of Mulian yinxi." (pp. 15-16)

Wang's observations can supplement what Hu Tiancheng has not dealt with in *The Yangxi in Jielong;* also, Wang's study helps explain why the story "Mulian the Monk Touring the Six Halls of the Purgatory" 目連僧遊六殿 appears in the *qingju* 清劇 texts of the *yangxi* in Zitong.

VII. Overall Comments (1)

Although different kinds of *yangxi* in Sichuan in general exhibit certain common characteristics, we have seen how the *yangxi* in Youyang, Jielong, Zitong and Jiangbei differ in both artistic form and ritual content. These ritual practices may even influence the *yangxi* in nearby counties, a notable point raised in a recent study of *yangxi* in Guizhou County.

The widespread presence of *yangxi* in southern Guizhou has been noted by Yao Guimei 姚桂梅 in her essay "Miscellaneous Reflections on the *Yangxi* in Qiannan" 黔南陽戲雜識散議 (1994).[14] *Yangxi* is especially popular in the villages of Luodian, Pingtang, Huishui, Fuquan, and Wengan counties. In October 1995, the *Minsu quyi* Series published another volume, *Yangxi in Guizhou* 貴州陽戲. The author, Huangfu Chongqing 皇甫重慶, spent eighteen months (from February 1993 to August 1994) doing field research in southern Guizhou. According to Huangfu, *yangxi* in Guizhou has a very prominent theme, the redemption of vows to the gods, which is also highly ritualistic in nature. Besides the use of masks as a characterization technique, the three saints, the Sichuan Master, the Earth Master and the King of Medicine are worshipped, sometimes together with Emperor Wenchang and the martial Saint Guan 關聖. *Yangxi* in Southern Guizhou is therefore deeply rooted in the culture of Sichuan. According to many *yangxi* performers, their "ancestors migrated from Sichuan to Guizhou." Some said their "ancestors first migrated from Jiangxi to Sichuan, then from Sichuan to Guizhou." From what he heard from these performers, Huangfu believes that "the *yangxi* of Guizhou probably came from Sichuan." (p. 17) In "The Cultural Background of Yangxi in Zitong," 梓潼陽戲的文

---

14 *Yiwen luncong* 藝文論叢, 1994.4: 62-67.

化淺識 He Gang and Yao Guangpu argue that the *yangxi* of Sichuan also spread to Yunnan: "During the reign of Tongzhi in the Qing Dynasty, a *yangxi* performer in Zitong, Ye Deqing 葉德青, led his troupe from Sichuan to Yunnan. In 1985, Liu Shiren 劉詩仁, an official for historical records from the Zhuang Nationality Autonomous County in Wenshan, Yunnan, wrote an article saying that 'Zitong drama' was brought into Yunnan by a performer from Zitong County, Mianzhou Prefecture, Sichuan. The *yangxi* of Zitong has a direct influence not only on the 'Zitong drama' of Wenshan, but also on the customs, music, singing tunes, titles, and dramatic form of the region."[15]   In addition, Zhao Dahong 趙大宏 in "The Yangxi and Chong Nuo Drama of the Han People in Taiping Village, Xichou County, Yunnan" 雲南省西疇縣太平村的漢族陽戲、衝儺戲 [16] points out that *yangxi* was present in Wenshan County, Yunnan; moreover, old manuscripts such as *A Complete Collection of Newly Recorded Yangxi* were kept in the home of a Zitong drama performer Chen Hongzhang 陳洪章. Zhao believes that A Complete Collection probably came from the *nuo* theatre troupes in the north region of southern Guizhou, since the Chen household had lived in northeastern Guizhou for three generations. However, this tradition could have been learned at any point along the journey the Chen family once took in their long history of migration, i.e. from Jiangxi to Hunan, from Hunan to Sichuan, and from Sichuan to Guizhou. The Chen family troupe still performs *yangxi* honoring the same deities, i.e. the Master of Sichuan, the Earth Master, the King of Medicine and the Emperor Wenchang (or the Emperor Zitong 梓潼帝君). Other similar deities like Meihua *Er Jie* 梅花二姐 (i.e. Plum Flower Sisters) and the Three Great Uncles and Aunts 三伯公婆, are also present. All this suggests a close affinity between *yangxi* in Yunnan and Sichuan.

Nowadays, besides Sichuan, Guizhou and Yunnan, *yangxi* is also popular in the Tujia and Miao autonomous zones and the Huaihua region in western Hunan. Here, *yangxi* is named after the counties, as in Fenghuang *yangxi* 鳳凰陽戲, Jishou *yangxi* 吉首陽戲, Dayong *yangxi* 大庸陽戲, Yuanling *yangxi* 沅陵陽戲, Huaihua *yangxi* 懷化陽戲, etc.

---

15 C.f. No. 8, p. 158. Liu's essay, "The Origins of Zitong Drama" 梓潼戲探源 was published in *Minzu yishu yanjiu* 民族藝術研究, 1993.2: 16-20.

16 *Min-su ch'ü-i*, 96 (1995): 3-126.

The origin of these *yangxi* varieties is closely related to the *nuo tang xi* 儺堂戲 and local lantern plays in western Hunan; at some point it was also influenced by Chenhe drama 辰河戲. After the fifties, professional *yangxi* troupes were set up in these counties; however, these performances differ significantly from local ritual drama in terms of structure, procedure and content, and they no longer resemble the *yangxi* in Sichuan, Guizhou and Yunnan.[17]

VIII. Overall Comments (2)

Apparently, *yangxi* in Hunan is not as intimately linked to *yangxi* in Sichuan as in the case of Guizhou and Yunnan. However, new discoveries are still possible if more efforts could be spent on traditional *yangxi* in the rural areas in Hunan. Tremendous results have been brought about by the use of anthropological and ethnological methods in the study of *yangxi* in Youyang, Jielong, Zitong and Jiangbei, without which our present understanding of *yangxi* in Sichuan, i.e. its general and regional character, would have been impossible. The four volumes discussed in this essay draw attention to the interesting fact that performers in Jielong, Zitong and Jiangbei unanimously claim that their ancestors came from Macheng County, Hubei (and most often from Xiaogan Township 孝感鄉). Performers in Youyang believe they are natives of Jiangxi, which coincides with the view of some performers in Guizhou. This phenomenon fits well with the great migrations in the Ming and Qing dynasties. If this is true, can we say that the vast regions of Hubei, Hunan, Jiangxi, Sichuan, Guizhou and Yunnan constitute a "*yangxi* belt" or "*yangxi* constellation"?

The four books discussed here are a vast resource of both oral and written literatures on *yangxi*. The authors have raised a lot of thought-provoking issues that deserve more in-depth research in the future. Needless to say, these publications have contributed greatly to the preservation of our cultural treasures.

---

17 See *A History of Chinese Opera: Hunan Region* 中國戲曲志‧湖南卷 (Beijing: Wenhua yishu chubanshe, 1990), pp. 108-109.

4

THREE BOOKS ON THE *DUANGONG* RITUAL OF JIANGBEI COUNTY, SICHUAN BY WANG YUE

Hsu Li-ling

1. *"Offerings to the God of Wealth": A Chinese Ritual Performance by the Tao Lineage of Shangxin Village, Shujia Township, Jiangbei County, Sichuan* 四川省江北縣舒家鄉上新村陶宅的漢族祭財神儀式. *Min-su ch'ü-i ts'ung-shu* 民俗曲藝叢書 (Studies in Chinese Ritual, Theatre and Folklore Series), No. 5, 1993. 368 pages. Abbreviated as *Offerings to the God of Wealth*.
2. *The "Altar of Congratulation" Ritual of the 'Fourth Precinct' Chen Household in Xiemu Village, Fusheng Township, Jiangbei County, Sichuan* 江北縣復盛鄉協睦村四社諶宅的慶壇祭儀調查. *Min-su ch'ü-i ts'ung-shu*, No. 6, 1993. 530 pages. Abbreviated as *Altar of Congratulation*.
3. *The Redemption of Vows to the Gods: The Huanyang Play as Performed for the Liu Household in Longgang Village, Shujia Township, Jiangbei County, Sichuan* 四川省江北縣舒家鄉龍崗村劉宅的還陽戲. *Min-su ch'ü-i ts'ung-shu*, No. 49, 1996. 322 pages. Abbreviated as *The Redemption of Vows to the Gods*.

I. Summary of Contents

1. Offerings to the God of Wealth

The subject of this study is a ritual performance in Jiangbei county from March 17th to 18th, 1992. This book consists of six chapters. Chapter One is a background introduction to Shujia Township Shangxin village and the Tao Lineage. Upon close reading, this chapter can in fact be divided into three, instead of two, parts. The first part is a brief account of the geographical location, topography and population of Shujia County. The description of the *duangong* 端公, the ritual master, in part two, is the main focus of this chapter. It introduces the local religious tradition with a detailed description of the practice of *duangong*. Also included is an account of the professional status and heritage of *duangong* in Sichuan and other details about the ritual. Background information concerning the Tao lineage is given in part three. Chapter Two gives further details about the origins of ritual titles and a historical account of the ritual performance. Research findings on Zhao Gongming 趙公明, the martial god of wealth (*wu caishen* 武財神), and the four gods of wealth (*siguan caishen* 四官財神) are also included. The final section briefly describes the procedure of the ritual, including observations of the ritual masters, the host and those who attended the ceremony.

Chapter Three is the main focus of the entire volume. There is a detailed description of the process of the ritual with explanations. Chapter Four provides further descriptions of the ritual company. This includes those who participated in the performance and their relationship as masters and apprentices, as well as the master's costume case, ritual instruments and drawings of deities. Chapter Five provides reproductions of drawings of the ritual setting without any explanatory notes. Five appendices are attached in Chapter Six. Appendix 1 consists of four charts, two of which are name lists of the monasteries, temples and practicing ritual masters in Shujia Township before 1949. The other two are hand-made maps of Chongqing City and Jiangbei County.

Appendices 2, 3 and 4 contain the scripts and the lyrics of the entire performance in seventeen parts. Appendix 5 briefly records a 'four gods of wealth' ritual (*tiao siguan lao* 跳四官佬) performed in Maliu Township 麻柳鄉, Jiangbei County, based on the author's field notes of late 1989.

2. Altar of Congratulation

This book is an account of an 'altar of congratulation' ritual performed in Fusheng Township, Jiangbei County, Sichuan Province on December 9th, 1992. It consists of four chapters. Chapter One is a brief description of the geographical environment of Xiemu Village where the ritual took place, and the sacred altar of the Chen household, the host family. The "Altar of Congratulation" ritual is "a kind of family worship where a ritual master is invited to the household to pay tribute to the god of the altar." In Chapter Two, a detailed description of the "altar of congratulation" ritual is given, including locally worshiped upper and lower altars, the origins of the god of the altar, and the religious ceremonies relating to these altars. In Chapter Three the author records in detail the entire process of the ritual, which involved a total of twenty-one parts, from preparation, "invoking the god" to "enshrining." In addition, the contents of the religious texts and lyrics for chanting are also included. Chapter Four gives brief biographical details of the members of the *duangong* company in charge of the ceremony as well as descriptions of the costume case, ritual instruments and ritual drawings of deities. The Appendix includes the texts of two *duangong* ritual plays, *Qianyuan County* 乾元縣 and *The Battle of Mount Qi* 戰岐山, and some religious texts used in the ritual. There is also a photograph of the ritual master's hand gestures.

3. The Redemption of Vows to the Gods

Practiced by the local people of Jiangbei County, Sichuan, *yang xi* 陽戲 is also known as *Wuyang shen xi* 舞陽神戲, a form of ritual play to fulfill vows to the gods. A family whose vows are answered has to invite a local *duangong* to perform *huanyang xi*, or the "redemption of vows to the gods" ritual to express their gratitude to the gods. This book is about a ritual performed in Shujia Township, Jiangbei County in

December 1992. There are altogether five chapters with an appendix. Chapter One is a brief account of Longgang Village (where the ritual took place), the Liu household (the host), and also the reasons for staging the play. Chapter Two traces the development of the ritual with a description of its twenty-four part structure, the taboos to be observed during the performance and the gods invoked in the play. Also mentioned in this chapter is *yin xi* 陰戲, a variation of *yang xi* performed in four parts of *Mulian* xi 目連戲. Chaper Three, the major chapter, mainly concerns the ritual itself. Instead of having the standard twenty-four parts, two more were added as the actual circumstances required. Chapter Four consists of brief descriptions of the performers, the costume case and ritual instruments. Chapter Five investigates the origins of the three most important gods: the Sichuan Master 川主, the Earth Master 土主, and the Medicine King 藥王. The Appendix, in seven sections, includes part of the ritual texts used and the text of the play, as well as the legends of the three gods according to the local oral tradition and related ritual performances.

II. Critique

As ethnographical records, these three volumes are very comprehensive in descriptive details and contain a valuable pool of first hand sources, e.g. hand-written ritual texts, scripts and hand gestures of ritual masters which have never been publicized. The discovery of these valuable records and materials is therefore the most distinguished achievement of these studies. However, there are areas which need further consideration:

1. Instead of first-hand description of the economic and cultural conditions of the target communities, the author employs a huge amount of statistical data for this purpose. This over-reliance on numerical data inevitably obscures the most important factor of all, human beings. In other words, despite their meticulous details, these studies fail to provide any realistic account of the way of life and thinking of the local people.

2. There is no mention of local architecture and the household design of the host family in these volumes. Since ritual is inseparable from the

place where it is performed, and the local architectural style is intimately connected with the lifestyle of the people and even their religious beliefs, the design and use of houses are expressions of the inhabitants' cosmic world views and religious beliefs. In *Altar of Congratulations*, for example, the author makes no attempt to account for the relationship between the local people's spatial and architectural concepts and the overall design of the sacred altars.

3. The author's interviews with ritual masters are strategically employed, but still there is no in-depth analysis in this regard. For example, what is the overall social habitat of the *duangong* ritual troupe? What changes have occurred before and after the Cultural Revolution? How do different *duangong* companies operate in relation to one another? Does any kind of competition or cooperation exist between them? What does the professional life of a ritual master look like? All this requires comprehensive field survey and analysis, not just brief interviews.

4. Descriptions of ritual instruments, layouts of sacred altars , ritual drawings of deities and costume boxes are too brief. In fact, these aspects of ritual performances are excellent raw materials for new discoveries about the legends and taboos of the *duangong* tradition. Had the author been able to limit his historical textual research (some of which has been quite contrived) and extend his inquiry into these areas, he could have avoided copying too much from already published findings as in the case of the legends of the three gods in *Redemption of Vows*.

It is always not easy to give a comprehensive account of a complex cultural phenomenon. Ethnographical records are but the most basic yet very limited method. Although in recent years there has been an imbalance between the quantity and quality of research studies on Chinese ethnic ritual performances published by Monograph series of Studies in Chinese Ritual, Theatre and Folklore, these pioneering efforts are made without precedents and within a very short time. The findings in these studies are an important source for future academic research, and they continue to stimulate interest among scholars in related areas.

Related References

Seven other publications related to ritual performances in Sichuan are listed below:

Duan Ming 段明. 1993. *Yangxi Performed with Masks: The Ritual Theatre of Xinglong Village, Xiaogang Township, Shuanghe District, Youyang County, Sichuan* 四川省酉陽土家族苗族自治縣雙河區小崗鄉興隆村面具陽戲. *Min-su ch'ü-i ts'ung-shu*, No. 4. 310 pages.

Hu Tiancheng 胡天成. 1995. *Vernacular Priest Plays of Jielong in Sichuan, Vol.1* 四川省重慶市巴縣接龍區漢族的接龍陽戲——接龍端公戲之一. *Min-su ch'ü-i ts'ung-shu*, No. 18. 490 pages.

——. 1995. *Vernacular Priest Plays of Jielong in Sichuan, Vol. 2: The Altar of Celebration in Jielong* 四川省接龍端公戲之二——接龍慶壇. *Min-su ch'ü-i ts'ung-shu*, No. 36. 258 pages.

——. 1995. *Vernacular Priest Plays of Jielong in Sichuan, Vol. 3: The Prolongation of Life Ritual in Jielong* 四川省接龍端公戲之三——接龍延生. *Min-su ch'ü-i ts'ung-shu*, No. 37. 408 pages.

——. 1996. *The Five-Day Buddhist Ritual of Commendation and Offering as Performed for the Family of Zhong Weicheng of Shuanghekou Township, Ba County, Chongqing, Sichuan* 四川省重慶巴縣雙河口鄉鍾維成家五天佛教請薦祭祀儀式. *Min-su ch'ü-i ts'ung-shu*, No. 48. 278 pages.

Yu Yi 于一. 1995. *The "Altar of Celebration" Ritual of Qingyuan Township, Lushan County, Sichuan* 四川省蘆山縣清源鄉蘆山慶壇田野調查報告. *Min-su ch'ü-i ts'ung-shu*, No. 31. 504 pages.

——. 1994. *The Yangxi of Zitong: A Report from Hongzhai Village, Maming Township, Zitong County, Sichuan* 四川省梓潼縣馬鳴鄉紅寨村一帶的梓潼陽戲. *Min-su ch'ü-i ts'ung-shu*, No. 11. 365 pages.

Other related articles were published in the journal *Min-su ch'ü-i*:

Wang Yue 王躍. 1994. "The 'Da Siguan Lao' Ritual of Jiangbei County, Sichuan: a Summary." 江北縣「打四倌佬」民間祭祀述要. 88: 213-228.

——. 1994. "The 'Yingmao Tidai' of the Hu Household of Datang Village, Shujia Township, Jiangbei County, Sichuan" 江北縣舒家鄉

大塘村胡宅的「迎茅替代」祭儀調查, 90: 321-354.

——. 1996. "The 'Hemei Shan' Ritual of Gaodong Village, Shujia Township, Jiangbei County, Sichuan" 江北縣舒家鄉高洞村的和梅山, 99: 91-126.

Hu Tiancheng. 1993 "Duangong Theatre: The Integration of Ethnic Tradition and Drama" 端公戲：民俗與戲劇結合的一種戲劇形態, 81: 87-102.

——. 1993. "The 'Guanyin Gathering' in Shuanggou, Xiaowan Cooperative, Xinwan Village, Jielong, Ba County, Chongqing City, Sichuan" 重慶市巴縣接龍新壪村小壪合作社雙溝觀音會調查報告, 85: 1-42.

——. 1994. "Crossing the Bridge: A Funeral Ritual of the Han People of Chongqing, Sichuan" 重慶漢族喪葬儀式中的過橋, 92: 735-780.

——. 1994. "The Worship of Nuo Niang: The Investigation the Longevity Rituals of 'Ying xiama' and 'Daonuo songsheng'" (welcoming and seeing off gods) 祈求延年益壽的儺娘崇拜——重慶市巴縣雙新鄉接壽延生的迎下馬和倒儺送聖之調查, 88: 93-124.

——. 1996. "The Alchemical Ritual for Seating the Masters and Gathering the Generals: A Taoist Ritual from Ba County, Chongqing City" 混和咒煉法術安師集將——重慶市巴縣道門壇班安師法事, 99: 127-178.

——. 1997. "Extending Blessing, Continuing Long Life and Long-Lasting Marriage: the 'Jie Shou Yuan' Ritual of Mudong Municipality, Banan District, Chongqing City, Sichuan" 接壽延福、偕老百年——重慶市巴南區木洞鎮六居委張淑英 "接壽緣" 儀式, 109: 87-114.

Hao Gang 郝剛 and Yao Guangpu 姚光譜. 1993. "The Cultural Tradition of the Yang Theatre of Zitong" 梓潼陽戲的文化淺識, 83: 149-168.

Duan Ming. 1996. "The Public Offering Ritual for Prosperity: The Guanyin Gathering of Shaba Village, Lishi Municipality, Jiangjin, Chongqing, Sichuan" 祈求物阜民豐的公眾性醮儀活動——重慶江津李市鎮沙壩村岩上觀音會記實, 103: 113-168.

5 a

THE ALTAR OF CELEBRATION RITUAL IN LUSHAN COUNTY, SICHUAN

John Lagerwey

1. Yu Yi 于一, *Field Report on the Altar of Celebration in Lushan County, Sichuan* 四川省蘆山縣清源鄉蘆山慶壇田野調查報告. *Min-su ch'ü-i ts'ung-shu* 民俗曲藝叢書(Studies in Chinese Ritual, Theatre and Folklore Series), No. 27, 1995. 254 pages.

Lushan County is located west of Mount Emei in Sichuan. As recently as the sixteenth century, this area apparently still had a substantial Tibetan population, but, thanks to Ming and Qing immigration, it is now entirely Han. Curiously, the *duangong* 端公 (vernacular priest) families for whom Yu Yi provides information as to origins, came in the early Qing from the same Xiaogan Township 孝感鄉 in Macheng County 麻城縣, Hubei as the practitioners described by Hu Tiancheng in the Jielong area near Chongqing (see my review of Hu's books in this volume). However, while basic rituals and the pantheon in the two traditions, as well as the standard heptameter verse, bear undeniable similarities, there are also major differences. The *duangong* of Lushan do not perform funeral rituals, for example; and the link between theatre and ritual is quite different: whereas in Jielong the relevant distinction is

75

between the "inner altar for ritual and the outer for theatre" in Lushan ritual and theatre simply alternate (p. 26), with rituals being performed in the morning and plays in the afternoon. Moreover, the theatre in Jielong contributes to the ritual trajectory, while in Lushan the subject matter of the theatre seems essentially unrelated to that of the ritual. The far more complex structure of the Jielong version is built around a central ritual involving the sacrifice of a pig and a banquet for the gods; Yu Yi makes no mention of any such ritual in Lushan. Finally, and most importantly, the Qingtan in Jielong was done to remove an old and install a new altar (*tan* 壇), a function not apparent in Yu Yi's account of the Lushan *Qingtan*.

Qingtan in Lushan were usually day-long rituals done by an individual family sometime during the three months of winter, "to thank the gods for a year's protection, an abundant harvest, and good health, as well as to ask for prosperity in the year to come." (p. 17) Old Year's Day was the preferred day for Qingtan in honor of the domestic "altar gods" (*tanshen* 壇神), said in the local monograph usually to be either Li Bing 李冰 or Zhao Yu 趙昱, "both of whom had won merit in the realm of flood control." (p. 19) There were also collective Qingtan, on the first day of the third month, for example; the people of Qingyuan Township 清源鄉 carried the gods from their "lineage temples" (*jiamiao* 家廟) to a central temple dedicated to the Holy Mother (Shengmu 聖母), where a *Qingtan* and "play for the gods" (*shenxi* 神戲) were performed. (p. 15) The *Qingtan* described in the present book also used to be done annually, on the fifteenth day of the eighth month, in honor of one Jiang Wei 姜維, a general under the Shu Han 蜀漢 said to have died in battle on that day. In the presence of the county leaders, *duangong* troupes — called "halls" (*tangkou* 堂口) — from the entire county came to perform inside a temple dedicated to Jiang Wei first built in the year 1109. In the year 1860, the altar used for this performance was officially designated the "central altar" (*zongtan* 總壇) in the county. An unwritten rule forbade doing *Qingtan* elsewhere in Lushan prior to the performance of the Altar-Opening (*kaitan* 開壇) ritual in the Jiang Wei pavilion (p. 20). A master who did not observe this regulation risked "offending the altar gods, bringing trouble to the entire family, and putting his own life in danger." (p. 44) Clearly, the *Qingtan* in honor of Jiang Wei opened the *Qingtan* "season"— a fact which suggests that the Lushan *Qingtan* was also designed to renew altars, as in Jielong. This view is confirmed by the fact that the *Qingtan* could only be performed in a temple or a house where there was an "altar base" (*tandeng* 壇蹬): "Pillars used to have a stone base, with a hole in which an altar flag could be inserted. The divine armies and generals dwelt there. The Altar-Opening consisted in opening this base and releasing the divine troops." (p. 44)

Classified as "supersitious"ever since 1950, the *Qingtan* is no longer performed. It was put on once in 1986 so that the Cultural Affairs Bureau could record and study it, and it is that version of the ritual that Yu Yi describes. Its program, given on pages 90-91, was basically the same as a traditional three-day program (p. 33), except that it was compressed into two days. The Lushan *Qingtan*, even in its maximalist, seven-day version, consisted of fewer than a dozen rituals and as many "lantern plays" (*dengxi* 燈戲). The chief rituals were the Altar-Opening, the Dispatch of the Troops (*fangbing* 放兵), the Earth Gods Sally Forth (*chu Tudi* 出土地), the Invitation of the Gods (*qingshen* 請神), the Lad Invites the Immortal Lady (*Tongzi qing Xianniang* 童子請仙娘), Keke Sallies Forth (*chu Keke* 出柯柯), Erlang Sallies Forth (*chu Erlang* 出二郎), Treading on the Nine Continents (*cai jiuzhou* 踩九洲), and the Return of the Troops to their Stations on the Altar (*shoubing zhatan* 收兵扎壇). Yu Yi provides rather minimalist descriptions of these rituals and seven plays, as well as orally reconstituted texts of the rituals. He also describes briefly opening and closing rituals called the Powerful Officer Anchors the Altar (*Lingguan zhentan* 靈官鎮壇) and the Powerful Officer Sweeps the Altar (*Lingguan saotan* 靈官掃壇) which were added if the ritual lasted more than three days. Carved wooden masks were worn by those representing Erlang, Keke–said to be from a "minority people" (p. 55) —the Powerful Officer, and the evil dragon (see below).

The ritual texts speak of the "teaching of the masters" (*shifu jiao* 師父教) and refer to Laojun 老君 as "the transmitter of all altars." (p. 109) He is also called Li Laojun of Maoshan 茅山 (p. 230), where the Lad is said to have studied magic (*xuefa* 學法; p. 178). It is at the foot of the Buddhist mountain Wutai shan 五台山, however, that the Five Camps (*wuying* 五營) are set up. (pp. 114, 137) But the most interesting figure in the Lushan pantheon is its unique Chuanzhu 川主, or Lord of Sichuan, one Yang Jin 楊揖, also called Yang Erlang 楊二郎. His mask, with its angry third eye, is set out on the central table throughout the *Qingtan*. At the beginning of the Erlang Sallies Forth ritual, the chief *duangong*, having first invited the god, picks up the mask and puts it on the *duangong* who is playing Erlang. At the end of the ritual, the master removes the mask from the kneeling player and returns it with equal reverence to its place on the main table. In the ritual Yang Jin saves his mother on Peach Mountain and then defeats the flood-causing "evil dragon" (*nielong* 孽龍) with the help of Guanyin. According to one version of Erlang's myth collected by Yu Yi, the Jade Emperor was too busy to judge a case for an importunate of lady, so he asked his nephew Yang Jin to do it for him. The Qingtan is in fact a representation of Erlang passing judgement (p. 43). In the text of the ritual itself, Erlang is portrayed as sitting in Jiang Wei's temple judging the dragon, who required the annual sacrifice of a young man and maiden in exchange for leaving the people in peace (p. 216).

According to one *duangong* interviewed by Yu Yi, the portrait of Zhenwu 眞武, the Perfect Warrior, hung permanently on his master's altar: "Because the ancestral Master Zhenwu can defeat and drive off demons, *duangong* worship him," his master told him; "when we wield a sword or starwalk *(gangbu* 罡步), we are the inheritors of the magic powers of Zhenwu." (p. 48) The master was no doubt referring to the walks on trigram-defined space in the ritual Treading on the Nine Continents (see the diagrams on pp. 60-72). On the painting which used to be hung up in the center of the Qingtan altar, Zhenwu was portrayed in the central part of the painting, below the Sanqing 三清, Doumu 斗母, and Guanyin; the central gods were flanked by stellar gods, twelve sisters, ten marshals, the earth god, and the god of walls and moats (pp. 40-41).

Repetitions and unclear or inadequate explanations — of the pictures at the back of the book, for example, but above all of the rituals themselves — make Yu Yi's work far less satisfying reading than that of Hu Tiancheng. Indeed, if we did not have Hu's far more detailed account, we would be at a loss to understand references in the Lushan rituals to Guo Sanlan 郭三郎 (p. 157), the Fifth Patriarch Master Luo 羅公五祖 (pp. 103, 108, 156), or the *tan* for "nourishing life" 養生壇 (p. 101; this is is no doubt an error for the "domestic animal altar" 養牲壇

described by Hu). Yu Yi has nonetheless provided us with precious documentation of a now-destroyed past.[1]

---

1   Born in 1928. Yu Yi is Assistant Director of the Sichuan Academy of Local Theatre. He has published books on lantern plays, Nuo, Yangxi, and masks in Sichuan.

5b

DUANGONG RITUAL AND RITUAL THEATRE IN THE CHONGQING AREA:

A Survey of the Work of Hu Tiancheng[1]

John Lagerwey

1. *Vernacular Priest Plays of Jielong in Sichuan, Vol. 1: Yangxi* 四川省重慶市巴縣接龍區漢族的接龍陽戲——接龍端公戲之一. *Min-su*

---

1 Born in 1936, Hu Tiancheng 胡天成 is Assistant Director of the Chongqing Institute for the Study of the Arts. In addition to the books reviewed here, he has published a collection of essays on Mulian theatre in Sichuan.

   As the title of my paper indicates, the focus of this review will be the first three books. If I have included the fourth book and two articles, it is at once to give a full overview of the work of one person's contribution to the Wang Ch'iu-kuei project and to be able to address one of the primary issues these materials oblige us to confront, to wit, the definitions of and frontiers between popular Buddhism, Taoism, and shamanism. There is also a certain geographical unity to the books and articles insofar as all describe ritual practices in Ba county: the Jielong township center is 61 kilometers from the Ba county seat (*Yangxi*, p.13; Hu unfortunately does not tell us 61 kilometers in what direction, nor does he include a map in any of his works) ; the Shuanghekou township center is 80 kilometers from the county seat (*Fojiao*, p. 5; a typo here has the text say "80 kilometers east and west of..."). It is also worth noting that the ancestors of the *duangong* "artists" whose work is described in the first three volumes and the ancestors of the Taoists who perform the Buddhist funeral ritual described in *Fojiao* all came from the same township in Macheng county, Hubei (*Yangxi*, p. 16; *Fojiao*, p. 12).

ch'ü-i ts'ung-shu 民俗曲藝叢書 (Studies in Chinese Ritual, Theatre and Folklore Series), No. 18, 1993. 489 pages. Abbreviated as *Yangxi.*

2. *Vernacular Priest Plays of Jielong in Sichuan, Vol. 2: The Altar of Celebration* 四川省接龍陽戲接龍端公戲之二——接龍慶壇. *Min-su ch'ü-i ts'ung-shu*, No. 34, 1995. 362 pages. Abbreviated as *Qingtan.*

3. *Vernacular Priest Plays of Jielong in Sichuan, Vol. 3: the Prolongation of Life Ritual* 四川省接龍陽戲接龍端公戲之三——接龍延生. *Min-su ch'ü-i ts'ung-shu*, No. 35, 1995. 417 pages. Abbreviated as *Yansheng.*

4. *The Five-Day Buddhist Ritual of Commendation and Offering as Performed for the Family of Zhong Weicheng of Shuanghekou Township, Ba County, Chongqing* 四川省重慶巴縣雙河口鄉鍾維成家五天佛教請薦祭祀儀式. *Min-su ch'ü-i ts'ung-shu*, No. 48, 1996. 278 pages. Abbreviated as *Fojiao.*

5. "A Report on the Guanyin Festival in a Jielong Village" 重慶市巴縣接龍新灣村小灣合作社雙溝觀音會調查報告, in *Min-su ch'ü-i*, 85 (1995) : 1-42.

6. "The Alchemical Ritual for Seating the Masters and Gathering the Generals: A Taoist Ritual from Ba County" 混合咒煉法術安師集將：重慶市巴縣道門壇班安師法事, in *Min-su ch'ü-i*, 99 (1996) : 127-170. Abbreviated as "Seating."

Hu's first three books constitute a unit, for as he says in his general introduction to *Yangxi* 陽戲, "leaping duangong" 跳端公 rituals are of three kinds, Yangxi (Yang theatre), Yansheng 延生 (prolongation of life), and Qingtan 慶壇 (altar celebration). While these three ritual types are clearly distinct, each having its own aims, pantheons, and rituals, they also involve many of the same basic rituals and, above all, share the same basic structure and certain fundamental characteristics. Structurally, all three last from late afternoon till after breakfast and are built around the central midnight offering of a "large pig" 洪豬 in a ritual called "return to the cooked" 回熟: rituals prior to it belong to the "first half" 上壇, those after it to the "second" 下壇. All three are "domestic" rituals, done in peoples' homes, and they involve a combination of ritual on the "inner altar" 內壇 and theatre on the "outer altar" 外壇. Some *duangong* do only inner altar rituals, others only outer altar plays, and still others are competent in both inner and outer forms. When these same *duangong* do funeral rituals of either Buddhist or Taoist inspiration they are called "Taoists." The leader of the "Taoist troupe" described doing a "Buddhist" funeral ritual in *Fojiao* began learning Yangxi, Qingtan, Yansheng, and "fasts for the dead" 陰齋 with his father at twelve years of age (*Fojiao*, p. 12). Finally, insofar as these three ritual sequences all involve the use of masks, they are not unrelated to Nuo 儺, indeed the ritual space is called a "Nuo altar" 儺壇 in one form of the Celebration ritual (*Qingtan*, pp. 11, 207, etc.).[2]

I. Yangxi

Hu Tiancheng goes briefly and inconclusively into the question of the origins and history of *Yangxi*. More interesting by far is the tale the *duangong* themselves tell: frustrated at seeing rich people always watching plays, a young cowherd in the Tang decided to organize a poor man's theatre, but he and his friends managed only to fight, not perform. Fortunately for them, the Lord of Sichuan 川主, the Earth Lord of Bishan 璧山土主, and the Medicine King 藥王 were just passing by and decided to teach the young men the story of how the Lord of Sichuan "defeated a dragon" 降龍 and the Earth Lord "captured demons" 收妖 on Cock's Ridge in Bishan. They learned very quickly and were told to go put on the play in temples. Afraid they would forget their lines, the gods came along to sit on the stage and "keep order" 壓陣. The play was such a success that the gods could no longer go along everywhere, so they came to be invited and represented by "god seats" instead. These Three Saints 三聖尊神 not only preside over the Yangxi, they put in masked appearances on the outer altar during the Invitation of the Gods. Their central importance suggests we have to do with a native Sichuan tradition, not one brought by the *duangongs*' ancestors from Hubei.[3]

---

2 Cf. the Chariot-welcoming 接駕 ritual in *Yansheng*, p. 307 ff., where the "Mother of Nuo" 儺母 plays a major role, but no reference is made to a "Nuo altar".

3 The Lord of the Earth is said, however, to have saved the people of Macheng, the place of origin of the *duangong* ancestors (*Yangxi*, p. 175), and the Medicine King cult apparently comes from a temple in Suzhou prefecture 湖廣省蘇州府燕子街藥王廟 in Hubei (*Yansheng*, p. 13).

Yangxi is a form of "vow repayment" 還願 or thanksgiving, for money, position, or marriage. It is (was) usually performed after the harvest. The first ritual, called Opening the Curtain 徹帳, sets the tone with its sequence of "opening" 開棚, "building" 造棚 and "sweeping the shed" 掃棚. Done by a single *duangong* on the inner altar, it belongs rather to the category "ritual" than to that of "theatre," but it is very theatrical ritual, in which the speech is of a highly performative kind: even the tree whose wood will be used to build the altar must be cut, and Lu Ban must be invited to do the building. Most of the description of actions is done in the seven-character lines which seem to characterize popular ritual throughout southern China, but there is also dialogue between the priest and the musicians: "What's going on here?", "The faithful are repaying a vow" (*Yangxi*, p. 100). "Do you want to hear the tale of the rooster who sweeps the shed?" — "Yes." — "Then give a tip" (*Yangxi*, p. 103). Such tips will be given throughout the *Yangxi*, and their analysis would no doubt make an interesting contribution to the study of systems of symbolic exchange.

Theatre begins in earnest in the second ritual, Opening the Altar 開壇, in which, after a more extended invitation of the gods to be "witnesses to the alliance" 證盟 (*Qingtan*, p. 106), the master goes to inform the stove god while, outside, the Maiden who Opens the Altar 開壇小姐 has come to cleanse the altar. In her dialogues with the priest, she announces the planting of a stick of incense, and the priest then plants it: for the Upper Three Religions, those of the Buddha, Laojun, and Confucius; for the Middle, Zhenwu, Guanyin, and Wenchang; and for the Three Saints of the Lower Three. That the theatrical has here taken charge of the ritual is clear from the fact that, if both an outer altar and an inner altar master perform, it is the text of the former that is used. The Dispatch of the Mandate (of invitation) 發牒 that follows gives an even clearer picture of the pantheon: the invitations begin with the Three Pure Ones 三清 and include the Officers of Merit of the Four Times 四值功曹, the cavaliers and foot-soldiers of the Five Ferocious Ones 五猖兵馬, the Great Emperor and ancestor of Thunder 九天應元雷祖大帝, and the "ancestral masters of the Buddhists, Taoists, and shamans" 佛道巫門宗師. The song goes on to tell of the five sons of Guo Sanlang 郭三郎, the Wuchang, going to "learn magic in order save the good people" 學法救良民 (*Qingtan*, p. 134). It takes them seven days to get to Maoshan 茅山, where the "master of magic" 法主 dwells in the upper of three caves. They learn the techniques of "walking on the dipper" 步罡, writing talismans, exorcism, destroying temples, and much more. As they leave, they run into five tigers, knock them over by reciting the "black tiger Xuantan formula" 黑虎玄壇咒, and then mount them. From Taiwan to Sichuan, the Wuchang ride tigers and do the dirty work of exorcism.

In the Formal Invitation 正請, an outer altar master plays the Earth God, who escorts the Three Saints to their seats on the altar. Each god in turn then comes to get his share of the "big pig" during the Taking of the Offering 領牲. That still involves theatrical outer altar masters, but then the inner altar priest takes over with a ritual designed to Release the Offering 放牲 and enable it (the pig) to be reborn a human. This inner altar ritual describes the actual slaying of the pig, the clean knife entering, the red knife coming out: "The host's repayment of his vow spells disaster for you" (*Yangxi*, p.181). But the *Diamond Sutra* 金剛經 will be read for the debristled, disembowled, and quartered pig, and he will be saved. The Three Saints now send the Earth God to Check the Shed 點棚, that is, the offerings in it. The comic dialogue between the drummer and the god is very similar to what may be heard in Lüshan 閭山 rituals performed by *saigong* 師公 in Taiwan, and one almost wonders whether it does not have the same rhythm. However farcical he may be, the Earth God also reveals himself to be an astute observer of popular religion: he is one of seven brothers, he tells us; the eldest is earth god of the Gate of Heaven, the second lives in the mountains, the third lived in a Buddhist temple but manhandled Guanyin and was driven out to become the god of the "mountain gate" 山門土地, the fourth is on a bridge and is prayed to for children, the fifth is in the field, in charge of cereals and animals, the sixth is the "god of good fortune" of the house, linked to longevity, and he himself is the earth god of theatre, who shows up whenever there is a vow repayment (food).

Afraid the percussion has attracted bad gods as well as good, the *duangong* invite Wang the Powerful Official 王靈官 to exorcise the house and protect it 鎮宅. For this ritual, the outer altar table is moved inside and joined to the inner altar table, and the ritual, says Hu, is done in an "extremely solemn, sincere, and theatrical atmosphere" (*Yangxi*, P. 198). Contradictory as that description may sound, I suspect it is extremely accurate, for Wang Lingguan is a fiercesome fellow with his iron whip, but it is the whole myth of Wang Long's leaving heaven to do battle with the northern rebels and being enfeoffed as Celestial Lord 天君 and told to go to protect the host's house that is played out theatrically here. It is followed by a thoroughly theatrical representation of the Road-opening 開路 done on the outer altar: the story of how Fang bi 方弼 and Fang xiang 方相 came to be used as road-openers by Jiang Ziya 姜子牙 is referred explicitly to the *Enfeoffment of the Gods* 封神榜 (*Yangxi*, p. 238).

Several rituals later, the gods are at last all assembled and served their banquet. Among the rituals that follow, the Compensation of Big-mouthed Yang 賞楊大口 deserves special mention: Yang is the inventor of *Yangxi*, and when he opens his big mouth, it is to swallow the epidemic gods (*Yangxi*, p. 327). Yang Qilang 楊七郎, the youngest of seven brothers, enfeoffed and granted a goat-hair brush by the Jade Emperor after having been killed by 108 arrows, now comes on to the ritual stage to Check the Documents 鉤願 and ensure nothing is missing of what had been promised. After the Three Saints have been escorted back from the inner altar to their homes, on the outer altar Zhong Kui drives away all lingering "perverse gods and wilderness ghosts" 邪神野鬼 and Wang Lingguan Sweeps the Altar 掃臺. The *Yangxi* ends with the Construction of a (reed) Boat 造船 and the Sendoff of the Gods 送神. The negative gods are sent off first, by the burning of the boat, which is sent east to the Yangzhou night market or north to Luoyang, and then the positive gods are dismissed. A Pacification of the Incense Burner 安香火 on the domestic altar consists in apologizing to the domestic gods for all the noise and disturbance and turning the house back over to their guardianship. Hu Tiancheng concludes his account with the texts of several additional outer altar plays.

II. Qingtan

The Celebration ritual may be done for a "domestic animal altar" 養牲壇, a Wutong altar 伍通壇, or a Sanxiao altar 三霄壇. The first and most common is for the wellbeing and protection of the family, its cereals, and its animals; the second is to prevent fires; the third is to prevent or end illness or "odd happenings". All three consist in the "destruction" 拆壇 of an old altar and then the "transfer" 遷壇 of a new altar to be installed like the old one to the right of the domestic altar. According to Hu, most old houses in Jielong had such an altar dedicated either to the Immortal Luo 羅公仙師 or to Marquis Zhao 鎮一元壇趙侯元帥 and Guo Sanlang 郭三郎, and they should receive the annual sacrifice of a pig (*Qingtan*, p. 1). During the ritual, a large stone serves as support 壇座 for the paper-on-bamboo seat 壇槍 of the "gods of the three caves" 三洞神靈: the gods of the upper cave take care of human beings, those of the middle cave of cereals, and those of the lower cave of animals. Five flags are stuck in the top of this structure for the "barbarian" troops of the five directions and their commander-in-chief, Guo Sanlang. The breaking down of the old and the moving in of the new altar are the key rituals, and they involve a remarkable number of secret instructions and mudras: they are esoteric rituals, at least partly of Tantric inspiration. The Sanxiao version, being particularly designed to put an end to untoward events caused by "little gods" 小神子, has a special ritual called Interdicting the Jar 禁罐 by means of which these troublemakers are sealed inside a jar.

After an Invitation which begins with the Dark Sovereign 玄皇, Zhang Tianshi 張天師, and Li Laojun 李老君 and includes a Laojun of Maoshan 茅山老君, Nagarjuna on the left 左壇龍樹王, and Zhenwu on the right 右壇眞武將,[4] the pig is carved up in accord with instructions given in the ritual. During the removal of the old altar, the inner altar master sings while outer altar masters play the roles of Zhaohou, Luogong, Wutong, and Guo Sanlang. The priest uses mudrās and steps to send the gods over a bridge to the waiting Earth God, who leads them out of the altar being disbanded. When he has removed the barbarian troops, the priest kneels to throw the blocks and determine whether all is well. He then walks the Dipper, exits the main gate, and does the nine-continent walk 九洲罡, carries the "divine seats" 神牌 out while blow-

---

4 The only other place I have encountered this combination of "Longshu on the left" and "Zhenwu on the right" is on the ritual paintings of Jianyang 建陽 in northwestern Fujian! See my "The Taoism of the Jianyang Region in Fujian" 福建省建陽地區的道教, in *Min-su ch'ü-i*, 84 (1993): 49.

ing on his buffalo horn 牛角, and pastes them up on the wall. A special ritual escorts the painting of the Saintly Mother and Commander-in-Chief 統兵聖母 to the temporary altar outside the house. The five barbarian armies are brought out in the next ritual, to Pacify the Military Camps and Construct the Fortress 安營紮寨. The outer altar version of this ritual is called Borrowing the Five Terraces 借五台. In theatrical style, first Guo Sanlang and then Zhaohou enter and introduce themselves: Zhaohou tells how, when he was born of a gourd, he had no interest in the "red dust" and went off to Maoshan to learn magic. He helped the Yellow Emperor 黃帝 defeat Chiyou 蚩尤 and was enfeoffed as the god of wealth, with the right to a fat pig and goat every third year 小祭 and to a virgin girl and boy 童男童女 every fifth 大祭.[5] Zhaohou then sends Guo Sanlang to each of the Five Peaks in turn in search of a new site for the military camps, but the local Earth God explains each time to Guo that that peak is too cold, too small, and so on. Finally, Mount Wutai in the center proves to be the right place, but its lord, a Chan Master called Wuda 五大禪師, has to be defeated in battle by Zhaohou before he will lend them the mountain:[6] The troops settle in.

After rituals for Protecting the House and Opening the Road, basically the same as those in the *Yangxi* sequence, a special ritual called Painting the Beam 畫樑 is performed. It comes in both inner and outer versions: the former contains fascinating insights into the exorcistic function of the main beam and the origin of the *duangong*'s buffalo horn in a rhinoceros fight observed by Xuanzang 玄奘 on his voyage to India; in the latter, Luban's disciple shows a decidedly greater interest in sex, food, and money than in finding the right tree to cut down or how to paint the beam. Once the beam has been painted, Guo Sanlang is invited to receive the new weapons, and then an Animation 開光 of the

---

5   Demanding the sacrifice of a virgin boy and girl is a standard motif in areas influenced by Lüshan Taoism, it is the mark of a "perverse god" who must be driven out by an exorcist after the latter has first gone to Lüshan to "learn magic." (see, for example, my "Notes on the Symbolic Life of a Hakka Village," in *Proceedings of the International Conference on Popular Beliefs and Chinese Culture* (Taipei: Center for Chinese Studies, Vol. 2, pp. 733-762).

6.   Taoist funeral ritual texts I first collected in Jianyang in 1990, and which Ye Mingsheng and I will soon be publishing in Wang Ch'iu-kuei's *Ziliao huibian* series, ascribe a remarkably similar role to Wutai shan.

Three Dark Lords of Magic 三玄法主 on the new altar is performed. Then at last it is time for the Banquet. Wine is poured for each of the Wuchang in turn as their respective flags are planted and the horn blown to summon the barbarian troops to come and "hold the fort". It is now past midnight and time to shake everyone out of his torpor with off-color jokes: three skits end with a Ritual Miss 法官小姐 giving money by turns to the kings of the Upper, Middle, and Lower Caves, the generals Tang 上洞王唐將軍, Ge 中洞王葛將軍, and Zhou 下洞王周將軍;[7] but before she manages to play her ritual function in that manner, she has to go through what can only be called "sexual harassment," most notably in the second skit, by the outer altar meat-starved and sex-starved monk and disciple of the inner altar Ancestral Master of Powerful Salvation 靈濟祖師.

In the rituals that follow, the Ancestral Master's troops take up their positions on the new altar and receive their sacrificial dues. An optional Mat-fabrication 造席 ritual contains fascinating material about the bamboo mat used by Taoists to send off memorials, by monks to worship the Buddha, and by the "disciple" 弟子 to "walk on the nine continents."[8] The same mat, rolled up, may in the following ritual play for Weapons-fabrication 造槍 be used to strike and cleanse the altar in the five directions. This ritual includes a whole series of steps, such as the One-footed Wutong Step 獨腳伍通罡, which lead in the end to the transportation of the troops across a river to come and guard the host's house.[9] After a Sacrifice to the Troops 祭兵 of the ancestral Master of Powerful Salvation, it is time to Transfer the Altar: the priest calls on his masters, who taught him on Maoshan, to move the altar in the Yin world

---

7 Actually, for some unexplained reason, the gift of money of General Zhou at the end of the third skit is omitted.

8 *Qingtan*, p. 126. Throughout, the priests refer to themselves as "disciples", using either the term just given or "disciple-gentleman" 弟郎 (for example, *Yangxi*, p. 231; *Qingxi*, p. 34). Both terms, which are typical of the Saigong tradition as far away as Taiwan as well, reflect the fundamental importance of "lineage masters" 宗師 in popular, exorcistic Taoism. See further below.

9 On the one-footed Wutong gods, see Ursula Cedzich, "The Cult of the Wu-t'ung / Wu-hsien in History and Fiction: The Religious Roots of the *Journey to the South*," in *Ritual and Scripture in Chinese Popular Religion: Five Studies*, edited by David Johnson (Publications of the Chinese Popular Culture Project 3, Berkeley, 1995), pp. 137-218.

while he does so in the Yang;[10] he then visualizes his personal master on Maoshan and does the Three Terrace Walk 三台罡 in order to go before the Three Dark Ones 三玄. Thus prepared, he builds divine wells, towers, and then altars in each of the five directions. The wells serve to trap demons and the towers to transmit messages to the central (control) tower inhabited by Laojun. Then, the red-hot altar support 壇墩 having been placed on a bridge, the priest blows vegetable oil on it so flames leap up and then picks it up and carries it on a Nine-continent Walk to its appropriate place. A whole series of mudrās brings the gods to their seats on the newly installed altar.

The troops are now invited to cross the bridge to the altar, followed by their commander-in-chief, the Saintly Mother. After a sendoff ritual, the priest Treads the Nine Continents 踩九洲; after summoning the troops with the buffalo horn, the priest speaks of the "divine skirts worn in the Three Religions" 三教穿神君. "My girl puts on a first skirt and refers to our Buddha, Śākyamuni, transmitting the true teaching on Vulture Peak 靈鷲山前傳眞教" (Qingtan, p. 163) ; the second skirt recalls the transmission of Taishang laojun's 太上老君 teaching on Jade Capital Mountain 玉京山, and the third that of Confucius. If the master wears these skirts, it is apparently because he will invite immortal women to walk the Nine Continents: as he describes it, it is a city full of vengeful souls, and the way there is full of dangers. As he is on his way, he tells the story of the world, from cosmogenesis with Pangu 盤古 — whose "body holds the Nine Continents in place" 身鎮九洲 — to how the world is governed by the Three Religions, Buddhism, Taoism, and Confucianism, in that order. (These are the "upper" Three Teachings, the "middle" being that of the Three Saints, and the "lower" that of Su Dongpo and two others; p. 165). The story of Fuxi 伏羲 and Nü Wa 女媧 is also told, of their birth from a gourd after the flood, and Nü Wa's reluctance to commit incest. They give birth to a "lump of flesh" 肉包 which Shennong 神農 chops up to produce the human race. The Nine Palaces and the Eight Trigrams, we hear, are located at the gate of the

---

10 This kind of reference to ritual action in the Yang (visible) world having its counterpart in the invisible Yin underworld of the masters is a typical feature of the *fachang* 法場 exorcism done by the *saigong* of northern Taiwan as well: see my "Les fetes des demons tombent par milliers: Le *fachang*, rituel exorciste du nord de Taiwan," in *L'Homme*, 101 (1978) : 101-116.

gods; they govern all things. Buddhist monks have their place in hell, and Taoists have their swords: "Only the family of the masters 師家 has no place to stay; soon they will be settled inside the city of the Nine Continents" (*Qingtan*, p. 168). This leads to a sequence of walks, first on the eight trigrams and then on the nine continents. It is from the central continent, occupied by Xuanyuan 軒轅, that a message may be sent 投文 (*Qingtan*, pp. 174, 178).

After a last ritual with off-color jokes involving the Ancestral Master of Powerful Salvation's disciple coming to Inspect the Fast 撿齋和尚, the Opening of the Jar and Red Mountain 開缸紅山 provides the troops with sustenance. The jar is a wine jar and the mountain is the priest's forehead, cut so as to bleed into the wine, which is then offered to the troops: "I congratulate the host, here's why: I cut my forehead to sacrifice to your soldiers" (*Qingtan*, p. 192).[11] The ritual sequence then concludes with exorcisms by Zhong Kui and Wang Lingguan.

Hu Tiancheng's equally detailed account of the Sanxiao celebration ritual would also repay a full summary, but we shall have to content ourselves with pointing out a few particularly important points. The first is that the Sanxiao are three Ladies from the precious mountain of Peach Garden 桃源寶山三霄娘娘, known respectively as Yunxiao 雲霄, Shanxiao 山霄, and Shuixiao 水霄:[12] In the Altar-destruction ritual they are more explicitly described as Yunxiao of the Upper, Shanxiao of the Middle, and Shuixiao of the Lower Cave of Peach Tree Spring 桃源洞.[13]

---

11 This "sacrificial realism" is also characteristic of Taiwanese Lüshan Taoists: as the Taipei master Zhu Kuncan 朱堃燦 once said to me, "Nothing is accomplished without blood-letting." While he was in this instance applying his ritual knowledge to the interpretation of Chinese history – the phrase was designed to explain why "we Taoists think highly of Wu Zetian" – it corresponds to what is readily obvious from a comparison of popular, exorcistic with more elite forms of Taoism: the latter has resolutely eliminated the blood sacrifices that characterize both popular religion and exorcistic Taoism. Traditionally, exorcizing Taoists in Taiwan would use either the blood of a cock's crest or that of their own tongue to consecrate the symbols they wrote.

12 One cannot help but wonder whether these goddesses in charge of illness are not yet another incarnation of the Shanxiao 山魈 demons described by Cedzich, *op. cit.*, Index, p. 259. An article by Zhang Sijie 張嗣介 on the worship of the Sanxiao epidemic goddesses in Ganzhou 贛州, Jiangxi, will be published in volume 7 of my "Traditional Hakka Society Series."

13 The Taoyuan Cave is, of course, fundamental to Yao Taoism, where it is the dwelling place of the dead. Interestingly, it is also the name of the one surviving Taoist hermitage on Wuyi shan 武夷山 in northwestern Fujian, and local Taoist funeral ritual manuscripts describe how the soul of the dead is brought, via Wutai shan, to Taoyuan Cave.

The second is the large number of references to Nuo. In one ritual, called Opening the Theatre Cave 開戲洞, the twelve gates of Taoyuan Cave are opened to allow the gods to come to the host's Nuo Hall 儺堂 (*Qingtan*, p. 207). A third feature of the Sanxiao ritual is the frequency of reference to Meishan 梅山 gods, as during the Taking of the Offering, when a whole series of Meishan gods is invited (*Qingtan*, p. 223). A fourth is the evident importance of the Zhengyi 正一 tradition: the priest's register title makes him a disciple of Zhang Tianshi (*Qingtan*, p. 230), and it is the same Zhang Tianshi who signs the crucial list of offerings on whose accuracy the efficacy of the entire ritual depends (*Qingtan*, p. 259). Finally, at the end of the ritual, the "little mountain" troublemakers must be shipped off in a reed boat. According to the text of this ritual, one of them — their leader? — in Qin times helped the First Emperor and then married Yunxiao... And when, before sending them off as the last act of the ritual sequence, the master sees the Three Ladies off, he must first "hide his body" 藏身:[14] clearly, the Sanxiao are themselves epidemic goddesses.

III. Yansheng

The first outer altar play provided by Hu Tiancheng in part four of *Qingtan* is the story of the "defeat of the basket snake" 降藍蛇 by one of Li Laojun's disciples, who has learned his magic on Maoshan. As such it bears comparison with similar stories involving Chen Jinggu 陳靖姑 in Fujian and Xu Zhenjun 許眞君 in Jiangxi. But we must move on to the third book in the *duangong* series, the *Yansheng*. Of the three ritual sequences, the Prolongation of Life ritual is the least theatrical, the most "liturgical". It comes in two basic types, one in "time of peace" 太平延生, the other in "time of emergency" 急救延生. Ths first, addressed to the Sovereign of the Eastern Peak 東皇, is planned well in advance and is in fact a vow-repayment; the second, addressed to the Ten Kings of hell 十王, is to pray for salvation from severe illness. The

---

14 Other obvious contexts for reading them would be that of the other Qingtan and Yangxi rituals in the same series (in Yunnan, Guizhou, and other parts of Sichuan) or, more generally, of Nuo ritual theatre and "leaping" 跳 rituals of all kinds.

latter kind is done by *duangong* who belong to the "Huainan school of Taoism" 淮南教，是道教之一種; the former "belongs essentially to Buddhism and is done by people whose office is that of a Taoist" 主要屬佛教，頒職是頒道士職 (*Yansheng*, p. 17). The "Buddhist Taoists" can do only the "peaceful prolongation", the "Huainan Taoists" can do both kinds.

As this sounds like nonsense, we do well to examine it more closely: in an earlier note (*Yansheng*, p. 26, n. 2), Hu Tiancheng had explained that "with respect to the *duangong* of Buddhist and Taoist schools, the people of Jielong call those who do funeral rituals 'Taoists' 道士, or 'ritual masters' 法師 (cf, *Fojiao*, p. 19)." Although Hu unfortunately nowhere explains who uses the term "*duangong*" and to refer to what, it seems fairly clear that "*duangong*" is the equivalent of *shigong*, as that term is widely used throughout southern China, that is, "specialist of domestic exorcisms", and that "Taoist" means locally, as it does in much of southern China, "funeral ritual specialist". Within the latter category — and in Jielong, apparently among the former as well, if we judge from the manuscripts and other ritual paraphernalia they use — there are both Taoist "Taoists" and Buddhist "Taoists". This latter classification as "Buddhist" or "Taoist" usually corresponds, as well, to how the ritual specialists themselves classify themselves, but the people pay no attention to that and simply use the word "Taoist" to designate a funeral ritual specialist. The potential for confusion is obvious, and Hu might have taken a little more care in dealing with this terminological problem. It would also have been nice to know just what is meant by the term "Huainan school of Taoism", as the term does not appear in *Yangxi* and *Qingtan*. To add even further to the confusion, there is a special Meishan version of the "emergency longevity" ritual (cf. *Yansheng*, pp. 14, 22, 321).

Moreover, the very first line of the first ritual of the supposedly "Buddhist" Yansheng ritual "in time of peace" reads: "A great wind arose on Longhu shan, the altar of the Heavenly Masters was transmitted directly to the *duangong*" 龍虎山前起大風，天師壇內傳端公 (*Yansheng*, p. 27). The memorial read in this Altar-opening 開壇 ritual speaks of "worshiping the Buddha and taking refuge in the Tao, performing a *Jiao* 醮 and making an offering" (*Yansheng*, p. 29). In the Respectful Invitation 禮請 that follows, the priest ascribes to himself a

Buddhist rank, but the invitation begins with the Taoist Three Pure Ones 三清 and Three Officers 三官 (*Yansheng*, p. 40). The officiant refers to himself as "Bowing with reverence to... all the masters who transmit Buddhism and magic 傳佛傳法 from the schools of Buddhism 佛門, Taoism 道門, and shamanism 巫門" (*Yansheng*, p. 43). Both Buddhist and Taoist scriptures and litanies are then recited to the assembled gods. By contrast, the Taking of the Offering is a more frankly Buddhist ritual: having recited his Buddhist register, the *duangong* invites the Sanbao, five directional Buddhas, and Wenshu before getting to the Three Pure Ones; farther along, he invites "the ancestral master Pu'an, lord of the religion of the Southern Spring 南泉教主普庵祖師, King Nagarjuna on the left, and General Zhenwu on the right" (*Yansheng*, p. 91). Hu Tiancheng provides a second version of this ritual in which the *duangong*'s register is Taoist (*Yansheng*, p. 93). In short, Hu is apparently right in saying there are "Buddhist" and "Taoist" versions of this "shamanist" *duangong* ritual.

The most interesting part of the "peaceful longevity" ritual is the "reed person" used as a substitute body. He first appears in the Making of the Reed (Person) 造茅, in which the reed person is placed facing inward on the outer altar and first "made", then painted, animated with a cock's blood, and led to worship the Sanbao 三寶 before being "seated" for the duration of the Yansheng. The "making" is accomplished primarily by the recounting of the reed person's mythical origins: when Song Renzong 宋仁宗 came to the throne, he wished to offer the head of one Zhang the Filial 張孝 to show his gratitude to Heaven, but Zhang proves to be an exiled Golden Boy 金童 star and, when his would-be captor sends his soul to heaven to speak to the Jade Emperor, he is told to make a reed man to replace Zhang the Filial, in whose clothes he should nonetheless be dressed. "The deceased master who makes the reed person has finished his work; the deceased master who paints him descends to the mundane world," continues the Daoguang 26 (1846) text, using a ritual technique typical of shamanistic texts of the Lüshan tradition as well. A Tongzhi 13 (1874) text of the same ritual, which would appear to have come from Hunan as it refers to the ritual taking place at night in Xiaogan township, gives a much more circumstantial version of the reedman tale.

The Redemption of the Soul 贖魂, also called Summons of the

Soul 招魂, which involves using a cock to lead the souls back over a bridge with "the earth god at its head, a general at its tail, and Guanyin seated in the middle" (*Yansheng*, p. 159), would also bear comparison with Lüshan rituals of the same kind. But it is the Exhorting the Reed Person 勸茅 which is the more interesting ritual. The Daoguang version, called Sacrificial Compensation of the Reedman 祭賞茅郎, gives a whole series of historical examples of people sacrificing themselves for others so as to show the *maolang* 茅郎 he is not alone in his sad fate. All this is said in a unique 3-3-4 character verse, a ryhthm not previously encountered. The reed person is then given food for his voyage by boat to Yangzhou: "We are sending you to that land of plenty 福國地, Yangzhou, thousands of miles from here, to the night market." The Construction of the Boat 造船 that follows is done facing outward by the inner altar master: this "divine boat of the five epidemics" 五瘟神船 is made from a cosmic tree that grew on Kunlun. Then Camp is Broken and the Fortress Overturned 拆營倒寨 before the Sendoff of the Gods 送神, which involves carrying the boat to an intersection in an open area for burning. The 1980's version of the ritual provided by Hu Tiancheng is much more explicit about the pleasures, mostly physical, of the Yangzhou market to which the epidemic, fire, and other troublemaking spirits are being sent.

One version of the "peaceful longevity" ritual is done for children who are in contradiction with one or another cosmic fores: this is the Barrier-crossing 過關 ritual well known in the Lüshan tradition as well. It is addressed, however, not to the Three Ladies 三奶, but to the Three Immortal Queen Mothers 三仙王姆, that is the immortal mothers of heaven, earth, and the waters under the earth. And as in the Yao 瑤族 Taoist ordination rituals, the barrier-crossing child must have twelve guarantors 保爺, whose main role in the ritual is to give tips 利是 to the players. Once the child has crossed the barriers of the Three Mothers, it is placed on the Queen Mother's Terrace: she asks the guarantors how many years of life they wish to guarantee; if it is 120 years, they must give 12 *yuan*, and the Queen Mother then gives this money to the child. Rice and water used as offerings are also placed by the child's pillow for a week and then used to produce cooked rice that the child eats. When the Barrier-crossing is finished, the *duangong* must ascend a sword ladder 上刀山 in order to present a memorial to the Three Mothers. Upon descending, he takes an axe to chop his way out of the Demon-gate Barrier 鬼門關, an act said to belong to "the teaching of Lord Lao" 老君教.

The "emergency" version of the Yansheng ritual is apparently what most impressed the Republican-era local monograph editor quoted by Hu Tiancheng at the beginning of this book:

> Whenever they fall ill or something untoward happens, the people here invite shamans and do an exorcism to drive it away. This is called a 'Nuo exorcism' 禳儺, and it must be done at night. Its technical name is 'teaching of the Master and the Mistress' 師娘教. They make two demon heads to represent the gods they worship. One has a red face and long beard and is called the Master 師爺; the other has a female face and is called the Mistress 師娘. They say it is Fuxi 伏羲 and Nü Wa 女媧. Before the ritual, they are placed on a bamboo stick which serves as their neck. At the top and bottom of the stick they place bamboo splinter circles, dress them in (real) clothes, and lean them against the ritual table on the left and right... To the right they set up a small table for the worship of the Wuchang, who are also represented by small images... In the middle of the night, the main shaman dances and swirls his sleeves, while a demon-masked young priest, accompanied by the Earth God leading the way, goes and comes following orders. This is called 'turning loose the Wuchang' 放五猖. The main shaman then crosses the threshold and blows the buffalo horn like a demon screeching. The spectators who hear this say there is sure to be a response... Wherever the sound of the horn reaches, young children are not allowed to sleep lest they answer in their dreams... Reeds must be cut to make a person of reeds...; having placed it in a reed boat, they go outside to burn it. This is called Exhorting and Dispatching the Reed Person, and they say it takes on the disasters as a substitute (for the sick person). (cited, *Yansheng*, p. 3)

According to Hu, the editor is referring to Grandpa 爺爺 and the Lady 娘娘, that is, "divine lord number two from Huashan" 華山二帝神君 and the Saintly Matron and Divine Lady 聖姆靈娘, who are dressed in the host's clothes and set up next to the ritual table on the inner altar (p.20). In some places, Hu adds, only the Mother is used, and that would seem to be the case in the ritual he describes, for while the Dispatch 發申 ritual does contain reference to sending invitations to Huashan, in the Chariot-reception 接駕 ritual that follows, only the Saintly Matron and Divine Lady, Mother of Nuo 儺母, is invited, "together with the troops of little mountain men 小山人 who protect her" (*Yansheng*, p. 307). These little mountain men used also to be represented by twelve small heads of wood; eggs are used instead now. A little farther on the same Republican-era ritual text mentions "the Master (whose painting is hung) on the rope and the Mistress who catches the Nuo" 纂上師公捕儺師母. It also refers to Huguang 湖廣 and to the Huainan teaching 淮南教. When, after many mudras and walks, the *duangong* finally goes to sit on the Seven Star Terrace 七星台, he says: "We bivouac the troops of the upper, lower, and middle caves of Peach Tree Spring; the disciple from the three caves of Peach Tree Spring 三洞桃源弟子 will seat you forthwith." (p. 321) These troops will then be sent to the three caves of Meishan 梅山, whose locks, each of a different kind of metal, it will be their job to break open.

IV. Fojiao

The funeral ritual described in *Fojiao* was not one for the just-deceased, called Sacrifice to the Blood-Soul 祭血靈, but for four persons who had died some years earlier. Such rituals are called familiarly "doing an old ritual" 做老道場 or, more officially, Sacrifice with Invitation and Offering 請薦祭祀 (whence the title of the book). It contained thirty-two separate rituals, as opposed to a Jielong township 接龍區 version Hu saw, which contained forty-seven (*Fojiao*, p. 2). Unfortunately, the report on the Jielong ritual, which was performed by one of the priests already encountered in the *duangong* books, has not yet been published. It would have allowed us to see what happens to a *duangong* when he turns into a "Taoist". According to Hu, moreover, the differences between the Jielong and Shuanghekou Township 雙河口鄉 funerals was considerable, especially in the Memorial-dispatch, Invitation, and Explaining the Fast 演齋 rituals (the villages, according to Hu, are separated by about 50 kilometers). Nonetheless, the principal Shuanghekou

"Taoist" also learned during his youth in the 1930s how to perform the three *duangong* rituals, and he also traces his ancestry back to Xiaogan township 孝感鄉 in Macheng county 麻城縣, Hubei (*Fojiao*, p. 12): we are still in the same cultural "space."

The thirty-three Taoists in Shuanghekou belong to nine separate troupes, all of whom perform Buddhist funeral rituals. The inner, Scripture Altar 經壇, is hung with paintings of Buddha, Confucius, Laojun, Guanyin, Wenshu 文殊, and Puxian 普賢, in that order. The chief officiant alternates between wearing a Vairocana cap 毗盧帽 and monk's robe 架裟 or a Buddhist cap 佛帽 and ritual robe 法衣. To cleanse the altar he invites Guanyin and asks her for her willow branch water before murmuring cleansing formulae and writing symbols over the water. The pardon sought in the Welcoming of the Honored One and Dispatch of the Pardon 迎尊放赦 comes from the Buddha in Western Heaven, and it involves sending a saintly monk to go fetch the pardon from the Buddha. To Open the Roads and Destroy Hell 開方破獄, recourse is had to Mulian 目連 and his pewter staff 錫杖. There is also evidence of Taoist influence, as in the use of Gongcao 功曹 to transmit documents, or in the sending of such documents to the Three Officers 三官 in separate rituals where the Sanguan may be said to reveal themselves as one of the principal means of organizing the local pantheon: the Officer of the Earth, for example, is first named among all the gods of hell, including Dizang 地藏, Yanluo 閻羅, and the Ten Kings; the Officer of the Waters heads the entire underworld bureaucracy of city gods, earth gods, local gods, and transporters of infernal money. But there can be no denying that this is an essentially Buddhist ritual being performed by local "Taoists".

The individual rituals described by Hu Tiancheng simply confirm that assessment. In the Sealing of the Altar 結界, for example, the seats of the Five Kings show them to be understood in accordance with the 24 + 1 energies 氣 of the standard Taoist scheme, but these forces are invited by means of Tantric "true words" 眞言, and the central Buddha in this scheme is Vairocana, who is said to live in the Realm of Yoga 瑜伽界 (*Fojiao*, p. 63). Once the Five Kings are in place, the actual sealing is accomplished by "covering and sequestering (inside) the red mouth" 掩押赤口: after first visualizing his master and hiding his body, the priest "orders the water," then uses a whole series of mudrā over the cup to seal it, burns the Five Kings' symbols into the water, puts salt, tea, rice, beans, and earth in the cup, then wraps a five-colored cloth over its mouth and places it upside down under the altar. The water, of course, must not leak out. In the Invitation ritual that follows, a welter of Buddhist gods, led off by Vairocana, are invited before the text finally gets to the Three Pure Ones, the Jade Emperor, Zhenwu, and all the earth and water gods of the underworld. Once the gods are in place, they are treated to the recitation of the *Prajñāpāramitā sūtra* 般若波羅密多心經.

In the Flag-hoisting ritual 豎旛, by contrast, it is the Jade Emperor who is asked to bless the living with good fortune: according to Hu, this is a "ritual of the banquet for the living" 陽醮法事 (*Fojiao*, p. 76). That is why the placard 榜 refers to the ritual as being "for the benefit of those in the light and those in darkness" 爲冥陽二利事, that is, the living and the dead (*Fojiao*, p. 32). Beneath the flag, a "divine seat of the heavenly lord Zhang of Sun Valley and the Five Thunders of the Unique Energy of Prior Heaven" 先天一氣五雷暘谷張天君神位 is set up. This ritual contains a most peculiar rite which is also widely used in western Fujian where the teachings of Pu'an still flourish, namely, the "knotting of the flag" 結旛. It consists in an extremely elaborate preparation of the flag's dangling tassels so that they will knot and so the knots can be cut off at the end of the entire funeral and used to divine the implications for the living and the dead of the ritual as a whole. Whether or not the flag knots, according to Hu, depends on the magic quality of the master's "painting" of the flag. After rites of self-cleansing and flag-fumigation, the master visualizes his masters, especially the one who ordained him, presses that master's birth date point in his left hand, imagines him as though he were present, unites with him, and then recites a formula for the transformation of his own body which ends, "Quickly, quickly, in accord with the celestial laws of Lady Green" 急急如女青天律令.

After this reference to an ancient Taoist book, the priest begins to write strange characters while reciting "true words", then takes up the brush to order the thunder generals to show their "true form", the gods to obey, and the demons to convert, for "those who do not obey will be smashed to smithereens." After tracing ten more characters with the word for "rain" on top, he at last writes on it the names of the Three Pure Ones, the Jade Emperor, and that of the Heavenly Worthy of the

Voice of Thunder which Transforms All 雷聲普化天尊. When the symbol of the Jade Emperor has been written on the tail of the flag, it is torn into five strips, on each of which is written a symbol dotted with blood taken from the crest of a cock and onto which are stuck cock's feathers. A small brass coin, salt, tea, rice, beans, and earth are then wrapped in the ends of the strips and tied in with five-colored thread. After some final mudrās and muttering, the flag is hoisted at last, and the master, while mingling the fingers of his left hand among the five dangling strips, says, "In ordering the angels of flag-knotting who respond to the flying message summoning the unique energy of prior heaven, I follow the ritual instructions of the ancestral master Pu'an" 吾奉普庵祖師法旨，敕召先天一氣飛捷報應結旛使者. All incurable diseases can be cured by this knotted flag (*Fojiao*, p. 91).

Hu also gives excellent descriptions of the Grand Invitation 大召請, in which the soul is led across a huge bridge made of nine tables, four stacked on five, of the Explanation of the Fast of the Ten Kings 演十王齋 — in which Renzong is wakened from a dream-visit to hell and told by Yanluo that his time has not yet come, but that there is a fast which can be used to escape from the suffering he witnessed — and of the Offering to Heaven 貢天, in which the priest reads a document that describes in minute detail the ritual he is doing. But the high point of this book is its meticulous description of the Crossing of the Lake of Blood Bridge 過血河橋. Disciples of Victor Turner looking for the "liminal" creation of *communitas* in Chinese rituals will find it here: performed in a field where the rice had been cut, way out behind and out of sight of the house, this ritual has the Taoist priest in the role of Mulian leading the mourners to the Gate of Demons, where the Yin and Yang realms meet 陰陽交界的鬼門關. Mulian gives the mourners a guided tour of one hell after another in search of their mothers (in the ritual described two mothers were involved) until they are found at last in the Lake of Blood hell. Each hell and what gets one there is described in the process, and when the mothers have been found in that grimmest of all hells reserved for women because they soil the earth with their blood in childbirth, Mulian asks the general who guards the entry to this hell why, since it takes both men and women to produce children, only women should be punished. The question goes unanswered, but the mourners symbolically drink the blood and so help save their mothers.

Many people, writes Hu, come from the neighborhood to watch these rituals, especially the Bridge-crossing, and when the harshness of life and the terrors of hell are described, they listen closely (*Fojiao*, p. 204).

V. Concluding Observations

That we have here first-rate ethnographic description no one who has ever attempted the genre would contest. These books are the product of judicious interweaving of text, observation (where possible), and interviews. There is no doubt room for questioning to author's use of texts ranging from the Daoguang era to the 1980s the reconstruct the now rarely practiced *duangong* rituals (and I as a reviewer have no doubt fallen into the carefully laid trap by paying even less attention to the differing provenance and dates of the various manuscripts and oral reconstructions). For those interested in investigating the legitimacy of these reconstructions and perhaps even sorting out the clearly complicated business of ritual schools, the announced publication of the complete texts in the *Ziliao huibian* is good news: Is the Huainan a local school or an import from Hubei? How common was (not is) it for *duangong* to do both their stock-in-trade exorcistic rituals and funeral rituals? What determined whether they did essentially Buddhist or basically Taoist versions of these rituals? These and many other questions should be easier to answer once we have all the texts.

But even without them, Hu's texts and descriptions enable us to make a number of observations. I shall make mine from the perspective of someone far more familiar with southeast than with southwest China, for that is the context within which, inevitable, I have read these books.[15] Two impressions in particular — one of similarity, the other of difference — compete in my mind for priority: what is very different is the distinctive interaction between a highly theatrical ritual and a highly ritualized theatre (I would not call it opera here) ; what is similar is the distinction between exorcistic masters and specialists of funeral rituals.

---

15 Other obvious contexts for reading them would be that of the other Qingtan and Yangxi rituals in the same series (in Yunnan, Guizhou, and other parts of Sichuan) or, more generally, of Nuo ritual theatre and "leaping" 跳 rituals of all kinds.

As I have already suggested several times above, the Chongqing *duan-gong* are clearly comparable to the *shigong* of much of the rest of South China:[16] This is not just a vague resemblance, based on their primarily "exorcistic" role. It is something that goes right to the heart of ritual structure and content: common rituals such as the Barrier- (or Bridge-) crossing, the Sendoff by Boat of epidemic gods, and the Sword Ladder Ascension; the staple seven-character verse, substitute reed persons, comic interludes involving the earth god, and the ritual use of off-color jokes; the predominant role of myth as opposed to cosmology in elite Taoist ritual, the concomitant importance of local gods as opposed to abstract cosmic forces,[17] and the *duangong* and *shigong*'s use of "disciple" 弟郎 as opposed to "minister" 臣 as the standard term of self-reference are some of the more obvious common features. Perhaps most surprising of all, given the very local character of these ritual traditions, is the degree to which the operative pantheons overlap in structure and content: they are systematically divided into upper, middle, and lower caves, and Laojun, the Queen Mother, and the Wuchang play very similar roles. The first is the ultimate master, who is said here to have studied on Maoshan; the second is the chief deity when children are involved, as in the Barrier-crossing; the Wuchang, five brothers astride tigers, are the primary exorcists. Though their surname is not Guo 郭 but Ge 葛, in a version of their story told in Changting county 長汀縣 in western Fujian, the story is essentially the same and serves to explain how each of the brothers came to be a specialist of one or other of the *duangong* / *shigong*'s basic ritual tricks.[18]

Of all these common elements, I would be inclined to focus on the word "disciple" as the defining term of these popular exorcistic traditions: whereas a "minister" is part of a bureaucratic metaphor and tradi-

---

16 The term *shigong* is the one most frequently used, but one also encounters terms like *shiye* 師爺 and *Shangong*. The latter term, found in many Hakka areas, is written, for lack of an appropriate character, *xigong* 覡公. It is worth noting that our Sichuan *duangong* also use the term *shigong*, as when they call on their masters to protect them in the Sanxiao Altar-destruction ritual: 掌壇師公劉太保 is the first in a long list of masters evoked.

17 On these points, see my "De la ritualite chinoise," in *Bulletin de l'Ecole francaise d'Extreme-Orient*, 79.2 (1992): 359-373.

18 This tale will be published in an article by Lai Jian 賴建 in the forthcoming volume 6 of my "Traditional Hakka Society Series."

tion, a "disciple" belongs to a local lineage. It is worth noting, in this regard, that the Republican-era monograph quoted by Hu Tiancheng refers to the *duangong* as belonging to "the teaching of masters and mistresses" 師娘教 (see above). The terms "shamanistic school" 巫門 and "teaching of the masters" 師教 are synonymous in these texts: "Don't say the plays from the master's house are not true; he too is a disciple of the Three Teachings" 莫說師家戲無眞，也是三教門下人, says the *duangong* as he approaches the city of Nine Continents in the *Qingtan* (p. 164). During the Altar-moving ritual in the same Qingtan sequence, the *duangong* mentions the "altar of the disciple" as one of three types: there are Buddhist and Taoist *tan*, and there is "the altar where the disciple makes transformations in all directions" 弟郎十方打化壇. In the Altar-destruction ritual of the sequence we read: "One ritual (*tan*) is barely done, another begins, but all the rituals were transmitted by Laojun; all the rituals were taught by Laojun, but they are so varied they still require a master" 一壇不了又一壇，壇壇都是老君傳，壇壇都是老君教，萬般還要師父傳 (*Qingtan*, p. 41). The text could hardly be more explicit: Laojun is the ultimate source, but the proximate and equally indispensable source is one's own master.

That is why it seemed to me important to include in this review the article on "seating of the masters and assembling of the generals" 安師集將. With its floodtide of "true words", symbols, visualizations, mudrās, and dipper-walking, it may be described as a maximal version of ritual at its most esoteric and, as such, not entirely typical, or rather, quite unlike the theatrical rituals of the three *duangong* books. Hu Tiancheng ascribes it to the Shenxiao 神霄 tradition; Tantric influences are rife. But what is most interesting is when and why it is performed: according to Hu, "*duangong* Taoists" 端公道士門 attach great importance to masters, especially to the "master of oral transmission" 口度師 ("Seating", p. 127). If the disciple does not treat his master with respect, his rituals will never be efficacious, he may even be punished by the gods. Once a disciple has been ordained and received his religious name 法號, he must worship the masters as well as the general associated with his own birthdate. Whenever he burns incense or makes an offering on his domestic altar, he must first burn it for them and give them the meat and wine first. On the last day of every year, he must invite the masters and their troops to take a two-week vacation, until the 15th day of the first month. Whenever he goes to do a ritual, he must inform them and ask for their protection, and when he returns, he must bring back a pair of candles, incense, and some paper money for them. They also have their seat on any temporary altar, and crucial items like the master's knife and the divining blocks must be put there when not in use. The disciple must dress and undress in front of them before and after every ritual. And before a major ritual sequence, he must do the "seating" rite described in the article. Hu observed this ritual when it was performed on the first day of the first month for a deceased Taoist as a prelude to a Yansheng Longevity sequence for the Taoist's son, to begin on the following day.

Along with these similarities there are also differences: the Lüshan Taoism of the Southeast is also not infrequently associated with theatre, but it is usually *Mu'ou* 木偶 puppet theatre. We know from Ye Mingsheng's 葉明生 studies in Shouning county 壽寧縣 in far northern Fujian that *Mu'ou* is normally performed by Taoist masters of the *shigong* variety,[19] and *Mu'ou* is also a standard form of theatre offered the gods during community *Jiao* 醮 in Taiwan, as well as in the Hakka parts of Fujian. Given the fact that such theatre is often performed on stages set up facing the gods, it is structurally very much like the "outer altar" in the Jielong rituals under review. *Mu'ou*, moreover, unlike most forms of "human theatre" 人劇, is an explicitly ritual and exorcistic theatre used, in Taiwan for example, to cleanse by exorcism the site of a fire or a drowning. Shouning *Mu'ou* quite simply replaces ritual: it is performed on an "altar" that must be constructed and then swept, not by Wang Lingguan but by Marshal Tian Du 田都元帥, a patron saint of theatre who also figures in the *duangong* plays of Chongqing (*Yangxi*, p. 325). Both traditions also have recourse to Zhong Kui 鍾馗 to drive out the "perverse gods and wilderness demons" (see above).

Many more parallels could no doubt be found, but they only serve to underscore the fact that the *duangong* ritual and ritual theatre of the Chongqing area are both very different from their Lüshan cousins. Comparison of what we have seen here with the Fachang exorcism of the *saigong* priests of northern Taiwan makes that very clear: the

---

19 Ye Mingsheng, "The Invitation of the Lady in the Yuanxiao Festival in Xiafang Village, Shouning" 壽寧縣下房村的元宵會與請婆神過關, in *Min-su ch'ü-i*, 90 (1994): 193-246.

Fachang, at least as it is now performed, contains but one theatrical ritu-al.[20] Performed directly on the altar area, it involves no distinction, as here, between "inner" ritual and "outer" theatre. Once Ye Mingsheng's full report on the *saigong* plays of Longyan 龍巖 in southwestern Fujian has been published (in the *Ziliao huibian* series), we may have to refine our analysis. But that will not change the fact that most Lüshan texts collected to date are relatively speaking low in theatrical content, and they are not inextricably or structurally linked to a ritual theatre tradi-tion. Why? — the frequent references to the "Nuo hall" 儺堂 in the *duangong* texts would seem to provide the obvious answer.

A final point: the *duangong* texts collected by Hu Tiancheng emphatically and repeatedly embrace the "three teachings". This is at least in part a reflection of the very obvious influence on these texts of popular literature of the *Enfeoffment of the Gods* variety. It is no doubt also a reflection of the popular (and late imperial) character of this the-atrical ritual tradition. But more is at stake here: in the first place, unlike Sanjiao movements associated with the elite, like that of Lin Zhao'en 林兆恩, for example, the "three teachings" tolerance evinced by these texts is not "cooked" but "raw", that is, it gives the impression of being a spontaneous, popular product, not the product of an intellectual elabo-ration. Perhaps the impression is wrong, but my sense would be that these texts reflect the realism of the people: in social reality, each of the three teachings played a clear and distinct role, and therefore for any rit-ual to be effective it quite naturally incorporated the pantheon and ethics of all three teachings. I suspect they reflect something else as well, and that is pervasive Tantric Buddhist influence. The Tantric fusion with the master required in the Flag-knotting ritual (see above) suggests that a primary source of this influence is the Pu'an school 普庵教. The com-plex ritual for Seating the Masters just evoked is the most radical exam-ple of Tantric influence, but it is also paradigmatic, at least if we judge by the visualizations of the master on Maoshan done in the Moving of the Altar 遷壇 ritual in the Qingtan (*Qingtan*, p. 142). Indeed, given the fact that the Qingtan ritual is all about the annual renewal of the altar, I

---

20 Its text has recently been published by Hsu Li-ling 許麗玲, "The Redhead Taoist Fachang Ritual for Improving Fortune in Northern Taiwan" 臺灣北部紅頭法師法場補運儀式, in *Min-su ch'ü-i*, 105 (1996) : 1-146.

would suggest it is quite simply a "lay" version of the *duangong*'s annual Seating of the Masters ritual. This would in turn intimate the existence of something like a Taoist "church" such as we assume to have existed in early Sichuan Taoism and to have survived in "minority", especially Yao Taoism.

But is *duangong* ritual theatre Taoist? Hu Tiancheng seems sometimes to take for granted that *duangong* are Taoists, as above when he spoke of "*duangong* Taoists". But on other occasions, as when he gives his general survey of the types of Yangxi troupes and their origins (*Yangxi*, pp. 33-40), he leaves all question of affiliation aside. You Zemin 猶澤民, for example, is the informant who has the widest competence: he is not only a good musician, but he can also do both inner and outer altar rituals, as well as "Yin fasts" 陰齋 for the dead. He is also the primary officiant in the "Guanyin Festival" described by Hu in a separate article (the ritual has a vaguely Buddhist coloration). Nowhere is he explicitly described as a Taoist, nor is it said that he thinks of himself as one. The people, as we saw, think of funeral ritual specialists as Taoists. In the context of the *duangong* rituals, the Buddha seems by and large to be higher than Laojun, and we have seen that the *duangong* refer to themselves in these texts as neither Buddhist nor Taoist but shamans: on what grounds call them Taoists? why not call them Tantric Buddhists?

The principal reason for considering them Taoists, as I see it, is the role of Laojun, especially the Laojun of Maoshan, source of the shamans' magic techniques. The case of the Queen Mother is not as clear, though I do think that a good case could be made for considering her (as Suzanne Cahill does) quintessentially Taoist. Nonetheless, given the incredible mix of gods in the various rituals, it could be argued that, at least as regards the pantheon, calling *duangong* ritual "Taoist" is begging the question. One might also point to the Taoist ritual register titles used by most of the priests: in all three *duangong* books the priest uses the very classic, elite Taoist Scriptural Register of the Five Thunders of the Three Caves of Highest Purity 上清三洞五雷經籙...便宜科事，臣 (*Yangxi*, p. 295; *Qingtan*, p. 27; *Yansheng*, p. 45).[21] While the lack of a

---

21 It should be noted, however, that the *Yangxi* and *Qingtan* register titles belong to the same Xianfeng (1851-1861) group of manuscripts, and the *Yansheng* text was written down by Yang Zhongli in the 1980s, on what basis Hu Tiancheng does not say: see the tables of manuscript origins and dates in *Yangxi*, pp. 57-58, and *Yansheng*, pp. 6-7.

fit between the elite title and the shamanistic reality might be understood to mean that such register titles don't prove much (or that they derive from the fact that these people do funeral rituals), the fact that in at least one Yansheng ritual, a Buddhist title is used — The minister so-and-so, disciple who inherited the teachings of Śākyamuni, the founder of the religion..." 欽稟...開教本師釋迦牟尼文佛金蓮座下，遺教弟子便宜科法事，臣 (*Yansheng*, p. 87) — suggests, on the contrary, a fairly clear sense of belonging. Hu does state — without really explaining what he means — that there are "Buddhist, Taoist, and shamanistic" versions of several of the Yansheng rituals (*Yansheng*, p. 12).

In a more general way, it is unfortunate that Hu does not discuss more clearly how the *duangong* see themselves. It is even more unfortunate that the central paintings 總眞神軸 hung during these rituals are poorly reproduced and nowhere explained (*Yangxi*, p. 484; *Qingtan* p. 358; *Yansheng*, p. 389). Clearly, we need more information if we are to discuss the question of religious affiliation intelligently. (Of course, we can also adopt the view that the question is irrelevant.) For my part. I provisionally consider it, like Lüshan, a form of Taoism, albeit with a heavy admixture of Tantrism, specifically of the Pu'an school variety. If that classification were to be confirmed, it would oblige us to rethink radically our views of "shamanism", "Taoism", and "Buddhism." I would add that, while it is all clearly enough "popular Chinese religion" — a term I continue to use without qualms — that does not make the question of the *duangong*'s religious affiliation an impertinent one.

In short, these marvellous ethnographic reports give us an excellent basis for thinking about cultural unity and diversity in that vast space to which we quite legitimately give the single name of "China," even though it is clearly no cultural monolith.

A REVIEW OF THE CELEBRATION OF THE BODHISATTVA RITUAL OF THE VERNACULAR PRIESTS OF THE ZOU LINEAGE IN POJI TOWNSHIP, ZHENXIONG COUNTY, ZHAOTONG REGION, YUNNAN BY GUO SIJIU AND WANG YONG

David Holm

1. Guo Sijiu 郭思九 and Wang Yong 王勇, *The Celebration of the Bodhisattva Ritual of the Vernacular Priests of the Zou Lineage in Poji Township, Zhenxiong County, Zhaotong Region, Yunnan* 雲南省昭通地區鎮雄縣潑機鄉鄒氏端公的慶菩薩調查. *Min-su ch'ü-i ts'ung-shu* 民俗曲藝叢書 (Studies in Chinese Ritual, Theatre and Folklore Series), No. 29, 1995. 244 pages.

Zhaotong 昭通 is located in the panhandle of far northeastern Yunnan, flanked by the barren uplands of the Bijie 畢節 Region of northwestern Guizhou to the south, and mountainous terrain adjoining the Jinshajiang 金沙江 river in southwestern Sichuan to the north. Zhenxiong 鎮雄 is the easternmost county in the Zhaotong Region, bordering on Guizhou and Sichuan. It is a poor and heavily populated county, lying at the foot of the Wumeng 烏蒙 Mountains. During the Nanzhao 南詔 period it was occupied by the Yi 彝, and during the Song a 'haltered-and-bridled' principality was set up there, which lasted until the conversion to direct Chinese rule during the Yongzheng (1723-1735) period in the early Qing. This 'haltered-and-bridled' principality involved only loose control by the Chinese state, while real power within the principality was retained by a hereditary Yi aristocracy. A commandery was established there during the Yuan, and Zhenxiong continued to be an important military post during the Ming. Poji is in the southeast of the county, and the parish seat is only seven kilometres from the Guizhou border. Three encampments were established there during the Hongwu period (1368-1398). The area is prosperous, relatively speaking, and the main crops include grains (maize, wheat, a small amount of rice, and tubers), tobacco, and rape-seed.

The local ethnic mix includes Han, Yi, Hmong, Bai, and Zhuang, plus the Caijia 蔡家, a group whose affiliation is yet to be determined. Of all these groups, the Yi have been in the area the longest, and politically have been the most powerful. The Han settlers came into the area after the end of the Yuan, coming mainly from Jiangsu, Jiangxi, Hunan, Hubei, Sichuan and Anhui, but also from Shandong, Shanxi, and Guizhou. They came either as soldiers or as camp followers, merchants, artisans, or refugees. Local families such as the Shen 申, Ji 吉 and Wang 王 date from the Ming; a further wave came in with Wu Sangui 吳三桂 when he invaded Yunnan, and there was further in-migration after conversion to direct Chinese rule.

Migrants both adapted to the new environment and tenaciously held onto their old culture. One mechanism for both was the native-place association (*huiguan* 會館) system. The authors give a brief overview of seasonal observances and taboos (pp. 7-9), and note that worship of the Buddhist goddess of mercy *Guanyin* 觀音, the God of Wealth (*Caishen* 財神), and Imperial Lord Zitong (*Zitong dijun* 梓潼帝君) was particularly prominent in the area; all three gods are included on domestic altars along with the usual hierarchy of Heaven, Earth, Ruler, Kin and Teachers (*tian di jun qin shi* 天地君親師). Some people however also set up a shrine and make offerings to the "God of the Altar" (*Tanshen* 壇神), in hopes of obtaining "support for the family and protection for the house" (*chi jia zhen zhai* 持家鎮宅) (p. 9).

Duangong 端公, which can be roughly translated as "vernacular priest," is the term used in this area for ritualists, regardless of whether they performed Buddhist, Taoist or Wuist rituals, though nobody locally could explain what it meant. There were two "lines of office" (*zhitiao* 職條) locally: 'civil offices' (*wenzhi* 文職) and "military offices" (*wuzhi* 武職). The former were Buddhist, while the latter were Taoist or *Wu* 巫 specialists. The label *Wu* was generally tabooed in favour of "Tao" because of the fear of being labelled as practitioners of illicit cults. Some priests could perform both Buddhist and Taoist (or *Wu*) rituals. Vernacular priests were generally held in high regard in the villages, being literate specialists.

Zoujia yuanzi 鄒家院子, the home of the Zou 鄒 lineage, was a single-surname village one kilometre from the township seat. According to their ancestral register, the Zou came from Jiangxi, and had been in the district for sixteen generations. The register includes a story of how their first ancestor in the district had cured the daughter of the local Yi chieftain of a strange illness caused by witchcraft, which suggests (though the authors do not say this) that the Zou may have owed their preeminent position in the district to subsequent patronage by the local Yi ruling clans. The Zou were originally practitioners of Taoist and Wuist ritual, but later also added Buddhism to their repertoire, partly in order to avoid the stigma of unorthodoxy. Another factor was that the Taoist and Wuist rituals are all performed during the winter, while Buddhist rituals are performed year-round. The troupe now makes most of its living by performing Buddhist rituals, even though it is universally recognised that they perform the best 'Celebration of the Bodhisattva' in the area.

The vernacular priests worship many gods, but priests were not in the habit of counting them or providing lists, and the authors present an overview which is based on the ritual process itself, rather than just interviews. Most of the gods invited for the 'Celebration of the Bodhisattva' are those whose names appear in the "Spirit Gate Ritual of Invitation" (*Shenmen liqing keyi* 神門禮請科儀) text that is included here as Appendix 10. The authors found it useful to distinguish between gods with images and gods without images; most gods were merely invited, with no visual image supplementing the text. Those with images were represented either on sacred scrolls hung up during the ritual (*shenbang* 神榜), or as statuettes (josses), or in the form of masks. For "Celebration of the Bodhisattva," mostly three scrolls were used (identification of the deities represented is given p.29 and cross-referenced to Plates 4-6). In this ritual they also employ the josses of the deities Generalissimo Duke Zhao (*Zhaogong Yuanshuai* 趙公元帥), the

Imperial Lord Zitong 梓潼, and the Crown Prince Bodhisattva (*Taizi pusa* 太子菩薩). The functions of the first two were wealth and male progeny, respectively, while the Crown Prince Bodhisattva, also called the Old Gentleman God (*Laolangshen* 老郎神), the Old Gentleman Crown Prince (*Laolang taizi* 老郎太子), or the Great God who Rules over Theatre (*Xizhu dashen* 戲主大神), was worshipped when the priests performed plays (a legend about the Crown Prince is retold on pp. 30-31). The masks are kept in a costumes trunk until use, and a ritual of animation (*kaiguang* 開光) is performed before the priest puts them on. For the duration of the performance, they are regarded as the concrete form of the divine presence.

The layout of the shrines and domestic altar of the head priest (*zhangtanshi* 掌壇師) of the Zou lineage is described. (pp. 31 ff.) Of particular interest is the shrine to the Altar God. The purpose of setting up this shrine is said to be the "garrisoning (i.e. suppression) of the spirits of those who died violent deaths" (*zhen lishen* 鎮厲神), with a view to seeking "peace and tranquillity in the family abode" (*jiazhai ping'an* 家宅平安). The identity of the various Altar Gods is discussed in a story told by Zou Yongfu 鄒永福 (pp. 32-33). Chief among them is the deity Sagely Lord Marquis Zhao (*Zhaohou shengzhu* 趙侯聖主), who is said to have assisted the emperor in the suppression of the ghosts of slain southern tribesmen during the Tang. Until fairly recently, offerings of human blood were made to this deity before the beginning of a Celebration of the Bodhisattva ritual. Other Altar Gods included Duke Luo the Great Dharma Teacher (*Luogong dafa laoshi* 羅公大法老師), and Marquis Zhao's generalissimo Monsieur Guo the Third Son (*Guoshi sanlang* 郭氏三郎). Investigations elsewhere indicated that Marquis Zhao was always included among the Altar Gods, though the identity of the others varied.

Another deity important locally is General of the Eight Barbarian Tribes (*Baman jiangjun* 八蠻將軍). This god is identified in Poji with the local Yizu and more specifically with the Yi chieftains, but his cult is quite widespread, being found also in other counties in the Zhaotong Region and further afield in northern Yunnan and southwestern Sichuan. His mask is that of a ferocious god (*xiongshen* 凶神). The authors point out that Han settlers moving into the area were dependent on the goodwill of the Yi, who were politically dominant over a long period. Even now, if the Celebration of the Bodhisattva is performed in a mixed Han-Yi village, the priests must obtain the permission of the Yi before the part of General of the Eight Barbarian Tribes can be performed. The attitude of the priests is strict and respectful, even if the General in the plays is a figure of fun. He is worshipped as Sagely Lord of the Earth (*Dipan shengzhu* 地盤聖主), i.e. as the Local Lord of the Earth (*tuzhu* 土主). In fact, as the authors go on to point out, he is the object of 'offerings to the souls of the slain' (*liji* 厲祭). The priest's performance of Celebration rituals is an archetypal "offering to the souls of the slain," that is, an offering intended for the ghosts of those who had died unnatural, violent or sudden deaths.

The third deity discussed at length is Miao Laosan 苗老三, "Hmong the Third," so-called because of local legends in which the Hmong are identified as the third of three brothers. Unlike the General of the Eight Barbarian Tribes, Miao Laosan is not invested with great power, and is primarily a figure of fun who appears with his wife Mrs Guess (*Niangcai* 娘猜) in flirtation skits.

Celebration of the Bodhisattva is a household-based ritual. It is performed either when a household has been enjoying exceptionally prosperous circumstances, or when it is adjudged that the gods have bestowed what was asked of them when making a vow, whether this was a request for male progeny, recovery from illness, or a favourable turn in family fortunes. The ritual is conducted in recompense, in order to "write off the lingering [debt resulting from a] vow" (*liaoque suyuan* 了卻宿願). "Bodhisattva" (*pusa* 菩薩) in this region is a general term, applied to all deities indiscriminately, and "Celebration (*qing* 慶) has the force of requiting the kindness and celebrating [the successful intervention of the gods]. " The ritual is normally performed in winter, beginning on a suitable day determined by formulae given on pp. 39-40; there is a general taboo on performing after the Establishment of Spring (*lichun* 立春), the solar term that falls usually around February 5th.

Preparations include the rearing of one or two pigs, to be used in sacrifice, and discussion between the household head and the priests so that the exact nature of the vow contracted is understood. The ritual is planned with this in mind: if the household has made a vow (called a *Zitong yuan* 梓潼願) for the birth of a son, then the Imperial Lord Zitong must be accorded his place as the chief deity addressed in the ritual, though in such cases "joint offerings" (*jianji* 兼祭) are always made to Generalissimo Duke Zhao. If the host also worships the Altar Gods, then the priests must add the ritual of offerings addressed to them. The latter may be performed separately, in which case such a ritual is called a Celebration of the Altar (*Qingtan* 慶壇). Invitations are also made to people to fulfil other offices, such as that of the Incense and Lamp Officer (*xiangdengshi* 香燈師), whose job it is to ensure continuity of incense and candles, and the Official Officer (*guanshi* 官師), who takes charge of guests, records gifts, and organises subsidiary help. The priests send along an Archival Officer *(wen'anshi* 文案師) to organise the ritual area and write out ritual documents. They also invite a butcher from the village to kill the sacrificial pigs and goats.

The rest of the book discusses two separate performances of the Celebration of the Bodhisattva, one at the house of Zhu Shaofei 朱少非 in Heishigou 黑石溝 in Bailuo 擺落 administrative village, Poji township (pp. 48-57), and one in the house of Hu Kairong 胡開榮 or Jigucao 吉谷槽 village, Dahe 大河 parish, Bijie County, Guizhou (pp. 57-73). The reason for this is that the offerings to the Altar Gods were not included as part of the ritual performed in the house of Zhu Shaofei, so the Celebration of the Altar ritual performed by the same troupe for the household of Hu Kairong was presented by way of a supplement.

The ritual performed in the house of Hu Kairong took place over five days, and the menu of 'altars' (*tan* 壇) performed included some twenty items, compared with the abstract list of twenty-seven items provided by the head priest. A good number of these ritual segments entailed performative elaboration, either through song-and-dance, spoken repartee, or full-scale performance of plays. For example, the "Garrisoning of the Stage" that took place on the morning of the third day, which involved the ritual sweeping of the stage area by the deity Efficaceous Official (*Lingguan* 靈官), included the play segment "Emplanting the Five Camps" (*Zha wuying* 紮五營). Other plays performed included Story of the Eight Barbarian Tribes (*Baman ji* 八蠻記), Story of the Aged Mother (*Laomu ji* 老母記), Great Journey to the Mountain of Yellow Flowers (*Da you Huanghuashan* 大游黃花山), Erlang Splits Peach Mountain to Rescue his Mother (*Erlang Pi Taoshan jiu mu* 二郎劈桃山救母), and Phoenix Camp (*Fenghuangying* 鳳凰營).

The account of the Celebration of the Altars ritual is also of interest and would repay close study. The authors conclude their volume with a short discussion of the mudrās used by the priests. Material in the appendix includes material on the ordination registers of the priests of the Zou lineage, both Taoist and Buddhist; a transcription of the placard for the shrine to the Altar Gods; the ritual text and diagrams for the Nine Continents ritual; the text for the Placing the Hay (*Luocao* 落草) ritual; the text for the Camp of the Wealth God ritual; the poem of the Hundred Flowers; the text of the ritual plays Phoenix Camp and Splitting Peach Mountain; and a photoreprint of the manuscript of invitation. Ninety-one photographs complete the volume, all of exceptional quality.

Critique

In spite of a few obvious omissions — such as a section on music — this volume is excellent. It is written in a particularly lucid style, and the information it contains is pertinent, coherent, and inherently interesting. The companion volume by Ma Chaokai is also excellent, and supplements this volume both in the provision of more systematic information about ritual details and in the provision of carefully edited texts. The authors' speculations are refreshingly well-grounded, and devoid of the arid historicism that characterises far too much of the writing of desk-bound Chinese scholars. A number of questions covered are likely to be of very general interest for the study of Chinese ritual traditions. The information provided on ordination registers should be consulted by all scholars interested in geographic variations in Taoist traditions. The material on the cult of the Altar Gods alone would be worth a special review article, particularly if combined with information about the Altar Gods in Sichuan and elsewhere. The cult of the General of the Eight Barbarian Tribes, of course, is found over a much wider area than the authors indicate; it is also found in the Pleasing the Nuo God ritual of eastern Guizhou and, one suspects, is probably found quite widely throughout southwest and south-central China. Particularly stimulating is the authors' observation that the Han in South China paid a continued endemnity, through ritual observance, for all the violent deaths of non-Han tribespepole caused over many centuries by the southward expansion of the Chinese state.

Bibliography

Ma Chaokai 馬朝開. 1997. *Collected Ritual Texts Pertaining to the "Celebrating the Bodhisattva" Ritual of Poji Town, Zhenxiong County, Yunnan* 雲南省鎮雄縣潑機鎮漢族慶菩薩. *Min-su ch'ü-i ts'ung-shu*, No. 56. 442 pages. Taipei: Shih Ho-cheng Folk Culture Foundation.

6b

A REVIEW OF THE YANGXI OF GUIZHOU:

THE THEATRICAL TROUPE OF THE DENG LINEAGE IN DASHANG VILLAGE, LIMU TOWNSHIP, LUODIAN BY HUANGFU CHONGQING

David Holm

1. Huangfu Chongqing 皇甫重慶, *The Yangxi Plays of Guizhou: Case Study of the Deng Family Troupe in Dashang Village, Limu Township, Luodian County* 貴州陽戲——以羅甸縣栗木鄉達上村鄧氏戲班爲例. *Min-su ch'ü-i ts'ung-shu* 民俗曲藝叢書 (Studies in Chinese Ritual, Theatre and Folklore Series), No. 38, 1995. 290 pages.

Luodian county is on the southern border of Guizhou, facing Tian'e 天峨 county in Guangxi on the other side of the Hongshui River 紅水河. The entire county is part of the upper reaches of the Hongshui River system, which in turn flows south and east into the Xijiang 西江. It was formerly the seat of a local chieftaincy,[1] and the inhabitants are predominantly Tai-speaking Bouyei, with some Hmong (*Miao*) communities in the mountains to the west of the county and comparatively recent Han migrants concentrated in the hill country to the north and the areas adja-

---

1 *Buyizu shehui lishi diaocha* 布依族社會歷史調查 (Bouyi Social and Historical Investigated. Guiyang: Guizhou minsu chubanshe, 1986).

cent to the main towns.[2] Limu township is located in these northern hills, and the village of Dashang is located in a valley five kilometres to the east of Bianyang 邊陽, a small market town on the main road between Luodian and Guiyang.

In fact, Dashang is a general name for an area that comprises nine hamlets, including Dashang, Huagao 化稿, Dapo 大坡, Pujiawuji 朴家屋基, Zhongzhai 中寨, and Dongna 董納, of which Dongna is ethnically Bouyei and Zhongzhai is Hmong (p. 4). The population of Limu parish is now about 75% Han, people whose forebears migrated to this district in large numbers in the seventeenth century, during the Ming-Qing transition (p. 8). All 100-odd families in Dashang are Han, with only a few women married in from Hmong, Kham (*Dong*), or Bouyei. Deng is the dominant surname in the hamlet, with a few Luo 羅, Wang 王, Li 李 and Shao 邵 (p. 12). Deng family graves occupy most of the surrounding mountains. According to family registers, the forebears of the Deng are said to have come from Linjiang 臨江 in Jiangxi. They went to Sichuan with the army during the Ming-Qing transition, then migrated from Sichuan to Meitan 湄潭 (east of Zunyi 遵義) in northeastern Guizhou. From there they migrated south via Guiyang and Bianyang, with five brothers settling first in Chenbo hamlet. They resettled in Dashang after driving out the local Hmong, with whom they engaged in a lawsuit. They have been in Dashang for 10 generations, or approximately 200 years (a list of generational names 字輩 is given on p. 12). The lineage register was destroyed during the Cultural Revolution, and re-written in 1988. There was at one time a Deng lineage hall, but it was converted to other uses during the 1930's. There was also originally a Temple of the Lotus Scripture (*Lianjingmiao* 蓮經廟) in the village, said to have sūtras that came from the Temple of Boundless Blessings (*Hongfusi* 宏福寺) near Guiyang. There is still evidence of Buddhist influence in the area: for funerals people call upon practitioners called 'gentlemen of the civil altar' (*wentan xiansheng* 文壇先生) or 'companions in benevolence' (*shanlü* 善侶). But more influ-

---

2   Qiannan Bouyizu Miaozu Guizhousheng Bianjizu, ed., *Qiannan Buyizu Miaozu zizhizhou zhi, di 4 juan: Minzu zhi* 黔南布依族苗族自治州志・第四卷・民族志 (Gazetteer of the Qiannan Bouyi Miao Autonomous Prefecture, Vol. 4: Nationalities Gazetter). Guiyang: Guizhou minsu chubanshe, 1993.

ential is the 'martial *nuo*' (*wunuo* 巫儺) cult and the worship of the Three Sages (*sansheng* 三聖). The Three Sages are the Lord of Streams (*Chuanzhu* 川主 - a name which also means the Lord of Sichuan), the Lord of the Earth (*Tuzhu* 土主), and the Medicine King (*Yaowang* 藥 王). The deity *Wenchang* 文昌, worship of whom also originated from Sichuan, is often added to form a foursome, the Four Sages (*Sisheng* 四 聖). Domestic altars make provision for offerings to a variety of deities (p. 13). Households worshipping the martial *nuo* make offerings to the Three Mountain Sprites (*sanxiao* 三魈) and Laozi (*Laojun* 老君) as the chief deities.

The earliest mention of *yang* plays in Guizhou comes from the Zunyi Prefectural Gazetteer of the Daoguang period (1821-1851), which links the performance of *yang* plays specifically with worship of the Three Sages, and refers to the practice of worshippers pasting up written vows in front of the gods, promising the performance of *yang* plays as recompense for relief from affliction. Apart from the Three Sages themselves, a connection with Sichuan is to be found in all Guizhou *yang* plays. Within Guizhou, *yang* plays are found mainly in Meitan, Tongzi 桐梓, Fenggang 鳳岡, Zheng'an 正安, Wuchuan 務川, Daozhen 道眞, Sinan 思南, and Yanhe 沿河 — all counties in the north and northeast which were originally part of Sichuan. The counties of Luodian, Fuquan 福泉, Weng'an 瓮安, Huishui 惠水, Changshun 長順, Pingtang 平塘, Jinsha 金沙 and Zhijin 織金 - all in present-day central and southern Guizhou - have never been part of Sichuan administratively, but in all these areas performers say their families came from Sichuan, or came from Jiangxi via Sichuan (p. 16). The chief deities also come from Sichuan. The Lord of Streams is identified as Erlang 二郎, and in *yang* plays Erlang is already an amalgam of two separate figures: Li Bing's 李冰 Second Son (Li Erlang 李二郎), and Yang Jian 楊戩 of *The Journey to the West and The Enfeoffment of the Gods* fame. Both figures are connected with Sichuan. The same applies to the other deities in the trinity. The fourth deity — variously identified as *Wenchang* 文昌 or the Sage *Guandi* (*Guansheng* 關聖) — the former in Zitong and Zunyi and the latter in Fuquan and Weng'an — are also closely connected with Sichuan.

The repertoire of ritual plays is very similar all over Guizhou. The play Erlang Humbles the Dragon (*Erlang jiang long* 二郎降龍) is found all over Guizhou, though under different titles and in somewhat varying lengths. Other plays in the Deng family repertoire include Erlang Rescues His Mother from Peach Mountain (*Taoshan jiu mu* 桃山救母), Han Xin Pursues Chu (*Han Xin zhui Chu* 韓信追楚), and Lady Mengjiang is Reunited with her Husband (*Mengjiang tuanyuan* 孟姜團圓). A manuscript containing scripts of these plays came into the possession of Deng Guofei 鄧國飛, the current leader of the troupe and head priest, at the time when he was ordained. The manuscript came from his father, and was probably transcribed sometime in the 1860's.

The organization unit in *yang* plays is called the "altar" (*tan* 壇) in Guizhou. This term refers to a special troupe that performs rituals and plays in recompense and redemption of vows. Typically, the specific occasions are when families are blessed with an increase in family members (*tian ren jin kou* 添人進口) through marriage, when a bride is brought into the family of her new husband. The instance of performance of *yang* plays that the author used as the basis of his analysis took place on the occasion of the celebrant's son's wedding. The "altar" requires transmission of appropriate religious practices (*tanpai* 壇派) of its members, that is, regular offerings to the relevant gods, and observation of the rules and taboos. In addition, the troupe ensures the transmission of the relevant skills, including ritual knowledge of the appropriate activity and skills in theatrical performance.

During the previous generation, the Deng family troupe was quite prosperous, performing as far afield as Huishui, Changshun, Qingzhen 清鎮, Ziyun 紫雲, and Tian'e in Guangxi. This carried on until the Cultural Revolution. In the middle 1950's the troupe was responding to some 40-50 invitations a year, and it split into two bands in order to cope with the demand.

Performance of *yang* plays requires around ten men, but the Deng troupe has some twenty names on the books, of whom thirteen frequently perform. Brief biographical details of current performers are given (pp. 19-20).

Transmission of the knowledge of how to perform *yang* plays is secret. Some details of the ordination procedure are given (pp. 24 ff). The ritual procedure and the list of prohibitions (p. 25) relate not only to the performance of rituals involving *yang* plays, but also to worship of the Altar Gods (*dingtan* 頂壇). According to local informants, there was a two-fold meaning to this term. For normal townsmen, the phrase was an abbreviation of the term "to support an altar for the Three Sages" (*dingyou Sansheng tan* 頂有三聖壇), that is, to practice worship of the Three Sages at their domestic altar. For families who worshipped the Three Sages, it was obligatory to invite a troupe to perform *yang* plays every time there was a new member of the family (i.e., a wife marrying in, or giving birth to a boy), regardless of whether or not there had been any prior pledging of vows (*xuyuan* 許願). Other families, that is those that did not worship the Three Sages, had the choice; if they chose to make and redeem a vow to perform *yang* plays, this was called "short-head vow" (*duantou yuan* 短頭願). For troupe members, "support of the altar" (*dingtan* 頂壇) had a more specific meaning, which was to take on the responsibilities of troupe leader. Once they were ordained, any troupe member could take on apprentices and become a presiding priest, but there was only one "presiding priest who supports the altar" (*ding tan de zhangtanshi* 頂壇的掌壇師) at any one time. This man was usually chosen by the man he succeeded, and inherited the responsibility for the leadership and welfare of the troupe. At the time he assumed these responsibilities, the leader (*dingtande* 頂壇的) also took over a shrine to the Three Sages, which was set up in his home to the right-hand side of the domestic gods. There used to be a small figurine on the wooden shelf of the shrine called the Crown Prince Bodhisattva (*Taizi pusa* 太子菩薩), but this was now no longer seen, though before performances the ritual segment "Installing the Crown Prince" (*an Taizi* 安太子) still had to be performed. The various duties of the troupe leader are listed on p. 28.

The Three Sages are worshipped in all parts of Guizhou where *yang* plays are performed. The Lord of Streams, the Lord of the Earth, and the Medicine King are gods of watercourses, the earth, and illness respectively. The three are regarded as equal in status, but the Lord of Streams is always mentioned first. The Lord of the Earth and the Medicine King do not have names or histories — the fullest expression of their names is Lord of the Earth of Wall Mountain (*Bishan tuzhu* 壁山土主) and Medicine King of Suzhou (*Suzhou yaowang* 蘇州藥王). The Lord of Streams is also called Erlang the God of the Water Inlet (*Guankou Erlang shen* 灌口二郎神). In *yang* plays, the Lord of Streams is the lord of watercourses, and also subdues demons and garrisons the four directions. The Three Sages serve as chief deities (*zhushen* 主神) and also as gods of the theatre (*xishen* 戲神). The term "gods of the theatre" however is also used locally for the twenty-four character roles in the twenty-four plays. The real 'god of the theatre' however is the Crown Prince Bodhisattva 太子菩薩, who is also called the Old Gentleman Crown Prince (*Laolang taizi* 老郎太子).

The Sagely Imperial Lord Guanyu (*Guansheng dijun* 關聖帝君) is worshipped especially in Fuquan and Weng'an along with the Three Sages. In Fuquan a special item in the repertoire is the play Going through the Passes (*Guoguan* 過關), which presents the story of how Guan Yu went through five passes in his search for Liu Bei 劉備, and killed six generals. This play is only performed by troupes that worship the Four Sages. After each victory, women waiting in the wings rush out with their children and whisk their children underneath Guan Yu's upheld sword. Other deities discussed at some length include the Efficacious Official Wang (*Wang lingguan* 王靈官), the Vanguard who Opens the Road (*Kailu xianfeng* 開路先鋒), and the Gruff General who Opens the Mountains (*Kaishan mangjiang* 開山莽將).

Only one scroll is hung up by this particular troupe during performances. It is a four-level ikon (the identity of the gods represented is discussed on p. 34). In addition a list of gods who have places at the offerings table (*shenghao* 聖號) is given on p.35, along with their honorific titles (*fenghao* 封號).

In Chapter Five the author discusses various reasons for performance, as well as methods of making vows (pp. 37-39). When the troupe arrives at the house to which it has been invited to perform, the first item of business is to confirm appointment of two persons to look after incense, candles, wine and tea (the "incense and candle officers" *xiangzhushi* 香燭師, as they are called locally) ; another young male to perform obeisance to the gods on behalf of the "owner of the vow (*yuanzhu* 願主) ; and fourthly a "kitchen-official" *chuguan* 廚官 to kill the pig. The author then describes how the inner altar (*neitan* 內壇) and outer altar (*waitan* 外壇) are set up, with details of how the statuettes are installed on the ancestral altar (p. 43). Afterwards, the god of the hearth (*Zaowang fujun* 灶王府君) and the Lady of the Cistern (*Yuchi furen* 玉池夫人) are installed in the kitchen (p. 46). The Crown Prince is installed by the troupe leader, after which the 'owner of the vow' puts a red envelope before the statuette.

The performance analysed is one that took place on 18-19 January 1994 (the 7th day of the 12th month) in a village up in the mountains ten kilometers from Dashang. The occasion was the marriage of Luo Anpin's second son, and the vow that was being redeemed was a "good vow for long life to the Three Sages" (*Sansheng changsheng liangyuan* 三聖長生良願). The performance of *yang* plays began the evening before the arrival of the bride's party and the culmination of the wedding ceremony. The performance itself was divided into the ritual proper (*fashi* 法事) — also called "proper plays" (*zhengxi* 正戲) — and 'decotative plays' (*huaxi* 花戲). Normally only 'proper plays' are performed, which requires one whole day (24 hours). Under special circumstances "decorative plays" are performed as well, in which case one and a half or two days are required.

Each ritual segment in the ritual is described in turn. Space does not permit more than the presentation of a list here:

1) Opening the Altar and Beginning the Invitations (*Kaitan qiqing* 開壇啓請), itself composed of the following sub-segments:
   Presentation of Incense (*Shangxiang* 上香)
   Sweeping the Marquee (*Saopeng* 掃棚)
   Illuminating the Marquee (*Liangpeng* 亮棚)
   Requesting Water for purification (*Qingshui* 請水)
   Audience with the Stove God (*Can Zao* 參灶)
2) Taking One's Seat in the Palace and Conveying the Writ (*Zuodian chuanwen* 座殿傳文), composed of the following sub-segments:
   Little Demons Announce the Stage (*Baotai xiaogui* 報台小鬼)
   Emergence of the Earth God (*Chu Tudi* 出土地)
   Emergence of the Officers of Merit (*Chu Gongcao* 出功曹)
   Taking One's Seat in the Palace and Conveying the Writ (*Zuodian chuanwen* 座殿傳文)
   Emergence of the Opener of the Road (*Chu Kailu* 出開路)
   Inviting the Divine Lad (*Qing shen tongzi* 請神童子)
3) Acceptance of the Offering (*Lingsheng yizong* 領牲一宗)
4) The Efficacious Officer (*Lingguan yizong* 靈官一宗)
5) Young Lady Liu Qing (*Liu Qing niangzi yizong* 柳青娘子一宗)
6) Selling Quack Medicines (*Hua yao yizong* 化藥一宗)
7) Erlang Parades on Horseback (*Zouma Erlang* 走馬二郎)

8) Return of the Cooked Offerings and the Payment of Money (*Huishu jiaoqian* 回熟交錢)

9) The Beating in the Shackles (*Qiaojia* 敲枷)

10) Seeing off the Gods (*Songshen* 送神)

11) The God of Wealth (*Caishen* 財神)

12) The Secular Play *Three People Seek Marriage* (*Chu huaxi Sanren taoqin* 出花戲三人討親)

13) Taking Leave of the Gods (*Cishen* 辭神)

14) Registering the Redemption of the Vow (*Gouyuan* 勾願)

15) Sending off the Gods (*Songshen* 送神)

Many segments of this ritual are dramatised to a greater or lesser extent. The stage conventions observed by the priests are particularly interesting. All priests bow to the statuette of the Crown Prince before going on stage, and burn sacrificial paper and *kowtow* at the altar to the Three Sages afterwards. Conventions for the priest performing the part of Erlang are particularly rigorous; this part was performed by Deng Guofei, the troupe leader. After each performance the priest sings a long penance (*chanwen* 懺文) as he kneels before the offering table in front of the altar to the Three Sages, in which he asks forgiveness for any mistakes made during the performance, and requests that the god return his souls (*sanhun qipo* 三魂七魄). The wording of the penance text is highly reflexive, playing on the ironies of the god's appearance in the form of a human actor. The priests are quite explicit about the ritual danger: when they are acting the part, they are the god's incarnation (*huashen* 化身), and their own soul has left their body for the duration. Their own soul will return to them only if they recite the penance.

The author goes on to describe various aspects of the performance of both proper plays (*zhengxi* 正戲) and decorative plays (*huaxi* 花戲), including performance techniques, dance steps and music. Appendices provide edited versions of the scripts of the four plays previously mentioned.

Critique

The information the author provides on the ways in which cult affiliations, whether handed down within families or within *yang* theatre troupes, should prompt a thorough reconsideration of what we mean when we talk about "Chinese popular religion." Particularly interesting is the author's discussion of what he calls "shamanic *nuo* beliefs" (*wunuo xinyang* 巫儺信仰) on pp. 35-36. There he notes that the various designations of cultic transmission he has encountered include Altars to Marquis Zhao (*Zhaohou tan* 趙侯壇), Altars to the Five Manifestations (*Wuxian tan* 五顯壇), Altars to the Five Ferocious Deities (*Wuchang tan* 五猖壇), Altars to Laozi (*Laojun tan* 老君壇), Altars to the Stone Step (*Shideng tan* 石磴壇), Altars to the Cummerbund (*Doudon tan* 兜兜壇), Altars to the Green Snake (*Qingshe tan* 青蛇壇), Altars to the White Tiger (*Bohu tan* 白虎壇), Altars to the Wild Boar (*Yezhu tan* 野豬壇), Altars to the Hillock (*Xiaoshan tan* 小山壇), Altars to the Lady Goddesses (*Niangniang tan* 娘娘壇), Altars to the Teacher's Wife (*Shiniang tan* 師娘壇), Altars to Wenchang (*Wenchang tan* 文昌壇), altars to Zitong (*Zitong tan* 梓潼壇), altars to the Three Mountain Sprites (*Sanxiao tan* 三魈壇), Altars to the Three Sages (*Sansheng tan* 三聖壇), altars to the Four Sages (*Sisheng tan* 四聖壇), and Altars to the Earth God (*Tudi tan* 土地壇). he provides sample photographs of scrolls for some of these altars in the back of the book, though he does not draw our attention to them in the main text. All these altars differ in order of ritual procedure, the gods worshipped, and the theatrical repertoire of the priests. The affiliation of the Deng family troupe is to the Altar to the Three Sages, and so differs from the troupe from the village of Huangtushao 黃土哨 in Fuquan county, also investigated by the author, which belongs to the Four Sages Altar. For the redemption of vows, peasant families must invite troupes in accordance with their own cult affiliations — that is, in accordance with which gods they worship (*ding he shen* 頂何神) on their domestic altar. When performance of ritual is required, they must normally invite a troupe of the same cult. There is common saying, "Two [sets of] gods are not worshipped under one roof" (*yi wu bu ding er shen* 一屋不頂二神). A description of the Return of the God of Happiness (*Hui Xishen* 回喜神) wedding ritual is given. Spirits worshipped by the incoming bride's family are sent back to her natal home, and the bride is not allowed into her husband's house until this is done. If the bride's family is of the same ritual affiliation as that of the groom, then this is not necessary. In general, households worshipping the Three Sages, Wenchang, Zitong and Guan Yu invite priests who perform *yang* plays, while households of other altars invite troupes that perform *nuo* plays (*Nuoxiban* 儺戲班). All this indicates that, in this part of China at least, religious affiliation is a serious matter that involves laypeople as well as priests, and is organized on the basis of patrilineal descent rather than common residence in a natural village. This is certainly a matter which deserves further exploration.

Also deserving further investigation is the question of "civil altar" (*wentan* 文壇) and "martial altar" (*wutan* 武壇) when applied to troupes performing *yang* plays. The author mentions this in passing, observing that the Deng family troupe used to be a "civil altar" troupe, capable of performing entire funerals, before they converted to 'martial altar' performance. No further details are given.

The author gives a well-organised exposition of the ritual, carefully noting the time at which each ritual segment began. This enables the reader, without much effort, to compile a synoptic table and gain a clear idea of how the author's discursive descriptions relate to the unfolding of the ritual process through time and space. Inclusion of a photocopy of the ritual manuscript enables readers to discover further details for themselves, though they should be advised to make a magnified copy of this material before attempting to work on it. Cross-references between the descriptions in the main text and the pages of the ritual manuscript would also have been helpful.

Less satisfactory is the treatment of two matters. One is the lack of any introduction to the various ritual implements used by the priests. We are left to guess whether or not a *chaofo* 朝佛 (lit. "court Buddha") is the same as an audience board (*chaoban* 朝板), and the *lingpai* 令牌 (lit. "sign of command") that is used to knock on the offerings table is nowhere described (see pp. 51-52). Detailed descriptions of these implements would have assisted greatly in comparing *yang* plays as performed in Luodian with *yang* plays elsewhere. Secondly, the captions on the photographic plates (pp. 265-290) are seriously uninformative. Readers should be warned that not all of the photographs pertain to the Deng family truope, or even the Luodian locale or even *yang* plays in quite a few cases. There is no photograph of the one sacred scroll that is used by the Deng troupe, though it can be seen in the background of the photographs on page 284. The photographs of the masks may or may not be of those in the possession of the Deng troupe, but it is certain that many of the scrolls are those pertaining to various forms of *wunuo* 巫儺 cults, rather than *yang* plays. We are not told where they come from. These are matters which would be very easy to put right.

Overall, in spite of the oversights mentioned above, this is an excellent volume. The presentation is particularly lucid, the details that are presented are pertinent and interesting in themselves, and the author's many years of fieldwork experience in various parts of Guizhou shine forth, enabling him to make regional comparisons that transcend the immediate locale. The account also raises indirectly issues of considerable importance for the understanding of Chinese theatrical ritual and so-called "popular religion."

6 c

A REVIEW OF THE CELEBRATION OF THE BODHISATTVA RITUAL OF THE HAN CHINESE IN POJI TOWNSHIP, ZHENXIONG COUNTY, YUNNAN BY MA CHAOKAI

David Holm

1. Ma Chaokai 馬朝開, *Collected Ritual Texts Pertaining to the "Cele-brating the Buddhisattva" Ritual of Poji Town, Zhenxiong County, Yunnan* 雲南省鎮雄縣潑機鎮漢族慶菩薩. *Min-su ch'ü-i ts'ung-shu* 民俗曲藝叢書 (Studies in Chinese Ritual, Theatre and Folklore Series), No. 56, 1997. 442 pages.

This volume is mainly a collection of texts and ancillary materials. It is based on a number of troupes of vernacular priests (*duangong* 端公) in Poji township, including the Zou 鄒 lineage that is the subject of the field report by Guo Sijiu 郭思九 and Wang Yong 王勇, and it can be considered as a companion volume to that report.

A relatively short main text covers a number of important ques-tions, such as the date of the establishment of Celebrating the Bodhisattva (*Qing pusa* 慶菩薩) in the area; various customs surround-ing this ritual and its evolution in northeastern Yunnan; the deities to which offerings are made; the ritual repertoire; performative aspects of the rituals; and a discussion of the process through which the textual materials in part two were collected and edited.

The second part of the volume is a collection of three main bodies of ritual texts: those for 'civil affairs' (*wenshi* 文事), 'proper rituals' (*zhengtan* 正壇), and 'Returning the Money' (*Huanqian* 還錢). The first two of these rituals are discussed in detail in the Guo and Wang volume, though under slightly different designations.

The bulk of the volume is taken up with appendices, viz:

1) the origin of the texts.
2) the layout of the ritual space and of the spirit tablets of deities worshipped in Celebrating the Bodhisativa and Returning the Money.
3) explanations of technical terms used by the priests.
4) text of an encomium to the Efficacious Official.
5) analysis of the division of labor for each ritual segment in Celebrating the Bodhisattva.
6) the mudrās used in Celebrating the Bodhisattva.
7) the use of various written documents, including *biao* 表, *shu* 疏, *die* 牒, *fu* 符 and *zhuang* 狀.
8) tables giving information about ritual texts, ritual programs, and number of priests participating in each ritual segment.
9) photographic plates 1-117.

Celebrating the Bodhisattva is a highly theatrical ritual in which, for at least some ritual segments, the priests wear masks from beginning to end, and conduct all important business of the ritual in the persona of the deities represented. Theatre, dance and ritual are combined into a single performative body, much as in *nuo*.

Celebrating the Bodhisattva has a history of almost 100 years in this locality, and probably reached its apogee in the late Qing and Republican periods. The author can confirm the Jiangxi origins of the Zou lineage, but happened also to read a report on "vernacular priest plays" (*duangongxi* 端公戲) in Jiangbei 江北, Sichuan, by Wang Yue 王躍. He discovered that the system of Taoist generational names (*faming zibei* 法名字輩) used in Jiangbei is exactly the same, character for character, as that found in the Taoist registers of the Zou lineage in Poji. He notes that Zhenxiong county was at various times under the administrative control of Sichuan. More importantly, there are pervasive similarities in plays, deities worshipped, and ritual structure between Jiangbei and Poji, which leads the author to infer that Celebrating the Bodhisattva arrived in Zhenxiong via Sichuan, and represents a tradition very close to that found in the environs of Chongqing.

Vernacular priests in Poji make a distinction between 'civil celebration' (*wenqing* 文慶) and "martial celebration" (*wuqing* 武慶). The former is devoted to the deity Imperial Lord Zitong (*Zitong dijun* 梓潼帝君), and the ritual segments Calling up the Troops (*zhaobing* 招兵), Releasing the Troops (*fangbing* 放兵) and Opening the Altar (*kaitan* 開壇) are not performed, since Zitong is not normally accompanied by spirit soldiers. The term 'martial celebration' refers to rituals performed for the God of Wealth (*Caishen* 財神) and the Altar Gods (*Tanshen* 壇神).

Returning the Money is a ritual also frequently performed by vernacular priests in the area. The deities invited and the order of performance are basically the same as for Celebrating the Bodhisattva. But whereas the latter is a ritual of thanksgiving (*chou'en* 酬恩), Returning the Money is an apotropaic ritual intended to dispel disaster (*jierang xiaozai* 解禳消災). A list of ritual segments is given on p. 8. Also provided is a systematic listing of the deities whose spirit seats are placed on each of the three altars in Celebrating the Bodhisattva.

Ma Chaokai is a local scholar recruited to the project, and he was able to visit Poji repeatedly in order to check matters of detail with the priests. The texts he painstakingly collected or had copied are the result of a great deal of elicitation and cross-checking. He found that many important aspects of the ritual performances were not written down in the ritual manuscripts — for example, the texts of the memorials and other written documents — and the priests themselves were often vague about the details of what they used to perform. Because no single group of priests now had a complete set of texts relating to Celebrating the Bodhisattva, he assembled texts from a number of groups in the area: the contributors for specific texts are listed in Appendix 8. Texts are presented in punctuated and typeset form, with a brief introduction describing the main contents of each.

Critique

Taken together with the field report produced by Guo Sijiu and Wang Yong, this volume provides additional information on quite a number of matters, as well as a compendium of ritual texts. The photographs also supplement those provided in the Guo and Wang book, e.g. by providing a photograph of the "well" constructed from rice-bowls and buffalo horns for the "Making the Well" ritual. Both volumes are well-produced, well signposted, and present a minimum of frustration to the interested reader. Together, they present a coherent body of material that would well repay detailed examination and analysis.

Bibliography

Wang Yue 王躍. 1992. "Vernacular Priests and Drama in Jiangbei County" 江北縣的端公與端公戲, *in Yuzhou yitan* 2.

Guo Sijiu 郭思九 and Wang Yong 王勇. 1995. *The Celebration of the Bodhisattva Ritual of the Vernacular Priests of the Zou Lineage in Poji Township, Zhenxiong County, Zhaotong Region, Yunnan* 雲南省昭通地區鎮雄縣潑機鄉鄒氏端公的慶菩薩調查. *Min-su ch'ü-i ts'ung-shu*, No. 29. 244 pages. Taipei: Shih Ho-cheng Folk Culture Foundation.

B.
SOUTHWEST CHINA: MINORITIES

7

RITUAL LITERALIZED:

A CRITICAL REVIEW OF RITUAL STUDIES ON THE NATIONAL MINORITIES IN GUANGXI, GUIZHOU, HUNAN AND SICHUAN

Ho Ts'ui-p'ing

This review article covers the methods and results of six volumes that report on ritual studies among four national minorities in four provinces of China. The four nationalities are the Tujia, Xilao, Maonan, and Miao and the four provinces are Hunan, Guizhou, Guangxi, and Sichuan. All six volumes are published in the series "Studies in Chinese Ritual, Theatre and Folklore" (see Table One).[1]

I. Table One: Volumes Reviewed

1. Duan Ming 段明, *The Masked Yangxi in Xinglong Village, Youyang*

---

1 This review is an abbreviated version of the Chinese version distributed and discussed at the "Conference on Ethnography in China Today: A Critical Assessment of Methods and Results," May 14-16, 1998. I gratefully acknowledge the comments on the original Chinese version given at that conference. The lengthier Chinese version is being revised for separate publication. I am also thankful to my husband James Wilkerson, who made helpful comments about language and argument.

Tujia and Miao Nationalities Autonomous County in Sichuan 四川省
酉陽土家族苗族自治縣雙河區小崗鄉興隆村面具陽戲. No. 4,
1993. 310 pages. Abbreviated below as *Tujia Masked Yangxi*.

2. Meng Guorong 蒙國榮, The *"Recompensing the Gods for Fulfilled
   Wishes" among the Maonan Nationality in Huanjiang County in
   Guangxi* 廣西省環江縣毛南族的「還願儀式」. No. 11, 1994. 365
   pages. Abbreviated below as *Maonan Recompensing the Gods*.

3. Wang Ch'iu-kuei 王秋桂 and Tuo Xiuming 庹修明, *A Field Report
   on the Nuo Exorcism for Calendrical Conflicts for Seniors among the
   Tujia Nationality of Huangtu Village, Dejiang County, Wenping
   Township, Dejiang County, Guizhou* 貴州省德江縣穩坪鄉黃土村土
   家族衝壽儺調查報告. No. 12, 1994. 528 pages. Abbreviated below
   as *Tujia Nuo Exorcism*.

4. Tuo Xiuming, Yang Qixiao 楊啓孝 and Wang Ch'iu-kuei, comp., *A
   Field Report on the Nuo Exorcistic Altar for Initiation into the Office
   of the Ritual Master among the Yilao Nationality in Cengong County,
   Pingzhuang Township, Guizhou* 貴州省岑鞏縣平庄鄉仡佬族儺壇
   過職儀式調查報告. No. 13, 1994. 426 pages. Abbreviated below
   as *Yilao Nuo Altar Initiation*.

5. Zhang Ziwei 張子偉, The *"Maogusi" of the Tujia Nationality of
   Shuangfeng Villiage, Heping Township, Yongshun County, Hunan* 湖南
   省永順縣和平鄉雙鳳村土家族的毛古斯儀式. No. 47, 1996. 397
   pages. Abbreviated below as *Tujia Maogusi*.

6. Yang Lan 楊蘭 and Liu Feng 劉峰, *A Field Report on Celebrating
   the Altar for Honoring Ancestors among the Miao in Xinguang
   Village in Guizhou* 貴州省晴隆縣中營鎮新光村硝洞苗族慶壇調查
   報告. No. 50, 1996. 311 pages. Abbreviated below as *Miao
   Celebrating Altar*.

These six books are a refreshing change from past publications on ritual
studies among China's national minorities. All the volumes share the
principle of "collect holistically, record honestly, and organize carefully"
and the goal of "striving against over-generalizing and unsupported
empty statements in publications" (Wang and Tuo 1994: 2). Each volume provides valuable first-hand field material and fills what has so far
been a yawning void for high-quality descriptions of local ritual traditions and ritual performances among South China's culturally diverse

national minority peoples.

All six volumes follow closely a general design set by and funded through Wang Ch'iu-kuei's project "Chinese Regional Theatre in Its Social and Ritual Context." Each volume reports on a single rite witnessed on site by the researcher or researchers as well as such aspects of that rite's social context as ethnicity, local society, and ritual genres. Close attention is also paid to the performing troupe's organization, inheritance, and the personal background of the individual members. In particular, a special effort is given to the collection and reproduction in appendices of liturgical texts and, for some, transcriptions of the actual performances.

In so doing the authors or compilers of the various volumes followed the directions given in *Manual for Writing Field Reports* provided by the Project. That manual directs that each report should contain: (1) an overview of the basic data of the village and its folklore; (2) basic data on the rites in general; (3) a detailed description of the process of the ritual performance, including the people, occasion, time and place; (4) the type of performing troupe (e.g. theatre troupe versus *nuo* troupe, for instance); (5) the performance and its theatrical genre; (6) a conclusion.[2] The considerable consistency among the various volumes results from close adherence to this outline. Over half of each monograph is given over to appendices, which is evidence of generous funding and a sophisticated understanding of the value of accuracy and primary source material. The appendices include, besides manuscripts and ritual texts, photos taken during the ritual performance, and especially photos of the different stages of each rite, the paraphernalia of the ritual specialists, and their altars.

I find this otherwise admirable effort to insure the authority and accuracy of the volumes through the imposition of a standard outline to be self-defeating in literalizing the ritual performances. First, the descriptions of the performances of a rite as unique events are literalized in the sense that the descriptions do not include discussion of the discontinuity of that performance with other performances of the rite. Second, the descriptions of the performances of a rite have an emotional and aes-

---

2 The author thanks Professor Wang Ch'iu-kuei for providing me with a copy of the Project's *Manual for Writing Field Reports*.

thetic superficiality that robs the ritual performances of their vitality. Also, announced intentions notwithstanding, descriptions of the ritual performances and local social context do not include sufficiently precise detail to show how specific ritual performances are integrated into the lives of the individual people, communities, and regions who make up the social contexts of the ritual performances. This gap between performance and context means that the descriptions fall short of the announced goal to describe one rite well, and so miss the possibility of learning what ritual theatre is really all about. At best the careful reader can, after considerable effort, fill in this gap by piecing together different parts of the book.

The review below will spell out the above points book-by-book. I will start with the five volumes on rites for "recompensing the gods for fulfilled wishes" (*huanyuan* 還願) and end with last volume on "dressing up as ancestors" (*Tujia Maogusi*).

II. Tujia Nuo Exorcism

The volume *Tujia Nuo Exorcism* records a *chongshou nuo* 衝壽儺 (*Nuo exorcism for calendrical conflicts for seniors*), which took place between six-thirty in the afternoon on February 18 and four o'clock in the afternoon on February 20, 1992. A Tujia national minority resident, Zhang Jintai, held a *chongshou nuo* exorcism for the birthday of his father, Zhang Yusheng, in Huangtu Village, Wenping Township, Dejiang County, Guizhou Province. The *chongshou nuo* exorcism only takes place for those over sixty. It differs from other birthday celebrations in including "religious ritual." The *chongshou nuo* exorcism can take only one day or last as long as three or four days depending upon the financial means of its host (p. 57). The performance described is an instance of the longer version.

After a brief introduction, the body of the book is divided into eight chapters followed by three pages of footnotes. The eight chapters cover:
1. The social cultural background and the ecological environment.
2. The host Zhang Jinta's family.
3. The ritual master of the *nuo* exorcistic altar Zhang Jinliao.
4. Preparations for the *chongshou nuo* (pp. 16-57), including descrip-

tions and figures of the altar and pictures of the altar being set up, the gods and goddess in the sacred scrolls, and so forth.

5. The ritual sequence (pp. 57-129) divided into:

   (1) Ritual activities (*fa-shi* 法事) (pp. 57-87).

   (2) *Nuo* altar plays (*nuo-tang xi* 儺堂戲) (pp. 87-111).

   (3) *Nuo* birthday congratulatory blessings (*zhu shou* 祝壽) (pp. 111-125).

   (4) Tearing down the altar (*shou tan* 收壇) (pp. 125-6).

6. The costumes and the paraphernalia used by the *Nuo* exorcistic altar.

7. *Nuo* music and dance in the performance.

8. The masks used in the *nuo* exorcistic plays.

After the body of the book, appendices include 26 liturgical texts and scripts (pp. 162-464), one genealogy (p. 465), several music recordings (pp. 466-476), and 100 pictures (pp. 477-528). The author concludes that this *chongshou nuo* exorcism follows the "procedure and structure" of "opening the altar inviting the gods, " "opening the grottoes entertaining the gods (people)" and "closing the altar and sending off the gods" (pp. 126-128).

Anyone familiar with Chinese-language publications on local culture and religious practices will appreciate the effort given by the series to fieldwork methodology, particularly in this volume with its appendices, which take up over seventy percent of the volume. The title clearly indicates that the book is about one ritual performance in a specific place. The appendices self-evidently stress the collection by the researcher of the actual liturgical texts used in the rituals reported upon. The volume's table of contents also speaks to the intention to place the ritual performance squarely within its sociocultural and performative context.

The source of the masks should be noted. Dejiang County is fortunate in the number and antiquity of the masks used in *nuo* exorcistic plays, with some dating back to the Qing dynasty. These masks are classified as valuable "cultural objects" (*wenwu* 文物) under the care and preservation of Dejiang County's Nationalities Committee (*minwei* 民委).³ The Nationalities Committee has collected most of the more

---

3 The author also provides a table listing the collected nuo "cultural objects" kept in the Dejiang County Nationalities Committee Office (p. 155).

valuable masks and related ritual paraphernalia. When local ritual masters perform *nuo* exorcistic rites they must borrow back the masks. The Nationalities Committee was also involved in the ritual performance recorded in this volume, including the borrowing back of several masks. The masks used in the ritual performance are listed in a table (pp. 156-7) by name and size. Photos of masks that are "cultural objects" are provided in the appendices (Photos 93 to 100, pp. 524-27).

The contribution of the book is curtailed by what I call the literalization of ritual performances. In recording the one specific performance, the author fails to indicate whether the *chongshou nuo* exorcism is related to the general life-cycle rites in that locality, and how it is related to other *chongshou nuo* exorcisms elsewhere in that locality. Though given a description of the longer version of the *chongshou nuo* exorcism, we are not told about less elaborate versions or, more to the point, what is the minimum required for a ritual performance to count as a *chongshou nuo* exorcism, and what is the minimal "ritual work" required in *chongshou nuo* exorcism to effect the "Recompensing the Gods for Fulfilled Wishes." We do learn, however, that the ritual specialist was asked to perform, and complied, awkward the "ritual work" of *shangdao* 上刀 (pp. 105-6). *Shangdao*, it so happens, is "ritual work" that is normally performed as exorcistic rites for children, not seniors. The author provided no explanation of the relationship between *shangdao* and *chongshou nou* is general.

On the other hand, the fascinating accounts of the origins of the main gods of the *nuo* exorcism — the *Nuo* father (*nuo gong* 儺公) and the *Nuo* mother (*nuo mu* 儺母) provide an example of insufficient detail concerning the social contexts (pp. 7-9). The various legends about the *nuo* father and mother include the themes that: (1) they are the primordial siblings from whom humanity was procreated; (2) they are the principal tutors for the emperor and queen; (3) they are lovers whose marriage was frustrated by others; and, (4) they are commoners who are killed for resisting oppression by the imperial court. Information is lacking, however, on the source or sources of these legends. Who transmits these stories (ritual masters, ritual specialists, commoners, men or women), and their social distribution are just as important as the contents of the stories.

III. Maonan "Recompensing the Gods"

The second book reviewed here on *huanyuan* 還願 (recompensing the gods for fulfilled wishes) is Meng Guorong's *Maonan Recompensing the Gods*. Meng Guorong tells us that the most important part of *huanyuan* is a ritual play for "singing and leaping for the gods" (*changshen tiaoshen* 唱神跳神) (p. 56). The bulk of the book is given over to a description of a *huanyuan* rite which took place in February 1993 in Wei'er Hamlet (*tun* 屯) Xianan Village, Xianan Township, Huanjiang Maonan Autonomous County, Guangxi Zhuang Autonomous Region 廣西壯族自治區環江毛南族自治縣下南鄉下南村委衾屯.

Following a brief introduction (pp. 1-8), the bulk of the book is divided into eight sections followed by appendices. Chapter One gives a general introduction (pp. 9-15), and Chapter Two gives a social, cultural and ecological overview of the Maonan nationality (pp. 16-58), including a summary of Maonan *nuo* exorcism plays (pp. 40-58). Chapter Three provides background about the family, troupe, and preparations for this particular performance of *huanyuan* (pp. 58-64). Chapter Four describes the altar and arrangements for the *huanyuan* rite (pp. 64-67); Chapter Five discussed the preliminary rites, starting on the afternoon of February 1 (pp. 67-69); and, Chapter Six the formal rites of singing and playing for the gods, beginning at eight-thirty in the morning on February 2 and lasting until dawn on February 4 (pp. 69-81). Chapter Seven gives a brief introduction to the music, dance, costumes and utensils used by the ritual specialists (pp. 81-86), while Chapter Eight introduces the masks and the legendary stories of each god being played at *huanyuan* (pp. 86-104). Chapter Nine consists of two pages of acknowledgments (pp. 104-105). Thereafter follow several pages of footnotes, references, and a name list of key informants (pp. 106-111). The rest of the volume is taken up with appendices in the form of tables, maps, figures, texts and scripts, and pictures. These appendices form almost two-thirds of the whole book (pp. 112-365).

Compared to *Tujia Nuo Exorcism, Maonan Recompensing the Gods* has a solid introduction (pp. 1-8) that provides a more comprehensive description of the ritual context, its performance and related rituals.

Comparing with the ritual genre of *shigong* 師公 theatre, popular among the Zhuang nationality, the author lists in his introduction six characteristics specific to *huanyuan* among mountainous Maonan villages. First, *huanyuan* is not equally popular throughout the Maonan nationality. Maonan in Ningshi City do not perform *huanyuan*, and the practice is not universal in all mountainous Maonan villages, such as that of the Meng family.[4] Secondly, a *huanyuan* performance counts as a *xi shi* (felicitous event), like weddings and birthday celebrations, but differs in including singing, dancing and chanting. Thirdly, *huanyuan* is performed at the host's house and on a household basis. Fourthly, ritual specialists wear masks to play gods at *huanyuan* performances. The singing is mostly in the Zhuang language, though some is also in the Maonan language. Chants and mantras are in the Han Chinese dialect of Desheng Township, Yishan County, which is incomprehensible to most Maonan.[5] Fifthly, *huanyuan* are performed by *shigong* ritual specialists, who either inherit the profession from their fathers or learn the skill from a ritual master. However, being a *shigong* is always a sideline to another livelihood. Sixthly, and especially different from the dialogue of the *shigong* theatre of the Zhuang, the Maonan *huanyuan* performances include references to modern history no earlier than early in the Republican era (1911-1949) (pp. 1-6).

Though the introduction takes steps in the right direction, the relationship between the performance and the people still leaves something to be desired. I feel in this case the influence of the Project *Manual*. For instance, in *Maonan Recompensing the Gods*, Meng Guorong loyally reviews Maonan life and sociocultural background, gives a map, describes the ritual masks, and describes the dance and music as instructed by the Project *Manual*. Unfortunately, the entire review is irrelevant to our understanding of the ritual. The maps (p. 112, p. 113) serve no apparent purpose in the volume. Similar frustrations occur

---

4 However, the author also says later in the book, that the *huanyuan* used to be the ritual activity that was "required to be held in each house at least once each generation"(p. 46). No comment is given to clarify the apparent discrepancy.

5 The author does not provide any information about where Desheng township, Yishan County is located in relationship to Xianan township, Huanjiang county where the *huanyuan* performance takes place.

with the four-page description of music, dance, costumes, and ritual objects (pp. 83-86) as well as the three-line description of the masks (p. 86).

Despite placing the *huanyuan* within its local context and other useful information already mentioned, the relationship between the February 1 through 4, 1993 *huanyuan* performance and the general Maonan sociocultural and ecological background is still not worked out in any detail.

On the other hand, some of the details provided are misleading. Meng Guorong even gives the time to the minute when the rite starts. Left out, however, is the significance of time for the ritual specialists, the host, and the audience. For instance, the troupe performed the play "The Earth God Accompanies the Three Goddesses" (*Tudi pei Sanniang* 土地配三娘) at eight o'clock in the morning, and "Hualin Xianguan Sends Off Yinhua" (*Hualin Xianguan song Yinhua* 花林仙官送銀花) at nine-thirty in the morning (pp. 76-77). Is this sequence prescribed or optional? Can they be performed at other times or in other sequences? By the same token, the last act of the first day is said to be "the ritual master accompanying the host who shoulders the flower child to the room" (pp. 74-75). Could this be postponed until the second day or maybe even the act of sending the "long life chicken" to the host (pp. 75-76)? Is there something about the play that dictates the time and sequence of its performance? Or are the times and sequence optional?

Finally, though documentation of the formal performance is given in great detail, what is counted in or counted out of the performance is up to the author. For instance, Meng Guorong describes how the altar is torn down after the ritual specialists complete their chanting, but also states that in the early morning they then go on to "recall the soldiers" (*shou bing* 收兵). However, between the tearing down of the altar and "recall the soldiers" there is improvisational "singing" (*dui ge* 對歌) which the author mentions but does not record or describe. Similarly, the stage talk or dialogue that is without a textual base is excised from the record of the performances. This is a clear bias in the descriptions of the performances. Why did this happen? I suggest this is a bias that arises from the "cultural heritage" viewpoint in ritual studies. This "cultural heritage" viewpoint takes preservation as primary, rather than studying the living aspects of the performance.

IV. Tujia Masked Yangxi

Duan Ming's *Tujia Masked Yangxi* is also about rituals for *huanyuan*. The book covers two performances of masked Yangxi (also called *tiaoxi* 跳戲 "Leaping Plays") which took place in Xinglong Village, Xiaogang Township, Shuanghe Region, Youyang Tujia and Miao Autonomous County, Sichuan Province. The first performance was held from twelve-thirty in the afternoon of February 7 through twelve-forty in the afternoon on February 9, 1993. The second performance was held from noon February 5 to one o'clock in the afternoon of February 6. In addition, however, Duan Ming also makes an effort in *Tujia Masked Yangxi* toward a more comprehensive understanding of the *yangxi* genre in Sichuan Province.

"Leaping plays" are held locally whenever people want to ask *Guansheng dijun* 關聖帝君 for blessing, to be rid of disaster, evil, and negative forces, request promotion and good fortune, healing, curing and protection of one's health, admission to high school, and to welcome the approach of felicitous events. Those who host the "leaping plays" do so to "recompense the gods for fulfilled wishes" (*huanyuan*) as a gesture of gratitude. If they fail to perform "recompensing the gods for fulfilled wishes," then disasters cannot be avoided and fresh disaster will visit that household (p. 20). For those who are praying for descendants and the protection of a pregnancy or for children, prayers should be directed to the Jade emperor (*Yu huang* 玉皇).

In studying the masked *yangxi* as a ritual genre, Duan Ming gives clear comparisons across Sichuan of various *yangxi* in the transmission of the offices and ritual knowledge, the size of the troupe, and the different styles of performance. He also tells the reader why the genre of the *yangxi* popular in the Youyang and Xioushan area are called "masked *yangxi*," and that not all the *yangxi* figures and stories in the Yang world are used in the Yin altars set up for funerals. The genre is called the "masked *yangxi*" because all male roles, but not the female roles, are played with masks.

After a brief introduction, the body of the book is divided into six chapters (pp. 1-89) covering:

1. The geographical environment and livelihood of Xinglong Village residents.
2. Some of the basic materials of the masked *yangxi*.
3. The structure and content of the "leaping plays," including that of a performance of "recompensing the gods for fulfilled wishes" and a performance of "rewarding the gods and worshipping the ancestors."
4. The structure and lineage of the altar troupe.
5. The attitude of the members of the altar troupe and the villagers toward leaping plays.
6. Conclusion.

Over two-thirds of this book is given over to appendices (pp. 90-310), including: the liturgical texts used at the two performances, the scripts and examples of the music scores, pictures of the masks, and scenes from the two leaping plays. Also included are scripts and texts not used in the two performances of leaping plays in Xinglong Village (pp. 198-242, pp. 244-249). These materials will be welcomed by those interested in gaining a wider comparative perspective.

By including two different performances, Duan Ming's *Tujia Masked Yangxi* provides a clearer explication of the structure of the ritual performances of the leaping plays. In general, there are three segments. The first and last sections are the more solemn and religious, while the middle section is more ludic and theatrical. The first section may including the rite "Inviting the Gods" (*qingshen* 請神), "Guanye Secures the Altar" (*Guanye Zhendian* 關爺鎮殿), and "Madam Pang Secures the Stage" (*pangshi fujen zhentai* 龐氏夫人鎮台). The last section will have the rite "Sending off the Gods" (*songshen* 送神), "Guanye Sweeps the Altar" (*Guanye saodian* 關爺掃殿), and "The Altar Master Throws the Eggs" (*zhangtan laoshi toudan* 掌壇老師投蛋). What happens in the middle section seems to depend to a great extent on the talents of the troupe. Also, the rites performed during the first and third sections may very depending upon when "leaping gods" is performed. The rites "Guanye Secures the Altar" and "Guanye Sweeps the Altar" are unnecessary when the performance takes place at the ritual master's home "because no evil would come, nor any ghosts dare to make trouble" (p. 62).

Though Duan Ming's *Tujia Masked Yangxi* gives a comparatively better picture of the structure of "leaping plays," important questions remain about it. For instance, the performance of a "leaping play" at the ritual master's house included the rites of "Inviting the Gods" and "Madam Pang Secures the Stage" in the first section, "Winter Plum Blossom" (*dong meihua* 冬梅花) in the middle section, and "Sending Off the Gods" in the last section. However, the expected "The Ritual Master Throws the Eggs" was missing. The only explanation we have is that this particular "leaping play" was for the annual "Rewarding the Gods and Thanking the Ancestors" instead of "Recompensing the Gods for Fulfilled Wishes." Instead the troupe performed "Frolicking All Around" (*wandeng wanxi* 完燈完戲) (pp. 61-64). We are told early in the book that the "leaping plays" for rewarding the gods and worshipping the ancestors need to be done before the conclusion of the local custom of "Recompensing the Gods for Fulfilled Wishes at the Lantern Festival." (*tiao yuan deng* 跳願燈) (pp. 13-14). However, no explanation is given as to whether the rite of "Frolicking All Around" has anything to do with the local custom of *tiao yuan deng*, nor do we know whether it is a required rite as "Inviting the Gods," "Madam Pang Secures the Stage" and "Sending off the Gods" are in all leaping plays for rewarding the gods and worshipping the ancestors. The readers' understanding of this masked *yangxi* still depends very much on which performance happens to be reported upon.

I mentioned earlier the value of the data on Chinese folk religion, and especially the unedited texts which appear as appendices. In this volume, however, Duan Ming's *Tujia Masked Yangxi* gives the script to "Winter Plum Blossom," a theatrical play performed at the home of the ritual master in an appendix, but only in outline form. This is in contrast to the inclusion of additional scripts that were not part of the actual performance.

The book contains fascinating comments on the people and community of masked *yangxi* performances. Duan Ming writes in *Tujia Masked Yangxi* about the general background of the people and the community (pp. 4-14), their "belief" in the power of the "leaping plays," and their fondness for the theatrical plays (pp. 73-84), but does so in an unconvincing way. The precise terms of the cohesiveness among the masked *yangxi*, the people, and their lives are not dealt with. For instance, there are fascinating and important comments in an interview with the ritual master in charge of the altar troupe, as well as the carver of the masks and the leader of the community, about the magical power of the masks, and dreaming as a source of knowledge for mask-carving and leaping plays (pp. 23, 28, 70). Only by pursuing points such as these at length and in detail can the descriptions of the people and the community come into convincing focus.

V. Yilao Nuo Altar Initiation

The fourth book on recompensing the gods for fulfilled wishes is *Yilao Nuo Altar Initiation* compiled by Tuo Xiuming, Yang Qixiao and Wang Ch'iu-kuei. *Yilao Nuo Altar* describes not only rites for recompensing the gods, but also a very rare initiation into the office of the ritual master of the *Nuo* Exorcistic Altar. The initiation took place in the Yang altar troupe in Pingzhuang Township, Cengong County, Guizhou Province. Xiao Guanghua 蕭光華, a novice who for years had been a disciple of the Yang altar troupe, was initiated into the office of ritual master with the approval of the ritual master of the troupe. At the same time, Xiao took the opportunity to perform the rite "Recompensing the Gods for Fulfilled Wishes" to become a ritual master. These initiation rites are rare even for *nuo* exorcistic altar troupes.

The bulk of the book is divided into eight chapters (pp. 1-164):
1. The socio-cultural and ecological environment.
2. An overview of the Yang Guoding *nuo* exorcistic altar troupe.
3. Preparations for the initiation rites for Xiao Guanghua.
4. The *nuo* altar and its masks and setup.
5. The *nuo* exorcistic rites.
6. Initiation rites.
7. The music and dance of the *nuo* exorcistic altar.
8. The customs and etiquette of the *nuo* exorcistic altar.

The appendices, which are sixty percent of the book, include thirty-two liturgical texts, a table of Cengong County folk artists, and photos (pp. 165-426).

Chapters Five and Six describe the particular ritual performance. Chapter Five divides the *nuo* exorcistic rites into three kinds: (1) ritual work (*fashi* 法事) (pp. 73-86); (2) the *nuo* exorcistic play (*nuoxi* 儺戲) (pp. 86-95); and, (3) the *nuo* exorcistic special skill (*nuoji* 儺技) performed by the novice in the initiation to the office of the ritual master (pp. 96-100). During the four days and nights of the ritual, twenty-seven ritual tasks, eight exorcistic plays, seven kinds of special skill (including stepping on a burning hot plough, balancing a burning tripod stand on the head, holding a burning iron in the mouth, dipping hands into burning oil in a wok, walking through burning charcoal, and ascending the knife ladder) are performed by the novice. A timetable shows clearly the arrangement and the sequence of the ritual work, the play, and the display of special skills (pp. 70-72). Thirty-two kinds of the liturgical texts used in the ritual are attached as appendices (pp. 165-373). Chapter Six describes the never before recorded rites of "passing on the magic work and succession to the office of ritual master" (*chuan-fa guozhi* 傳法過職). The series of rites (pp. 101-121) "interconnected talismans and rituals" (*fufa xiangtong* 符法相通), "inter-linked flesh and blood" *(xuerou xianglian* 血肉相連), and "inter-linked blood and vessels" (*xuemai xianglian* 血脈相連) establishes a relationship between the novice and the ritual masters of the exorcistic altar.

The book pays special attention to cross-indexing between the text and the pictures, photos, and liturgical texts in the appendices. This makes the volume much more accessible and interesting than the three books reviewed earlier. However, a problem remains concerning the relationship between the ritual performance and the people for whom the rituals are performed. For instance, the "interconnected flesh and blood" between ritual masters and novice is performed through the medium of the exchange of several *pai* cloths from their *paidai* 牌帶 (p.103). This *paidai*, which is an emblem of office of ritual master in the *nuo* exorcistic altar, is made by the novice before he is initiated by the invited "thirty-six unmarried young girls." Red, yellow, blue, green, purple, orange and greenish blue clothes, embroidered with characters, flowers and grass patterns, are used (p.31). After the initiation, repre-sentatives of the old women in the village congratulate this *paidai* emblem of office (p. 114). In other words, this initiation ritual is unique and arresting not only in the relationship between the ritual master, the troupe, and the novice, but also in their relationship to their surrounding community.

VI. Miao Celebration Altar

Yang Lan and Liu Feng's *Miao Celebrating Altar* is the last of the five volumes under review which cover ritual performances for "recompensing the gods for fulfilled wishes." The book is a delight to read. The subject is the "Celebrating Altar" (*qingtan* 慶壇) among the "Laba Miao 喇叭苗" in Xiaodong hamlet, Xinguang Village, Zhongying Township, Qingling County, Guizhou Province. The main body of the book describes a "Celebrating Altar" rite performed between about eight-thirty in the evening of January 12 to almost four o'clock in the afternoon of January 13, 1994, and was divided into fifty-six rites and four *nuo* exorcistic plays. Yang Lan and Liu Feng tell us that *qingtan* for *huanyuan* ("Recompensing for Fulfilled Wishes") for the ancestors is specific to the Laba Miao, though it is also used, as elsewhere, for *huanyuan* for the gods (p. 122). Laba Miao attribute misfortune to the disrepair of an altar or failure to build an altar for the ancestors (*dong zhu* 洞竹, literally "grotto bamboo") (pp. 48-51, p.106). *Qingtan* is often promised when making wishes for dispelling misfortune.

Once more the main body of the book is shorter than its appendices, this time taking up slightly less than half the length of the book. The appendices include pictures and liturgical texts. Yang Lan and Liu Feng indicate that the relationship of *qingtan* to the Laba Miao is through the latter's beliefs in *sandong taoyuan* 三洞桃源 (supernatural and ancestral beliefs). Yang Lan and Liu Feng follow the Project *Manual*, though not mechanically, by dividing the book into ten chapters. The first chapter provides excellent descriptions of the sociocultural context and ecological environment as well as Laba Miao history and relations with such other ethnic groups as the Miao, Buyi, Yilao, and Yi. Today's Laba Miao are the descendants of soldiers sent about 600 years ago to conquer Yunnan during the Hongwu reign in the Ming dynasty. These soldiers stayed as a military colony in Qinglong County, Guizhou Province. The ancestors of the Laba Miao of Xiaodong Village were from the Huguang area, but linguistically and culturally were Miao who had long lived interspersed among the Han (pp. 7-8). Chapter Two gives an overview of the *qingtan* and its history. Chapter Three describes the composition of the altar troupe, Chapter Four the altar troupe paraphernalia, including especially masks and costumes; and Chapter Five the background of the performance of *qingtan* in Xiaodong hamlet. Chapter Six provides the preparations done for the *qingtan* performance in Xiaodong hamlet. Chapter Seven gives an account of how the altar is set up; Chapter Eight describes the ritual stages in the the *qingtan* performance in Xiaodong hamlet, and Chapter Nine the music and dance used in the *qingtan* ceremony. Chapter Ten gives the conclusion.

The texts and appendices in this volume are consistently better than the others reviewed here; this book succeeds exactly where the other five books fail. That is, this book successfully handles the relationship between people and performance. It is especially informative in the social and historical background information it provides on the relationship between the Laba Miao and *qingtan*.

The author lays out convincing evidence of the relationship between the Laba Mjiao, *taoyuan sandong* beliefs, and Ming dynasty military colonies. The authors accomplish this in part by the close comparison of place names in the liturgical texts *lutuji* 路途記 and their distribution in space. Doing so enables them to show a close correspondence between those localities where *qingtan* are prevalent and the route for imperial communication during the Ming and Qing dynasties that ran from Hunan through Guizhou and on into Yunnan. The authors furthermore found written records of five thousand households of military colonists (*wei suo* 衛所) in those localities from the Ming and Qing dynasties and learned that they were subdivided first into subunits of one thousand (*qianhu suo* 千戶所) and then one hundred (*baihu suo* 百戶所) military colonist households. The areas where these troops were stationed are the same areas where there is substantial evidence of altar troupe activities (pp. 21-22). The author also suggests that the Laba Miao in the Zhongying area are the descendants of those who were originally stationed in Nanwei in Guizhou. *Qingtan* activities became the ethnic symbol of the Laba Miao only after they started their military settlement in Guizhou, where they lived among the other Miao ethnic groups, the Yilao, the Yi and the Buyi (pp. 8-9, 21-27). *Qingtan* is from their original inheritance of *qing niangniang* (慶娘娘) activities in the western part of Hunan (pp. 28-29, 32-33) where their ancestors were from.

Other scholars will want to look in greater detail into the authority of the correlations suggested by Yang Lan and Liu Feng's *Miao Celebrating Altar*. What I stress here is that, right or wrong, their hypothesis does address the central issue of the relationship between people and ritual performances. The evidence even supports the hypothesis in the additional sense that it helps make sense of such liturgical texts as the *lutuji*, where that text describes how the ancestors (both male and female) enter the altar area (pp. 88-92, 120, 193-207).

Unfortunately, however, the contemporary relationship of the people to the ritual performances includes much that is simply not covered because it is contemporary rather than indicative of past practices. Especially interesting would be a more thorough description of the relationship between the emotional and efficacious aspects of the ritual performances. For instance, if one reads closely the scripts of *shiliu hua* 石榴花 and *lutuji* in appendix three (pp. 193-215), one cannot but admire the rich vibrancy and, as Victor Turner would have called it, the *communitas* of the ritual performance. However, the description of this aspect is limited to only three words: enthusiastic, highly-spirited, and extraordinarily energetic (p. 133).

VII. Tujia Maogusi

In contrast to the other five books reviewed above, Zhang Ziwei's *Tujia Maogusi* is not a field report. *Maogusi* ritual performances are prevalent among the Tujia nationality in Yongshun County and Guzhang County, Hunan Province. Zhang Ziwei's *Tujia Maogusi* is evolutionary in approach (e.g. pp. 15, 35, 92, 119-120, 120-123, 176-181, 182-183), with modern accounts of the ritual performances being used to draw conclusions about an earlier way of life. This view of ritual performance ignores the fact that the *maogusi's* modern history has alternated, since at least the 1950s, between appropriation for use as an emblem of the Tujia nationality and as a target for eradication during periods of political turmoil.

Zhang Ziwei describes state intervention into the *maogusi* as beginning no later than the Qianlong and Jiaqing reign periods of the Qing dynasty (1736-1820). Local histories are quoted to show that the *maogusi* was already considered obscene and lewd by that time. The state banned *maogusi* many times, especially from the Yongzheng reign period (1723-1735) on, after Chinese officials replaced local native officials. The *maogusi* was "discovered" in the late 1950s and early 1960s during a nationwide survey of folk art, and was described as a survival of archaic forms of Chinese primitive dance, music, and fertility worship (pp. 2-4, 95-96). The tables turned during the Cultural Revolution, and the ritual masters in charge of the *maogusi* performances were humiliated and even tortured. With liberalization and a more tolerant attitude toward nationality customs, the Yongshun County Cultural Office choreographed the *maogusi* into twenty-four standardized motions on the basis of written records from the 1950s and early 1960s and the performances of elderly people willing and able to perform (pp. 95-96). Ritual masters are no longer involved in the contemporary performances of the *maogusi*, where it is a part of annual ancestor worship performances (*sheba ri*) (pp. 40-41, 70-71).

The Tujia term for *maogusi* is *babuka* or *babukari*, which means "hairy ancestors" or "dressing up as hairy ancestors" (p. 37).[6] The author argues that *maogusi* should be understood as an exorcistic play of "dressing up as ancestors" after the annual ancestral worship rite in the early spring. In conclusion, the author defines *maogusi* as follows: "*Maogusi* is a kind of primitive theatre that combines worship, singing, and dancing together, originally in the *sheba* hall (the village level *tuwang* 土王 shrine). In *maogusi*, villagers dress up as ancestors who lived during the fishing and hunting era [of cultural evolution]" (p. 175).

After a five-page introduction, the main body of the book is divided into six chapters:

1. Overview of Shuangfeng Village and its beliefs.
2. Overview of the ritual performance, and especially *sheba ri* ancestral worship activities, *maogusi* performances, and their historical development. This review gives a picture of the highpoints in historical development and spatial distribution in various counties, townships, and villages. It also discussed performance, organization, plays, and

---

6 The author only uses Chinese characters, instead of a romanization or IPA transcript, to record this Tujia terms. I thus romanize from the Chinese characters.

dates in the *sheba ri* activities and times of the *maogusi* performances in these places. The Shuangfeng Village *sheba ri* activities took seven days and nights, and seven and a half natural villages or hamlets took turns sponsoring each night's activities.

3. The evening ritual activities are described in comparative detail. These activities include: inviting the ancestors to the *sheba* hall; purifying the hall; dancing the hand-waving dance (*baishou wu* 擺手舞); singing the *sheba* origin songs; and, performing the *maogusi*. The plots of the *maogusi* plays differ each night (pp. 75-79), including plots of "meat chasing, " "fish catching, " "wife capturing," "studying," and "*zuo yangchun* (做陽春)." The former three plots Zhang Ziwei cites as evidence of the ancestors belonging to a fishing and hunting stage of social evolution. The plot of "studying" reflects the stage of the civilized life. The plot of *Zuo yangchun* describes how order is established out of chaos through the ritual specialist *tima*'s singing.

4. Accounts are given of the performance troupe, including the names and ages of *maogusi* performers, life histories of some performers, legends about the ritual master *tima*, and various ancestral figures in the *sheba* hall.

5. Descriptions are given of the performance and its theatrical forms, including dance, songs, make-up, and costumes.

6. Discussion of the hypothesis that the *maogusi* is a "living fossil" in the history of theatre.

The appendices include all "relevant" written material which Zhang Ziwei collected from the village and local histories. This material includes all the inscriptions he could find in the ancestral halls and temples; all accounts in the Yongshun County local history about the ancestral temples, worship, poetry, customs, founding ancestors of the village, and materials on the local native officials (*tusi* 土司). The appendices also include several *sheba* songs, not all of which were performed, transcripts of three *maogusi* plays romanized in the Tujia language and with Chinese translation (pp. 237-261), as well as some transcribed texts whose origin and use are not stated (pp. 262-318).

In all, the book gives a good overview of the custom of performing *maogusi* at a regional level, and some historical background about its development. The author suggests the custom of playing the "hairy ancestors" as a reflection of the hybridity of the local population, which involves not only the Tujia, but also Han and the natives before the Tujia were there. However, in addition to using a rather vulgar evolutionary theory to assume the existence of the "primitives" in the "hunting and gathering stage" without demonstrating it, the book also fails in its coherence.

A cursory look at Zhang Ziwei's *Tujia Maogusi* shows that it follows the Project *Manual*, though closer scrutiny suggests to that there is little connection between the headings and the contents under those headings. For instance, in the account given under the heading for the section on "performance troupe, " Zhang Ziwei's treats ordinary villagers who played in *maogusi* for Shuangfeng Village only as if they were the paid ritual specialists in the Han exorcistic altar troupe (pp. 92-94, also Appendixes 4 and 5). Any villager who has ever played in *maogusi* is listed in the name list. In addition to listing names and ages, each person usually has a *maogusi* role assigned. However, there is no description of how the *maogusi* players were selected and their roles assigned. Under the heading for the section "the life history of important artists, " there is nothing that relates directly to their lives as performers. For instance, the author gives the life history of Peng Yingfa as: "male, 58 years old, Tujia nationality, elementary-school cultural level, and two-term Shuangfeng Village head. He is the *sheba* hall master for *sheba ri* activities. He plays the role of the beast in *maogusi*" (p.107).

Zhang Ziwei sometimes is overzealous in following the "suggestions" of the Project *Manual*. These excesses should have been caught during the editorial process. The same could be said about the appearance of paragraphs that have little or nothing to do with the section's topic. For instance, in Chapter Three, where the general content is *maogusi* performance, suddenly Zhang Ziwei gives a three-line paragraph (p. 85) about the parade in *sheba ri* activities, not the *maogusi* performance. Chapter Four is about the performance troupe, but suddenly starts with descriptions of the ritual specialist *tima*, his legends and deity scrolls.

VIII. Conclusion

Of all the volumes under review, only Yang Lan and Liu Feng's *Miao Celebrating Altar* raises a thesis or theoretical viewpoint which explains the lived relationship between people and ritual performance. Zhang Ziwei's *Tujia Maogusi* raises arguments about the relationship between the *maogusi* performance and the people, but it is more about the dead than the living. The other four books can only be read as fieldwork reports of one or two rituals. The appendices each of them provide will probably be much more useful than the main body of the volumes. All five volumes on "recompensing the gods" should be of great interest and use for comparing the different texts. They might best be approached by beginning with the appendices. This is just another way of saying, however, that the descriptions tell us less about the ritual performances than do the original texts themselves.

The effort in making the above volumes possible should be appreciated and the authors congratulated. The flaws I have noted could well be the result of an epistemological bias of viewing rituals as cultural objects or commodities that can be extracted from the lives of the people, community, or nationality. The volumes under review are, largely though not wholly, themselves a cautionary tale about the dangers of formalism, particularism, and objectification of rituals as cultural relics.

8

RITUAL, CONTEXT, AND IDENTITY:
THE LINGMU RITUAL OF THE LIANGSHAN YI PEOPLE IN SICHUAN

Liu Tik-sang

1. Wang Kang 王康 and Jike Zehuo Shihuo 吉克・則伙・史伙, *A Review of the Lingmu Ritual in Luojiu Village, Lizi Township, Xide County, Liangshan Yizu Autonomous Department, Sichuan Province* 四川省涼山彝族自治州喜德縣李子鄉倮糾村的靈姆. *Min-su·ch'ü-i ts'ung-shu* 民俗曲藝叢書 (Studies in Chinese Ritual, Theatre and Folklore Series), No. 36, 1995. 258 pages.

The Yi 彝 are one of China's fifty-six national minorities. More than six million Yi live spread across four provinces in Southwestern China (Wang and Jike 1995: 1; see also Wu 1991: 43-48). Although the Yi are classified as an official ethnic group, communities in different regions speak tens of mutually unintelligible "dialects" in six major language categories (Fang 1984: 6, 8-12; Liu 1995: 15). In China, Sichuan Liangshan is the largest Yi settlement area (Fang 1984: 3), it is also where Wang Kang and Jike Zehuo Shihuo conducted their research on the *lingmu* 靈姆 death ritual. The aim of this paper is to review their book on this ritual.

A Yi funerary ritual, *lingmu*, consists of three parts: the soul establishment rite (*liling* 立靈), the rite of offering to the soul (*gongling* 供靈), and the soul sending rite (*songling* 送靈) (Wang and Jike 1995: 17, 47-48, 67). Wang and Jike's ethnography is a detailed account of the third part of a twenty-five year-long Yi death ritual in 1993. Through in-depth interviews and field observations the authors elicited data on the general background information of the Yi and the village, the ritual, local histories, and myths. The documented *lingmu* was for a couple who had died seven and twenty-five years ago respectively. Because the couple had died so long ago, the ritual was not one of mourning, but a happy occasion where horse racing, wrestling, and singing contests were held for the kinsmen and friends. People believed that after the *lingmu* ritual, ancestors' souls were sent to heaven and became deities who could protect their offspring and bring the host family prosperity.

This ethnography is organized in six chapters with six appendixes. The first two chapters give a general background of the Yi village and the *lingmu* ritual. Chapter three is about the ritual itself, and the fourth chapter is a description of the organization of ritual specialists who performed the *lingmu* ritual. Ritual scriptures and the ways of reciting are illustrated in chapter five. Some of the scriptures used at the ritual have been transcribed in the Yi language and further translated into Chinese. In the concluding chapter, a functional approach is adopted to explain how the *lingmu* ritual fulfils the Yi people's psychological, social, and entertainment needs. The description of the ritual is further enriched by the six appendixes that provide details from the ritual participants and informants, as well as musical notations, sketches, maps, photos, and scriptures.

Although the whole manuscript is only about one ritual, the general background of Yi culture and society is provided. The ritual is presented in such a way that all the items are in clearly defined categories and systematically ordered.

I. The *Lingmu* Ritual

The first part of the ritual took place in the youngest son's house, performed by ritual specialists called *bimo* 畢摩. The process was first to inform deities that the family was going to arrange the ritual. Members of the family and the house were purified. A goat was offered to gods and ghosts to request them not to take their ancestors' souls away during the ritual. Then offerings were made to the ancestors. The final ritual in the house was to settle the ancestral souls into their positions within the home to signify the ending of the indoor ritual (Wang and Jike 1995: 67-75).

The second part of the ritual was arranged outdoors in an open space in the village. The couple's two tablets were the foci of the ritual. The *bimo* first informed the gods and ancestors about the ritual they were going to perform. Then a purification rite was performed to prepare the two ancestral souls for the last meal on earth before they were sent to heaven. After the offering of a meal, another purification rite was performed immediately to ensure that the two ancestors did not bring along any polluted substances to heaven. The rite afterwards was to eliminate any harmful effects on offspring that might be caused by their ancestors' wrongdoings. The two ancestral souls were then transferred symbolically from the old tablets to the new ones. A rite was performed to demonstrate that the family's descent line, known as incense and fire (*xianghuo* 香火), had been maintained by the family's male members. The next rite prepared the ancestral souls to leave their offspring; this was also the time for the souls of the dead couple to reunite and again have a sexual relationship. The participants in the ritual exchanged sexual jokes and the ritual specialists recited a scripture concerning sexuality. This was the only time throughout the ritual when people spoke about sex. During the final rite, the ancestral tablets were put into a small wooden coffin, so that the souls of the couple could join their other ancestors in heaven, and leave their offspring's territory. After these rites, the host family lit firecrackers to mark the ending of the ritual (Wang and Jike 1995: 75-97).[1]

---

1 Wang and Jike explain that the third part of the *lingmu* ritual was to send the small coffin, with the ancestral souls, *nage* 娜格, inside, to the ancestral cave to join the other ancestors. However, as the two authors did not study this part of the ritual, it is not included in their monograph (Wang and Jike 1995: 97-98).

II. Conceptual Categories

To describe the ritual Wang and Jike employ such basic social and cultural categories as the lineage, religious specialists, geomancy, concepts of the soul, and the implementation of taboo. A patrilineal organization constitutes the background of the religious activity.

The Yi lineage group, *jiazhi* 家支, is considered the general basis for Yi social organization. Without exception, the Yi in Luojiu Village organize themselves into *jiazhi*. The principle of patrilineal descent is demonstrated by the "father-son linked names" system (*fuzi lianming* 父子連名): a man's second given name becomes his son's first given name. In addition to the patrilineal descent principle, the *jiazhi*'s membership is further defined by the practice of *jiazhi* exogamy; the wives from other *jiazhi* marry in and the daughters marry out to other *jiazhi*. A *jiazhi* is the fundamental unit that protects and helps individual families when they face difficulties, whereas the lineage headmen are responsible for resolving minor conflicts among lineage members. When there are serious problems, *jiazhi* meetings are held where members of the lineage can express their concerns and opinions. Wang and Jike regard the *jiazhi* as a democratic organization in that the headmen achieve their positions purely by their own ability (Wang and Jike 1995: 9-11).

Bimo, ritual specialists from the local community, are hired to perform the *lingmu* ritual. All the *bimo* are full-time farmers, who perform rituals on part-time basis. Although they work part-time, their training system organizes them into an occupational category. One has to be trained to become a *bimo*; to learn to recite standard scriptures and perform standard rituals, in which local variations of these "standard" scriptures may be employed. Although a *bimo* could acquire his training from any other *bimo*, most are trained by their fathers. Thus, the line of training overlaps with the line of descent. This particular kinship-based *bimo* training pattern is revealed clearly in the "father-son linked names" pattern among *bimo*.

The *bimo* are classified into two segregated categories based on the nature of the rituals they perform: the sacred worship ritual (*jiexing jisi*

潔性祭祀) and exorcism (*xiongxing fashi* 凶性法事). A *bimo* who performs sacred rituals can switch to exorcism if he decides to stay in the latter category forever. This means that a *bimo* who deals with exorcism can no longer perform sacred worship rituals. Within each of the two categories, the *bimo* are divided into ranks of high, middle, and low. A *bimo* in a lower rank is promoted when he gains experience or his ability improves (Wang and Jike 1995: 26-28). When *bimo* are hired to perform in a ritual, the required number of *bimo* varies according the scale of the ritual. A *bimo* of high rank usually engages his lower ranking *bimo* associates to help in rituals. However, there are informal networks of cooperation among *bimo* that allow them to handle rituals on various scales (Wang and Jike 1995: 106-107).

All the Yi ritual scriptures are written in the Yi language. To become a *bimo*, one has to master this language. Most of the *bimo* spend much time to study the written language, and routinely hand-copy ritual scriptures (Wang and Jike 1995: 110-111, 137). These activities suggest that the *bimos'* ritual techniques, professional networks, and knowledge of cultural traditions define their own professional organization.

The Yi have a tripartite concept of soul which exists in three forms: *yi* 依, *na* 娜, *nage* 娜格. After death, the *yi* wanders between heaven and earth until a *lingmu* ritual has been conducted. The *na* is the part of the soul that joins the deceased's ancestors immediately after death. Like the *yi*, it can settle in heaven only after a *lingmu* ritual has been conducted. The *nage* resides in the corpse or in the bone-ash after cremation; it moves to the soul tablet after the rite of offering to the soul (*gongling*) has been held. The *lingmu* ritual transfers the *nage* to the ancestral cave (*zulingshan* 祖靈山) where all the ancestral souls finally settle (Wang and Jike 1995: 34-35).

The Yi believe that one can benefit from the ancestors' supernatural power through the mechanism of geomancy, "wind and water." The Yi must pick a good location to establish their ancestral cave, which brings the family prosperity. The location of the ancestral cave is a secret to outsiders. The Yi never relocate the site of their ancestral cave unless they move to another area themselves (Wang and Jike 1995: 32-33).

There are rules of prohibition during the *lingmu* ritual that all the participants, including the *bimo*, must observe. Wang and Jike note that there are different levels of prohibition observed by various participants. The chief *bimo* has to forego sexual activity three days before the ritual and he is only allowed to consume cigarettes, wine, tea, and eggs. The other *bimo* are not supposed to engage in sexual activity during the time of the ritual (Wang and Jike 1995: 124). Members of the host family should not engage in sexual activity three days before the ritual, should not be involved in any physical conflicts the year before the ritual, and may not acquire their ritual offerings through robbing or cheating (Wang and Jike 1995: 124). The plants used in rituals have to be collected from designated ritually clean areas. The Yi raise their own ritual animals to ensure that the animals have a "clean" raising history. Animals are considered to be polluted if they are acquired by illegal means or have abnormal biological traits. All the ritual instruments must be purified before the ritual (Wang and Jike 1995: 124-125). Women are not allowed to touch any ritual instruments, to approach any ritual specialists, or to enter ritual sites, since the Yi believe that ritual pollution also comes from them (Wang and Jike 1995: 125).

III. Similarities to South China?

When I summarize Wang and Jike's ethnography, of course I see it through my own South China lens. With a very limited knowledge of Yi culture, I assume that the Yi in Sichuan and people in South China have their own distinctive cultural characteristics in the areas of patrilineage, ritual specialists, ancestral worship, concepts of the soul, and ritual taboos. The major difference, I believe, is the context, in which people manipulate their social and cultural categories and through which they interact with each other.

In South China, the patrilineage, which is the same as the Yi's *jiazhi* to a certain extent, is the major form of social organization (Freedmen 1965, J. Watson 1975, R. Watson 1985). With a genealogy, common ancestors, ancestral estates, and ancestral graves, male lineage members and their married-in wives are linked together. They practice surname exogamy and patrilocal residence: men who share the same surname stay in their settlements and get their wives from outside, while women marry out to other lineages. The ancestral estate, usually in the form of land, constitutes the economic core of a lineage. The income from these ancestral estates is used to fund the annual ancestral worship activities at the ancestral halls and graves, while the extra profit is usually shared by the lineage members. A genealogy records the members of the lineage, thus defining who has claims on the ancestral estates. The ancestral estate has the function of maintaining the ancestors' names as the major lineage symbols, and financing collective activities within the lineage. When the imperial state did not enforce its power at the local level, lineages were the governing organizations of local society.

People in South China believe that one has multiple souls in two different categories: three *hun* 魂 and seven *po* 魄. According to Potter (1970:149), most people are not certain about the exact nature of these souls. However, some believe that their ancestors' souls reside in the grave, in the ancestral hall, and in the domestic ancestral tablet. These three locations become the places where people practice ancestral worship. Belief in geomancy provides a utilitarian explanation of ancestral worship. People believe that the geomanic force, as qi or *longmai* 龍脈 in the natural environment, can be captured and transferred by manipulating the direction and location of houses and ancestral graves (see Potter 1970, R.Watson 1988). Ancestors can benefit their offspring if the ancestral hall is built on a good geomanic site; or descendants can acquire benevolent aid by finding a good site for the ancestors' secondary burial. Geomancy links members of the lineage to their ancestors.

An ancestor can bring bad luck to his offspring by his death. A corpse produces death pollution, *shaqi* 煞氣 which can harm both offspring and unrelated observers, so people try to avoid it (J. Watson 1982). However, the offspring of the dead cannot entirely avoid the pollution since they participate in the death ritual. The one who inherits most from the dead takes a dominant role in the death ritual, and thus takes on more of the potentially harmful supernatural power. The *shaqi* is distributed along the line of descent, and bound to the patrilineal inheritance pattern (J. Watson 1982: 169-72).

In this male-dominated lineage system, women often play a subordinate role. The idea of pollution is attached to women, who are considered unclean, as they regularly produce menstrual blood (Ahern 1978). It is common that in South China most of the communal rituals are performed by men, while women are relegated to the role of observers. Although women cannot participate in important communal rituals, their role is sometimes ambiguous. They sometimes monitor the process to ensure that the rituals are arranged properly. A second ambiguity is that, while women are considered polluted, it is women who maintain the lineage by bearing the lineage's new members.

In South China, the *jiao* festival is the common regional ritual to purify the region, renew the cosmos, and bring the area prosperity (Saso 1989). Most *jiao* 醮 festivals are organized once every ten years. But some occur at one-year, three-year, seven-year, or sixty-year intervals. A *jiao* festival is a year-long activity, with the ritual representatives picked by divination at the beginning of the year, and the main part of the festival, lasting for five to seven days, occurring at the end of the year. Ritual specialists are hired and a Cantonese opera[2] or a puppet show is put on. The number of ritual specialists and the scale of the performance vary according to the budget of the festival. A large scale *jiao* festival may involve many local lineages and villages. It is often an important event to express the unity of a regional alliance. However, it is usually the members of the dominant lineage in a region who organize the ritual.

During the festival members of the community have to observe rules of prohibition. All the community members consume only vegetarian food, while the ritual representatives in addition must not engage in sexual activities. However, the ritual specialists do not have to follow the rules of prohibition when they are not in the ritual territory.

In South China, people hire *nam mo* 喃嘸, or Taoist priests, to perform communal and domestic rituals. The priests perform standardized rituals according to their uniform ritual handbooks.[3] Unlike the *bimo*, these priests have no special affiliation with a particular lineage or village, but perform rituals for whomever hires them. A simple domestic ritual can be conducted by a single *nam mo*. However, more are hired if

---

2 See Ward 1979 for her study of the ritual aspect of the Cantonese opera.

3 I have studied *nam mo* ritual activities in Hong Kong's New Territories in the last several years. For their roles in the Cantonese funeral, see J. Watson 1988.

the ritual is large, like a *jiao* festival, and senior priests are required to head communal rituals. Although these priests do not belong to any formal organizations, they have their informal networks in recruiting members for large-scale religious activities. These networks are reinforced by the apprentice training system of new *nam mo*. Like a *bimo*, a senior *nam mo* has several juniors working under him. To become a *nam mo*, one has to work as an apprentice for several years learning how to recite scriptures, play musical instruments, learn body movements, and make paper products for rituals. One can become a senior member of the profession after he acquires the recognition of most *nam mo*. In sum, the *nam mo* in Hong Kong's New Territories are related through apprenticeship.

In this very short description, I have attempted to illustrate that similar social and cultural categories can be found in the South China context. Both the Yi and the Cantonese societies have patrilineages, religious specialists, and share some similar cultural concepts. I am not suggesting that socio-cultural explanations developed in South China can be applied to the Liangshan Yi case without any local consideration. Religious activities are conducted within the framework of local social organization, and reflect people's views of the cosmos and the supernatural world, while revealing the social structure of the society. The interpretations of geomancy, pollution, and ancestral worship make sense only if they are explained in South China's social and cultural context. In the Liangshan case, without the local context, all the concepts become simply categories. We cannot see the social and cultural meanings of the Yi ritual.

IV. Identity: An Alternative Significance

Wang and Jike trace the origin of the Yi in Sichuan Liangshan back to two ancestors who entered the region two thousand years ago (1995: 3). They claim that although people may have developed some minor ritual details with local characteristics, every Yi group in the region practices a very similar *lingmu* ritual (1995: 4). Because they share the apical ancestors and practice the same religious rituals, Wang and Jike assert that, as one of the state-designated national minorities, the Yi are a single homogenous ethnic group sharing many similarities.[4]

The *lingmu* ritual studied by Wang and Jike was hosted by a family. However, it is obvious that the family was not the focus of their research. The interactions among participants in the ritual are not discussed in the book. What the authors wanted to find out was a "standard" and an "objective" representation of the *lingmu* ritual. It seems to me that the two researchers intended to de-contextualize their findings, to extract the valuable "Yi traditions" while leaving the "superstitious" people aside.

The Yi have had a written tradition for many centuries, although there are hypotheses arguing that the language has a history of five hundred to six thousand years (Ma 1989: 139-140). In their language, the Yi ritual scriptures have recorded their heritage, worldview, and moral system. Since 1949, Putonghua (and written Chinese) have been defined as the official language in China, and so the opportunity for the younger generation to learn the Yi language was minimal until 1980, when the government approved a standardized Yi language (Wang and Jike 1995: 1), which has become a "legitimatized symbol" to distinguish the Yi from the Han Chinese who had suppressed them for centuries.

In the last two decades, numerous research results on the Yi have been published, and a significant number of manuscripts have been published as monographs of the Series on the Study of Yi Culture. Jike and Liu Yiuhan, chief editors of the Series, have jointly contributed their works (Jike et al. 1990) to the Series. In their book, *Between Gods and Ghosts: A Self-portrayal of a Yi Priest*, Jike records his father Jike Erda Zehuo's oral life history, which includes their lineage's genealogy, religious practices, myths, production activities, and the management of land and slaves. Liu was responsible for organizing and coordinating the materials for the book. Liu describes Jike's father as a saintly man who keeps important Yi values and traditions (Liu 1990: 2). This is a book by and about the Yi.

As it is stated in one of the Series' general prefaces, the Series aims to establish a "Yi School":

... the publication of the 'Series on the Study of Yi Culture'

---

4   See Harrell 1995 for a discussion of the process of the formation of a Yi history.

announces the establishment of the 'School of Chinese Yi Culture' and the 'Theory on Yi Culture'... (Cheng 1990: 28)

Professor Liu Yiuhan also wrote for the Series a general preface. In the third revision of the preface, with the subtitle of "Promoting the Chinese Yi's Excellent Cultural Tradition," Liu emphasizes that the Yi School should have its special research orientations: (i) the Yi scholars study Yi themselves, (ii) Yi studies are situated within the Chinese or global, context, and (iii) the contemporary field research is used to trace Yi history (1995: 14). Whether or not these suggestions are implemented, these are statements asking Yi scholars to study their own culture and society, and further to reconstruct their own ethnic history.

Wang and Jike's research is about a Yi religious tradition believed to have been sustained throughout Yi history and across contemporary Yi communities. With their strong background in Yi culture and society, the researchers completed their field research in 20 days (Wang and Jike 1995: 5). The rich details of the manuscript make it a possible ritual handbook for organizing *lingmu* rituals. The manuscript obviously has its role in standardizing the religious practice, thus contributing to the Yi scholars' project of constituting a homogenous Yi identity.

References

Ahern, Emily M. 1978. "The Power and Pollution of Chinese Women," in *Studies in Chinese Society*, Arthur P. Wolf, ed., pp. 269-290. Stanford: Stanford University Press.

Cheng Zhifang 程志方. 1990. "Reviewing the Founding of the School of Chinese Yi Culture: A Critique of the Publication of the Series on the Study of Yi Culture" 論中華彝族文化學派的誕生——評「彝族文化研究叢書」的出版, in *Between Gods and Ghosts: A Self-portrayal of a Yi Priest* 我在神鬼之間——一個彝族祭司的自述, Jike Erda Zehuo 吉克 · 爾達 · 則伙, Jike Zehuo Shihuo 吉克 · 則伙 · 史伙, and Liu Yiuhan 劉堯漢, pp. 28-44. Series on the Study of Yi Culture. Kunming: Yunnan People's Press.

Fang, Guoyu 方國瑜. 1984. *The Yi History* 彝族史稿. Chengdu: Sichuan People's Press.

Freedman, Maurice. 1965[1958]. *Lineage Organization in Southeastern China*. London: Atholone Press.

Harrell, Stevan. 1995. "The History of the History of the Yi," in *Cultural Enocunter on China's Ethnic Frontiers*, Stevan Harrell, ed., pp. 63-91. Seattle: University of Washington Press.

Jike, Erda Zehuo (Oral Presentation), Jike Zehuo Shihuo(Recording), and Liu Yiuhan (Organization). 1990. *Between Gods and Ghosts: A Self-portrayal of a Yi Priest*. Series on the Study of Yi Culture. Kunming: Yunnan People's Press.

Liu, Yiuhan. 1995. "General Preface: Promoting the Chinese Yi's Excellent Cultural Tradition" 總序──弘揚中華彝族優秀文化傳統, in *Autobiographies of Yi Shamans* 彝巫列傳──禹步，巫步；步虛聲，巫歌聲, Li Shikang 李世康, pp. 1-39. Series on the Study of Yi Culture. Kunming: Yunnan People's Press.

Ma, Xueliang 馬學良 et al. 1989. *Cultural History of the Yi* 彝族文化史. Shanghai: Shanghai People's Press.

Potter, Jack M. 1970. "Wind, Water, Bones, and Souls: The Religious Life of the Cantonese Peasant," *Journal of Oriental Studies*, 3.1: 139-53.

Saso, Michael R. 1989. *Taoism and the Rite of Cosmic Renewal* (Second Edition). Washington: Washington State University Press.

Watson, James L. 1975. *Emigration and the Chinese Lineage: The Mans in Hong Kong and London*. Berkeley: University of California Press.

──────. 1982. "Of Flesh and Bones: The Management of Death Pollution in Cantonese Society," in *Death and the Regeneration of Life*, Maurice Block & Jonathan Parry, eds., pp. 155-86. London: Cambridge University Press.

──────. 1988. "Funeral Specialists in Cantonese Society: Pollution, Performance, and Social Hierarchy," in *Death Ritual in Late Imperial and Modern China*, pp. 109-134, James Watson and Evelyn Rawski, eds., Berkeley: University of California Press.

Watson, Rubie S. 1985. *Inequality among Brothers: Class and Kinship in South China*. Cambridge: Cambridge University Press

──────. 1988. "Remembering the Dead: Graves and Politics in Southern China," in *Death Ritual in Late Imperial and Modern China*, James L. Watson and Evelyn Rawski, eds., pp. 203-227.

Berkeley: University of California Press.

Ward, Barbara E. 1979. "Not Merely Players: Drama, Art, and Ritual in Traditional China." *Man*, 14.1: 18-39.

Wu, David Y.H.吳燕和. 1991. "The Development of Chinese Anthropology and the Issue of Ethnic Classification in China" 中國人類學發展與中國民族分類問題, *Bulletin of the Department of Anthropology* 考古人類學刊, 47: 36-50.

9

A REVIEW OF PLEASING
THE NUO GODS IN
CENGONG COUNTY, GUIZHOU

David Holm

1. Wang Ch'iu-kuei 王秋桂 and Tuo Xiuming 庹修明, *Pleasing the Nuo Gods in Laowuji Hamlet, Cenwang Village, Zhuxi Township, Cengong County, Guizhou* 貴州省岑鞏縣注溪鄉岑王村老屋基喜儺神調查報告. *Min-Su ch'ü-i ts'ung-shu* 民俗曲藝叢書 (Studies in Chinese Ritual, Theatre and Folklore Series), No. 37, 1995. 408 pages.

I. Content

Cengong 岑鞏 County is located in easternmost Guizhou on the northern flank of the Wuyang 潕陽 River, the valley of which traditionally has formed a major transport route between Hunan and the uplands of central Guizhou. This is now where the Hunan-Guizhou railway is located. Thus Cengong, and the whole of what was formerly the prefecture of Sizhou 思州, faces east towards Hunan, and shares many cultural traits with contiguous parts of western Hunan (Xiangxi 湘西). Though administratively it has now been incorporated into the Southeastern Guizhou Miao 苗 and Dong 侗 Autonomous Zhou, culturally it would seem to have little in common with counties further south.

The ethnic mix in Cengong is Han along with Gelao, Kham (Dong), and Hmong (Miao). No information is provided about which particular branch of the Hmong are resident in this district, but such facts are readily obtainable elsewhere. According to old people in the village, Laowuji used to be a large fortified village inhabited by 'mountain-valley barbarians' (*dongman* 洞蠻) — an imprecise term — but was laid waste by Chinese armies during the Ming. The early inhabitants moved away, and the area was a wasteland for a long while. The village was eventually resettled by a mixed population. Two of the surname groups in the village, Xiang 向 and Zhang 張, are Hmong from western Hunan, four — Deng 鄧, Liu 劉, Wu 吳 and Huang 黃— are Kham from Mayang 麻陽 and Xinhuang 新化 in Hunan, and the 'big surname' group, the Zhou 周, are a Han family said to be from Jiangxi. In fact, though, locals draw a distinction between 'local' and 'outsider' Zhou: the latter are Han and trace their ancestry to Zhou Zhongrong 周仲融, one of the commanding generals in the military campaigns at the beginning of the Ming; the former are the descendants of local non-Han people, who adopted the Zhou surname when they sought protection from Zhou Zhongrong during the campaigns of extermination against minority peoples in Sizhou during the Hongwu 洪武 reign period (1368-1399). They became Han and combined their ancestral records with the Zhou at that time, claiming ancestry from Jiangxi.

The sacrificer, Zhou Daoming 周道明, came from a family that was originally Kham, but was adopted into the Han lineage of the head priest (*zhangtanshi* 掌壇師) Zhou Liangzhong 周良忠. Like those in their adopted lineage, the Zhou of Laowuji had made a 'Vow to the Nuo Altar to Please the Nuo Gods' (*Xi nuoshen nuotan yuanjiao* 喜儺神儺壇願腳); they made offerings of incense and paper at home, and twice every three years engaged a *nuo* troupe to perform Pleasing the Nuo God. This was only one of a variety of kinds of vows made. 'nuo vows' (*Nuo yuanjiao* 儺願腳) was the name given in Cengong to a kind of *nuo* vow made by families that redeemed the vow with performances of *nuo* plays (*Nuotangxi* 儺堂戲) (p. 9). Other types of vow are the '*nuo* spoken vow' (*Kouyuan nuo yuanjiao* 口願儺願腳), which involves offerings to gods of the world of the sky, earth and water (*Tian di shui yangshen* 天地水陽神) and is intended to ameliorate the effects of family disputes; and the '*nuo* vow to the Xiao sisters' (*Xiaoyuan nuo yuanjiao* 霄願儺願腳), for which offerings are made to Divine Sisters of the Cloudy Empyrean in Heaven (*Tianshang Yunxiao zimei shen* 天上雲霄 姊妹神) and prayers are made for Riches, Honour, and Peace (p. 9). The *nuo* 儺 gods are worshipped if things are not going smoothly, or if the family suffers from strange illnesses, or if there is a sudden death. The purpose of the *nuo* offering (*Nuoji* 儺祭) is to expel nefarious influences and pestilence, pray for blessings and peace, and make recompense to the gods. There are specific gods for specific ailments: for reflux and diarrhoea one invites the Lower Altar Gods of the Five Peaks (*Wuyue xiatan* 五岳下壇), for strange illnesses and sudden illnesses on invites the Gods of the Seven Continents and Five Temples (*Qizhou wumiao shen* 七洲五廟神), and so on (p. 15).

The hereditary priests of Zhou Liangzhong's lineage call themselves the Jiangxi Jade Emperor Cult (*Jiangxi Yuhuang pai* 江西玉皇 派), and pay reverence to Zhou Fabing 周法兵 of the Eastern Jin (286-367 CE) as their founder. The troupe is an 'altar troupe of the martial teaching' (*wujiao tanban* 武教壇班), and mainly performs Pleasing the Nuo God, but can also perform Assault Nuo (*Chong nuo* 衝儺) rituals (p. 40). Some interesting details are given about the transmission. The Zhou are a Nuo-vow altar-group (*Nuoyuantan* 儺願壇), while a subsidiary line (the Yang lineage troupe) are a Xiao-vow altar-group (*Xiaoyuantan* 霄願壇) and perform mainly civil rather than military rituals. The point of this is that the Yangs are not in command of the complete transmission. They can help the Zhou perform the Redemption of Vows to Ancestors (*Huan zuyuan* 還祖願), but cannot perform this ritual by themselves even for the ancestors of their own lineage. The chief deities of a Xiao-vow altar-group are the Sisters of the Cloudy Empyrean, Yunxiao 雲霄, Shanxiao 山霄, and Shuixiao 水霄. Pleasing the Nuo God however has Father Nuo (*Nuogong* 儺公) and Mother Nuo (*Nuomu* 儺母) as its chief deities, deities who are conventionally identified with the sage-emperor Fu Xi 伏羲 and Nüwa 女媧 (p. 26). In fact, the Zhou are related through marriage to the Yang, the Ding and the Liu. Affinal relations were clearly important in the hierarchy of liturgical transmission, and we are given some details about villages of residence on p. 26; unfortunately a map is needed to start working out some of the patterns between the ritually dominant Zhou and their ritually subordinate affinal lineages.

Pleasing the Nuo God is a ritual that is conducted mainly in the period between September and Qingming (approximate date April 5th). There is a relatively set repertoire, lasting three to five days. The 'host families redeeming the vow' (*huanyuan zhujia* 還願主家) are the lineages of the Zhou, Liu, Ding and Yang. It is thus a closed activity confined to lineages whose member families have made the appropriate vows. It is not commodified, and recompense to the performers is in accordance with the economic circumstances of the host family (p. 32). It is interesting that the family of Zhou Daoming was chosen to be the 'host family' for this performance partly for geographic convenience, but mainly because he was part of Zhou Lianzhong's branch of the Zhou, and enjoyed a relationship of descent with him. Zhou Daoming had also made a Pleasing the Nuo God vow, so he was fully qualified to serve as host for an intra-lineage ritual. If he had not fulfilled these conditions, the ritual would not have fulfilled its function of protecting later generations (*yin sun* 蔭孫). Even for a demonstration performance with outsiders present, if the ritual was seen not to fulfil the function of 'making reverence to the ancestors above, and providing shade to the descendants below' (*shang jing zuxian, xia yin zisun* 上敬祖先，下蔭子孫), it would have been regarded as a waste of resources, and would have made people laugh at the priests, thereby having a serious effect on the reputation of the priests of the *nuo* transmission in the district as a whole (p. 53).

The ritual itself took place over three days, with ten ritual segments performed on the first day, nine on the second, and eight on the third. The arrangement of the ritual segments was marked by logical progression. An outline follows below (names of segments in parentheses are the special performances of supernatural tricks by Xiao Guanghua 蕭光華):

First day

Invitation to Departed Masters
Issue of the Invitation
Reception of the Gods
Construction of the Bridge

Bivouacking of Soldiers
(Kicking Knives)
Harmonising the Gods in the First Primordial
(Fire Belching)
(Bamboo Splitting)
Sending forth the Five Chang
Acceptance of Offerings
and Harmonising the Gods in the Middle Primordial, Releasing the
Gods in the Last
Primordial, and Paying Respects to the Plays

Second day

Morning Invitation
Request for Water and Respects to the Hearth
The White Offering
Running the Limit
(Groping in a Panful of Hot Oil)
(Stepping on a Red-Hot Plowshare)
(Climbing the Ladder of Swords)
Eighth Young Gentleman Presents Offerings
The Mountain-Opener

Third day

Mountain-Opener
Vanguard with the White Flag
The Earth-God of Liangshan
(Rubbing Red-Hot Iron)
(Crossing the Sea of Fire)
The Divine Judge Records the Performance of the Vow
Settling the Dragon and Expressing Thanks to the Soil
Sending Off the Gods

The general character of the Pleasing the Nuo God ritual is one of
light-hearted merrymaking. Humorous lyrics abound in many of the
above ritual segments, usually taking the form of seven-syllable verse.

There is a great deal of folkloric material here that would well repay closer study.

Since this is a *nou* ritual, it is worth taking a closer look at the characteristics that are specifically *nou*. In fact, the ritual process in broad outline is similar to that of other varieties of "popular religion" in the south of China, following a standard pattern that involves invitation to the gods, reception in the sacred space, presentation of offerings, prayers and plays, and finally, after the fulfilment of ritual obligations and the recording of the redemption of the vow in the record-book, the final sending-off of the gods and the conclusion of the ritual. What is specific here is the identity of the chief deities, Father Nuo and Mother Nuo. As elsewhere in Guizhou, these deities are represented in the ritual by small carved wooden heads, much like the heads of puppets. When the ritual area is being prepared, the heads of Father Nuo and Mother Nuo are set up in the same row as the spirit tablet of the deity Jade Purity on the main offering table; their heads are placed on the top of two poles (p. 63). Their images also appear in the third row of the scroll of Jade Purity 玉清, along with Pangu 盤古 and directly underneath Jade Purity. Father Nuo and Mother Nuo are said, according to legend, to be identified as Fu Xi and Nüwa. It is not clear, however, whether this was simply what the priests recounted to the investigators, outside the ritual context, or whether it was given some kind of manifestation in ritual. The myth of divine incest between Fu Xi and Nüwa has it that they were brother and sister who survived a great flood by floating in a medicine gourd, and that they were obliged to become man and wife in order to repopulate the world. This myth is widespread throughout southwest China. We are told that Father Nuo and Mother Nuo are worshipped as the progenitors of humankind, and that they are treated in a familiar fashion during this ritual, even as the butt of jokes. However, there seem to be no traces of the flood myth or the incest story in the ritual segments in which Father Nuo and Mother Nuo play a major role, such as the Welcome to the Gods as they Dismount (*ying shen xia ma* 迎神下馬). One question for further investigation is, therefore, the exact status of this identification in *nou* ritual. The wider question, of course, is the possibility that the identity of Fu Xi and Nüwa has been grafted onto older figures of non-Han origin. This is a question that would have to be investigated for the southwest region as a whole, and across a wide range of minority cultures.

The earliest reference to Pleasing the Nuo Gods comes from the manuscript 'Register of the Names of Masters in Successive Generations', the text of which is included as Appendix 4. There, there is a passage connecting this ritual to Zhou Fabing, an adept who is said to have lived during the Eastern Jin and to have brought this ritual to Sizhou prefecture. The authors go on to observe that the Grand Exorcism ritual of the Han imperial court probably became widely dispersed among the general populace at around this time, and that the ritual Pleasing the Nuo God developed as a result of this process. As corroborating evidence of this theory, the authors cite worship of the Immortal Dong Zhong (Dong Zhongxian 董仲仙), identified as the famous Western Han philosopher Dong Zhongshu 董仲舒, in the context of the Pleasing the Nuo God ritual (p. 18). The present form of Pleasing the Nuo God, then, is a combination of the exorcism of the court with the culture of the non-Han peoples who inhabited the Sizhou area. There are a number of points that could be made about this theory, the first of which is that it is generally unwise to accept genealogical claims at face value. While none of the above is particularly implausible, it is obvious that a great deal more work will be needed to present it in convincing fashion. Future discussion of the supposed influence of non-Han cultures should be informed by the ethnography of the relevant peoples.

II. Critique

As Professor Wang points out in his Foreword, the investigations that gave rise to the present volume were undertaken under the auspices of collaboration between National Tsing Hua University in Taiwan and the Guizhou Nationalities College. Because of limitations of time, the performance that was recorded and analysed by a joint team of investigators was one that had been 'organised,' rather than one which occurred naturally in its village setting. It is greatly to the editors' credit that the concrete ways in which this performance was organised, and the role in this process of the Cengong County Cultural Office (Cengong xian wenhuaju 岑鞏縣文化局) and other county-level government departments, are all made explicit, thus enabling the reader to begin to unravel which aspects of the performance might have been changed as a result of this official involvement. For instance, we are given details about preliminary negotiations between the Guizhou Nationalities College and county government officials on p. 52, and the considerations that led to the performance being located at Laowuji and the family of Zhou Daoming being chosen as the 'redeemer of the vow' on p. 53. We are given the programme of ritual events, as first worked out with county officials (pp. 79-82), and told how this program was changed in actual performance by the priests (pp. 82 ff). Timing ritual sequences during daytime hours for the convenience of postgraduate students was another concession. The presence of Xiao Guanghua, a *nuo* "artist" who had performed in Beijing, was the result of a decision by officials to include in the program his spectacular "*nuo* tricks," such as "crossing the sea of fire" and "treading on a red-hot ploughshare;" he and the other men in the troupe, we are told, were from different localities and had no previous experience of collaboration. It may be ironic that the more lurid demonstrations of 'supernatural powers' recounted in this volume were included at the behest of the government, but this can be seen as part of an unofficial craze for 'supernatural powers' and *qigong* 氣功 that swept China-including high government circles-during the early 1990's. All of this provides readers with a refreshingly frank account of how collaborative fieldwork frequently has to be conducted in the People's Republic of China. At the same time, the information about folklore and performance assembled in the present volume is very rich, and it is my view that the integrity of this material is not seriously compromised by the circumstances.

This is a volume, however, that needs to be read in conjunction with the authors' previous book on *nou* in Dejiang 德江 County (See the bibliography for this chapter). In fact the authors presuppose some familiarity with their previous book, though they refer readers to it explicitly on only one occasion (to refer them to legends about Father Nuo and Mother Nuo). The layout of the earlier volume, for instance the presentation of information about the deities invited down to the altar ("Dejiang" pp. 22-44), is more accessible and reader-friendly.

The needs of any readership, specialised or nonspecialised, would have been much better served by providing more cross-referencing, and also providing adequate maps. There is one miserable little sketch-map on p. 6. We are given a great deal of detailed geographic information on pp. 20 ff. about the three routes taken by the deities Vanguard, Sacrificer and Mountain-Opener from the Peach-Orchard Grotto to eastern Guizhou, with a wealth of place-names which the authors have painstakingly located (pp. 21-23). The authors conclude on the basis of this that, among other things, the *Xi Nuoshen* ritual came from Taoyuan 桃源 county in Hunan, arriving at Yuping 玉屏 in eastern Guizhou before spreading throughout the Sizhou region. This is certainly important. While the story sounds plausible enough-though one wonders about the ready identification of Taoyuan with the mythical Peach-Orchard Grotto — it will be difficult for readers to gain a clear picture of what the authors are talking about, and thus gain some appreciation for the force of their argument, without a map to give them the necessary overview. Many of the identifications of local village place-names come from the *Toponymic Gazetteer of Cengong County* (貴州省岑鞏縣地名志), an internal publication which scholars and students may have difficulty in consulting without making a trip to Cengong. Ordinarily, reports such as this should endeavour to provide maps showing the location of all placenames mentioned in the text, including those of natural villages.

There are remarkably few minor errors. The transcription of the altar-placard (*tanbang* 壇榜) on p. 42 will need to be checked against the photographic record, (not much was legible from the photograph provided (Plate 3)), but it is at least clear that the first two characters on the right-hand couplet are reversed (they should read '*Tanshen*' 壇神 rather than '*Shentan*' 神壇). There are two errors of transcription in the passage on Zhou Fabing (compare pp. 17-18 and p. 298). The photograph of the troupe members (Plate 2) also shows signs of having been doctored.

In all other respects, this volume is fully up to the high standards set for the series. Taken together with other volumes in the series documenting the *nou* drama of northeastern Guizhou, it provides us for the first time with adequate documentation for ritual practices that have come to take on a cultural importance in China that extends far beyond the confines of mountain villages.

Bibliography

Wang Ch'iu-kuei and Tuo Xiuming. 1994. *"Nuo in Celebration of Long Life" among the Tujia Nationality of Huangtu Village, Wenping Township, Dejiang County, Guizhou* 貴州省德江縣穩坪鄉黃土村土家族衝壽儺調查報告. *Min-su ch'ü-i ts'ung-shu*, No. 12. 528 pages. Taipei: Shih Ho-cheng Folk Culture Foundation.

C.
EASTERN CHINA

10

THE MASKED EXORCISTIC THEATRE OF ANHUI AND JIANGXI

Kenneth Dean

This review treats the *nuo* altar performances and plays of Anhui and Jiangxi that have been described in the following four books in Wang Ch'iu-kuei 王秋桂, ed., *Min-su ch'ü-i ts'ung-shu* 民俗曲藝叢書 (Studies in Chinese Ritual, Theatre and Folklore Series). Taipei: Shih Ho-cheng Folk Culture Foundation, 80 vols.

1. Mao Limei 毛禮鎂, *Jiangxi sheng Wanzai xian Tanfu xiang Chixi cun Hanzu Dingxing de 'tiaoxia'* 江西省萬載縣潭阜鄉池溪村漢族丁姓的跳魁 (*Tiaoxiao [Hopping Goblins]: The Nuo Plays of the Ding Lineage of Chixi Village, Tanfu Township, Wanzai County, Jiangxi*). No. 7, 1993. 198 pages. Hereafter *Hopping Goblins*.
2. Wang Zhaoqian 王兆乾 and Wang Qiugui 王秋貴, *Anhui sheng Guichi shi Liujiex iang Yuanxi cun Cao, Jin, Ke Sanxing Jiazu de Nuoxi* 安徽省貴池市劉街鄉源溪村曹、金、柯三姓家族的儺戲 (*The Nuo Plays of the Cao, Jin, and Ke Lineages of Yuanxi Village, Liujie Township, Guichi County, Anhui*). No. 8, 1993. 231 pages. Hereafter *Yuanxi Nuo*.
3. Wang Zhaoqian, *Anhui Guichi Nuoxi Juben xuan* 安徽貴池儺戲劇本

選(*Selection of Scripts from the Exorcistic Drama of Guichi, Anhui*). No. 40, 1995. 680 pages. Hereafter *Selected Plays*.
4. Yu Daxi 余大喜 and Liu Zhifan 劉之凡, *Jiangxi sheng Nanfeng xian Sanxi xiang Shiyou cun de Tiaonuo* 江西省南豐縣三溪鄉石郵村的 跳儺(*The "Leaping Nuo" of Shiyou Village, Sanxi Township, Nanfeng County, Jiangxi*). No. 45, 1996. 194 pages. Hereafter *Leaping Nuo*.

The materials in the four books under review are exceptionally rich and detailed.They provide case studies of *nuo* exorcistic performances and plays in Anhui and Jiangxi. Each study describes a temple dedicated to the gods of *nuo* exorcism (*Nuoshen miao* 儺神廟 or *Nuo tang* 儺堂). All of these temples keep collections of masks of several deities. These masks are worn during performances at New Year's designed to solicit blessings from the gods and exorcize demonic influences. In southern Anhui, in several villages the villagers perform a set of plays, some of them quite ancient in form and performance style, while wearing the masks, before sending off the gods and storing away the masks for another year. Annotated texts of these plays are provided in *Selected Plays*. Some of these rare plays are similar in form to Ming dynasty *shuochang cihua* 說唱詞話 (chantefable) versions, as noted in Wang Ch'iu-kuei's paper for the conference. Thus, they are of great importance for the history of theatre in China. In the two case studies dealing with *nuo* performances from northwest Jiangxi, the theatrical side is far less developed, but certain characters are acted out, and mock battles and processions are held. A distinguishing characteristic in all of these instances is the lack of outside ritual specialists.

What is the distribution of specifically designated *nuo* temples with masked dances in south and central China? Tanaka Issei claims that this ritual/performance tradition spread across southern Anhui and northwestern Jiangxi, as well as eastern Hunan (see note 4 below). The *Zhongguo minzu minjian wudao jicheng* 中國民族民間舞蹈集成 volumes on Anhui, Jiangxi and Hunan all provide detailed descriptions of *nuo* dance performances. The Jiangxi volume begins with over 100 pages describing *nuo* performances in the Fuzhou 撫州 region southwest of Nanchang 南昌 (pages 53-171). Subsequent sections are devoted to western Jiangxi, i.e., the Pingxiang 萍鄉 region (171-209) and the Wanzai 萬載 region (210-236). A final section covers the *nuo* dances of

Wuyuan 婺源 in northeast Jiangxi (east of Jingdezhen 景德鎮 which borders Huizhou in Anhui). Another source on Jiangxi *nuo* exorcistic dances is the recent study of Liukeng 流坑 village, in central Jiangxi (Le'an county 樂安縣).[1] Deng Wenqin 鄧文欽 claims that there was only one *nuo* temple to be found in southern Jiangxi or Gannan, namely the Fuzhu Temple of Guantou village of Huangshi township in Ningdu county 寧都縣黃石鄉罐頭村福主廟.[2] From these sources one can conclude that Nuo performances were widespread across northern and central Jiangxi (Yichun 宜春 and Shangrao 上饒), but that they do not appear to be common in predominantly Hakka areas of Gannan.

The Anhui volumes describe the Guichi *nuo* dances (vol. 2, 991-1018) as well as those of Qimen 祁門 county in the Huizhou 徽州 region (1019-1056). The Hunan volume mentions the performance of *nuo* dances in several regions including Hengshan 衡山 and Chenzhou 郴州 (bordering on Jiangxi), and notes that the gazetteers of these regions contain frequent references to *nuo* exorcistic dance and processions (vol. 2, 1084-1179). Clearly more research needs to be done to try to delimit the scope of this trans-regional ritual tradition. One hopes that further research in Anhui, southern Henan, Hunan, and western Jiangxi, will help determine the spread of a highly significant and conceivably very ancient form of communal ritual performance.

I. Summary of the contents of the volumes reviewed

The *Yuanxi Nuo* volume provides a detailed description of *nuoxi* performances by three lineage groups, the Cao and the Jin of Gaoxi village

---

1 Zhou Luanshu 周鑾書, ed, *Qiannian yicun: Liukeng lishi wenhua de kaocha* 千年一村：流坑歷史文化的考察 (*A Study of Liukeng's Historical Culture: A Thousand Year Old Village*. Nanchang: Jiangxi renmin chubanshe, 1997). This is primarily a village history, focusing on lineage organization, which is graphically represented in the layout of the village. One section discusses *nuo* ritual performances in the village.

2 Deng Wenqin 鄧文欽, *Ningdu yichu teshu de miaohui xisu* 寧都一處特殊的廟會習俗 ("The temple festivals of Ningdu"), in Luo Yong and John Lagerwey eds., *Gannan diqu de miaohui yu zongzu* 贛南地區的廟會與宗族 (*The Temple Festivals and Lineages of the Gannan Region*. Hong Kong: Hakka Studies Association, EFEO, 1997), pp. 48-56.

縞溪村, and the Ke of Xu village 徐村 in Guichi, Anhui. This is primarily a description of *nuo* ritual dances, processions, and theatrical performances that took place on Lunar 1/13, 1991, and another performance on New Year's of 1992, with additional information gathered in a visit of August, 1991. The book is organized as follows: first, the geography, population, lineage histories of the three lineages (excellent use is made of Qing editions of lineage genealogies and other local historical records), basic economics and livelihood of the region (again very thorough, based on *xiang*-level sources), beliefs and customs, annual rituals, and temple organization of the village. Next the Nuo festival of New Year's is described, with sections on the timing, organization, funding, participants, audience, and supervision of the festival. The ritual process is next outlined, followed by a section on the performance of the exorcistic plays, with sections on the performance troupe, the process and structure of the performance, and its artistic qualities. Musical scores for a few lines from *Liu Wenlong* 劉文龍 and *Meng Jiangnü* 孟姜女 are provided on pages 91-93. Appendix One lists the characters in *Liu Wenlong*. Appendix Two provides the layout of the ritual masks as set out by each of the three lineage groups discussed in the book. Maps of Liujie township and of Yuanxi village are given on pages 110-111. A map of the *nuo* procession routes within Gaoxi village on lunar 1/13 to the ruins of the Great Temple, and the procession route to the minor *she* (altar of the soil) of lunar 1/15 are given on pages 112-113. Pages 114-174 provide vivid photographs covering the village setting, selections from local genealogies, the nearby caves, the lanterns prepared for the festival, the offerings, the procession (including masked figures), the incense heads, the dancers, the musicians, the performance of the plays (with the *Xiansheng* 先生 (masters) sitting backstage singing and reciting much of the text), the martial arts choreography, the procession to the ruins of the temple, and the ritual masks. Pages 175-231 provide photographs of manuscripts of an invocation to the gods (the *Qing yangshen bu* 請陽神簿), and the scripts of the *Xue Rengui zhengdong* 薛仁貴征東 and the *Hua Guan Suo* 花關索. The book is written in an elegant style, with many classical allusions. The conclusion points to the sexual content underlying the Nuo rites, rather in the manner of Zhu Xi's 朱熹 interpretation of the *Shijing*. And like Marcel Granet as well, the authors celebrate the "orgiastic rites of spring." Caves and lanterns are interpreted as sexual symbols, and the authors highlight the celebration of vitality in these village festivals.

If the *Yuanxi Nuo* volume presents a vibrant and lively account of specific performances of exorcistic drama in the Guichi area, the *Selected Plays* gives a comprehensive treatment of the Nuo ritual traditions in the area, in addition to providing annotated editions of the following seven plays: 1) three versions of *Liu Wenlong*; 2) one version of *Hefan ji* 和番記; 3) three versions of *Meng Jiangnü*; 4) one version of a Bao Gong play (*Chenzhou tiaomi ji* 陳州糶米記; 5) one version of *Hua Guan Suo*; 6) one version of *Xue Rengui zhengdong*; 7) two versions of *Zhang Wenxuan* 章文選. The lengthy appendix (pages 521-646) provides a very useful overview of Guichi exorcistic opera. Photographs are given on pages 647-680.

(Brief summary of a few of these plays): In *Liu Wenlong*, the hero goes off to take the exams, and is given an official post by the emperor. A minister requests that Liu marry his daughter. Barbarian troops attack the border, and Liu is dispatched to fight them. He is defeated and surrenders. Meanwhile, his father forces his wife to remarry a rich man. The earth god then appears, and Liu returns home, whereupon the Jade Emperor saves the day and reunites Liu and his wife's soul.

In the *Meng Jiangnü* plays, the officials call up villagers for the draft. Fan hides in a willow tree and spies Meng taking a bath. They fall in love on the spot. But Fan is forced to depart, and so Meng too sets off to search for him at the Great Wall.

In *Zhang Wenxuan*, Bao Gong 包公 is assigned to judge the case of Zhang, an examination candidate who has traveled to the capital with his wife. The Empress' brother spies her at an inn, seizes her, and eventually kills her. Zhang appeals to Bao Gong who declares his judgement by summoning her soul.

The Appendix to *Selected Plays* gives information in chart form on the clusters of villages and lineages that perform *nuo* plays and rituals together in the region. *Nuo* plays are performed by thirty-seven different groups, consisting of eighty-one villages in eleven *xiang* 鄉 (townships). This same chart (pages 528-533) gives the dates of the Nuo performances of the respective village clusters. Another two charts (pages 602-604; 606-607) show the theatrical repertoire of each of these groups. These groups have between thirteen and forty-eight masks each. The links between many of these village clusters and the Western Temple of Prince Zhaoming 昭明, editor of the *Wenxuan* 文選, are discussed; this was a major pilgrimage site in the area between lunar 8/12-8/15, and probably was at the head of an extended division of incense networks. Other temples are mentioned in the voluminous local lineage genealogies and local historical writings, including the Qingshan miao 青山廟, collectively constructed in the 1330's by a nine-village coalition, and repaired and rebuilt repeatedly throughout the Ming and Qing by this coalition. A lengthy prayer used in some village *nuo* processions in this area, the *Qing yangshen bu* 請陽神簿, lists all the nearby temples and their gods, whether they are still standing or not.[3] Thus there appear to have been several levels of local temple networks in the area. Even the *tudigong* 土地公 shrines are arranged in a hierarchy, with a small shrine at the mouth of the stream, and a larger temple in the heart of most villages. There was also the vast collection of monasteries on nearby Jiuhua shan 九華山, center of the Dizangwang cult. Unfortunately, although there is some mention of *shigong* 師公 and *duangong* 端公 vernacular priests, it is not clear to what degree they were involved in village rituals or the *nuo* performances, although they appear to have some connection with local Mulian 目連 performances. It would be useful to know more about such traditions in this area, in order to better understand the autonomous village ritual tradition.

Some of the *nuo* troupes are formed on the basis of branches within a single lineage (see the chart on page 548). Detailed comments on the organization of these troupes are given on pages 549-50. Funding is primarily on a per capita basis, with individuals contributing three to five yuan each. In one example, eighty-six households took part in supporting the *nuo* rites. Whenever a household has a child (son?), they place a special lantern in the village temple, and other families desirous of children 'steal' these lanterns from the temple, but must supply new ones if they are successful.

The *nuo* processions are occasions for the re-assertion of settlement rights and inter-lineage relations. Thus, four lineages converge on the ruins of a temple, but the Yao 姚 are considered the host, so they wor-

---

3 These are extremely articulate and elegant prayers (see the example on page 564).

ship first. The other three come in one by one and bow before the Yao lineage leaders. The entire exchange is highly formalized; one group waits across the river for another to complete their obeisances, and only enters when they have left the way clear.

A chart on page 541 compares stylistic features some of the lines from the Meng Jiangnü plays from Guichi with songs from Dunhuang. There are two principal styles of lines in the plays, one is seven syllable *changci*, with some lines starting off with three character lines, while the other is the more standard seven word *changci* line. There is extensive influence from Ming *chuanqi* 傳奇 in the repertoire as well, and many *qupai* 曲牌 are from *Qingyangqiang* 青陽腔 or *Gaoqiang* 高腔.

The *Leaping Nuo* volume covers exorcistic processions and rituals in Nanfeng, Jiangxi. This is a very primitive form of Nuo, the authors contend. The *Leaping Nuo* is performed every New Year's between the first and the sixteenth of the month. The authors describe the consecration of the masks by the lacquerer, and the subsequent Daoist consecration service is also summarized. The itinerary of the processions is specified, and the texts of the poems recited at each spot along the procession route are given. A few comparisons are made with the related *nuo* traditions of two nearby villages (where the gods like to eat but not to play). Most important, however, is the description of ritual performance, which is divided into four parts: 'raising *nuo*,' 'performing *nuo*,' 'collecting *nuo*,' and 'rounding off *nuo*.' In the 'collecting *nuo*' section, the troupe goes from house to house to drive off "harmful vapors" (*xieqi* 邪氣). Masked performers playing the Mountain Opener, Zhong Kui and Dashen 開山、鍾馗、大神 strike blows into all the corners of the house with iron chain halberds, and arrest any lingering demons. The authors examine the background of this tradition, and so next they discuss a local source entitled *Discriminating the Nuo Spirit* (*Nuoshen bianji* 儺神辨記), from a Qing Tongzhi period (1862-1874) Yu lineage genealogy from a nearby village, Jinshacun (Jinshacun Yushi zupu 金沙村余氏族譜). The authors also quote Liu Tang's 劉鐋 Song dynasty poem entitled "Observing the Nuo 觀儺詩." The book finally reproduces another interesting brief text, the *Record of the Founding Masters Throughout the Ages of the Ganfang Nuoshen Association* (*Ganfang Nuoshenhuichuan qijiao lidai zongshi pu* 甘坊儺神會傳啓教歷代宗師譜), then presents a map of Shiyou village, along with thirty-six photos of the Nuoshen temple, the procession, the masked dance (two choreographies are recorded on pages 186-187), and the masks themselves.

Mao Limei's *Leaping Goblins of the Ding lineage* is written in a lively, anecdotal style. Based on visits on March 16, 1992, September 15, 1992, and February 28, 1993, she first provides basic information on Wanzai county in western Jiangxi, and on Chixi village. She provides extensive information on the Ding lineage — its history and its current ritual observances. She next describes the "Sandbridge Nuo Temple" (Shaqiao Nuoci 沙橋儺祠), founded in the early Ming, and dedicated to Great General Ouyang of the Golden Armor 金甲歐陽大將軍 and twenty-four *sha* 煞 spirits. All of these gods are represented by large carved wooden masks set on thrones in the temple. Mao Limei explores the legends of these gods, the offerings and ceremonies performed for them, and the dramatic performances associated with their worship. The author describes the traces of their consecration. Mao gives the brief texts and certain musical scores for the passages performed by some of the characters. These are as follows: the Mountain-opener, the Earth-treader, the Vanguard, the Envoys of the Four Divisions of Time, the Green-faced Warrior, Generalissimo Yang, Third Lady Bao (Bao Sanniang) and Guan Suo in a Flowery Costume (Hua Guan Suo), the Little Demon who wriggles through a hoop, the Divine Judge who seizes a little demon, Guan Gong (performed with two different masks), the Divine Boy, the Tale-telling Official, the City God, the Yamen Runner, the God of the Soil, the Recruiting Officer, the God of Thunder, the four Great Heavenly Generals, and the Grand Assembly. Mao Limei goes on to describe 'repayment of vows' rites and the 'sweeping of the home' carried out in individual homes by the God of Thunder, Zhong Kui, and the Four Great Heavenly Officials. In the appendices she provides a map of Wanzai county, and a sketch-map showing the location of the lineage hall, two temples (including the Nuoci) and a Buddhist monastery. She gives the texts of the divinatory poetry of the temple. She also provides the text of a Tongzhi period carved placard hanging in the Nuo temple which has an inscription of a memorial and a more recent prayer. Sketches of the temple, and of some *mudras* are included. She also gives the texts of "fragrant scrolls" – probably handwritten pledges pasted on the walls of temple. A set of photographs of the Nuo temple, the masks, the procession, and some of the performers round out the volume. Mao Limei relies a great deal on interviews in this book, but she carefully identifies each informant.

II. Alternative Contexts: Theoretical and Historical Implications

Tanaka Issei's 1993 work, *Chugokū fukei engeki kenkyū* (*Chinese Shamanistic Theatre*) gathers several case studies related to those given in the four books under review.[4] He provides introductions to the Jiangxi tradition of village exorcistic dance and performance (including notes on the two Jiangxi sites studied by Mao Limei and Yu Daxi and Liu Zhifan). He also describes the Anhui Guichi exorcistic dramas covered in more detail by Selected Plays and Yuanxi Nuo. We can be grateful for the far more detailed and complete accounts provided in the four volumes reviewed.

Tanaka Issei has never been one to shy away from sweeping generalizations. In his 1993 volume, he has arranged over twenty case studies into a continuum ranging from "The Original Form of Village Exorcism" (represented primarily by examples of village tiaonuo 跳儺 or tiaoxiao 跳魈 from northern Jiangxi) to "The Developed Form of

---

4 Tanaka Issei's 1993 volume includes notes on exorcistic masked performances in several villages in several counties of northwest Jiangxi: Under the rubric "Village exorcism in Pingxiang county, Jiangxi 江西省萍鄉縣" he covers the following seven sites — 1) Xiabu xian Tantang cun 下埠鄉潭塘村; 2) Lashi xiang Luqian cun 臘市鄉爐前村; 3) Paishang xiang Maoyuan cun 排上鄉毛圍村; 4) Mashan xiang Xiaheng and Wenquan cun 麻山鄉下亨、汶泉村; 5) Chishan xiang Shitongkou cun 赤山鄉石洞口村; 6) Dongyuan xiang Shiyuan cun 東源鄉石源村); 7) Wanzai xiang Tanbu cun 萬載鄉潭埠村; 8) Nanfeng xiang Shiyou cun 南豐鄉石郵村, 9) Wuyuan xiang Changjing cun 婺源縣長徑村. Under the section entitled "The transformation of village exorcism into Theatre — The Martial Arts Performances" he also provides additional information on 10) Shuinan cun, Nanfeng xiang 南豐縣水南村, Jiangxi. Under the title "The Developed Form of Village Exorcism" (Part 2, Chapters 1-6, pages 355-763), Tanaka provides information on the exorcistic performances and theatrical performances of the following villages in the Anhui Guichi region: 1) Yao lineage rituals of Liujie xiang Yin cun and Maodan cun 劉街鄉殷村，茅坦村姚氏; 2) Liu lineage rituals of Nanshan cun in Liujie xiang 劉街鄉南山村; 3) Wang lineage rituals and theatre from Chaxi cun in Liujie township 劉街鄉茶溪村汪氏; 4) Yao lineage rituals and theatre from Shanli and Shanwai cun in Liujie xiang 劉街鄉山里山外姚氏; 5) the Zhang lineage rituals and theatre of Taihe cun of Liujie xiang 劉街鄉太和章氏村。

Village Exorcism" (beginning with Guizhou Dixi 貴州地戲 and evolving into Anhui Nuoxi 安徽儺戲) to "The Transformation of Village Exorcism — the retrogression of mask theatre" (represented by the Shanxi shangu 山西扇鼓 performance at Renzhuang village in Quwo county 山西省曲沃縣任庄村 and the various Nantong tongzixi 南通童子戲 as well as the Zhao Hou altar rites of Guizhou 貴州省織金縣綺佰村趙侯壇). A supplementary section of the book discusses the diffusion of "family *nuo*" from Han society (represented by the *Dacheng* 打城 (harrowing of hell) rites of southern Fujian and Hainan) to the minority areas (represented by the "passing through the gates of hell" and the "greeting the exorcistic deities" rites of the Tujia in Guizhou). This is an attempt to understand exorcistic theatre on a continuum ranging from primitive communal possession performances via masked theatre to fully self-conscious theatre that nonetheless remains shamanistic.

Tanaka Issei's ideas appear to have evolved slightly since his earlier efforts to classify Chinese theatre according to Marxist categories. In his earlier work he distinguished three venues (noblemen's palaces, rural ancestral halls, and urban markets/fairs) in which he claimed to be able to find distinct generic differences. These were refined stylized plays for nobility, plays emphasizing morality for ancestral venues, and more licentious, entertaining plays for market fairs. He further argued that the same play was performed at different levels of class and culture, using different versions of the script, or improvising around a skeletal script.

In his 1993 study, Tanaka moves away from an exclusive focus on class analysis to a typology based on the intersection of class, lineage and territoriality. He distinguishes three levels of each of the latter two modes of social organization. In the case of the lineage these are: 1) stem or joint; 2) lineage branch organizations; 3) fully developed lineage organizations collectively worshipping a founding ancestor. For territorial organization the three levels are a) scattered, isolated villages; b) village alliances (formed by irrigation, etc); and c) villages clustered around a central market. He suggests that the stem family units are controlled by mid-to-low class landlords, while the branch or complete lineage formations were under the control of upper-class landlords. The village alliances were controlled by peasant householders while the markets were in the hands of the merchants. Tanaka is especially interested in those cases in which a powerful, complete lineage dominates scattered, non-allied, non-market centered villages. In these cases, he suggests that the lineages had control over ritual theatre, and principles of kinship dominated territorial modes. When this control is weakened by the growing independence of tenant farmers, theatre begins to evolve away from its ritual origins. When the pull of the market wrenches social relations entirely away from kinship domination, ritual theatre transforms into "free-market theatre." On the other hand, when lineage domination over stem-families fades away, the plays associated with marriage and funerals give way to more varied forms of family entertainment (birthday plays, etc.). Tanaka Issei also uses this tension between kinship and territorial ties to divide Nuo exorcistic performances between what he calls "*tang nuo*" 堂儺 ([ancestral] hall exorcisms) and "*xiang nuo*" 鄉儺 (village exorcisms).

Although *Chugokū fukei engeki kenkyū* (*Shamanistic Theatre in China*) is over 1200 pages long, it is still difficult for Tanaka Issei to provide enough socio-historical context for each case study to demonstrate the applicability of his class, lineage, and territorial variables. One could point to other factors underlying the preservation of unique ritual and performance traditions, such as a strong sense of local tradition. While we may find Tanaka Issei's categories too confining, it nonetheless provides a productive way to read the four volumes under discussion by paying close attention to the specific forms of social organization and ritual networks they describe. Here we find very rich materials for study of lineage organizations, territorial cults, and collective performances. We see the dominance of lineage forms, but also find traces of larger territorial cults in the ritual circuit to the West temple of Prince Zhaoming near Guichi city and in the processions in Jiangxi Nanfeng. The performance of exorcistic ritual and theatre in relation to the territorial cult is mediated in all the places covered by lineage membership. The lack of a need for ritual specialists (except for the consecration of the masks — which is done in Anhui by the laquerers) deserves special consideration.

The materials presented in the Anhui volumes could be productively linked up with recent research on the socioeconomic and cultural historical studies of the Anhui region (especially Huizhou). Several of the lineages described in the *Selected Plays* and *Yuanxi Nuo* moved to Guichi from Huizhou at the end of the Ming or the early Qing. These

materials provide a more detailed look at the activities of local Anhui
lineages. The economic aspects of similar lineages through the Ming
and Qing are recorded in the account books included in the *Huizhou
qiannian qiyue wenshu* 徽州千年契約文書. The long-term finances of
local territorial cult organizations of this region have also been studied
by Japanese scholars. Thus these materials provide a perfect opportunity
to compare contemporary financing and managing of culture with the
forms and finances of similar groups over a several hundred year period.

These local materials allow us to achieve a more complex view of
the relationship between lineage, territorial cult, and performance traditions than we find in Harriet Zurndorfer's 1989 study. There she points
to the rise of *Yiyangqiang* 弋陽腔 as the defining expression of localism
in Huizhou society. Yet in the *Selected Plays* and the *Yuanxi Nuoxi* we
see the much more complicated survival of local ritual and theatrical traditions. Local tunes mix with *Qingyangqiang*, and chantefable styles
survive alongside archaic modes of theatrical performance (masked
actors, the open presence on stage of the *xiansheng*, the potential danger
to the actor playing the role of Zhou Cang 周倉 if his sword dance is not
brought to a stop at the right moment, the elements of humor when the
children in one village are allowed to take up the sacred masks and
become *xiaogui* 小鬼 while Zhong Kui tries to catch them but mostly
catches young women in the audience by mistake, etc.).

Furthermore, the *Selected Plays* and the *Yuanxi Nuo* make a fundamental contribution to the study of Chinese religion and literature. Not
only are these texts crucial for the study of the history of Chinese theatre, they also provide one of the clearest examples of the unbreakable
link between exorcism and entertainment, between ritual and opera, that
can be found in the world. The literary quality of the texts is impressive,
and the performances, although archaic, are compelling.

The music is also very interesting. The local tunes used in many
nuo performances are so local that they do not even have *chupai* names.
The *nuo* dance has been the subject of a specialized study by Brandl.[5]
Several video recordings have been made of the *nuo* exorcistic performances by ethnographers like J. Pampineau and Brandl. Several videos
that were produced in conjunction with the *Minsu quyi* project are
housed in the archives at National Tsinghua University in Hsinchu,
Taiwan.

There were of course many other ritual and theatrical traditions that traversed the Chizhou 池州 region. Several of these would leave a mark upon the style of local exorcistic drama. Thus for example, Zheng Zhizhen 鄭之珍 actually composed his extraordinarily influential Mulian play, the *Quanshanji* 勸善記, in Chizhou, not far (twenty miles) from the site of the performance of the exorcistic plays of Guichi in Anhui. From there the Mulian plays would spread throughout the regional traditions of China.

Bibliography

Brandl, Rudolf and Wang Zhaoqian. 1997. *Geisterasken im Erdgottkult in Anhui (China), Band IV: de Nuotanze*. Orbis Musicarum.

Dong Zhenya 董振亞, ed. 1995. *Zhongguo minzu minjian wudao jicheng: Anhui juan* 中國民間舞蹈集成 · 安徽卷, 2 vols. Beijing: Xinhua shuju.

Li Chenggang 黎承剛. 1990. "Chizhou Nouxi biaoyan jilue 池州儺戲表演紀略" (Notes on the performance of exorcistic drama in Chizhou), *Min-su ch'ü-i*, 70: 159-183.

Li Jian 李堅 ed. 1992. *Zhongguo minzu minjian wudao jicheng: Jiangxi juan* 中國民族民間舞蹈集成 · 江西卷, 2 vols. Beijing: Xinhua shuju.

Mao Limei 毛禮鎂. 1993. *Jiangxi sheng Wandai xian Tantu xiang Chixi cun Hanzu Dingxing de 'Tiaoxiao'* 江西省萬載縣潭埠鄉池溪漢族丁姓的跳魈(*The Leaping Goblins of the Han Ding Lineage of Chixi Village, Tanpu Township, Wanzai County, Jiangxi*), No. 7. 198 pages. Taipei: Shih Ho-cheng Folk Culture Foundation.

McDermott, Joseph P. 1999. "Emperor, élites, and commoners: the community pact ritual of the late Ming," in J.P. McDermott ed., *State and Court Ritual in China*, pp. 299-351. Cambridge: Cambridge

---

5 Rudolf Brandl and Wang Zhaoqian, *Geisterasken im Erdgottkult in Anhui (China), Band IV: de Nuotanze*, Orbis Musicarum, 1997. Brandl develops an intriguing form of choreographic analysis, which he has apparently linked to computer simulation models as well (personal communication). However, his comments on the socio-psychological functions of the Nuo drama are less sophisticated. See also the list of dances in *Selected Plays*, pp. 583-584.

University Press.

Sheng Jie 盛捷. 1985. "Jiangxi Nuowu diaocha baogao" 江西儺舞調查報告(Introduction to a Survey of Exorcistic Dance in Jiangxi), *Minzu minjian wudao yanjiu* 民族民間舞蹈研究, 1985.2.

Tanaka Issei 田仲一成. 1993. *Chūgaku fukei engeki kenkyū* 中國巫戲劇研究(*Chinese Shamanistic Theatre*). Tokyo: Tokyo Daigaku Toyo Bunka Kenkyujo Hokoku.

Wang Ch'iu-kuei 王秋桂, ed. 1992. *Zhongguo Nuoxi Nuowenhua yanjiu tongxun* 中國儺戲儺文化研究通訊(*Research Newwletter on Chinese Exorcistic Drama and Chinese Exorcistic Culture*), Vol. 1. Taipei: Shih Ho-cheng Folk Culture Foundation.

_____. 1993. *Zhongguo Nuoxi Nuowenhua yanjiu tongxun* 中國儺戲儺文化研究通訊(*Research Newsletter on Chinese Exorcistic Drama and Chinese Exorcistic Culture*), Vol. 2. Taipei: Shih Ho-cheng Folk Culture Foundation.

Wang Zhaoqian 王兆乾 and Wang Qiugui 王秋貴. 1993. *Anhui sheng Guichi shi Liujie xiang Yuanxi cun Cao, Jin, Ke sanxing jiazu de nuoxi* 安徽省貴池市劉街鄉源溪村曹、金、柯三姓家族的儺戲 (*The Exorcistic Drama of the Three Lineages Cao, Jin, and Ke of Yuanxi Village, Liujie Township, Guichi City, Anhui*). No. 8. 231 pages. Taipei: Shih Ho-cheng Folk Culture Foundation.

Wang Zhaoqian. 1995. *Anhui Guichi Nuoxi juben xuan* 安徽貴池儺戲劇本選(*Selection of Scripts from the Exorcistic Drama of Guichi, Anhui*). No. 40. 680 pages. Taipei: Shih Ho-cheng Folk Culture Foundation.

Wang Minli, ed. 1991. *Zhongguo minzu minjian wudao jicheng: Hunan juan* 中國民族民間舞蹈集成・湖南卷, 2 vols. Beijing: Xinhua Shuju.

Yang Qixiao 楊啓孝. 1993. *Zhongguo Nuoxi Nuowenhua ziliao huibian* 中國儺戲儺文化資料彙編(*Collected Materials on Chinese Exorcistic Drama and Chinese Exorcistic Culture*). No. 1. 439 pages. Taipei: Shih Ho-cheng Folk Culture Foundation.

Yu Daxi 余大喜 and Liu Zhifan 劉之凡. 1996. *Jiangxi sheng Nanfeng xian Sanxi xiang Shiyou cun de tiaonuo* 江西省南豐縣三溪鄉石郵村的跳儺(*The Leaping Exorcism of Shiyou Village, Sanxi Township, Nanfeng County, Jiangxi Province*). No. 45. 194 pages. Taipei: Shih Ho-cheng Folk Foundation.

Zhou Luanshu 周鑾書, ed. 1997. *Qiannian yicun: Liukeng lishiwenhua de kaocha* 千年一村：流坑歷史文化的考察(*A Study of Liukeng's Historical Culture: A Thousand Year Old Village*). Nanchang: Jiangxi renmin chubanshe.

Zhongguo kexue yanjiuyuan Lishi yanjiu suo 中國科學研究院歷史研究所. 1991-93. *Huizhou qiannian qiyue wenshu* 徽州千年契約文書 (*A Thousand Years of Huizhou Documents*). Shijiazhuang: Huashan Wenyi Chubanshe.

Zurndorfer, Harriet. 1989. *Continuity and Change in Chinese Local History: The Development of Hui-chou Prefecture 800-1800*. Leiden: E. J. Brill.

II

RECENT DEVELOPMENTS IN THE STUDY OF CHINESE RITUAL DRAMAS:

AN ASSESSMENT OF XU HONGTU'S REASEARCH ON ZHEJIANG

Paul R. Katz

The books from the *Min-su ch'ü-i ts'ung-shu* 民俗曲藝叢書 (Studies in Chinese Ritual Theatre and Folklore Series) being reviewed here are listed below in order of publication in the Series:[1]

1. Xu Hongtu 徐宏圖 & Wang Ch'iu-kuei 王秋桂, ed. & comp., *Zhejiang sheng Mulian xi ziliao huibian* 浙江省目連戲資料匯編 *(Mulian Plays from Zhejiang: A Collection of Materials)*. No. 21, 1994 (hereafter referred to as Xu & Wang 1994). 621 pages.

2. Xu Hongtu, ed., *Shaoxing jiumu ji* 紹興救母記 (*"Mulian's Mother Rescued": A Mulian Play from Shaoxing*). No. 22, 1994 (Xu 1994). 293 pages.

3. Xu Hongtu, *Zhejiang sheng Dongyang shi Mazhai zhen Kong cun Hanren de Mulian xi* 浙江省東陽市馬宅鎮孔村漢人的目連戲 *(The*

---

1 Translations of titles are based on C.K. Wang, "Studies in Chinese Ritual and Ritual Theatre: A Bibliographic Report." I wish to thank Professor Wang for showing me this manuscript. See also *Abstracts of the First Sixty Volumes of "Studies in Chinese Ritual, Theatre and Folklore Series"* (Taipei: Shih Ho-cheng Folk Culture Foundation, 1997).

Mulian Play of Kong Village, Dongyang Municipality, Zhejiang). No. 23, 1995 (Xu 1995a). 203 pages.

4. Xu Hongtu, *Zhejiang sheng Pan'an xian Yangtou cun de xifang le* 浙江省磐安縣仰頭村的西方樂 (*"Delights of the Western Region": A Buddhist Play from Yangtou Village, Pan'an County, Zhejiang*). No. 24, 1995 (Xu 1995b). 248 pages.

5. Xu Hongtu, *Zhejiang sheng Pan'an xian Shenze cun de lianhuo yishi* 浙江省磐安縣深澤村的煉火儀式 (*The Bonfire Play of Shenze Village, Pan'an County, Zhejiang*). No. 25, 1995 (Xu 1995c). 196 pages.

6. Xu Hongtu & Zhang Aiping 張愛萍, ed. & comp., *Zhejiang Nuoxi ziliao huibian* 浙江儺戲資料匯編 (*Nuo Dramas from Zhejiang: A Collection of Materials*). No. 55. 1997 (Xu & Zhang 1997).180 pages.

7. Xu Hongtu, ed., *Shaoxing jiuchao jiumu ji* 紹興舊抄救母記 (*"Mulian's Mother Rescued": An Old Manuscript Mulian Play From Shaoxing*). No. 59. 1997 (Xu 1997). 149 pages.

Perhaps the best kept secret of sinology or Chinese Studies today is that we no longer study "China", at least in terms of culture and society. A key turning point occurred when the late Michel Strickmann (1942-1994) published his penetrating and at times scathing review of Michael Saso's work on Taoism in the 1980 issue of the *Harvard Journal of Asiatic Studies*. Strickmann concluded his review by setting forth an agenda (complete with relevant bibliographic citations) for the study of Fujian's cultural history, and by logical extension the histories of other provinces in China. By that time, social scientists in Taiwan and Hong Kong (including Philip Baity, Stephan Feuchtwang, Maurice Freedman, C. Stevan Harrell, David Jordan, Li Yih-yuan 李亦園, Liu Chih-wan 劉枝萬, Daniel Overmyer, Gary Seaman, James and Rubie Watson, Arthur and Margery Wolf, etc.) had already compiled an impressive body of knowledge, while G. William Skinner had also published his work on market systems and macroregions based on field research in Sichuan.[2]

---

2 For data on even earlier efforts by Chinese folklorists, see Hung Chang-tai, *Going to the People: Chinese Intellectuals and Folk literature, 1918-1937* (MA, Cambridge: Harvard University Press, 1985).

In Taoist studies, Kristofer Schipper led the way with his detailed studies of the Taoist master Ch'en Jung-sheng 陳榮盛 as well as the religious system of Tainan and its environs, while in sinology broad-minded scholars such as Derk Bodde, K.C. Chang 張光直, Wolfram Eberhard, Piet van der Loon, and Edward Schafer had begun to explore China's cultural history at the local and regional levels. In the two decades since Strickmann's review was published, additional path-breaking research has been done by Ch'iu K'un-liang 邱坤良, Chuang Ying-chang 莊英章, Kenneth Dean, David Faure, Hamashima Atsutoshi, David Holm, David Johnson, Susan Naguin, Kanai Noriyuki, John Lagerwey, Li Feng-mao 李豐楙, Lin Mei-rong 林美容, Steven Sangren, Sawada Mizuho, Helen Siu, Michael Szonyi, Tanaka Issei, Barend ter Haar, Wang Mingming 王銘銘, Barbara Ward, Robert P. Weller, James Wilkerson, Ye Xian'en 葉顯恩, and Yü Chün-fang 于君方. The research these scholars have done thus marks a watershed in our ability to view China as a collage of vibrant local and regional cultures.[3]

The gradual opening of China to ethnographic and historical research during the 1980s and 1990s constituted an immense boon for those interested in researching China's cultural history at the local level, and scholars from all fields wasted little time in taking full advantage of it. One shining example of the fruits such research can bear has been the work of the Shih Ho-cheng Folk Culture Foundation, undertaken mainly under the auspices of C.K. Wang (Wang Ch'iu-kuei). The journal *Min-su ch'ü-i* 民俗曲藝 (founded in 1980 by Ch'iu K'un-liang; C.K. Wang assumed the editorship beginning with the 61st issue in 1989), regularly features articles and special issues on Chinese rituals and ritual dramas, topics which have also been thoroughly explored at a number of important conferences sponsored in part by the Foundation over the past few years. In addition, newsletters on Chinese *nuo* dramas/culture (*Zhongguo Nuoxi, Nuo wenhua tongxun* 中國儺戲儺文化通訊; 1992, 1993) and rituals (*Zhongguo yishi yanjiu tongxun* 中國儀式研究通訊; 1995, 1997) have effectively summarized the results of research on

---

3 See the two part series of essays entitled "Chinese Religions: The State of the Field," *Journal of Asian Studies*, 54.1 (February 1995): 124-160, 54.2 (May 1995): 314-395, edited by Daniel L. Overmyer. See also Anna Seidel, "Chronicle of Taoist Studies in the West 1950-1990," *Cahiers d'Extrême Asie*, 5 (1989-1990): 223-347.

these topics. Perhaps the crowning achievement of the Foundation has been the on-going publication of a series of texts, collections of materials, and field reports entited *Min-su ch'ü-i ts'ung-shu* (Studies in Chinese Ritual Theatre and Folklore Series), funded in large part by the Chiang Ching-kuo Foundation and the National Science Council of Taiwan. The results of this publication project have been truly impressive, and the importance of the *Series* in enhancing our understanding of Chinese local and regional cultures can hardly be exaggerated. Reviewers from all over the world have rightly lauded the *Series* as "a project that will bring glory to its sponsors for generations to come" and "one of the most important monuments to Chinese culture to have been published this century." The *Series* has also been commended for its methodological rigor, with one reviewer noting that all the authors in the *Series* have undergone special training in fieldwork methods.

This review focuses on the seven volumes in the *Series* comprising the results of Xu Hongtu's research on the rituals and ritual dramas of Zhejiang province. I summarize the contents of these volumes, praise their strengths and criticize their weaknesses. The review concludes with suggestions that Xu's research on Chinese rituals and ritual dramas might be made more accessible to the entire academic world, so that scholars may fully appreciate the importance of what has been accomplished.

Xu Hongtu's career has been notable for his accomplishments in the study of Chinese culture in general, and local ritual drama traditions in particular. Xu graduated from the Chinese Literature department of Zhejiang Teacher's College in 1968, and taught at a middle school in Pingyang County from 1967 until 1983. Since 1984, he has been on the research staff of the Zhejiang Provincial Institute of the Arts, and has also been an editor of the Zhejiang section of the *Zhongguo xiqu zhi* 中 國戲曲志. In addition to the publications reviewed below, he has written two books on Chinese drama, and over forty articles about drama and ritual dramas.[4] Xu has also helped complete two volumes on Zhejiang's liturgical traditions, which will soon be published as part of

---

4 Including articles published in volumes 84, 92, and 100 of *Min-su ch'ü-i*. Xu and other scholars have also published numerous useful articles on Zhejiang ritual dramas in the series *Zhongguo minjian wenhua* 中國民間文化.

the *Zhongguo chuantong keyiben huibian* 中國傳統科儀本彙編.

Xu Hongu deserves the highest commendation for undertaking such thorough research on one of China's most important provinces. Beginning in the Neolithic era, Zhejiang was home to advanced cultures such as Hemudu and Liangzhu (see below), and has remained one of China's socioeconomic and cultural heartlands up to the present day. Xu's broad-based historical research and detailed field studies on Zhejiang's ritual and dramatic traditions have gone a long way towards helping us better understand this province's bountiful cultural history. In the pages below, I plan to discuss Xu's research according to type of publication, not order of publication. Accordingly, I start with the two collections of materials, proceed to the two edited scripts of Mulian operas, and conclude with the three field reports.

I. Collections of Materials

The collection of materials on Mulian dramas from Zhejiang, co-edited by Xu Hongtu and C.K. Wang (Xu & Wang 1994), represents an accomplishment of some note.[5] The first such work devoted to the Mulian dramas of a single province, its 600-plus pages contain a wealth of data which is sure to spark further research on Zhejiang's cultural history. The text itself is divided into the following parts:1) Introduction (pp.13-24); 2) Records of Mulian dramas in local gazetteers (26-59); 3) Records of Mulian dramas in works about drama in Zhejiang, including two lengthy descriptions of mime performance (60-181); 4) Excerpts from late imperial scripts and the writings of contemporary literati, including Wang Yangming 王陽明, Qi Biaojia 祁彪佳, and Zhang Dai 張岱 (182-202); and 5) Assessments of modern scholars, from Lu Xun 魯迅 to Xu Hongtu himself (203-464). There is also an appendix containing a report on Mulian dramas by the cultural authorities of Sui'an 遂安 County (465-474), as well as three tables (474-513),[6] 214 illustra-

---

5 For more on Mulian dramas, see David Johnson, ed., *Ritual Opera, Operatic Ritual* (Berkeley: University of California Press, 1989), as well as Hou Jie's review in this volume.

6 Including Tanaka Issei's "Comparative Table of Eleven Mulian Scripts" on pp. 496-513, which is erroneously listed in the Table of Contents as starting on p. 465.

tions (515-570), and twenty-five scores (571-621). The materials derive from a broad range of primary and secondary sources, and have been painstakingly transcribed. The entire work constitutes an invaluable research aid for scholars working on Zhejiang's cultural history.

Despite the quality of scholarship in this volume, however, the introduction is somewhat disappointing. In general, introductions to scholarly writings (including collections of materials) are of the utmost importance in ensuring that the reader can both understand the topic under discussion and appreciate the significance of previous and current research on this topic. Accordingly, most introductions attempt to achieve the following goals: introduce the topic, summarize previous research while also presenting any new breakthroughs by the author/editor, and assess the nature of the sources used in studying the topic, particularly their strengths and weaknesses. Unfortunately, the introduction to this collection of materials merely opens with some speculative comments about the origins of Mulian dramas in Zhejiang, and then proceeds to describe their geographic distribution. The scholarship is thorough and detailed, but does little to help the reader grasp the nature and overall significance of the wealth of data presented in the next 600 pages. Important questions regarding the geographic distribution of Mulian dramas are also left unanswered. According to the Introduction, Zhejiang has six types of Mulian dramas. Based on the data presented in both the Introduction and the text itself, it is abundantly clear that these dramas were (and still are) most frequently performed in the northern and central regions of Zhejiang, particulary Hangzhou 杭州, Jinhua 金華, Ningbo 寧波, and Shaoxing 紹興. One would also have hoped that Xu and Wang would have gone on to explain the factors behind such a geographic distribution, but this problem is not discussed at length. The criteria underlying the above-mentioned system for classifying Mulian dramas are also unclear. Does such a system reflect the ideas of the performers themselves or the scholars who have studied them? It is also regrettable that Zhejiang's dialect sub-regions, which have been thoroughly researched by historical linguists, are not considered as factors contributing to this distribution.[7]

---

7   The extent to which the above-mentioned regional ritual drama traditions overlap with macroregions has yet to be determined. However, it is important to note that G. William Skinner origi-

Another important problem which the introduction neglects to mention involves the process by which materials were chosen for inclusion. This is particularly apparent in the section on local gazetteers. On reading through this section, it soon becomes apparent that most of the accounts cited are about Ghost Festival rites, while less than one-third (16 out of 67 entries) actually mention Mulian dramas by name (4 out of 7 entries for Shaoxing, 4 for Hangzhou, 3 for Ningbo, 3 for Jinhua, 2 for Wenzhou 溫州, and none at all for Lishui 麗水, Jiaxing 嘉興, Taizhou 台州 and Zhoushan 舟山). While gazetteers are infamous for omitting much useful data for the study of local culture, there seems to be no reason to assume that mention of Ghost Festival rituals must indicate the presence of Mulian dramas. Indeed, the data presented in subsequent sections of the collection reveal that Mulian dramas were only rarely performed in Lishui, Jiaxing, Taizhou, and Zhoushan. The 1930 edition of Sui'an's county gazetteer even states that Mulian dramas were infrequently staged there, and then only as a response to natural disasters (Xu & Wang 1994:35).

Criteria for inclusion and categorizaton of materials are also a relevant issue for the longest portion of the book, assessments of modern scholars. For example, the writings of Lu Xun, Zhou Zuoren 周作人, Zhou Yibai 周貽白 and others are clasified as "Miscellaneous Discussion" (*zatan* 雜談), while articles by Xu Hongtu, Xu Sinian 徐斯年, and Luo Ping 羅萍 are classified as "Critical Discourses" (*pinglun* 評論). Again, the reader does not know how this classification system came to be formulated. We are also at a loss as to why certain articles by Xu Hongtu and Luo Ping were selected for inclusion in the collection, while others were left out. Clearly not every scholarly paper could have been included, but one would like to be somewhat informed of the overall editorial process behind such an important academic project.

The collection of materials on Zhejiang *nuo* dramas (*Nuoxi* 儺戲) edited by Xu Hongtu and Zhang Aiping 張愛萍 (Xu & Zhang 1997) is

---

nally intended macroregions to be used only in the study of urbanization in nineteenth-century China. While it is true that some scholars have adopted macroregions in their research on China's social and cultural history, there seems to be no compelling reason to chose macroregions over dialect regions as a means of understanding the development of local/regional cultural traditions.

much shorter than the Mulian collection (only 180 pages in length), but no less important. This collection provides a wealth of data on various exorcistic rituals and ritual dramas which have been performed and in some cases continue to be performed in Zhejiang. The collection itself is divided into three parts: 1) Gazetteer entries (pp. 16-38); 2) Accounts by literati from the Song through Qing dynasties (pp. 39-47); and, 3) Assessments by modern scholars (pp. 48-153). There is also a lengthy appendix full of photographs of the masks used in some *nuo* dramas, as well as actual modern performances.

The introduction to the collection (pp. 2-15) is markedly better than that of the Mulian collection, particularly since Xu and Zhang start out by defining what they mean by *nuo* dramas. The authors choose a broad definition covering all manner of "dramatic performances to thank the gods" (*choushen xi* 酬神戲), including dramas performed at funerals and exorcistic dramas performed during epidemics or other crises (Xu & Zhang 1997: 2). However, this definition turns out to be highly problematic for two important reasons. The first reason is that not all the rituals described in the volume are dramas. One striking example involves Wenzhou's boat expulsion festival, the subject of my first book, which is treated in some detail on pp. 31-33, 45-47, and 136-146. This mammoth weeklong festival, which centered on the cult of the plague fighting deity known as Marshal Wen, did indeed feature all manner of dramatic performances, including exorcistic ritual dramas. However, to treat the entire festival as a *nuo* drama does not make sense in light of the wealth of data we have for this event. The second problem with Xu and Zhang's definition is that in almost all the sources currently available, particularly local gazetteers, the term *nuo* is used as an exonym by local officials to label rituals or ritual dramas which are known by very different autonyms to the people of Zhejiang.[8] One of the most intriguing sections of the introduction may be found on pp. 11-14, where Xu and Zhang provide a month-by-month description of *nuo* dramas based almost exclusively on local gazetteer accounts. However, a careful reading of these texts, as well as other works cited in the collection, soon

---

8 For more on problems social historians face when dealing with autonyms and exonyms, see Barend ter Haar, *The White Lotus Teachings in Chinese Religious History* (Leiden: E.J. Brill, 1992).

reveals that in each and every case the term *nuo* is used as an exonym or label, often applied by officials in an attempt to impose their interpretation upon rites known by other autonyms frequently mentioned in the very same passages. Thus, one must conclude that the very use of the term *nuo* dramas in this volume is open to question; why not simply call these performances "exorcistic ritual dramas?" It also seems a great pity that despite the literally thousands of pages of scholarship produced concerning so-called *nuo* rituals and *nuo* dramas, we have yet to reach a clear consensus as to what exactly we are studying.

The rest of the introduction calls our attention to an extremely important question — the interaction between northern and southern cultures in ancient China. Until relatively recently, most scholars had assumed that "Chinese" culture developed in the central plains region, particularly the area along the Yellow river, and was gradually transmitted southwards by Han Chinese officials, soldiers and settlers. However, archaelogical research in south China during the 1970s and 1980s has uncovered a massive body of data to challenge such assumptions, and the significance of this data is only now beginning to be fully apreciated throughout the field. In the middle section of their introduction (*Ibid.*: 1-11), Xu and Zhang rely on an impressive range of archaeological research (some of which is included in the collection; see for example pp. 107-108) to assert that Chinese *nuo* rituals and *nuo* dramas originated with the Hemudu and Liangzhu cultures and then spread northwards, contravening conventional wisdom which states that these rites developed in north China and spread southwards. To support their claims, Xu and Zhang point out that the renowned Liangzhu jades((particularly *cong* 琮)have four eyes (one pair divine or human, one pair animal), the same number of eyes featured on bearskin masks used by Fangxiang 方相 exorcists in ancient north China (*Ibid.*: 4-5). They also call our attention to the *Taotie* 饕餮 patterns and Taotie creatures featured on many Liangzhu jades, as well as the fact that some ancient texts compare the exorcistic characteristics of the spirits Taotie and Fangxiang (*Ibid.*:6). Xu and Zhang also note that ancient writings describe the Yue people of south China (including Zhejiang) as frequently employing shamans to worship ghosts, and that the Liangzhu culture placed great importance on mortuary rituals, rites which frequently involved *nuo* rituals (in *north* China; *Ibid.*: 6-7). Finally, archaeological research by K.C. Chang and other scholars indicating that Liangzhu jades were used in north China is also cited in some detail (*Ibid.*: 7-9). Xu and Zhang then conclude that the ancient *nuo* rites of the Liangzhu culture appeared before the *nuo* rituals of the central plains, and that the "shamanistic *nuo* culture" (*wunuo wenhua* 巫儺文化) of the Xia, Shang and Zhou dynasties was based on Liangzhu culture (*Ibid.*: 9-10).

Having been trained as a social historian and not as an archaeologist, it is difficult for me to comment intelligently on such a key problem. I would only note that neither scenario-southward transmission from north China or northward transmission from south China-appears to be undergirded by a convincing body of evidence. In the present case, the fact that the Hemudu or Liangzhu cultures interacted with northern cultures such as Yangshao, Dawenkou, and Longshan does not prove that one culture's rituals or ritual dramas decisively shaped the other's. Furthermore, Yangshao pottery also appears to feature masked figures, making one wonder if perhaps two distinct traditions (*nuo* or otherwise) might not have appeared at roughly the same time (cogeneration)? At any rate, Xu and Zhang deserve credit for bringing this important problem to our attention. One hopes that future archaeological research may help resolve it.

II. Scripts of Dramatic Performances

Xu Hongtu has performed a great service to the field by editing a Shaoxing version of the drama entitled "Mulian's Mother Rescued." The script for this play, which unfortunately is undated, consists of eight *juan* comprising 107 scenes. The plot describes how Mulian's father, Fu Xiang, cheated the local poor and was punished by the Jade Emperor, who sent down a baleful star to drive him into bankruptcy. Fu repented and became a Buddhist, but his wife, Ms. Liu, committed all manner of heinous sins against that religion. Upon her death, she is cast into purgatory, where she undergoes the most hideous of tortures. Happily, her son, Fo Luobo (literally "Turnip") goes on a quest to find the Buddha and ends up being converted to Buddhism by the bodhisattva Guanyin 觀音. He then enlists the aid of various Buddhist patriarchs and rescues his mother from the underworld.

The script for this play circulated among Shaoxing performers of Mulian dramas for generations, before being collected in 1956 by an organization of performers entitled "the Home of Shaoxing Artists" (Shaoxing yiren zhi jia 紹興藝人之家). This organization then gave the script to the Zhejiang Bureau of Culture, which included it as volumes 76-79 of a mammoth collection (for internal; *neibu* 內部; circulation only) of Zhejiang dramas entitled *Zhejiang sheng xiqu chuantong jumu huibian* 浙江省戲曲傳統劇目彙編 (1958). One would like to know more about the history and functions of these two organizations, particularly since the original manuscript apparently disappeared while in their possession (Xu 1994: 9, 11). In editing "Mulian's Mother Rescued", Xu Hongtu relied on the 1958 edition of the script, as well as another version in a 1962 collection of Shaoxing dramas (*Ibid.*: 10-11, 12). Four other versions were also consulted. Xu's edition presents the script largely in its original form-the only changes involve punctuation, the correction of incorrect or variant Chinese characters, and the use of end notes to explain dialect words (the entire drama was meant to be performed in the Shaoxing variant of Wu dialect). This reviewer's lack of training in Chinese drama makes it difficult to systematically evaluate the quality of the editing, but it seems to have been thorough and meticulous. However, Xu might have considered placing the explanations of dialect words in parentheses in the text, instead of endnotes.

My only other criticism, admittedly minor, involves Xu's introduction. As in the case of the collections of materials described above, the introduction merely summarizes the contents of the material studied, but fails to explain its significance or why it was chosen. Apparently numerous scripts from Zhejiang were collected by performers and the state during the 1950s and early 1960s. How many of these were Mulian dramas? Why was this particular script selected for inclusion in the *Min-su ch'ü-i ts'ung-shu*? Due to its length? The quality of the script? Because it was frequently performed? We can only guess. Xu's introduction does inform us that this text contains some scenes apparently lacking in other versions of Mulian dramas (in Zhejiang or all of China?), but the significance of this fact is left unexplored. Xu might also have included some information about the importance of the Shaoxing Wu dialect during actual performances. All in all, though, the preservation and editing of this text represents an important achievement in the study of Chinese local dramas.

More recently, Xu Hongtu has edited another version of a Shaoxing drama entitled "Mulian's Mother Rescued," which was published last year (Xu 1997). Based on a sacrificial colophon appended to the end of this script (see Xu 1997: 8, note 1), Xu concludes that this particular edition was written in 1883, and belonged to an organization of Taoist priests known as the Jingyi Tang 敬義堂. Xu does not tell us about how this volume came to be in his possession — was it given to him by Taoists, a colleague, or one of the above-mentioned organizations which collected such scripts? Xu does indicate that the eminent scholar Zhao Jingchen 趙景琛 once possessed a copy of this script, but does not state whether or not this is the very script published in the Series. Both Xu and Zhao argue that this script may have been in circulation as early as the Ming dynasty (*Ibid.*: 5, 8 note 2). Xu makes a convincing effort in comparing this particular script to others from Shaoxing, pointing out that while the plot structure is roughly the same, the score and spoken parts of the 1883 script are different, and the entire text is marked by the addition of a number of comic acts. Again, Xu is to be commended for his ability to thoroughly edit this text while also respecting its original dialectical and vernacular features; but one also wishes that Xu had told us more about why this script was chosen for publication. He does indicate its popularity, its age, and its links to Taoist performance traditions in Zhejiang (*Ibid.*: 5-6), but does not indicate whether it was these or other factors which merited this particular script being published. In particular, one would like to know if more such texts exist, if they have already been published, and if there are plans to publish them in the future. In fact, the first of the three field reports discussed below is also about a Mulian ritual drama performed by a Taoist troupe.

III. Field Reports

The three field reports published by Xu Hongtu represent the fruits of painstaking research and exhaustive fieldwork. They not only describe a wide range of ritual dramas, but also provide important data on the socioeconomic conditions of the areas in which these are performed. In addition, they also include thorough descriptions of the performers, from biographical data on key troupe members to a detailed inventory of costumes, props, instruments, etc. Xu's narrative and analysis are also supplemented by maps of the field sites, as well as texts, scores, illustrations, photographs, and line drawings which aid the reader in understanding in detail how such ritual dramas are performed. All in all, Xu's reports clearly constitute an achievement of major importance.

Despite the diversity of ritual dramas covered, Xu's three field studies have a number of points in common. To begin with, they all focus on the Jinhua sub-region of central Zhejiang, although why Xu chose to do fieldwork here and not in other areas of Zhejiang possessing extant traditions of ritual drama (i.e., Shaoxing or Ningbo) is unclear. All three reports also adhere to a single organizational structure. Chapter One describes the field site, Chapter Two gives background information on the ritual, Chapter Three presents an account of the ritual, Chapter Four provides information on the performance troupes (be they actors or religious specialists or both), and Chapter Five recounts the details of the performance. This structure is generally effective, but also presents some problems, especially since the interested reader is obliged to continuously flip back and forth between chapters Three and Five in order to piece together the details of a particular ritual or ritual drama performance. Xu's presentation of the data might have been more coherent had he chosen to place the accounts of the rituals and dramas together. Inasmuch as Xu himself states that the subject under investigation is ritual drama, to artificially separate the description of the performance into two chapters (one for ritual, one for drama) seems somewhat inconsistent.

There are also a few minor flaws in all three reports. The tables of contents do not indicate the presence of endnotes and bibliographies, while the maps are merely sketches traced by hand. The former problem can be easily solved, but inasmuch as this series is in part a study of local cultural traditions, one sincerely hopes that the editors of future volumes will be able to find sufficient funding to produce maps of professional quality.

The first field report (Xu 1995a) describes a Mulian drama performed in 1992 by a Taoist troupe in Kong Village of Dongyang Municipality on the nineteenth day of the second lunar month (the birthday of the bodhisattva Guanyin). Xu spent one month in Kong Village doing fieldwork on local ritual dramas. This particular Mulian drama was performed at the Luoqie Gong 落茄宮, a local temple and regional pilgrimage site dedicated to Guanyin, and accompanied an annual Taoist ritual to save the souls of dead males entitled "The Civilized Ritual of Merit of the White Crane Riding the Mist" (Baihe jiawu wenming gongde daochang 白鶴駕霧文明功德道場).[9] Xu also mentions an extant Taoist rite for the souls of dead females, entitled "The Ritual of Merit of Lotus Flowers Riding the Mist" (Lianhua jiawu gongde daochang 蓮花駕霧功德道場), which might be an interesting subject for future research (Xu 1995a: 14, 17, 64-65).

Chapter One introduces Kong Village, a mountain community of 320 people, the vast majority of whom bear the surname Chen (what happened to the Kong's, if in fact any ever lived there, is not explained) (*Ibid.*: 2). Although Xu states that Kong Village is relatively isolated and backwards, he also presents data indicating that the villagers engage in a thriving trade in Chinese medicines (as do the inhabitants of the other two communities described below), and that the Luoqie Gong is a bustling pilgrimage site (apparently becoming so during this century) (*Ibid.*: 2, 4, 21, 23-24, 37, 74-75). Chapter One also provides a thorough account of the Chen lineage, as well as important data on local marriage and adoption practices. The Luoqie Gong and its ritual association are also described in some detail, as are the village's annual ritual observances. The only problem with Xu's presentation of the data in this chapter (as well as subsequent ones) is that information on the local economy, temple histories, etc. is sometimes presented without any annotation (*Ibid.*: 4, 8, 54). Furthermore, Xu occasionally places too much faith in genealogies as sources to date events in village history, particularly in cases where the dates given are five to six centuries before the genealogy was written (see for example (*Ibid.*: 3)). Fortunately, these problems occur less frequently in the description of Yangtou village, and have been almost completely eliminated in the account of Shenze Village (see below).

Chapter Two gives background information on the White Crane rit-

---

9 The term "civilized" was only recently added to the ritual's title as a nod to government policy (Xu 1995a: 17). Xu's reports mention a number of interesting phenomena pertaining to the relationship between state and society in post-Cultural Revolution China (see below).

ual. Xu cites a wide range of late imperial sources on mortuary practices in Zhejiang, but most of the data derives from the Qing literatus Fan Zushu's 范祖述 late nineteenth century account of Hangzhou customs entitled *Hangsu yifeng* 杭俗遺風 (*Ibid.*: 18-19). It is not at all clear that such practices were identical in Dongyang or Kong Village; the one passage Xu provides from the 1828 edition of the Dongyang county gazetteer contains a thorough account of local mortuary practices but does not metion the White Crane or related rites (*Ibid.*: 20-21). The remainder of the chapter has important information on the temple committee of the Luoqie Gong, as well as the areas pilgrims to the temple come from.[10] Data on temple expenditures are also provided.

The two most intriguing, and in some ways disappointing, sections of this chapter are where Xu presents the result to his interviews in the field. For example, Xu makes the interesting observation that many worshippers can accompany the chanting of scriptures to Guanyin recited during the rites, but that young people seem less interested in them (*Ibid.*: 25). However, he also identifies and quotes both the village headman and a member of the temple committee (both have the surname Chen), and both staunchly maintain that their village's ritual is not some form of "superstition"(*mixin* 迷信) (*Ibid.*: 23-24; see also a similar statement by the Taoist priest in charge of the ritual quoted on p.51). These statements sound exactly like what some uncertain informants tell ethnographers during the initial interviewing phase, and raise some questions about Xu's fieldwork, particularly since Xu himself refers to the entire performance as "superstition" on p. 37 while informing us that some of the interviewing was conducted during so-called "villager discusson sessions"(*cunmin zuotan hui* 村民座談會).

Chapter Three presents a brief account of the White Crane ritual, which lasted from the evening of the eighteenth day of the second lunar month to the afternoon of the nineteenth. One of the penitential liturgies used in this rite is also photographically reproduced in the appendix on pp.108-161. Xu begins by presenting the layout of the Luoqie Gong and the Taoist altar (the latter was set up in the village assembly hall, apparently due to a lack of space). Biographical data on each member of the

---

10 The work of Lin Mei-rong and other scholars on so-called "ritual spheres" (*jisi quan* 祭祀圈) might have been helpful here.

Taoist troupe is also furnished. The actual description of the ritual consists mainly of excerpts from relevant scriptures and songs; terms are
not explained and few details are provided as to how the rituals were
performed. Xu does inform us that this very same Taoist troupe then
proceeded to perform Mulian opera throughout the night of the nineteenth, but the opera is not discussed until Chapter Five. Chapter Three
ends with brief descriptions of the Taoists' ritual implements, as well as
summaries of villagers' stories about Guanyin's miraculous powers.

Chapter Four contains some of the most interesting and important
information of this field study, especially concerning the Taoists who
perform both the rituals and dramas. We learn that this troupe, headed
by a Taoist/ actor named Zhu Fuyu 朱福雨 (born in 1928), was formed
during the Republican era (the exact date is not given), and performs
both Buddhist and Taoist rituals and dramas (*Ibid.*: 43; see also p. 72).
Xu also informs us that Zhu was arrested and his performances outlawed during the Cultural Revolution, but that they continued to persist
in secret (*Ibid.*: 43-44). In recent years, the troupe has engaged in over
200 performances (*Ibid.*: 44). Biographical data on the Taoists/actors
and musicians is also provided (*Ibid.*: 45-46), some of which overlap
with data presented on p.28. While the troupe formerly consisted solely
of men, four actresses have recently been admitted. Membership is
divided relatively evenly among individuals with the surnames Chen,
Ma, and Zhu. Data on the troupe's scroll paintings and other items,
patron deity (the Celestial Master Zhang Daoling), and performance
taboos is also furnished. Perhaps the most interesting part of this chapter
is a lengthy biography of Zhu Fuyu, which tells how he started life as a
peasant, became a devout Buddhist after a miraculous cure of his mother's eye disease, and studied Taoist rites under the tutelage of a Taoist
master from Kong village (*Ibid.*: 49-52). This autobiography, plus Xu's
reconstruction of the entire Mulian drama based on interviews with Zhu
(*Ibid.*: 81-107), rank as Xu's most significant achievements in this field
study. Xu also provides brief accounts of Mulian opera troupes in
Yongkang and Shaoxing (*Ibid.*: 52-56, 65), troupes which appear well-
worthy of future study.

Chapter Five features a brief description of the stage, as well as a
synopsis of the plot. Xu then gives information about props, costumes,
instruments, and songs, followed by a four-page summary of the perfor-

mance (*Ibid.*: 60-63). No scores are provided. He also tells us that the troupe possesses masks used in performances, but that many have been lost and that those which survive are not of good quality (*Ibid.*: 57), a fact which may explain why no photos of these masks are included in the book's appendix.

The book's conclusion contains a thought-provoking discussion of Guanyin's links to the cult of the dead, which draws in part on the Chinese translation (in Taiwan) of Glen Dudbridge's book on the Miaoshan 妙善 legend. Xu also quotes in full two Guanyin scriptures which are still chanted by Buddhist women of Kong village while performing the drama entitled "Delights of the Western Region" (*Xifang le* 西方樂), which happens to be the subject of the next field study to be reviewed here. Xu also summarizes a salvation ritual (*po diyu* 破地獄) performed by a troupe with links to Zhu Fuyu's (*Ibid.*: 72-74), and supplies a photographic reproduction of the liturgy on pages 162-187.

Xu Hongtu's second field report concerns the Buddhist drama "Delights of the Western Region" as performed in Yangtou Village of Pan'an County during a prophylactic offering rite known as the "Star of Great Peace" (*Taiping Xing* 太平星) or worshippind the stars (*Baixing* 拜星), which is held in order to express penance and avert misfortune. These ritual dramas were staged a mere three days after the completion of the Mulian drama in Kong Village, and Xu must have expended considerable energy in order to do such detailed fieldwork on both of them. Xu commences the three-page introduction to this work by claiming that the Yangtou version of "Delights of the Western Region" is a unique (*duju tese* 獨具特色) ritual drama, but does not explain what exactly this uniqueness involves. His claim seems a bit odd, particularly since his own data indicate the presence of such performances throughout the area (Xu 1995a: 66; Xu 1995b: 1, 43; Xu 1995c: 24, 25, 37). The remainder of the introduction presents important information about Pan'an county, data which might have been effectively combined with that in Chapter One. Xu also identifies one of the most important tutelary deities of the region and patron deity of the "Delights of the Western Region" troupe, Hugong dadi 胡公大帝, who is said to have been a Song dynasty scholar-official from the area named Hu Ze 胡則 (965-1039). The only sources Xu relies upon, however, are the 1883 edition of the Yongkang county gazetteer and the 1986 gazetteer on

Yongkang customs (also, like many of Xu's sources in all three volumes, a *neibu* publication) (Xu 1995b: 2-3, 52, 54). To his credit, though, Xu did look up Hu Ze's biography in the *Songshi* 宋史 (see *juan* 291, p. 9941) by the time he completed the third field report (Xu 1995c: 30, 67, 71-72, 95). Xu's neglect of the importance of local cults and the role of religion in constructing local culture and society constitutes one weakness of his work.[11]

Xu's data about Yangtou Village presented in Chapter 1 are much more complete and systematic than in the previous volume. Yangtou Village is a mountain community of 771 people, almost all of whom have the surname Ma. Xu furnishes a detailed description of Yangtou's geographic features, as well as its settlement history. Based on an 1838 edition of a Ma genealogy, Xu argues that Yangtou was settled in the thirteenth century. However, at least two of the dates contained in a biography of Yangtou's founder Xu cites appear to be incorrect, and the date for another genealogy Xu uses(Guangxu xinghai 光緒辛亥)never even occurred (the *xinghai* years closest to the reign of the Guangxu emperor were in 1851 and 1911) (Xu 1995b: 6, 52). A substantial body of data are also presented concerning local production and income, although a table describing these data for the years 1988-1992 is presented without any annotation (*Ibid.*: 10). Xu's description of the Ma lineage is both stimulating and thorough. Lineage rules are quoted at length, and Xu provides examples based on informant accounts of how these rules were enforced. The history of the Ma lineage hall, its organization, and its rites are also effectively presented. Chapter One concludes with a lengthy and colorful account of the area's main temples and rituals, including the fire-walking rite examined by Xu in his third and final field report.

Chapter Two presents important background information on the "Star of Great Peace" ritual (and the "Delights of the Western Region" drama as well). Based on informant accounts, Xu concludes that these ritual dramas originated at the end of the Ming dynasty during the bloody rebellion of Li Zicheng 李自成 (*Ibid.*: 22). They were apparently

---

11 "For more on these issues, one should consult the work of Eugene Cooper, who has done extensive research in this part of Zhejiang." See for example his *The Artisans and Entrepreneurs of Dongyang County* (Armonk, NY: M.E. Sharpe, 1998).

first performed only for families, then for groups of families, and finally on behalf of the entire village (*Ibid.*: 22-23). The villagers' concern with ritual purity may be seen by the fact that three days before the ritual dramas commence everyone must abstain from meat and sexual intercourse. The entire village is cleaned up, and all villagers perform ritual ablutions as well. Xu also informs us of an interesting change affecting the organization of the ritual dramas. Whereas in the past authority rested in the hands of those men who ran the Ma lineage hall, beginning in 1992 members of the Ma lineage who also served as local party and administrative leaders were placed in charge. However, inasmuch as some of these men (and/or their wives) had performed and continued to perform in the ritual dramas, this change does not appear to have adversely affected local performances (*Ibid.*: 24, 25). Xu does indicate that while the party/state apparatus does tolerate these performances it also continues to be concerned about such "superstitions," and that the villagers and their leaders where very careful about avoiding any untoward incidents during local performances (*Ibid.*: 28-29).[12]

It is also in the course of reading Chapter Two that we first discover that Xu Hongtu has not been the first to study Yangtou's ritual dramas. On page 23, Xu notes that a team working on the Zhejiang volume of the collection on Chinese folk dances entitled *Zhongguo minzu minjian wudao jicheng* 中國民族民間舞蹈集成 recorded the entire "Delights of the Western Region" performance. In fact, when we turn to this volume's three appendices, we find that two of them (including musical scores and drawings of costumes, props, and dance steps) were published in 1990 as part of this collection. (*Ibid.*: 57-92, 154-167).[13] There is nothing wrong with researching a site that has already been studied, and in many ways Xu's work appears to surpass that done for the folk dance collection. It is also important to note that Xu does provide a detailed reconstruction of the performance of "Delights of the

---

12 For more on the complex relationship between religion and the state in modern China, see Kenneth Dean, *Taoist Ritual and Popular Cults of Southeast China* (Princeton: Princeton University Press, 1993); and, Julian F. Pas, ed., *The Turning of the Tide. Religion in China Today* (Hong Kong: Oxford University Press, 1989).

13 See also Xu 1995c: 102-127, which in this volume's table of contents is not even labelled as being from the *Zhongguo minzu minjian wudao jicheng*.

Western Region" in Appendix 2, based on interviews with the troupe's leader, Ma Shentai 馬深泰 (born in 1946) (see Xu 1995b: 93-153). Nevertheless, Xu should have explained to his readers how his field research for this book and the third field study discussed below drew upon or surpassed the folk dance collection. The logical place for such an explanation would have been the introductions to these books.

The "Star of Great Peace", performed from 9:00 a.m. to 7:00 p.m. on the twenty-second day of the second lunar month, and during the morning of the twenty-third, is the subject of Chapter Three. Xu's description of this ritual, which in some ways resembles the *Lidou fahui* 禮斗法會 of northern Taiwan, is more detailed than that of the previous volume, and contains important passages from the liturgies used by Ma Shentai. The high quality of Xu's fieldwork may also be seen through his interviews with informants concerning the efficacy of these rites, which are quoted at length (Xu 1995b: 37-39). Xu informs us that the "Delights of the Western Region" drama is performed during the night of the twenty-second, but does not actually describe this rite until Chapter Five. He also mentions a boat expulsion(*songchuan* 送船), but does not give any detailed information as to its staging (*Ibid.*: 32, 37, 50; slightly more data may be found in Xu 1995c: 85-86). Two very well-drawn illustrations of the altar and procession routes are provided (Xu 1995b: 172, 173), although no credit is given to the artist who drew them.

Chapter Four, concerning the performers, is rich in detail. Xu provides a fascinating picture of the history and development of the troupes that perform Yangtou's ritual dramas. For example, we learn that most of the performers are women while most of the musicians are men, that performance traditions are frequently passed down from mother to daughter or mother-in-law to daughter-in-law, and that women who marry out of the village often transmit these traditions to their affines (*Ibid.*: 42-43) This chapter also contains detailed biographical information on Ma Shentai and the leading actress of the troupe, Jin Taonü 金桃女 (born in 1951).[14] Ma, a native of Yangtou, is a peasant with a lifelong interest in local religious traditions who has participated in the village's ritual dramas for many years (exactly how long is not clear). Ma trans-

---

14 I am not certain whether this is her real or stage name.

mitted his knowledge to his wife, a spirit-medium named Chen Meixian 陳美仙, who is also an actress in the troupe. Ma also appears intensely dedicated to preserving local traditions. He assisted in the compilation of the folk dance collection metioned above, and has won two prizes from the local cultural authorities. Jin Taonü was born in nearby Shenze Village (the site of the fire-walking rites described below), and from an early age participated in local performances (including that village's version of "Delights of the Western Region" and dramas sung in Anhui dialect). Her reasons for joining Ma's troupe are unclear, but she has gained renown for her portrayal of Mulian in local Mulian dramas, and has also won two prizes from the authorities (*Ibid.*: 41-42).

Chapter Five contains a brief description of the "Delights of the Western Region" drama (the text of the performance may be found in *Ibid.*: 93-153). A total of twenty-nine different dramas are performed during the night of the twenty-second, including Mulian dramas, two different dramas about the Eight Immortals, scenes from the *Journey to the West* and the *White Snake*, dramas about the Northern and Southern Dippers, etc. (*Ibid.*: 44-46). Detailed data, including numerous photographs in the appendices, are also provided about costumes, props, and musical instruments. All in all, the wealth of information presented here is a gold mine for all scholars interested in local dramatic performances in China.

Xu Hongtu's final field report is by far the finest of the three. While the English "Bibliographic Report" for the *Series* translates the term *lianhuo* 煉火 as "tempering fire" or "bonfire play", a more appropriate rendition might be purification (or purging) by fire, because what actually occurs is a fire-walking ritual. This ritual is staged every year in Shenze Village of Pan'an County on the thirteenth day of the eighth lunar month or the ninth day of the ninth lunar month (the Double Yang or Chongyang 重陽 Festival). The rite that Xu saw, and he spent two weeks researching in the field, was held during the Double Yang Festival of 1992. Xu's introduction immediately captures the reader's attention with a breath-taking account of the fire-walking, which describes a Taoist priest performing cathartic and fire-quenching rites around the blazing coals, following which a spirit-medium leads over fifty worshippers across the coals a total of three times. Xu also notes that this rite can be held during natural disasters, but varies on whether it is mainly to ward off epidemics or fires (Xu 1995c: 1, 2, 19, 29, 30, 61-62). Only in the book's conclusion does he provide a thorough typology of this ritual, which informs the reader that depending on the occasion fire-walkings can be held to ward off epidemics, fires, or insects (*Ibid.*: 83-91). Xu's analysis of this rite might have been clearer had this typology been provided in the book's introduction.

Shenze Village's historical development and current conditions are the subject of Chapter One. Xu's account is both clear and convincing, and most of the data are scrupulously accounted for in the notes. Shenze appears to be the largest community Xu has studied, consisting of 2,489 inhabitants, the vast majority of whom bear the surname Chen. Xu also provides interesting data on local marriage and adoption customs, particularly pertaining to uxorilocal marriage and female adoption (*Ibid.*: 10, 11, 15, 34). Lineage organization and lineage rules are also described in some detail (*Ibid.*: 10-18). Chapter One concludes with a brief account of the village's annual rites and its seven temples, as well as their four main festivals. Of these, the first rite(known as "Welcoming the [Gods of the] Altar" or *ying'an* 迎案) is described in great detail, while brief summaries are given of the third("Welcoming the Giant Paper Horse" *ying da zhima* 迎大紙馬) and fourth(eye-opening, dedication, *kaiguang* 開光); the second("Welcoming the Giant Flag" or *ying daqi* 迎大旗) is not described at all (*Ibid.*: 19-21). Xu's description of these rites is indicates an extremely high level of participation in local ritual dramas by both village men and women (*Ibid.*: 20-21, 36-37).

Chapter Two provides important background information on the fire-walking ritual, which Xu, based on informant accounts, dates back to the Song dynasty (*Ibid.*: 29). Xu also describes the participants, the committee in charge of organizing the firewalking and the expenses involved in staging this event. Xu's account informs us that in Shenze fire-walkings are frequently performed to cure diseases, and are staged not only for the entire village but for individual households as well. Rites for individuals are not called *lianhuo* but "Crossing the Fire" or *guohuo* 過火. Xu provides a description of one such rite, but does not indicate when or where it was held. According to Xu, only ritual specialists may fire-walk during these rites, and they must also climb a ladder of swords and bathe in a pot of boiling oil. The fire-walker then grasps a torch in one hand and a sword in the other, and proceeds to capture all demons in the household and trap them in a small grass boat, which is then burned on the outskirts of the village (*Ibid.*:30-31,85-86).[15]

Some of the data presented in this chapter concerning local specialists and participants is a bit unclear. For example, Xu states on page 40 that those who cross the burning coals are stark naked(*chi tiaotiao* 赤條條), only to note one page later that these men are only naked from the waist up.[16] The identity of the ritual specialist in charge of the rites, Zheng Changmao 鄭長茂 (born in 1938), is also unclear. At various points in this chapter and other parts of the text he is referred to as a "mountain man"(*shanren* 山人), "Taoist priest"(*daoshi* 道士), "ritual master" (*fashi* 法師) or "ritual master/mountain man"(*fashi shanren* 法師山人)(*Ibid.*: 1, 37, 44, 67, 68, 229) belonging to the Zhengyi 正一, Lingbao 靈寶, or Zhengyi Lingbao 正一靈寶 movements (*Ibid.*: 7, 34). Xu never clarifies whether these terms represent autonyms used by ritual specialists or exonyms used by the villagers.[17] Furthermore, Xu states that in the past a family of Taoists with the surname Qiu had been in charge of the rites, and that Zheng Changmao is the first man from Shenze to have been initiated into their tradition (*Ibid.*: 34). How the Qiu's came to transmit their knowledge to an outsider is not dealt with until Chapter Four.

Chapter Two also contains highly significant data on how the fire-walking ritual has changed since the founding of the People's Republic of China in 1949. Xu states that Shenze's fire-walking rite was outlawed that very year, but that the villagers continued to hold it in secret. Open performances were only held after 1980, and in 1981 the entire ritual was recorded for inclusion in the Zhejiang volume of the *Zhongguo minzu minjian wudao jicheng* (*Ibid.*: 31-32). A key figure in the revival of this rite has been a cultural official named Chen Yougen 陳友根 (born in 1948; see biographical data on pp. 34-35), who helped arrange

---

15 The conclusion to this rite sounds strikingly similar to boat burnings held for individuals suffering from disease held in Zhejiang and other parts of south China as early as the Song dynasty. See my *Demon Hordes and Burning Boats: The Cult of Marshal Wen in Late Imperial Chekiang* (Albany: SUNY Press, 1995).

16 In addition, photographs on pages 243-244 describe the fire-walkers as half-naked when they are fully clothed.

17 See the reviews in this volume by Brigitte Baptandier, Hsu Li-ling, and Li Feng-mao for more nuanced analyses of Taoist specialists and the roles they play in local society.

the 1981 performance and subsequent stagings, and has shown a profound interest in other local ritual dramas. Chen also appears to have
been one of Xu Hongtu's key informants. Chen has very interesting
ideas about the cultural significance of the fire-walking rites. For example, he thinks that they need to be "neater" (*zhenggi* 整齊), that some of
the Taoist rites can be eliminated, and that the entire ceremony needs to
tone down its religious elements in favor of entertaining ones (*Ibid.*: 32,
37; Xu concurs with these ideas on page 38). Chen also expresses an
interest in making a documentary of the fire-walking (*Ibid.*: 41), and
even arranged a performance at the Pan'an county seat in 1993 (*Ibid.*:
32). It would be interesting to read a field report of Shenze's fire-walking
as it is performed today, and see whether or not it has changed since 1992.

The fire-walking rite is vividly described in Chapter Three. Xu's
account is based on a number of liturgical texts which are photographically reproduced in the book's appendices (whether they belong to
Zheng or the Qiu family or both is not clear). Two altars are set up, a
"Dragon Altar" (*Longtan* 龍壇) to the east of the fire (which burns
down to hot coals) and an "Altar to Heaven" (*Tiantan* 天壇) to the west.
A stage for dramatic performances (see below) is set up to the north of
the Dragon altar. Zheng Changmao inaugurates the rites at the Altar to
Heaven by summoning various Taoist deities, following which he
plunges tridents into the ground at the four corners of the fire-walking
area. Taking his sword in hand, he then performs rites to purify the ritual
area (these are apparently sung, but no scores are provided). Zheng then
sacrifices a chicken, following which various martial spirits are summoned.[18] A *fafu* 發符 ritual.[19] for summoning deities and writing charms
is also performed,[20] and Zheng reads a memorial which is then burned.
Then, in a loud voice, Zheng summons various Taoist, Buddhist, and
local deities (including Hugong dadi), with the audience shouting out

---

18 Many of the rites Zheng performs seem similar to marionette ritual dramas in Taiwan, which are
   described in detail by Song Jinxiu, *Kuilei yu chusha* 傀儡與除煞 (Taipei: Daoxiang chubanshe,
   1994).

19 This ritual has also been studied by Zhu Jianming, who has done research on Jiangsu's ritual
   dramas. See the review of Zhu's work by Poul Andersen in this volume.

20 The deities summoned in this and other rites are not all Taoist but include Buddhist and popular
   ones as well.

answers in the affirmative to his questions. Moonblock divination is also performed to ensure that all the deities are present. Finally, Zheng drinks from a bowl of water, and after pacing, writing charms in the air, chanting mantras and making mudras, spits it onto the coals from the east, west, south and north (*Ibid*.: 44-58).

Zheng's rites are followed by two simultaneous instances of collective possessions. At the stage, the two performance troupes (one which performs "Delights of the Western Regions" and one which performs a masked dance known as "The Big Head Dance" or *Datou wu* 大頭舞) begin to dance in rhythmic motions to induce possession by their deities. This striking example of the overlap between ritual and drama in China deserves much further discussion (which deities possess which performers? for how long?), but unfortunately no further information is supplied. At the altar, the spirit medium Chen Yangmen 陳楊門 (born in 1937) takes charge. Chen, referred to as *jiangtong* 降佃 or *tiaotong* 跳佃(*tong* 佃 appears to be a variant of *tong* 童), is possessed by Hugong dadi and in his voice proceeds to exhort the other fire-walkers(*lianhuo zhe* 煉火者) to exert themselves to the utmost and fear not. Gongs are sounded and the other fire-walkers go into trance, whereupon Chen distributes steel tridents and incense burners to them. Then, holding a bowl of water in hand, he proceeds to the eastern side of the coals and spits some water on them. This is also done in succession at the western, southern, and northern sides. Finally, Chen leads the fire-walkers across the coals from north to south to west to east. After a brief rest, they cross the coals a second and a third time, following which ordinary worshippers are permitted to cross (*Ibid*.: 40, 58-60, 66-67).[21] Xu notes that the ritual area is laid out according to the Eight Trigrams, but does not explain this until the last paragraph of the conclusion (*Ibid*.: 60, 92).

The rites do not conclude with the fire-walking, though. After the coals have been crossed, Zheng Changmao performs a rite entitled "Sweeping away Xiao Demons"(*saoxiao* 掃魈), which is apparently designed to expel various insects (*Ibid*.: 61-62, 89).[22] Finally, a Pudu 普

---

21 Xu reports that mostly young men cross the coals on the spur of the moment. He considered crossing the coals, but decided not to.

22 The term *xiao* 魈 is also used in south China to refer to one legged mountain sprites later worshipped as the Wutong 五通. For more on this cult, see Ursula-Angelika Cedzich, "The Cult of

度 rite for hungry ghosts is held.

Chapter Four also describes various ritual implements, and contains very interesting informant interviews about the efficacy of fire-walking. One particularly graphic account describes how a young man was possessed by fox demons (in *south* China, no less!) and suffered frequent wet dreams until participating in a firewalking (*Ibid.*: 65). Another story tells of a Buddhist monk who tried to hide items in the coals to trip the fire-walkers but ended up being exposed. As a result, Buddhists from a local monastery are required to provide food to the fire-walkers (*Ibid.*: 65-66). It would be very interesting to learn more about the social tensions behind this story.

The performers of the rituals and dramas are described in Chapter Four. This chapter also contains biographical data on Zheng Changmao, Chen Yangmen, and Chen's predecessor Chen Maotian 陳茂天 (born in 1915). Zheng's biography is particularly interesting, as we learn that he was born in a neighboring village and came to Shenze through uxorilocal marriage. As a youth, he performed in local dramatic troupes, and after arriving in Shenze became an apprentice of the Taoist master Qiu Xianzhong 邱顯忠 (1919-1990). We are also told that the Qiu's came from a Taoist village and were considered to be of "mean" status (*dijian* 底賤). For twenty-four generations they did not transmit their teachings to outsiders. One of Qiu Xianzhong's sons, Qiu Zhangzhu 邱章竹 (Born in 1930) is still a practicing Taoist, so why the elder Qiu chose to transmit his knowledge to Zheng is not clear. Xu observes that Zheng is younger and less skilled than Qiu Zhangzhu, but that he will soon be his senior's equal (*Ibid.*: 74-75).

Chapter Five concerns the dramas performed during the fire-walking ritual, specifically "Delights of the Western Regions" and "The Big Head Dance." Some information on costumes, props, and masks is given (see also the photos in the appendices). However, most of the chapter is not devoted to describing these rites but instead presents the

---

the Wu-t'ung/Wu-hsien in History and Fiction." In David Johnson, ed., *Ritual and Scripture in Chinese Popular Religion. Five Studies* (Berkeley: Publications of the Chinese Popular Culture Project, 1995), No. 3, pp. 137-218; and, Richard Von Glahn, "The Enchantment of Wealth: The God Wutong in the Social History of Jiangnan," *Harvard Journal of Asiatic Studies*, 51.2 (1991): 651-714.

fire-walking ritual a second time (*Ibid.*: 79-82). It is here that Xu's decision to treat rituals and dramas as separate units in separate chapters sems particularly confusing.

The conclusion is a masterful work, which not only provides the typology of fire-walking goals mentioned above but also a wealth of comparative data on fire-walking and other fire rituals among Han Chinese and other ethnic peoples in China. Examples from Europe and Japan are also discussed, based on a sizeable body of secondary literature.

Based on the information presented above, we can conclude that Xu Hongtu's research is praiseworthy in the true sense of the word. While this review has at times been critical, I wish to emphasize my profound respect for Xu and his work. Those of us who have devoted a portion of our lives to the study of Chinese culture may differ in terms of goals and methods, but we remain united in our commitment to both appreciating and preserving the subjects of our research. It is in this light that I would like to conclude with a brief discussion of the accessibility of the data presented in these and other volumes in the *Series*. The proposal for the conference about these volumes held in Hong Kong in May of 1998 rightly pronounces one of its goals as being "to inject these field studies into the main-stream of Chinese studies". Unfortunately, however, the current manner in which data on Chinese ritual dramas has been presented in the *Series* makes it difficult to achieve this worthy goal. The volumes are not numbered, no information about their authors in presented, the provinces being researched are not introduced, there is no glossary of specialized or technical terms, and no abstracts or bibliographies of relevant works in Asian and Western languages are included (a brief bibliography of relevant secondary scholarship on the history of Zhejiang religion and society is appended to this review). As a result, the extremely significant data these works contain ends up being accessible only to specialists in ritual studies who read Chinese. Even qualified scholars from other areas of sinology would have a hard time reading through all the data, not to mention students or other nonexperts. Future publications can be designed to correct these matters, but what about the 60 volumes published to date? I would recommend the publication of a research guide for each province studied. This research guide would include a brief introduction to the province's history and development (including professionally drawn maps and up-to-date tables for statistical data), albeit focusing on the areas where ritual dramas were studied. Background information on the researchers who have produced the data should also be included. Lengthy summaries in English (and perhaps French and Japanese) could also be written for each volume of the *Series* covered by a particular research guide. Each guide would also contain a glossary in which technical terms are clearly defined, as well as an annotated bibliography of relevant works in Asian and Western languages which future scholars researching these topics could consult at will. Thus, the entire acadmic world would be better able to understand and appreciate the significance of what the *Series* has accomplished.

Bibliography

Boltz, Judith. 1987. *A Survey of Taoist Literature: Tenth to Seventeenth Centuries*. Berkeley: Institute of East Asian Studies.
———. 1993. "Not by the Seal of Office Alone: New Weapons in the Battle with the Supernatural," in Patricia B. Ebrey and Peter N. Gregory eds., *Religion and Society in T'ang and Sung China*, pp. 241-305. Honolulu: University of Hawaii Press.
Brook, Timothy. 1993. *Praying for Power: Buddhism and the Formation of Gentry Society in Late-Ming China*. Cambridge, Mass.: Harvard University Press.
Cedzich, Ursula-Angelika. 1985. "Wu-t'ung: Zur bewegten Beschichte eines Kultes," in Gert Naundorf, et al., eds, *Riligion und Philosophie in Ostasien. Festschrift für Hans Steininger zum 65. Geburtstag*, pp. 33-60. Wurzburg: Könighausen and Neumann.
———.. 1995. "The Cult of the Wu-t'ung/ Wu-hsien in History and Fiction," in David Johnson ed., *Ritual and Scripture in Chinese Popular Religion. Five Studies*, pp. 137-218. Berkeley: Publications of the Chinese Popular Culture Project, No. 3.
Chan, Leo Hak-Tung. 1993. "Narrative as Argument: The *Yuewei caotang biji* and the Late Eighteenth-Century Elite Discourse on the Supernatural," in *Harvard Journal of Asiatic Studies*, 53.1: 25-62.
Day, Clarence. 1940. *Chinese Peasant Cults: Being a Study of Chinese*

Paper Gods. Shanghai: Kelly & Walsh, Ltd.

Dong Chuping 董楚平. 1988. *Wuyue wenhua xintan* 吳越文化新探. Hangzhou: Zhejiang renmin chubanshe.

Eberhard, Wolfram. 1968. *The Local Cultures of South and East China.* Leiden: E. J. Brill.

Gernet, Jacques. 1962. *Daily Life in China on the Eve of the Mongol Invasion, 1250-1276.* Stanford: Stanford University Press.

Hansen, Valerie. 1990. *Changing Gods in Medieval China, 1127-1276.* Princeton: Princeton University Press.

Hu Pu'an 胡樸安 ed. 1923. *Zhongguo quanguo fengsu zhi* 中國全國風俗誌. Shanghai: Guangyi shuju.

Huang Shi 黃石. 1979. *Duanwu lisu shi* 端午禮俗史. Taipei: Dingwen shuju.

Johnson, David. 1980. "The Wu Tzu-hsü *Pien-wen* and its Sources," in *Harvard Journal of Asiatic Studies,* 40: 93-156, 465-505.

————. 1985. "The City God Cults of T'ang and Sung China," in *Harvard Journal of Asiatic Studies,* 45: 363-457.

————. ed. 1989. *Ritual Opera, Operatic Ritual: "Mu-lien Rescues his Mother" in Chinese Popular Culture.* Berkeley: Publications of the Chinese Popular Culture Project, No. 1.

Kanai Noriyuki 今井德幸. 1985. "Sōdai Sessai no sonsha to dōshin 宋代浙西の村社と土神," in *Sōdai no shakai to shūkyō* 宋代の社會と宗教, *Sōdai kenkyūkai kenkyū hokoku* 宋代研究會研究報告, volume 2, pp. 81-108. Tokyo: Kyūko Shōin.

Katz, Paul R. 1995a. *Demon Hordes and Burning Boats: The Cult of Marshal Wen in Late Imperial Chekiang.* Albany: SUNY Press.

————. 1995b. "The Pacification of Plagues: A Chinese Rite of Affliction," in *Journal of Ritual Studies,* 9.1: 55-100.

Kuhn, Philip A. 1991. *Soulstealers: The Chinese Sorcery Scare of 1768.* Cambridge, Mass.: Harvard University Press.

Lao Gewen 勞格文（John Lagerwey）& Lü Chukuan 呂錘寬. 1993. "Zhejiang sheng Cangnan diqu de Daojiao wenhua"浙江省蒼南地區的道教文化. *Dongfang zongjiao yanjiu* 東方宗教研究, 3: 171-198.

Li Feng-mao 李豐楙. 1994. "Xingwen yu songwen: wenshen xinyang yu zhuyi yishi de yiyi" 行瘟與送瘟：瘟神信仰與逐疫儀式的意義, in *Proceedings of the International Conference on Popular Beliefs and Chinese Culture,* volume 1: 373-422. Taipei: Center for Chinese

Studies.

Lin Yongzhong 林用中 & Zhang Songshou 張松壽. 1936. *Lao Dongyue: Miaohui diaocha baogao* 老東嶽：廟會調查報告. Hangzhou: Zhejiang yinshuaju.

Naquin, Susan & Evelyn Rawski. 1987. *Chinese Society in the Eighteenth Century.* New Haven and London: Yale University Press.

Rankin, Mary B. 1986. *Elite Activism and Political Transformation in China, Zhejiang Province, 1865-1911.* Stanford: Stanford University Press.

Schoppa, R. Keith. 1982. *Chinese Elites and Political Change: Zhejiang Province in the Early Twentieth Century.* Cambridge, Mass.: Harvard University Press.

Shiba Yoshinobu. 1970. *Commerce and Society in Sung China.* Trans. Mark Elvin. Michigan Abstracts, No. 2. Ann Arbor: University of Michigan Press.

———. 1977. "Ningpo and its Hinterland," in G. William Skinner ed., *The City in Late Imperial China*, pp. 391-439. Stanford: Stanford University Press.

Stein, Rolf. 1979. "Religious Taoism and Popular Religion from the Second to Seventh Centuries," in Holmes Welch a& Anna Seidel eds., *Facets of Taoism*, pp. 53-82. New Haven & London: Yale University Press.

Tanaka Issei 田仲一成. 1968. *Shindai chihōgeki shiryo shū* 清代地方劇史料集. Tokyo: Tōyō bunka kenkyūjo.

Ter Haar, Barend. 1995. "Local Society and the Organization of Cults in Early Modern China: A Preliminary Study," in *Studies in Central and East Asian Religions,* 8: 1-43.

Von Glahn, Richard. 1991. "The Enchantment of Wealth: The God Wutong in the Social History of Jiangnan," in *Harvard Journal of Asiatic Studies,* 51.2: 651-714.

Wu Cheng-han. 1988. "The Temple Fairs in Late Imperial China." Ph. D. dissertation, Princeton University.

Xiao Bing 蕭兵. 1992. *Nuo-Zha zhi feng: Changjiang liuyu zongjiao xiju wenhua* 儺蜡之風：長江流域宗教戲劇文化. Nanjing: Jiangsu renmin chubanshe.

Ye Dabing 葉大兵. 1991. "Wen Yuanshuai xinyang yu Dongyue miao-hui" 溫元帥信仰與東嶽廟會, *Min-su ch'ü-i,* 72/73: 102-128

————. 1992. "Wenzhou Dongyue miaohui poxi" 溫州東嶽廟會剖析, in *Zhongguo minjian wenhua* 中國民間文化, Volume 5, pp. 235-251. Shanghai: Xuelin chubanshe.

Yü Chün-fang. 1981. *The Renewal of Buddhism in China: Chu-hung and the Late Ming Synthesis.* New York: Columbia University Press.

————. 1992. "P'u-t'o shan: Pilgrimage and the Creation of the Chinese Potalake," in Susan Naquin and Yu Chün-fang, eds., *Pilgrims and Sacred Sites in China*, pp. 190-245. Berkeley: University of California Press.

Zhejiang fengsu jianzhi 浙江風俗簡志. 1986. Hangzhou: Zhejiang renmin chubanshe.

Zhejiang minsu yanjiu 浙江民俗研究. 1992. Hangzhou: Zhejiang renmin chubanshe.

Zhejiang wenhua shi 浙江文化史. 1992. Hangzhou: Zhejiang renmin chubanshe.

12

ACHIEVEMENTS IN THE STUDY OF THE TONGZI RITUAL DRAMA IN JIANGSU

Zhu Qiuhua

In order to promote the study of local drama and ritual in China, the monograph series of Studies in Chinese Ritual, Theatre and Folklore (*Min-su ch'ü-i ts'ung-shu* 民俗曲藝叢書) has published three special volumes on this topic; namely

1. Cao Lin 曹琳, *Jiangshu sheng Tongzhou shi Henggang xiang Beidian cun Hushi shang tongzi yishi* 江蘇省通州市橫港鄉北店村胡氏上童子儀式 (*The Tongzi Ritual of the Hu Family in Beidian Village, Henggang Township, Tongzhou Municipality, Jiangsu*), No. 31, 1995. 504 pages. Abbreviated as *Tongzi*.

2. Huang Wenhu 黃文虎, *Jiangsu Liuhe xian Ma'an xiang Wuxing cun Song zhuang he Maji zhen Jianshan cun Gongying hanren de jiapu xianghuo shenhui* 江蘇六合縣馬鞍鄉五星村宋莊和馬集鎮尖山村龔營漢人的家譜香火神會 (*The Genealogical Register Incense and Fire Festival of Songzhuang in Wuxing Village, Ma'an Township and of Jianshan Village in Maji Town, Liuhe County, Jiangsu*), No. 41, 1996. 289 pages. Abbreviated as *Genealogical Register*.

3. Cao Lin, *Jiangsu sheng Nantong shi Zhadong xiang hanren Gongyuan cun de mianzai shenhui* 江蘇省南通市閘東鄉公園村漢

人的免災勝會 (*The "Great Festival to Avert Disaster" of Gongyuan Village, Zhadong Township, Nantong Municipality, Jiangsu*), No. 42, 1996. 321 pages. Abbreviated as *Great Festival.*

At about the same time, a number of articles on rituals to dispel pestilence (*nuo* 儺) in the Jiang-Huai region 江淮 were published in the journal *Min-su ch'ü-i*. These include:

1. Cao Lin, "The Tradition of '*Nuo*' in the Jianghai Plain Region: An Overview of Southern Tongzi Ritual" 江海平原上的古儺餘風——南通童子祭祀活動概覽, in *Min-su ch'ü-i*, 70(1991): 183-216. Abbreviated as "Overview".

2. Zhang Guoji 張國基, "A Preliminary Study of the Incense Drama of Liuhe" 六合香火戲初探, in *Min-su ch'ü-i*, 88(1994): 117-140. Abbreviated as "Preliminary Study".

3. Shi Hanru 施漢如, Zhang Ziqiang 張自強 and Yang Wenchun 楊問春, "The '*Nuo*' Ritual and '*Nuo*' God of Nantong" 南通儺祭與儺神, in *Min-su ch'ü-i*, 88(1994): 141-168. Abbreviated as "Nuo God".

4. Cao Lin, "Demigod and Sanjian Jian: An Interpretation" 神人・三尖讜釋, in *Min-su ch'ü-i*, 88(1994): 169-198. Abbreviated as "Interpretation".

5. Zhang Guoji, "An Introduction to the Ritual Music of the Hongshan Sect of Liuhe Shamanism" 六合巫教洪山派儀式音樂簡述, in *Min-su ch'ü-i*, 102(1996): 1-30. Abbreviated as "Introduction".

Nuo rituals to dispel pestilence in the region between the Yangzi and Huai River 淮河 are generally called *tongzi* drama. Based on extensive field research in the region, these articles cover a wide range of issues concerning *nuo* ritual, a continuation of the ancient tradition of *nuo* and the predecessor of *tongzi* drama. The publications I have cited above bring to light the rich cultural content and unique artistic form of these rituals, as well as the transition from ritual to local drama.

I.

The Nantong 南通 region is located in the southeastern part of the Jiang-Huai plain. *Tongzi* ritual, a kind of shamanism, has a long historical existence. One kind of such practices is the "Tongzi Gathering" 童子會, a communal ritual to drive away pestilence. "Ascent of the

Shamans" (*Shang tongzi* 上童子) is part of *nuo* ritual hosted by individual families. *Tongzi* is a case study of this ritual hosted by the Hu household. It records in detail the historical background and customs of Tongzhou City, and the socio-cultural environment of Beidian Village. In light of the origin and organization of *shang tongzi*, it highlights the seventy-six "rituals (執事)" (pp. 95-101) of the *shang tongzi* ritual, particularly the performances of these rituals and the dramatic characteristics of these performances. Also included are the play scripts and the lyrics used in the ritual. The author collected a large quantity of source materials to establish the long historical tradition of *nuo* shamanism, and found that both the ritualization of drama (*yi xi gou yi* 以戲構儀) and the dramatization of ritual (*yi xi jia yi* 以戲夾儀) are integral to *tongzi* ritual itself. *Nuo* is also the result of the mutual influence of Wu 吳 and Chu 楚 cultures from time immemorial. In the appendix, examples of tunes, gongs and drums, and copies of the so-called "hand-written scripts of the underworld" are also given.

Genealogical Register can be divided into three parts. The first part is a brief account of Liuhe county, i.e. the natural environment of Song Village 宋莊 and Gongying 龔營, and the local culture and customs, including the family and social backgrounds of the Zhang and Xu households in charge of the genealogical incense fire festival. The second part introduces the festival in Liuhe, including the names, categories, historical origin and procedures. The third part is a detailed description of the twenty categories of genealogical register incense fire festival (*jiapu xianghuo shen hui* 家譜香火神會). It is obvious that many of these categories are either the prototypes or transformations of ancient ritual music and dancing, the popular stage performances (*xinong* 戲弄) of the Tang dynasty, or miscellaneous proto-dramas of the Song dynasties. This discovery is a great contribution to the study of the origin of drama. The appendix consists of the biographies and heritage of more than one hundred ritual performers and a collection of sacred books (*shen shu* 神書). There is also a list of examples of the dancing and singing involved in the more representative parts of the ritual, i.e. the performance of "dancing ladies" (*tiao niangniang* 跳娘娘) and "releasing a memorial" (*jie biao* 解表).

Great Festival is about the shaman culture in Nantong, where the influence of Wu, Yue, and Chu cultures has been predominant over the centuries. In Nantong, there are more than fifty kinds of religious gatherings to dispel omens and receive good fortune, and *tongzi* ritual is a combination of shamanism and medicine. This book records the complete process of a triumph over pestilence gathering supported by solid research on its historical origin and ceremonial structure, including the performing troupes and biographical details about the performers. Attention is drawn to the performance style, singing and the use of gongs and drums, costumes and props to illustrate the characteristics of the ritual and its dramatic form. The author also verifies the relationship between the "sanjian" (literally three spikes) sacred crown 三尖神冠 and shamanic *nuo* culture. The appendix consists of a list of the rituals of the *tongzi* gathering, the handbook of the butcher, and manuscripts of the "black pig" dedication ceremony (*wuzhu kaiguang* 烏豬開光), the "table of the celestial immortals" (*tianxian biao* 天仙表), the wine offering ceremony, and ritual writings. In particular, from certain loosely constructed dramatic scenes in the lyrics of the wine offering ceremony we can discover the original appearance of a *tongzi* gathering.

"Overview" traces the historical origin and development of *tongzi* ritual in Nantong based on local historical records. Its description of the different kinds of leaders involved in *tongzi* gatherings and *shang tongzi* worship complements the other two volumes by the same author, i.e. *Tongzi* and *Great Festival*. "Preliminary Study," on the other hand, traces the development of incense ritual drama from shaman practices in its early phase, and the way in which it assimilated ancient myths and legends into *nuo* dancing in a dramatic form. "'*Nuo*' God" is devoted to *nuo* worship and *nuo* deities. The author analyses the various kinds of *tongzi* rituals and their structure, and suggests that the *tongzi* ritual in Nantong originated from the shaman culture of ancient Chu and the shamanism of the Yue people in the Jiang-Huai region. According to the author, the *nuo* god of Nantong has two identities, i.e. the Great Emperor of the Eastern Mountain (Dongyu dadi 東嶽大帝), god of the altar, and the Boddhisatva *Dutian* (Dutian pusa 都天菩薩), a deity with the magical power to dispel omens and bestow blessings. "Interpretation" is basically a historical study of the three-spike official cap (*sanjian gongcao mao* 三尖功曹帽) worn by the *tongzi* character. It is an official cap with many folds made of yellow paper. With the support of a wide range of historical sources, the author concludes that this distinctive headwear originated from worship involving animal horns in pre-historic times. In the *nuo* ritual of the Zhou 周 dynasty, the "sanjian" costume was used alongside the beast mask of the exorcist, *Fangxiang-shi* 方相氏. "Overview" delineates the use of music in the ritual of the Hongshan shaman sect, including the characteristics of its musical composition and performance, a extremely important aspect in the study of shamanic cultures.

II.

According to the ancient text *Yugong* 禹貢, Jiangsu is part of the Xuzhou 徐州 and Yangzhou 揚州 region. In the Spring and Autumn period, before the founding of the state of Wu, it had once belonged to the states of Yue 越 and Chu respectively. The Chu people believed in the supernatural and shamanism, and Chu culture had a great impact upon the entire Jiangsu region. In the Jiang-Huai region, the stone engravings of Jiangjun Cliff 將軍崖 in Lianyun Bay 連雲港 show scenes of shaman activities and the ritual dance "The Grand Emperor's Dance to Worship Heaven."[1] In the historical records of Nantong, there is an entry about a person called Pan the Broken Head (*lantou* 爛頭) who "was good at mastering gods and demons" in around 957 AD (during the reign of the Zhou state in the Five Dynasties period).[2] According to the *Liuhe xianzhi* 六合縣志 (local history of Liuhe) written during the Jiajing 嘉靖 reign of the Ming dynasty (1522-1567) "on the fifteenth day of the first month of the New Year, lanterns would be hung at all road intersections and temples. Either the people would strike their gongs to perform shaman dance, or neighbors would gather together holding lanterns in their hands... until the thirteenth or seventeenth day of the new year."[3] During the Qing dynasty, Li Dou 李斗, a

---

1 Zhu Qiuhua, *Hai zhou qu lun* 海州曲論 (Beijing: Beijing zhongguo xiju chubanshe, 1992), p. 3.

2 Cao Lin, "The Tradition of '*Nuo*' in the Jianghai Plain Region: An Overview of Southern Tongzi Ritual," in *Min-su ch'ü-i*, 70(1991): 185.

3 Huang Wenhu, *The Genealogical Register Incense and Fire Festival of Songzhuang in Wuxing Village, Ma'an Parish and of Jianshan Village in Maji Town, Liuhe County, Jiangsu* (Taipei: Shih Ho-cheng Folk Culture Foundation, *Min-su ch'ü-i ts'ung-shu*, No. 41, 1996), p. 11.

native son of Yizheng 儀征, vividly described his impressions of the *nuo* ritual in the Huai river region in his *Memoirs of a Cruise to Yangzhou* 揚州畫舫錄:

> The local customs here favor *nuo*; the natives like to go barefoot with their hair loosened. Most often, *nuo* is a kind of incense burning, but during group worship, it is called *ma pi* 馬披. At the time of *ma pi*, the sound of gongs and drums is very loud. The first to arrive will receive blessings, or the so-called *kai shan* 開山 (mountain opening) gong. Chickens are killed for their blood in a ceremony called *jian sheng* 剪生 (cutting living things). Afterwards, a dance performance is staged where one can see ghosts and demons here and there like apparitions. Day and night the entire city basks in unreserved exhilaration.[4]

After the mid-Qing period, this kind of well-wishing ritual gradually merged with dramatic art until its complete transformation into local drama. The hand-written copy of the Yang drama 揚劇 *Mr. Zhang Divorces his Wife* (Zhangsheng xiuqi 張生休妻), for example, dates back to 1784 AD (the *shenchen* year of the Qianlong 乾隆 reign);[5] and in Li's *Memoirs* it is obvious that this sort of worship was once a very popular practice in this region. In 1919, ritual incense drama was staged for the first time in Shanghai, by what was later known as the "Great Company of Weiyang" 維揚大班. Due to its lofty music and the exclusive use of gongs and drums instead of strings and flutes, it was also known as "*da kai kou*" 大開口 or the "big opening the mouth". This performance still retained much of the antique quality of *nuo* ritual. After 1936, the Great Company joined forces with the "Drama of Weiyang" 維揚文戲 or "*xiao kai kou*" 小開口 (i.e. the "small opening the mouth"), another dramatic form in Yangzhou. The two seemed incompatible at first but later on they evolved into a new dramatic form called *Yang* drama 揚劇, the second most important genre in Jiangsu.[6]

---

4   Li Dou 李斗, *Memoirs of a Cruise to Yangzhou* (Yangzhou: Jiangsu Guangling guji keyinshe, 1984), p. 347.

5   *A History of Chinese Opera: Jiangsu Region* 中國戲曲志·江蘇卷 (Beijing: ISBN Centre of Beijing, China, 1992), p. 130.

Other genres like *huai* drama also have their origins in incense drama. According to the historical records of Jianhu 建湖 county, in 1488 (the first year of Hongzhi 弘治 in the Ming dynasty), a *tongzi* actor named Hu Ren 胡仁 performed "*tongzi* praying for repentance", a ritual drama to prolong blessings and dispel pestilence.[7] The tone for the songs sung by the *tongzi* character is called "the tone of incense". The tone used in the upper river region (Huaiyin 淮陰) is usually high and lofty and that in the lower river region (Salt Municipality 鹽城) is relatively low and subtle. In about 1860, the transformation of *huai* drama from *tongzi* rituals to independent operatic performance was basically complete, and *nuo* ritual became separated from local drama.[8] On the other hand, the *huaihai* drama 淮海戲 and the *liuqin* drama 柳琴戲 of the northern Huai region were also influenced by the ritual music of the *taiping* song 太平歌 and the elbow drum 肘鼓子, which in turn have their roots in *nuo* music.[9] From what we have discussed so far, we can see that almost every dramatic genre in the Jiang-Huai region has its roots in *nuo* ritual.

Although ritual drama is so influential and popular in Jiangsu, in the past *nuo* drama as the prototype of so many forms of local drama received very little attention from drama experts. In recent years, however, *nuo* has become a very popular topic among researchers once again. Studies on the "earth drama" (*dixi* 地戲) of Guizhou, the *Guan Suo* drama 關索戲 of Yunnan, the *tiao wuchang* 跳五猖 (leaping of the five generals of the East, South, West, North and Centre, commonly called the Five *Chang*) of Anhui, and the *nuo tang* drama 儺堂 of Hunan, among others, have produced very good results. However, we do not yet see any comparable research on the *tongzi* drama of the Jiang-Huai region. From 1986 onwards, hundreds of drama professionals began their work on the *History of Chinese Opera: Jiangsu Region*, which sparked their interest in the relationship between local drama and *nuo* ritual in Jiangsu. The publication of *Tongzi, Genealogical Register and Great Festival* by *Min-su ch'ü-i*, as well as essays like "Overview,"

---

6 *The Dramatic Genres of Jiangsu* 江蘇劇種 (Nanjing edition, 1992. Jiangsu Culture Bureau, 1983), pp. 121-123.

7 *Ibid*, pp. 96-97.

8 *Ibid*, pp. 97.

9 *Ibid*, pp. 132, 162.

is a good example of the fruitful results of recent studies in *nuo* ritual and the local drama in Jiangsu. Significant advance has been made in the study of Chinese drama, i.e. its origin and historical development, and a comprehensive understanding of the relations between *nuo* culture, anthropology, religion and ethnology. These publications, moreover, form a pool of valuable resources that will not only facilitate further research in the primitive culture of humankind, but also promote understanding of the ancient culture of China.

III.

All these publications are the result of critical and scientific studies of first-hand sources collected through rigorous field research. As we all know, source materials are the prerequisite for scholarly research; usually they determine the quality of a particular work. Some researchers shun the hardship of field studies; some will simply elaborate on hearsay evidence or put forward subjective conjecture after reading a few historical documents. Hence, their conclusions are partial and hollow in meaning, if not absolutely wrong. The three volumes and the essays discussed here, on the other hand, have a very solid foundation in concrete field research, through which the authors gained access to genuine, first-hand sources. Their analyses and conclusions are both meaningful and illuminating. More importantly, our knowledge of local dramatic forms like *tongzi* drama relies heavily on the performing artists themselves; hence the old saying, "Where man lives, art lives; where man lives not, neither does art." This special quality of *tongzi* drama, or any kind of ritual drama, makes comprehensive field study even more urgent and indispensable. Recovery of valuable first-hand sources and in-depth analyses, therefore, are the major contribution of these publications.

　　Nuo ritual drama is extremely rich in cultural meaning. It is intimately connected to every aspect of the social life of the local people. In studying *tongzi* drama as a social phenomenon, we have to pay attention to the natural environment, religion, and the economy and culture of the local community so as to understand the dynamic relationships between these factors. For instance, in *Tongzi*, the author traces the evolution of its locale: from the geographical development of Tongzhou city to the human geography of Beidian village, from the setting of the holy altar to the entire process of the ritual, and from the leaders to the titles of plays. Throughout the book the author bases his observations on solid facts, not subjective conjecture.[10] In *Genealogical Register*, the author meticulously delineates the internal structure of the *tongzi* ritual and devotes almost eighty per cent of the text to source materials, e.g. biographies of incense masters, sacred books, visual illustrations of the ritual dance "*tiao niangniang*" and "*jie biao*," as well as singing tunes and photographs. All this enables the author to present his own observations in an objective and factual manner. This is also characteristic of the other publications discussed in this essay.

IV.

Tongzi drama is an integrated and multidimensional popular art form. The publication of books and research papers like *Shang Tongzi* and "Overview" not only offers glimpses into the origin and development of *tongzi* drama in Jiangsu and the Huai River region, but also reveals the rich cultural content of *nuo*, and therefore paves the way for further inquiries into the relationship between *tongzi* drama and ritual. These studies also help establish the complex relationships between *tongzi* drama on the one hand, and ethnology, sociology, religious studies, and medical and health practices on the other.

According to the sources contained in the publications we have noted above (including local historical records, oral literature of performing artists, and sacred scriptures), *tongzi* drama originated from the *nuo* ritual of rural people (*xiang ren nuo* 鄉人儺). As a form of ritual drama, *tongzi* drama has had a surprisingly long historical existence. Its antique simplicity embodies the primitive character of Chinese drama, a kind of "living fossil" in the study of aesthetics. In the mid-Qing period, this sacred art gradually evolved into a form of secular entertainment

---

10 Cao Lin, *The Tongzi Ritual of the Hu Family in Beidian Village, Henggang Township, Tongzhou Municipality, Jiangsu* (Taipei: Shih Ho-cheng Folk Culture Foundation, *Min-su ch'ü-i ts'ung-shu*, No. 31, 1995).

and finally became a type of local drama. However, the performance of *tongzi* drama still bears traces of *nuo*.

From the perspective of ethno-cultural studies, *tongzi* drama in its early phase was primarily a form of shamanism. It had the power to drive away evil and illnesses and also served the function of vow fulfillment. In this respect, *tongzi* drama belongs to the realm of primitive religion and culture. In the Jiang-Huai region, *tongzi* drama is like a huge portrait of local customs commonly used in rural activities like New Year blessings, welcoming deities and dispelling demons.

As far as ethno-religious studies are concerned, it is widely held that *tongzi* drama is basically a kind of shamanism.[11] Some others have pointed out that the *tongzi* practitioner may identify himself as Confucian or one of the Bing teaching 秉教.[12] In light of the publications we have discussed so far, we understand that *nuo*, like Daoism, is the product of humans' primitive perception of nature and themselves; whereas Daoism itself evolved from shamanic practices. As it developed, *tongzi* drama and Daoism then gradually came together. From what we know about the many deities in the *nuo* ritual and the titles of *tongzi* plays, it is clear that *tongzi* drama is closely linked to Daoism.

The relationship between *tongzi* drama and traditional health and medical practices is explained in *Tongzi*. It contains details of the historical practice of "shaman doctors" who, as *tongzi*, are primarily responsible for dispelling evil and healing. The *tongzi* performer always displays his special skills during a ritual. One example is the *zhan dao* 站刀, where the actor has to stand barefoot on the blade of a hay-cutting knife as he tours around the village for six hours. In performing the "striking knife" [kan dao 砍刀], also known as "chopping knife" [zhan dao 斬刀], the *tongzi* character will use an iron knife to cut into his upper arm. He will bleed heavily and so it is believed that evil will be driven away. The *tongzi* actor will also perform "spade insertion" (han chan 含鏟) in which a hot, burning spade is put into his mouth; then the *tongzi* will go from place to place to drive away evil. These special effects are unnerving but they do not really hurt the body. As such,

---

11 Huang Wenhu, *op. cit.* p. 61.

12 Shi Hanru, Zhang Zhiqiang and Yang Wenchun, "The '*Nuo*' Ritual and '*Nuo*' God of Nantong," *Min-su ch'ü-i*, 87(1994): 155.

tongzi performances are an excellent case for research in ethnic art and traditional healing.

Nuo is a widespread cultural phenomenon in Chinese culture. *Tongzi* drama has a very long history in Jiangsu, and its unique artistic style has influenced not only Jiangsu but many other regions in China. The study of *tongzi* drama in the Jiang-Huai region, however, is still in an embryonic stage. For a long time, *nuo* culture has caused many misunderstandings precisely because we have little or no knowledge of the primitive culture and its "science" that *nuo* represents. We have to realize that not only Chinese but other civilizations have undergone the historical transformation from a shamanic culture to a modern one. The three books and other essays we have considered here have proven that this is true, and their contribution to future scholarship has to be duly recognized.

13

LÜSHAN PUPPET THEATRE IN FUJIAN

Brigitte Baptandier

The three books by Ye Minghseng 葉明生 reviewed here are playscripts, field reports and a research statement. They introduce a specific kind of ritual puppet theatre of Fujian, connected with the cult of one of the most important goddesses of this province, Chen Jinggu 陳靖姑, and with a specific Daoist ritual tradition: the *Lüshan pai* 閭山派 ("*Lüshan* sect") preponderant in Fujian.

Ye Mingsheng presents data from two places: Shanghang 上杭 (in Minxi 閩西), *Gaoqiang kuilei xi* 高腔傀儡戲 *Luandan kuilei xi* 亂彈傀儡戲 and Shouning 壽寧 (Daiyang 岱陽 village, in Mindong 閩東) *Siping kuilei xi* 四平傀儡戲. He then introduces two plays: the *Furen zhuan* 夫人傳 and the *Nainiang zhuan* 奶娘傳. Both retell the legendary life and deeds of Chen Jinggu, first adept of the *Lüshan pai*, Lüshan, Daoist ritual tradition .

The first book *Minxi Shanghang Gaoqiang kuilei yu Furen xi* 閩西上杭高腔傀儡與夫人戲 in the *Min-su ch'ü-i ts'ung-shu* 民俗曲藝叢書 (Studies in Chinese Ritual, Theatre and Folklore Series), is an elaboration of fieldwork and historical and sociological data on the relations between the puppet ritual theatre tradition of the Furen goddess in

243

Shanghang, enriched with different interesting supplements and ritual texts. The two other books (1996 and 1997) are mainly composed of the text of each puppet theatre script. Each of them provides in addition a documented introduction of about 40 pages.

I would like, first, to make a few general remarks on these three books. Then I will review in more detail the third book (Fujian Shouning *Siping kuilei xi nainiang zhuan* 福建壽寧四平傀儡戲奶娘傳 (*The Biography of the Nainiang in the Siping Puppet Theatre in the Shouning District of Fujian. Min-su ch'ü-i ts'ung-shu*, No. 60, 1997. 278 pages), and only present the contents of the first two.

I. General Remarks

Considered together, the three books by Ye Mingshang certainly provide a great deal of valuable information and interesting points of view. Among others I shall raise three main fields of interest. Ye Mingsheng focuses on a specific local ritual puppet theatre, he provides original and integral play scripts, and he expresses a crucial point of view on the relations between ritual and theatre. I shall try to express a constructive critical point of view, mainly concerning his third point.

Focusing on this specific tradition of *Lüshan* ritual puppet theatre, Ye provides important historical and sociological information as he traces the emergence of the "genre," its different branches and strata, the encoding of the characters that transformed the rituals in theatre tradition. He gives details on the puppets, and on the artistic skillfulness in playing them. He provides also information on the different styles of music that he briefly compares. Then, in a detailed description of the ritual staging, he provides valuable fieldwork data on the ritual objects used during the performance and on the written talismans that help create the sacred area.

He also offers some general information about the sociological context of this theatre: the associations connected with both the cult and the puppet theatre, the times of the year when the theatre is performed, and the occasions that require it, namely, public *jiao* 醮 rituals enacted in temples, and private rituals set at home, to heal or exorcise.

Of course the "heart" of this research is the publication "for the first time," Ye says, of the texts of the two plays, *Furen zhuan* and *Nainiang zhuan*. They come with indications about the characters performing, and the style and the music of each sequence. Music scores and other items that constitute precious data for further detailed analysis of the theatre corpus itself are also presented. In addition, Ye compares the summaries of different texts which introduces a further formal / structural-analysis of the variants in the Lady's legend.

The third point is of great interest me, as Ye Mingsheng adopts a double point of view in discussing the ritual aspect of this theatre: on the one hand, rituals are embedded in the play, and on the other hand the theatre play itself and its performance are, in effect, ritual. The first point of view obliges him to underline the relations between the so called "popular" beliefs, the oral traditions connected with them — that is to say the mythological context — and their transmission by way of a many faceted literature, among which the ritual texts, similar to poems or songs, provide complete sequences of the play. Thus, the reader, if he or she is familiar with this traditional context and knows this ritual tradition, may appreciate the intermingling of play and ritual and the close relationship of this theatre with the ritual life of people. If the reader is new to the field, then he will at least become aware of the intimate formal relations between this puppet theatre and the shamanistic *Lüshan* sect rituals (*Lüshan jiao*, or *Furen jiao*), notably the *wangshi jiao* 尫師 教 and the *shiye tiao haiqing* 師爺跳海青, even if he will not be able to understand clearly what this refers to in the religious practices of every-day life.

Ye argues that this theatre itself is an efficacious ritual ceremony for healing and exorcism. It reminds me of what a Daoist master told me in 1993 in Gutian 古田, after an official conference on *Chen jinggu wenhua* 陳靖姑文化 held in Fuzhou and Gutian (Ye and I both participated), when he understood that the theatre play of the Lady was going to be performed in a theatre hall and not in the temple where he had come to see it: "the theatre of the Lady," he said to me, "is the whole performance of her ritual tradition, and no one should perform it without actually wanting to enact those rituals;" that is to exorcise or heal. Ritual theatre is not a new topic, but few people have shown the richness of this particular ritual and theatrical tradition, a tradition that has been considered as mere "superstition" in China for a long period, when even to enact the play was forbidden. However, in spite of his explicit intention to contextualize and analyze the plays and rituals in their social and historical dimensions, Ye has produced a monographic outline of this puppet theatre that leaves the reader expecting more on ritual. Of course, one has to infer the origins and connections of those different productions: beliefs, mythology, cult, rituals and theatre, but this important narrative tradition — theatre or ritual — should also be submitted to the demanding question of meaning. If this is not undertaken, the anthropological aim may be missed and give way to a kind of folklorisation that would deny what even a cursory glance at these materials is sufficient to show: the extraordinary complexity of the semantical networks produced by cultures.[1] The danger would be that most of the readers might find here only a collection of old legends, Daoist folklore, and references to a survival from the past, only perceptible through theatre plays in "modern" society. Nothing is said about its relationship to everyday life. There is also the difficult question of the meaning of ritual. Since it is impossible to dissociate theatre / ritual / and cult, an elaboration of the meaning becomes necessary so that the intrinsic message of this tradition is not betrayed.

Regarding the question of the meaning of rituals one has usually to avoid two traps: presenting a meaningless folkloristic narrative, or looking for codified interpretations (symbols) that hide essential mechanisms. If those traps are avoided, then the question "does ritual have meaning?" becomes obsolete, which, in my point of view, *does not mean* that there is no meaning, but that the essential meaning is not codi-fied, and that one must look for it in another way. This is how rituals might become the prism through which to question other aspects of social activity. This is what Ch. Malamoud does for ancient Indian rituals and what K. Schipper and F. Staal undertook for Chinese and Indian rituals.[2] I would

---

1 I would give the following definition of folklore (Charuty 76): a collection and conservation of beliefs and archaic customs, signs of a past social stage.

2 Dan Sperber (1974) defines symbolical knowledge by the epistemological status of the propositions that express it: statements intended to establish the pertinence of other apparently irrelevant concepts.

   He gives an instance from his fieldwork in Dorzé society: "If a Dorzé friend tells me that women's pregnancy lasts for nine months I think: well, they know it. If he adds: But in such and such clan it lasts for eight or ten months, I think: it is symbolical. Why? Because it is not true.

like to make a comparison with dreams. Since Freud, everybody knows that they should not be interpreted by using codified symbols ("clés des songes"), but by elaborating their own discourse. But if Freud did not give any place to symbolism in the first edition of *l'Interprétation des rêves*, it is because condensation and deplacement — that is to say metaphor and metonymy — are sufficient to explain the structures of the unconscious and to show that the object of repression is not an affect but a "significant".[3] This is precisely what has to be done with the ritual theatre that Ye Mingsheng presents. This is why, although his work is indeed a valuable ethnography of this theatre tradition, it is also not completely satisfying from the point of view of myth and ritual. Two examples taken from Ye's book illustrate what I mean.

Strangely enough, it is only at the very end of the third book (p. 276) that Ye Mingsheng discusses the human elements of his fieldwork. After his research work in Minxi Shanghang (1992-93), Ye Mingsheng thought that the story of the *furen* 夫人 retold there was not actually what he considered to be the "true one," that is the one he had heard at home, in Shouning district, the one that made sense to him. I have heard this kind of remark many times on the field and I also know very well that feeling! I think that this impression of Ye that the Shanghang version was not the "true" one should have been analyzed carefully. In fact, what is the "true" version of those legends? What is the human truth within them that goes far beyond the search for their origins, their history and the retelling of old mythologies? Then Ye wanted to know what kind of theatre would be played in Shouning. He finally met Wu Naiyu 吳乃宇, Master of *Lüshan liyuan jiao* 閭山梨園教 puppet theatre of the Bao'an tan 保安壇, at Daiyang village. This master was taught since his childhood and performs every year on the 15th of the first month. He wrote the six books of the play for Ye Mingsheng (1993-95) and it was finally published in 1997.

(Of course)...Not all errors seem to me symbolic, and any symbolic discourse is not necessarily erroneous" (1974: 15). Sperber makes another statement: "people looking for the meaning of symbols look at the source of the light and they complain that they are dazzled. But it is not the light that has to be looked at but what it enlightens. The same for symbolism, a universal system that organizes the memory by focusing the attention" (1974) (my translation).

3   As G. Charuty stresses (1992: 97).

The second example comes from the *Shanghang gaoqiang kuilei xi* book (p.138), where Ye discusses the ritual sequence *qing potai shen* 請 破胎神, an invitation to the *potai* divinity, the one who "breaks the womb." He explains that this sequence goes back to the legend of Lin Jiuniang 林九娘, Chen Jinggu's child, by breaking the egg of the demon snake. In fact Lin Jiuniang is the *potai shen*. But this remark is only a first step toward the interpretation. If one stops here with this setting of circular connections between theatre, ritual and myth, has one explained why people still perform this sequence today? Is it out of faith or "superstition?" Is it because old people still remember the creation of the Min territory legends here embedded? Or is there another specific sociological, logical discourse present, conveyed by a metaphorical discourse? I think the latter is the case. This ritual and theatrical sequence of the *qing potai shen*, that goes back to the mythical episode (snake's egg), belongs also to the complex ritual performed for children, *guoguan* 過關, or *kaiguan* 開關, "crossing or opening of the passes," that Ye himself mentions in his books as one of the important rituals of this *furen* theatre and of the *Lüshan* tradition. But he nonetheless stops at that point, when in fact this ritual, through the exorcism of the demon of the passes, *guansha* 關煞, deals with the assimilation of the child to the father's lineage, and its progressive learning of the maternal universe. Actually, the ritual deals with the construction of the identity of the child, its place within the patrilineage and a certain conception of destiny.[4] Even if we deal here with a theatre play and not with the complete *guoguan* ritual, remember what Ye himself says: this play may be performed at home for the private benefit of women and children as a ritual... Here is its meaning, embedded within the play. This is what is enacted when the theatre is performed, as the Daoist master said.

Only the experience of "otherness" may generate the pertinent questions to look in another way at this corpus of beliefs and usages.

---

4   Within the crossing of the passes ritual, *guoguan*, the Daoist master sings a longer sequence that explains more in detail how the child has been "stolen by another mother." Then, the Daoist officiant has to break her womb to set the child free and get it back to its patrilineage. Within the *guoguan* ritual, this sequence of invitation of the divinity who breaks the womb, *qing potai shen*, is enacted by the pretended breaking of a cup — the womb — to send back the child to its own parents. The metaphor and its meaning are obvious here. See Baptandier 1994, pp. 560-563.

The correlation between the mythological/ritual discourse and the proper sociological encoding that expresses the people's usages, opens the path to the meaning. Of course the myth also deals with this same meaning, but the "egg of the serpent" by itself, at least as a symbol, does not say much explicitly about it. Myth and ritual are steps toward the interpretation, but one more step should be done to analyze the ritual metaphor used to enact the structures of the local society: kinship, difference of the sexes and so on are what the "symbol's light" gives us to see. Those are the proper meanings of the ritual and of the legends, their human ("true") meaning, expressed within the very discourse of the people.

Ye Mingsheng is from Shouning and so is reporting on his own culture, which is difficult to do. What goes without saying for a native person because he belongs to the culture he describes, is precisely what deserves explanation and further research by outside readers. This is why I believe that Ye should have opened his research to some comparison, and quoted other authors dealing with research on theatre, ritual and even the Lady's cult itself. That would have enlarged his point of view, completed his analysis, and given access to other methodological approaches. This would have also underlined more accurately the specific value of his own research. Ye Mingsheng has been trained as a scholar of fine arts and theatre, which gives a special value to his contribution on this important theatrical tradition. The necessity of a comparison is indeed what J. Lagerwey underlines about most of the books in this series: "These articles must be read together with the works of academic anthropologists and local history, which supply what local informants cannot: a critical regard."[5] I personally would prefer to emphasize the necessity of a comparative and interdisciplinary approach. This would have allowed a broader use of these data. This material is not a "precious witness to a past that has long since disappeared and that continues to survive now only in the memories of the old" as Lagerwey says about most of the ethnographic data in the different volumes here published. It seems to me that this tradition and representation system of

---

5   John Lagerwey, "The Structure and Dynamics of Chinese Rural Society," in Hsu Cheng-kuang 徐正光, ed., *Proceedings of International Conference on Hakkaology: History and Socio-Economy* (Taipei: Institute of Ethnology, Academia Sinica, 2000), pp. 17, 14.

south China is still very much rooted in peoples', minds and will still survive some time after the disappearance of the theatre play itself. Nowadays this theatre and its rituals are the very discourse, even though fragile, of the tradition of this society. We should not reduce them to silence once more by ignoring their meaning while they are still being performed. "One should not perform this theatre without being willing to enact its rituals," said the Daoist master.

II. A Review of the Shouning Nainiang Zhuan

Let me now review the book *The Biography of the Nainiang in the Siping Puppet Theatre in the Shouning District of Fujian.*

This is the text of the six books of the Shouning *Lüshan Liyuan jiao Nainiang zhuan*, each one divided in five to seven *pai* 拍, measures or *chu* 齣, acts (218 pages), written out by Wu Naiyu and annotated by Ye. This book is one version of the "biography," the legend and deeds of Chen Jinggu, the main adept of the Daoist *Lüshan pai*; how she went to Lüshan and came back to catch the demons of Min, particularly the *changkeng gui* 長坑鬼, how she performed a ritual for the rain to fall, and how she finally became a goddess. There is also an interesting Introduction (40 pages) which deserves a review of its own.

In the first part of this introduction, the "Context of the Creation of the *Nainiang zhuan,*" Ye Mingsheng provides a historical statement of popular beliefs in and the creation of the cult of the goddess Chen jinggu. He quotes such steles as the one written by Zhang Yining 張以寧 [6] He traces how the temples, their networks and social activities emerged, how the cult and its beliefs spread throughout Min society. He explains how this cult is intimately associated with the *Lüshan* sect Daoist tradition and its shamanistic rituals, as Chen Jinggu herself went to Lüshan to learn this ritual tradition. This context of specific beliefs and mythology, of a cult and its social network of temples and associations, of Daoist masters and their rituals is the context from which slowly emerged what Ye Mingsheng calls a "popular literature."

---

6 Quotation from Huang Qiquan 黃啓權, "Cong difangzhi jizai tan Chen Jinggu" 從地方志記載談陳靖姑, in *Chen Jinggu Wenhua Yanjiu* 陳靖姑文化研究, p. 96, 1993.

A few citations of other studies of this topic would have provided a comparative perspective.

There follows a detailed discussion of the diversity of the tradition itself. From the mainstream of the legends in Gutian and Fuzhou, the heart of the cult, issued all the variants in different places of the network, temples and associations, retold in the whole province. Ye Mingsheng provides a framework for this "popular literature," the first step, he says, toward the theatre play. First are notes the books of songs and poems about the Lady, written in verses of seven words. He divides them in three categories: books for the faithful ladies, books for the Daoist masters of the *Lüshan* sect, and for the *Lüshan* sect *Liyuan jiao* masters, such books as the "Book of the Pagoda Tower of the Lady" (*Nainiang ta ben* 奶娘塔本), and "Book of the Incantations of the Lady" (*Nainiang zhou ben* 奶娘咒本). For me, Ye does not show clearly enough the nature and particularity of the rituals within which those texts are sung as ritual sequences. It would be quite fascinating to present a complete vision of the play: not only to note the places where ritual sequences are embedded — mainly *qingshen* 請神 sequences — but what these rituals refer to. No doubt that they are all poems, which is quite interesting. Finally the last category is the one of song books for processions when the image of the goddess is taken out of the temple during the festivals.

A second kind of popular literature reviewed by Ye Mingsheng is the corpus of so called "novels" (*xiaoshuo* 小說), strange stories and mirabilia like the *Linshui pingyao zhuan* 臨水平妖傳 and the *Mindu bieji* 閩都別記. Ye says these came later so that "they could not influence the emergence of the theatre." To me this is a strange approach, as Ye himself explains that most of the episodes of these books came from the same ground of beliefs, mythology and rituals. Actually they are the mythology of the cult. So even if they were published later, their "oral" texts do not differ much from the others. Legends, popular literature — that is, mainly rituals — gave birth to the formalization of the *Nainiang zhuan* text of the theatre play during the Ming dynasty.

In the following section of the Introduction, Ye Mingsheng deals with the birth and development of the Lady's *kuilei xi* tradition, commenting that "This puppet theatre comes from the Daoist altar where theatre-rituals are performed." Three branches are presented like the three steps of the formalization of the present tradition: *Wangshi kuilei xi* 尪師傀儡戲, *Liyuan jiao* and *yeyou* 夜遊. *Wangshi jiao* is the name for the ritual healing and exorcising tradition of *Lüshan*. Here again are three ritual subdivisions of the *Lüshan* sect, first the *Yutang zhengpai* 玉堂正派, the literate branch close to the *Lingbao* 靈寶 tradition. Next is the *wujiao* 武教 ("martial branch") whose masters wear the red head-dress and the skirt of the goddess, and finally the *Lüshan Liyuan zhengjiao* 閭山梨園正教, whose masters are the puppet theatre masters. They are mostly for children (*guoguan*) or women. One or two masters perform with eighteen puppets in this ritual tradition. The *Wangshi jiao* has six branches, six grottos, each of which produces theatre plays: *Furong dong* 芙蓉洞 ("the Hibiscus grotto"), the *Linshui dong* 臨水洞 with the *Nainang zhuan* and the *Pingyao zhuan*, the *Nanchao dong* 南朝洞, the *Shuiguo dong* 水國洞, the kingdom of water with the Mazu theatre, *Tianfei zhuan* 天妃傳, the *Zijin shan quanzhuan* 紫金山全傳 and the *Huangbi tong* 黃碧洞. The *Wangshi* ritual theatre itself had no theatre music and codified roles of its own, it was only the "prehistory" of the *kuilei xi*, a kind of staging of the ritual, as Ye puts it. When it was integrated with theatre melodies and roles, then it became real *kuilei xi*. This happened in the beginning of the Ming dynasty, in the Yiyang district of Jiangxi province, when the *Yiyang qiang* 弋陽腔 spread throughout the Bamin area with its variant the *siping qiang* 四平腔. It is always with an accompanying drum, and sounds very much like Daoist music, which is why the Hibiscus and *Linshui* grottos adopted this music. It is like a branch of the *Wangshi kuilei jiao*, staged for theatre plays.[7] The *yeyou* gradually dissociated itself from the ritual altar. Though of the same origin it nonetheless became an entertainment.

In the second part, Ye Mingsheng gives a summary of the play text and a detailed listing of the main characters (roles / types). In this theatre play there are eight main characters called the *bajiaoqi* 八角齊. Those are: *chou* 丑, *jing* 淨, *sheng* 生, *dan* 旦, *wai* 外, *za* 雜, *fu* 夫 and *tie* 貼. Some other companies have ten characters. Previously there were eighteen persons for these roles. As this number does not fit the codes of the *shen xi* 神戲, ritual theatre it has been changed to twenty-

---

7 Cf. Ye Mingsheng 1997, p. 18.

four puppets (symbolically like the twenty-four sky mansions) or thirty-six (like the thirty-six constellations). Ye Mingsheng also gives details on the roles of the thirty-six actors. Some of the puppets do not play one of the eight main roles: these are themselves gods. Among them is the *nainiang* 奶娘 as a goddess and as a ritual master.

Ye also gives details of the different kinds of music and tunes played: *siping* 四平, *daotan* 到壇, *guochang* 過場, and *minge* 民歌. Then comes a short section that I think is very interesting and could open the field to other developments. It is a presentation of the different kinds of language used here: mandarin *guanhua* 官話, *baihua* 白話 and local expressions and language. It comes with a short summary of the different language particularisms with a comment on how they give access to the study of local society and local history.[8] This attention to the particularities of language in the text is carried on through the notes.

Finally, the last part deals with the *Nainiang wenhua* 奶娘文化 (Nainiang culture): society, religious characteristics and style. This is the sociological context in which Chen Jinggu lived according both to legend and history: her family, the official society, gods and common people. Ye introduces her as the benevolent goddess of the country.

Then he comes again to the analysis of the relations between theatre and ritual, once more giving examples of theatre embedded in the rituals and the reverse, ritual sequences in theatre play, in a somewhat circular demonstration.

The two other books are as follows:

(I.) *Minxi Shanghang gaoqiang kuiilei yu Furen xi* 閩西上杭高腔傀儡與夫人戲 (*The Gaoqiang Kuilei Theatre of Shanghang in Minxi, and the Furen Theatre*), 295 pages, No. 33, 1995. This book is in eight parts:

1. Village fundamental beliefs.
2. Data on *kuilei xi* ritual.
3. Organization of the *kuilei xi* ritual: organization, ritual objects, ritual sequences, talismans, repertory, texts and interpretation.
4. Associations and beliefs about *kuilei*.
5. Presentation of the associations for theatrical performances.
6. The artistic aspects of *kuilei xi*.

---

8 Cf. other examples of such research topics in Pimpaneau 1997 and Baptandier 1991.

7. *Furen* theatrical performances.

8. Conclusion: A) Shanghang *kuilei xi* and Fujian *kuilei xi*; B) Beliefs about Chen Jinggu in Fujian and the *kuilei* theatre of the Lady; C) Emergence of the Shanghang *gaoqiang kuilei furen xi*.

There are several supplements and annexes:

1. A) Planning and repertory of a *shanghang gaoqiang kuilei xi* company; B) comparison between *Luantan kuilei xi* (*furen zhuan*) summary and *Gaoqiang kuilei xi* (*furen zhuan*) summary; C) list and roles of members of the company.

2. A) *Shanghang gaoqiang kuilei xi* ritual books; B) *Shanghang gaoqiang kuilei xi* (*furen zhuan*): *qingshen*, and *songshen* 送神 ritual texts.

3. Music of the *Gaoqiang kuilei xi* of Shanghang.

4. Maps and photos.

(II.) *The "Biography of the Lady" in the Luantan Puppet Theatre of Shanghang* (Fujian Shanghang luantan kuilei xi Furen zhuan 福建上杭亂彈傀儡戲夫人傳), No. 44, 1996. 420 pages.

Here are the fifteen sections of the *Furen zhuan*, each one preceded by a short resume of the story. Before this text comes a thirty-six page Introduction, as follows:

1. Sociological background of beliefs about the *Furen*: A) Relations with the Lady's cult; B) Activities of the Lady's association; C) Beliefs about the goddess (3 subdivisions: a) exorcisms and fertility, b) pregnancy and giving birth, c) the Crossing of the passes, *guoguan* ritual (with no description or analysis of the ritual).

2. Formation of the Lady's theatre: A) Theatre and popular oral tradition; B) Theatre and Daoism (3 subdivisions: a) the activities of the Daoist altar, b) the *San furen zhuan* 三夫人傳 and the *Furen jing* 夫人經, c) the "Shiye tiao Haiqing" which is actually the story of the protagonists Chen Haiqing 陳海青 and his sister Chen Jinggu, Lin Jiuniang and Li Qianjin 李千金 or Sanniang, going to *Lüshan* to learn the rituals and exorcisms; C) Time of emergence of the theatre.

3. Evolution of the play (*xiju Lüshan*) "Furen zhuan:" A) The *Gaoqiang kuilei xi* and the *Furen zhuan*; a.) The ritual manifestations on the *kuilei xi* stage; b) Relations between *kuilei xi* and *Furen zhuan*; B) The *Furen zhuan* within the *Luantan qiang* tradition.

4. Artistic particularities of the *Furen zhuan*: A) Length and construc-

tion; B) Characters; C) Style of the play; D) Skillfullness in the handling of the puppets; E) Psychology.

5. *Furen zhuan* religious culture: A) Among the *Lüshan jiao*, the *Furen jiao*; B) Praise of Lüshan and contempt for Maoshan, which is an interesting point on the rivalries still very perceptible in the field between these Daoist traditions; C) *Furen zhuan* and the "three religions."

6. Glossary and commentary.

Bibliography

Baptandier, B. 1988. La Dame du Bord de l'Eau. *La féminité à travers un culte du sud de la Chine.* Société d'ethnologie. Nanterre, France.

——. 1991. "Le pont Loyang. Des mots, des humains et des dieux," in *Langage et Société, Métaphor et diglossie en contexte ethnologique,* No. 57.

——. 1994. "Kaiguang Ritual and the Construction of the Child's Identity," in *Popular Beliefs and Chinese Culture.* Taipei: Center for Chinese Studies Research Series, No. 4.

——. 1996. "Le rituel d'ouverture des passes (*kaiguang*). Un concetp de l'enfance," *L'Homme 137, Chine, Facettes d'identite.* Paris.

——. 1996. "The Lady Linshui: The Way a Woman Became a Goddess," in Meir Shahar and Robert Weller eds., *Unruly Gods: Divinity and Society in China.* Honolulu: University of Hawaii Press.

Charuty, G. 1992. "Anthropologie et psychanalyse: le dialogue inachevé," in G. Althabe, D. Fabre, and G. Lenclud eds., *Vers une ethnologie du présent.* Paris: Maison des Sciences des Sciences de l'Homme.

Ch'iu K'un-liang. 1991. *Les aspects rituels du théâtre chinois.* Paris: Mémoires de l'Institut des Hautes Etudes Chinoises, vol. XXXIII. Collège de France. Institut des Hautes Etudes Chinoises. De Boccard.

Dean, Kenneth. 1993. *Taoist Ritual and Popular Cults of Southeast China.* Princeton: Princeton University Press.

Lagerwey, John. 2000. "Structure and Dynamics of Chinese Rural Society," in Hsu Cheng-kuan ed., *Proceedings of the Four*

International Conference on the Hakka. Taipei: Institute of Ethnology, Academia Sinica.

Loon, Piet van der. 1977. "Les orgines rituelles du théâtre chinois," in *Journal asiatique,* CCLXV: 141-168.

Pimpaneau, J. 1983. *Promenade au jardin des poiriers, l'opéra chinois classique.* Paris: Musée Kwok On ed.

———. 1997. *Des poupées à l'ombre. Le théâtre d'ombres et de poupées en Chine.* Paris: Universite de Paris 7. Centre de Publication Asie Orientale. Diffusion: L'Asiathéque.

———. *Chine. Littérature populaire. Chanteurs, conteurs, bateleurs.* Paris: Edition revue et corrigée Philippe Picquier.

Schipper, K. 1977. "Neighborhood Cult Associations in Traditional Taiwan," in William Skinner ed., *The City in Late Imperial China.* Stanford: Stanford University Press.

———. 1989. "Mu-lien Plays in Taoist Liturgical Context," in David Johnson ed., *Ritual Opera, Operatic Ritual.* Berkeley: University of California Press.

Staal, Fritz ed. 1985. *Agni: The Vedic Fire Ritual.* Berkeley: Asian Humanities Press.

14

A REVIEW OF YE MINGSHENG'S STUDY OF THE LÜSHAN SECT IN LONGYAN, FUJIAN AND ITS RITUALS

Li Feng-mao

I.

As the first volume of the "Collection of Traditional Chinese Ritual Texts," Ye Mingsheng's 葉明生 full-length study of *nuo* drama and *nuo* culture is a comprehensive representation of this regional ritual and popular religious culture. *The Ritual Texts of the Guangji Altar of the Lüshan Sect in Dongxiao Town, Longyan Municipality, Fujian* 福建省龍巖市東肖鎮閭山教廣濟壇科儀本 (Taipei: Hsin Wen-feng, 1996) consists of a large collection of ritual texts together with the author's in-depth analysis of the relationship between the Daoist altar troupes and the local community. Ye's book is one of the most fruitful results of current research on *nuo* culture in Mainland China, and can serve as a 'model' for related projects in this area.

Due to reasons both historical and social, Ye Mingsheng has not received the kind of academic training one might expect of anthropological researchers in the West. Ye's closest affiliation is local drama research. Ye worked in the Beilu Theatre Group in Shouning county of Fujian for a long time, where he gained professional knowledge of local theatre, and hands-on experience in stage production. Due to his long-time experience in the field, Ye was able to work on the editorial board for *A History of Chinese Opera: Fujian Province* 中國戲曲志・福建卷. In mainland China, the "Four Great Compendia" project (*Si da jicheng gongcheng* 四大集成工程) has brought together a group of cultural workers who dedicate themselves to the recovery through field work of still extant folk dramas. Local drama is often connected to popular cult worship, and temple festivals and rituals always involve dramatic performance; moreover, some Daoist priests and followers of ritual teaching (*fa jiao* 法教) will perform religious mini dramas (*xiao xi* 小戲) from time to time. As a result, it is not surprising that in China it is always drama specialists who take the initiative to study the activities of the "miscellaneous Daoist priests" (*za san daoshi* 雜散道士) as part of their historical research on traditional opera.

In the initial stage of their research, many academics and cultural workers on the Mainland, consciously or subconsciously, subsumed religious customs under the dramatic genre. In fact, what we commonly call "*nuo* culture" has a long historical usage, referring to the kind of religious culture that integrates Daoism, shamanism and drama in different times and places. The Lüshan Sect 閭山教, for example, is the same as ritual teaching; it is a very popular religious sect in Fujian. Its origin is similar to those of the *duangong* 端公 and *shigong* 師公 vernacular rituals in other regions, although each has evolved through time into unique local religions. The *shigong* practices in Longyan are primarily based on the ritual teaching of Lüshan, but it has also brought in certain Daoist elements from the Orthodox Unity sect (*Zhengyi jiao* 正一教) in Jiangxi and various local shamanic practices in other areas. According to Ye, the ritual way (*fa dao* 法道) is a form of ancient and widespread local ritual teaching.

From the "Epilogue" we understand that the present volume is the result of several factors. In the first place, the large-scale research project "Chinese Regional Theatre in Its Ritual and Social Context" has set a standard methodology for all its participants. The supervision and funding commitments of Professor Wang Ch'iu-kuei 王秋桂, the organizer, made possible the co-operation of Ye and Liu Yuan 劉遠. In collecting oral and documented sources, Ye's professional knowledge in drama was best employed when extended to religion and rituals. In light of this standard methodology, generalizations and abstract theoretical discussions were avoided.

The starting point of Ye's study is a Guangji altar 廣濟壇 (Altar of Inclusive Salvation), from where other altars, their mutual relationships and the historical backgrounds of their activities are also investigated. The eleven chapters of the book are systematically arranged: background introduction is given in the first three chapters, "Origins of Ritual Altars" "Altar Troupes and Daoist Priests," and "Altar Rituals;" the main body covers the important aspects of ritual altars, namely "Hand-written Texts of the Ritual Altars," "Magic Charms," "Ritual Drama," "Ritual Music," "The Organization of Ritual Altars," "Ritual implements" and "Ritual Costumes;" the final chapter "Other Related Issues" is an investigation of the Lüshan Sect. Supporting evidence, such as ritual texts and other related sources, is given at the end to provide a more comprehensive view of the subject. It also satisfies the basic requirements of this large-scale research project.

II.

I would like to mention some major contributions and characteristics of the results of Ye and Liu's hard work:

1. The Collection and Preservation of First-hand Sources on Daoist Rituals

For decades, and especially during the Cultural Revolution, popular religions such as lay Daoism (*huoju dao* 火居道), especially the *shigong* practices of ritual teaching, have been suppressed by the government, and so many precious sources have been lost. Ye and Liu have managed to preserve in a fairly substantial way the existing sources through extensive interviews and surveys. Particularly noteworthy is the recovery of rarely known sources such as documents of ordination and transmitting ritual teaching (*chuandu kaofa* 傳度考法), and the secretly transmitted talismans and invocations of lay Daoist altars.

2. The Regulations and Organization of the Transmission Lay Daoist Altars (taodan 道壇)

Ye and Liu clearly delineate the transmission of lay Daoist ritual altars (by family inheritance or apprenticeship) and their genealogies according to the *chuandao kaofa*, demonstrating the institutionalization of this transmission. This suggests that ritual teaching is a well-organized local religion. The authors also trace the social origins of the organization of the altar troupes in order to explain the "mysteries" of the cult. This kind of research facilitates our understanding of lay Daoism and regional Daoist and ritual teaching.

3. The Actual Procedures of Daoist and Lay Rituals

Instead of a complete record of the actual process of Daoist and ritual teaching rituals, the present volume contains a series of tables on rituals for different occasions as a supplementary explanation. A shortcoming of this kind of presentation is that it does not clearly list the procedures of different rituals. Although some of these rituals are no longer practiced, the procedures as dictated from memory by the *shigong* still contain great research value, such as the ritual to dispel epidemics. It is possible that since it is difficult to do field research on the actual procedures of these rituals, the authors had to resort to summary tables as an alternative approach.

4. Explanations of Ritual Items

With the cooperation of the *shigong*, the authors have collected important information about the layout of the altars as well as the costumes and talismans used in the rituals. The combination of visual presentation and verbal explanation results in a vivid representation of the ritual altars used on both ordinary and festive occasions, which in turn draws attention to the ways in which ritual texts are used in the actual process of a ritual.

5. The Spread and Transformations of the Transmission of Ritual Teaching

The transmission of lay Daoist altars emphasizes popular festivals of community renewal (*jiao* 醮). Moreover, certain *zhai rituals* 齋科

are connected to Buddhism instead of Daoism. These regional variations have to do with the popularity of Buddhism in the local area, an
aspect only lightly mentioned by the authors. In fact, the dynamic relations between ritual teaching and Buddhism can be further explored in
the direction of a history of regional religions, as in the discussion of
relationships between ritual teaching and the practice of spirit-mediums
(*tong ji* 童乩).

III.

Ye and Liu and the *shigong* are aware of changes in the ritual teaching,
and of the possibility that it may be lost. This is why they have cooperated to preserve it for future generations. However, after the destruction
of the Cultural Revolution, many secret incantations such as those used
in writing ritual talismans are no longer recorded because their meaning
is lost, so only the forms of the talismans have been preserved. Also,
the secret methods used in reciting invocations have been lost, so only
the words remain. One of the biggest regrets is that since Lüshan has
been considered more "superstitious" than Zhengyi 正一 Daoist sects,
only certain general descriptions have been preserved.

A major emphasis of this volume is the collation of primary
sources, whereas the explanations and analyses serve to reconstruct their
history. Since the researchers themselves do not specialize in Daoism or
ritual teaching, their historical investigation has certain inevitable short-
comings. On the other hand, the authors have a professional understanding of the ritual performances, based on their knowledge of ritual
drama and music. For example, Ye's exhaustive research on *nuo* drama
is itself a good source of materials on religious drama. Ye's study also
opens the way for further research in popular arts and crafts as they are
intricately related to ritual altars, as for example, the meaning of the
content of sacred scroll paintings (*shenzhou* 神軸), the subject matter of
paper crafts, and by extension whether they are made by painters and
artists or by the ritual masters themselves.

In this first volume in a series, Ye and Liu have achieved a major
breakthrough in current research on *nuo* culture in China. One hopes
that the accumulation of knowledge through case studies of this kind

will lead to the development of Chinese theories on the subject. In China, there are many cases similar to the *shigong* in Longyan; for researchers in Chinese religions, the mainland is a fertile territory waiting to be explored. Ye's excellent study, as we have seen, has laid the foundation for further research in the future.

15

TAOIST RITUAL IN THE SHANGHAI AREA

Poul Andersen

I.

1. Zhu Jianming 朱建明, *Shanghai xian Shengtang daoyuan chi qi Taiping gongjiao kaozha jishi* 上海縣聖堂道院及其太平公醮考查紀實 (*The Shengtang Taoist Temple of Shanghai County and its Rite of Public Offering of Great Peace*), *Min-su ch'ü-i ts'ung-shu* 民俗曲藝叢書 (Studies in Chinese Ritual, Theatre and Folklore Series), No. 9, 1993. 216 pages.

2. Zhu Jianming and Tan Jingde 譚敬德, *Shanghai Nanhui xian Laogang xiang nongjia duqiao yishi chi qiao wenhua* 上海南匯縣老港鄉農家渡橋儀式及橋文化 (*The Ritual of "Leading the Soul acorss the Bridge" in a Family of Laogang Township, Nanhui County, Shanghai, with a Discussion of the Culture of Bridges in China*), *Min-su ch'ü-i ts'ung-shu*, No. 43, 1996. 247 pages.

One of the oddities of modern western theories of ritual, especially as applied to Chinese culture, has been the tendency of many scholars to cast suspicion on the notion of meaning in ritual. A dominant school of thought, which counted among its adherents some of the most influential specialists on Taoist liturgy, defended — at least for a while — the radical view that ritual was essentially "meaningless."[1] It is tempting to exclaim with Confucius: 禮云禮云，玉帛云乎哉？(*Lunyu*, Book 17, 11). Arthur Waley translates this as "Ritual, ritual! Does it mean no more than presents of jade and silk?", thus inserting the verb "to mean", which is absent in the original.[2] In fact, what the sentence says is "Ritual, ritual! Is it [nothing but offerings of] jade and silk?" And I would take the implied answer to this rhetorical question to be that, ideally, it certainly is much more than that; it is what it expresses and what it means to those who perform it. Interestingly, the Han dynasty commentator, Zheng Xuan 鄭玄 (127-200), explains the sense as follows: "It means (言) that ritual does not simply exalt [offerings of] jade and silk, what it values is bringing peace to the ruler and regulating the people."[3]

Ever since the *Xunzi* (early third century BC) and the earliest Chinese ritual classics, especially the *Liji*, the topic of the meaning of ritual has been a focus of attention in Chinese philosophy. The key terms are the two modern homophones *yi* 義, 'righteousness,' and *yi* 意, 'intention,' which — though originally apparently pertaining to quite separate semantic fields — in early texts also seem to be used very much interchangeably for the concept of meaning, just like in the earliest dictionaries, notably the *Shuowen jiezi* 說解文字 by Xu Shen 許慎 (c. 100 AD), where both of them refer to the meaning of words or char-

1 See for instance Frits Staal, "The Sound of Religion," *Numen* 33 (1986), p. 186, where he advances the opinion, said to be shared by himself and Kristofer Schipper, that "Taoist ritual consists of networks of relationships that are as rich and varied as those of Vedic ritual. These structural relationships can be fruitfully studied by syntactic methods, in which semantic interpretation plays almost no role."

2 Arthur Waley, *The Analects of Confucius*, New York: Vintage Books, 1938, p. 212. Note that Rodney Needham exploits this quote in a disquisition about the alleged "meaninglessness" of ritual based on this translation; see his "Remarks on Wittgenstein and Ritual," *Exemplars*, Berkeley: University of California Press, 1985, pp. 149 and 159-160.

3 所貴者安上治民. *Lunyu jinzhu jinyi* 論語今註今譯, Mao Zishui 毛子水, ed., Taipei: Shangwu, rev. ed. 1984, p. 271.

acters.[4] A basic metaphor for the ideal action of the ruler, used in the *Xunzi*, is that of the dance — which in itself is conceived of as of a kind of prototype of ritual action. The import of this ritual action is described in the following passage about "the meaning of the dance," in Chapter Twenty of the *Xunzi, Yuelun* 樂論, "A Discussion of Music":[5]

> How do we come to know the meaning of a dance? ... Our eyes not seeing for themselves, our ears not hearing for themselves, we look down and up, we curl and stretch, we advance and retreat, we quicken and slow — in all we are strictly ruled. We exhaust the strength of muscle and bone, constraining ourselves to the converging rhythms of gong and drum without the slightest deviation — and gradually the meaning becomes clear.

It seems that in all the classical passages that are characterized by this tenor, and that in a similar way refer to meaning as emergent within the participants, the term for meaning invariably is *yi*, 'intention,' another important example being the story in Chapter Six of the *Zhuangzi* about the "outrageous" behavior of the two masters Meng Zifan and Qinzhang at the funeral of their friend Sanghu. Having observed this behavior, the disciple of Confucius, Zigong, asked them: "May I inquire whether it is in accordance with the rites to sing with the corpse right there at your feet?" The two of them glanced at each other and smiled, saying: "What does he know about the meaning of the rites?"[6] It would

---

4 Of course, the basic formula for defining meaning used in this dictionary is the simple juxtaposition in a nominal predicate construction: X Y 也, "X means Y", and the more explicit terms for meaning are called upon only in general discussions (where *yi*, "intention", seems to be the common term), and to express special circumstances, such as two characters "having the same meaning", *tongyi* 同意, or (in a rare instance) the specific construction of a character "making no sense", wu yiyi 無意義. For the latter, see *Shuowen jiezi zhenben* 說文解字真本, *Sibu beiyao* ed., Shanghai: Zhonghua shuju, 1927-1935, j. 1 下, p. 17a.

5 *Xunzi jishi* 荀子集釋, Li Disheng 李滌生, ed., Taipei: Xuesheng shuju, 1979, ch. 20, p. 464; translated in Robert Eno, *The Confucian Creation of Heaven: Philosophy and the Defense of Ritual Mastery*(New York: SUNY Press, 1990), p. 180.

6 是惡知禮意. *Zhuangzi* 6, *Zhuzi huiyao* ed., j. 3, p. 10b. Cf. A. C. Graham, *Chuang-tzu. The Seven Inner Chapters and other writings from the book Chuang-tzu* (London: George Allen & Unwin, 1981), p. 89. It may be added that Burton Watson, in his translation of the above passage

appear, in other words, that early Chinese philosophers of different schools share a concept of the meaning of ritual, which relates this to the experience of those who participate in it, and to the overall intentionality, and the attitudes, expressed through it. It would be easy to demonstrate, furthermore, that throughout the subsequent history this concept of the meaning of ritual has represented a very dominant aspect of the view of ritual in Chinese culture in general.

Whether or not this notion of the meaning of ritual can in any objective, "scientific" sense be said to represent the actual meaning of ritual, it certainly is quite representative of the way that the Chinese tend to think about it, even in the present day. As it happens, a similar notion of the meaning of ritual is expressed also in the rubrics of ritual, for instance in the Taoist *jiao* 醮 liturgy, where a central act in all major rituals is the reading of a written document which has the form of a memorial addressed to the supreme deities presiding over the ritual in question and over the liturgy as a whole. As is well-known, the document gives the time and place of the event, and mentions the name and title of the officiating high priest; it identifies the community on whose behalf the liturgy is carried out, and lists the names of the heads of all the households involved; it briefly describes the full program of rituals included, along with a statement of the possible specific purposes of holding the ceremony at the time in question, for instance the specific calamities that need to be redressed; and it ends with a general prayer for blessing

---

from the Xunzi, instead of "the meaning of the dance" has "the spirit of the dance"— a rendering that would seem only to underscore the interpretation suggested here (see *Basic Writings of Mo Tzu, Hsun Tzu, and Han Fei Tzu*, New York: Columbia University Press, 1967, p. 118). Somewhat more problematic is his translation as "the meaning of ritual" of the phrase *li zhi li* 禮 之理, which occurs in the preceding chapter nineteen of the *Xunzi, Lilun* 禮論, "A Discussion of Rites" (*Xunzi jishi*, ch. 19, p. 428; *Basic Writings*, pp. 94-95). Interestingly, the whole passage in question is adopted by Catherine Bell as the motto for her new book, *Ritual: Perspectives and Dimensions* (New York: Oxford University Press, 1997), p. vii, where she quotes it from the rendering of Burton Watson and with no reference to the original, and where she associates it with her agenda of a critique of the emergence of the concept of 'ritual' as "a category for depicting a putatively universal phenomenon" (pp. xi-xii). In fact, the phrase *li zhi li* should probably rather be translated as "the principle (or perhaps: essence) of ritual", and in any case the passage clearly seems concerned, not so much with giving advice about the right way of *talking* about ritual (as suggested by Bell), as it is with the proper and enlightened way of *doing* ritual.

from the supreme deities.[7] The technical term for the reading of this document, which as mentioned occurs in all major rituals of the *jiao* liturgy (and has its direct counterpart in the Taoist funeral liturgy), is *ruyi* 入意, "entering the intention."

The notion of the purpose of ritual expressed in such documents as representing the "meaning" of ritual certainly seems to be supported by the way that the ordinary people of the relevant Chinese communities tend to talk about it. I do not, of course, wish to suggest that what the Taoist priests mumble in classical Chinese, as they recite a memorial behind the closed doors of the temple during a *jiao* ceremony, is generally registered — let alone understood — by the members of the community on whose behalf the liturgy is carried out, nor even necessarily by those of them who are allowed to be present inside the temple during the ceremony as representatives of the community. What I do wish to say, however, is that the priests themselves no doubt typically understand what they are reading (at least when they choose to pay attention to it), and that in fact quite commonly some of the leading members of the community have had a hand in the actual formulation of the document, as it usually is decided upon in the negotiations between the high priest and the local leaders prior to the event. Others clearly take their clues from what they see and what they hear, and no doubt often notice (if they are present at the ceremony), when their own name is mentioned. In any case, the performance in a number of ways speaks for itself and is designed to be expressive of a certain content and to show the execution of a certain sequence of acts. This is not to deny the importance of esoteric rubrics in Taoist liturgy, but to emphasize that mystification is not all. Quite the contrary it is my experience from the field that the explanations offered by the common members of the community, of why they organize and carry out these activities, often sound like a generalization of the specific purposes spelled out as elements of the highly specialized Taoist ritual.

It often seems warranted to speak of a certain unity of interpretation in the community as a whole, a fact that seems to contradict state-

---

7 See for instance Kristofer Schipper, "The Written Memorial in Taoist Ceremonies", Arthur P. Wolf, ed., *Religion and Ritual in Chinese Society* (Stanford: Stanford University Press, 1974), pp. 309-24.

ments such as Rodney Needham's in the article mentioned above concerning the reasons given by participants in ritual for carrying it out. The most common finding, he claims,

> is that those who take part in ritual can give no reasons for it; they say that it is their custom ... In other instances an acknowledged local authority, such as a priest or some other celebrant of ritual, gives a traditional reason, and other participants acquiesce; in that case, the reason is to be regarded as being itself part of the ritual, not as an independent excogitation providing a rational explanation for the performance of the ritual. In yet other instances, different participants may give conflicting reasons; in such a case there can sometimes be acceptable evidence of cogitation, but there is no means of deciding which explanation is the correct one, and there are certainly no grounds to presume that the most rational explanation (if that can be isolated) will provide the real reason for the behavior.[8]

Now, whether or not it makes any sense whatsoever to speak about the "real reasons" for the performance of rituals (and it should be noticed that Needham ends by siding with Waley, who states that there is no such thing), there certainly often is plenty of "(ex)cogitation", as Needham labels it, with a word that seems to correspond fairly well to what is meant by 'the interpretations offered by the participants themselves.' Whether this is true or not, I would like to suggest that (at least as far as Taoist liturgy is concerned) these interpretations are very far from being as random as suggested by Needham and others. There are important constraints, both in the actual structures and expressions of ritual, and in the minds of the participants (including the dominant ideological structures, and the traditions of interpretation transmitted within the community). It is these constraints on interpretation that should be made the focus of research on meaning in ritual, rather than the misleading concept of a permanently fixed "inherent meaning"— a concept that all too easily becomes an alibi for denying the presence of meaning in ritual altogether.

---

8   Needham, pp. 157-158.

Ritual cannot be rightfully termed "meaningless", based on the sole premise that it does not possess "inherent meaning". Even in the absence of such inherent meaning the interpretation of ritual is far from a total free-for-all, but rather — like the interpretation of literary works — an exercise that is bound by the "text" as it is given, and the correctness of which (far from being completely ephemeral) can be measured against the evidence found in this text.[9] Just as with a literary work there is no single, "true" interpretation which would exclude all others, nor any requirement for any given interpretation that in order to be valid it must be supported by everybody in the community. The absurdity of imposing such high standards on meaning in ritual perhaps becomes most apparent if we perform a thought-experiment based on the analogy between ritual and theatre. Is it conceivable that for instance a student of the works of Shakespeare would base his search for the meaning of these works on interviewing select members of the audience leaving the theatre after a performance (together with interviews with the director, the actors, the stage crew, etc.) — and having discovered a certain lack of agreement between the answers obtained would declare that Shakespeare's plays were "meaningless" (or even "inherently meaning-less")?

In any case, no matter what status is accorded the interpretations of the participants themselves (and it should be noticed that the participants include the liturgists who originally established the forms under discussion, as well as those who have changed them through history, that is, the "creators" of the rituals in question), it seems incontestable that these interpretations in many ways influence the actual performance. They are relevant for the way in which performances take shape, develop, and are modified over time, and for this reason alone are worthy of our attention and important to study.

II.

The first book by Zhu Jianming is to be commended for the systematic

---

9 Compare Umberto Eco, *The Limits of Interpretation* (Bloomington: Indiana University Press, 1990), especially pp. 1-63.

attention it pays to this crucial aspect of ritual, that is, for the frequent references to the interpretations of the event offered by the participants themselves, and especially for the lengthy reports of the interviews with the various categories of participants concerning their understandings of the purposes and effects of the ceremony, and their individual motivations for participating. To this reviewer these parts represent the most valuable contribution of the book, and — it should be said — they further demonstrate the huge advantage for this kind of fieldwork which accrues from the fact that the scholar conducting it is in a fundamental way familiar with the way of life of the people of the community, since he is Chinese himself.[10] I shall end this account with a more detailed discussion of these parts of the book, and also in this connection point to what appears as missed opportunities in this respect. However, prior to this an overview of the descriptive core of the book is in order.

The topic of the book is the *Taiping gongjiao* 太平公醮, "Communal Offering for Great Peace," which is performed annually on the fifteenth of the seventh month in the lunar calendar, that is, on the day of the Middle Prime, *zhongyuan* 中元, in the Taoist temple Shengtang daoyuan 聖堂道院, located in the township of Sanlin 三林 in the suburban district of Pudong 浦東, south of the city of Shanghai and east of the river Huangpu 黃浦. The history of the temple goes back to the end of the Northern Song dynasty and is documented in two stone inscriptions, of which the oldest, the *Guishe bei* 龜蛇碑 in the eastern part of the middle courtyard, Zhong tianjing 中天井, was carved in 1159, when the temple had been rebuilt after its destruction (ill., p. 157, full text included as app. 1, pp. 75-77). Having been abolished during the Cultural Revolution and used to house some minor industries, a plan for the restoration of the temple was drawn up by local Taoist priests in 1986, and toward the end of the following year the first of the newly-made statues, representing Guanyin, was consecrated in a large-scale *kaiguang* 開光 dedication ceremony.

The book begins with an account of the community which supports the temple, its history, demography, and economy (pp. 3-5), and contin-

---

10 Zhu Jianming was born in Wuxi 無錫, Jiangsu, in 1944, and has studied at Fudan University in Shanghai. He has published extensively on various kinds of Chinese theatre and currently holds a position as Assistant Researcher at the Shanghai Research Institute of the Arts.

ues with a sketch of the historical vicissitudes of the temple (pp. 5-7). It proceeds with a very detailed description of the whole complex of buildings and the various sacred objects, statues of deities, and even couplets, *yinglian* 楹聯, to be found in them at the present time, all supported by a large number of diagrams and photographs at the end of the book (pp. 8-18; ill., pp. 146-188). It is a "great temple in three stages," *sandai dadian* 三埭大殿, and the main deity, *zhushen* 主神, housed at the center of the third and innermost stage, is Zhenwu 眞武 or Xuantian shangdi 玄天上帝, the supreme Taoist god of the northern heavens, whose residence is flanked to the west by the Palace of the Three Pure Ones, Sanqing dian 三清殿. The author does not venture into an analysis of the very rich structure of the total pantheon of this temple complex, and thus, for instance, the crucial importance of the local deity, Shi xianggong 施相公, whose residence is found in the far eastern end of the middle stage of the temple, becomes clear only later in connection with the description of the ritual activities on the festival day, where also a series of highly interesting legends of this god is reported (pp. 42-44). In general, however, this opening description of the social and physical context of the event is both competent and thorough, and thus very satisfying.

The same is true for the account of the community of Taoists who are in charge of ritual activities in the temple (pp. 18-28). They all belong to the School of Orthodox Unity of the Shanghai area, *Haishang Zhengyi jiaopai* 海上正一教派, but they are further classified as either *Yuannei* 院內 or *Yuanwai daoshi* 院外道士. The first category, which is also labeled *Yuandao* 院道, comprises the eight Taoists who are formally affiliated with the temple as members of its "organizing committee", *guanli zu* 管理組, and who appear to be obligated to offer their services only within the temple and for a fixed remuneration. The book gives the biographies of each of these eight Taoists and further lists the names, ages, and places of origin of twelve "external Taoists", who may be invited to assist at large-scale events such as the annual *Taiping gongjiao*, but who otherwise appear mostly to do their business in the communities outside the temple. It is clear from this biographical material that another distinction, namely that between Taoists who have been ordained (and therefore have a "ritual name", *faming* 法名) and the so-called "ordinary Taoists", cuts across the dividing line between the categories of "internal" and "external Taoists", but no information is included concerning the circumstances of such ordination (except for the fact that in general those Taoists who have studied with a master are said to have completed their education after a fixed period of five years).

A further label encountered at every turn is that of *sanju daoshi* 散居道士, "Taoist living scattered [among the people]", but unfortunately without any direct statement of the reference of this term. It is clear from the biographies of the "internal Taoists" that several of them have in earlier phases of their lives supported themselves as *sanju daoshi*, the obvious implication being that, as Taoists formally affiliated with the temple, they are no longer to be considered as such, even though none of them actually live in the temple. In a concluding paragraph we are told that since the Republic, the Taoists of suburban Shanghai have to a large extent been *sanju*, also called *huoju* 火居 Taoists, and that for economic reasons even those Taoists who "are in temples," *zaiyuan* 在院, have "largely been scattered into all directions to perform activities in the countryside" (p. 24). However, the text continues, since the Taoists of the Shengtang daoyuan only do ritual inside the temple, they necessarily must obey the various regulations of the temple and cannot at will perform activities in the villages. As for the "external Taoists", their situation is quite different and much more free in this respect, and although the government does not approve of ritual activities in the homes of the rural population, the phenomenon of Taoists being invited to do this still is very widespread. It may be suggested, perhaps, that this whole discussion leaves it very much an open question which Taoists actually do what, and that the term *sanju*, completely devoid of its original meaning, is being used here more as a vague indication of a range of activities that the authorities view very negatively, while tacitly allowing them to continue to exist. In other words, the term *sanju*, having by now been adopted basically as a pejorative term in the language of official propaganda, should probably be either avoided or else given a strict redefinition in scholarly discourse.

The first of the "internal Taoists" mentioned in the book is the seventy-two year old Tang Shunchang 唐順昌, who is the leading master, *daozhang* 道長, of the temple, and who has been the driving force behind its restoration (see pp. 18-19). Most of the couplets carved in the new buildings were devised by him, and he supervised the copying of the scriptures that form the reconstructed collection of the temple. He is said to be especially skilled in ritual dances and the steps of Yu, *Yubu* 禹步, a fact that is given added significance by a remark to the effect that what distinguishes "ordinary Taoists" from those who have been ordained is that "they do not know ritual dances," *buhui fawu* 不會法舞 (p. 21). Indeed, this special importance of ritual dances in the Taoism of the region is underscored by a discussion of the attitudes of the Taoists toward their individual styles of performing the steps of Yu, which each of them ostensibly consider as a special skill essential to their livelihood, *kanjia benling* 看家本領, not to be transmitted to outsiders (p. 45). Tang Shunchang is referred to throughout the book as a main informant of the author, and one would have appreciated an account of his interpretation of the crucial position of dances in the ritual system. Something similar may be said about the somewhat surprising (and unexplained) regulation mentioned in the book as having been issued by the Taoist association of Shanghai, stipulating that, as a general rule, talismans should only be preserved and not used in actual ritual (p. 28).

The rituals performed at the temple are divided into the two main categories of "communal offerings," *gongjiao* 公醮, and "private offerings," *sijiao* 私醮, the latter being further subdivided into services for the living and for the dead. However, apart from a list of names of rituals and parts of ritual, along with the remark that programs of services are combined from these elements according to the needs of the patrons of ritual, *zhaizhu* 齋主, no inkling is given in the book concerning the contents and circumstances of such "private offerings" (pp. 28-29). The general trend in the development from the earlier more complex and lengthy ceremonies (which for both main categories might last as long as seven, ten, or fifteen days) to shorter and simpler ones is underscored in the book (pp. 29 and 31). The precedent of the *Luotian dajiao* 羅天大醮 performed by the 63rd Celestial Master, Zhang Enpu 張恩溥, in Shanghai in 1932 is mentioned, but we are told that since the 1950's such large-scale ceremonies have all but disappeared in the Shanghai area and been replaced by the *Taiping gongjiao* lasting one day and one night. Indeed, in 1991 a further simplification of the system was introduced in the Shengtang daoyuan, when the duration of the ceremony was reduced to only one day, starting at eight o'clock in the morning and ending around six or seven in the evening.

Some more information about the historical development of Taoist ritual in the Shanghai area would have been very desirable in this connection, especially concerning the program of the *Taiping gongjiao* and its place in the liturgical system of the Shengtang daoyuan. The book includes an appendix by one Hu Zhixin 胡志新 (app. 3, pp. 81-84), which — though marred by errors to the point of making the reader doubt its reliability — contains the interesting claim that since the Ming dynasty the main festival at the temple, *miaohui* 廟會, comprising three days of Taoist ritual, *zhaijiao fatan* 齋醮法壇, has occurred around the date of the fifteenth of the third month in the lunar calendar. One wonders whether this festival should be viewed as the predecessor of the current *Taiping gongjiao*, and what might have caused the change in date. It is of course beyond the scope of a field report from one particular locality to give answers to larger questions of this nature, but let it be stated here nonetheless that we very much lack a clear idea of the distribution of liturgical systems over the map of China, in terms of their religious affiliations as Taoist, Buddhist or both, their places in the ritual calendar near the day of the Middle Prime, zhongyuan, or closer to the winter solstice etc. The *Taiping gongjiao* of this suburb of Shanghai is marked as belonging on the day of the *Pudu* 普度 by its emphasis on the rituals and scriptures related to the hell of the Blood Lake, *Xuehu* 血湖 (the *Pudeng yishi* 普燈儀式 described on pp. 48-54), and the *Liandu yishi* 煉度儀式, which aims at the salvation of "orphaned souls", *guhun* 孤魂 (pp. 54-58). One would like to know whether this orientation is typical of the Taoism of the Shanghai area or perhaps a specialty of the Shengtang daoyuan, in which indeed the cult of Guanyin figures prominently (see pp. 9-10 and 67-68), but the book gives no clues in this regard.

This "syncretistic" flavor of the temple and the festival notwithstanding, it should be noticed nonetheless that the central part of this "communal offering" is very much an example of "bottom line" Taoist liturgy. As is very often the case, the shortening and simplification of a liturgical program not only eliminates a good deal of *interesting* material, but also has the effect of demonstrating what are the most important, the indispensable parts of ritual. It ought not really be a surprise to anybody that what we are left with here as the key elements of this minimal program of a *jiao* are the ritual dances and the "presentation of the memorial," *baibiao* 拜表 (pp. 44-48). Fortunately they are well represented by the ritual manual, which is reproduced *in toto*, *Zhaijiao baibiao chaoke* 齋醮拜表朝科 (app. 8, pp. 127-143), and by a series of photos (pp. 204-209). The description of the actual performance leaves much to be desired and is far from demonstrating any real expertise in Taoist ritual on the part of the author. The account of the central ritual of presenting the memorial is limited to a simple listing of labels for the parts of the ritual included (which furthermore bear no clear relation to the above-mentioned ritual manual), and matters get only worse when, at the end of the description of the whole program of performances, he concludes with a section allegedly intended to explain the import of some of the most fundamental of these parts of ritual, or the basic concepts of effects achieved through ritual acts. The most intriguing terms of the above-mentioned listing, for instance, the *Huangmen guan kemu* 黃門冠科目, are simply repeated without being explained, while the more common and accessible term "the transformation of the body," *bianshen* 變身, is given the weak interpretation of serving to convey the idea of "the contact between ordinary humans and divine immortals", and the "externalization of the [inner] officials," *chuguan* 出官, is said to serve the purpose of "pacifying the dwelling and driving away of baleful influences," *zhenzhai qusha* 鎮宅驅煞 (pp. 58-59). Admittedly, it is not the task of a field report of this kind to enter into a comparative study of Taoist ritual, but it nonetheless should be mentioned that much improvement could have been achieved through a consultation of the growing body of literature on Taoist ritual in the Shanghai area, by scholars such as Chen Yaoting 陳曜廷, and even the video-tapes of such ritual made by Chen Dacan 陳大燦.[11]

As mentioned earlier, the book does much better when it comes to accounting for the interpretations and motivations for participating in the ceremony of the ordinary members of the community. We are told that the older people, as part of their preparations, would explain to their children, as well as to skeptical neighbors, the religious meaning of the festival of the Middle Prime, according to their own beliefs and understandings (p. 35). At the same time it is made clear that large numbers of people will burn incense for the most varied reasons, each hoping there-

---

11 *Zhongguo daojiao zhaijiao* 中國道教齋醮(Shanghai: China Record Company, 1987).

by to obtain some specific benefit from the divine world, and all of them adding to the festive atmosphere in the temple (p. 36). A special case is made of the patron of ritual, Zhang Linfang 張林芳, a local woman of fifty-two years of age, who runs a small private clothing factory, and who, by virtue of her relatively high contribution to the festival (600 元), and her involvement in its organization and execution, is endowed with the status of "chief sacrificer," *zhu jiren* 主祭人, of the *Taiping gongjiao*.

The high point of her involvement falls in the initial part of the program, in the separate ceremony performed in the Palace of the King Ascending to Heaven, Shangtian wang dian 上天王殿, in front of the niche with the statues of Shi xianggong and his wife. The climax of this ceremony is the wiping of the statues performed by Zhang Linfang, when she has climbed up and entered into the niche, using towels that are handed to her from individual members of the community and following their individual instructions concerning the exact spot to be wiped. It is believed that the towels thereby acquire healing powers against illnesses corresponding to the spot in question. In spite of the strenuous exertion, Zhang is never replaced in this task, and indeed, according to an elderly bystander, is assumed to possess a special skill which makes it possible for her to connect with the gods in this particular way (pp. 40-41). In her own account, given in the week after the festival, she confirms that in her view the fact that everybody expects her to get especially involved in the activities also reflects the "decree of the gods", *shenxian de zhiyi* 神仙的旨意, but adds that in fact this accords very well with her own purposes, since by being the person who gets closest to the gods she also expects to be the one most likely to receive their blessings (p. 61).

The book contains a series of interviews with women of the community concerning the meaning of the Blood Lake rituals, which in a very interesting way relate this part of the service with specific women's problems connected with childbirth and menstrual bleeding (pp. 52-54). It further gives a number of interpretations of the final *Liandu* ceremony, provided by two of the leading Taoists and by Zhang Linfang, through which the ceremony is related specifically to the purpose of saving the souls of those who were killed during the Japanese bombing without warning of Shanghai on August 13, 1937 — the anniversary of which in 1991 coincided with the day of the Middle prime and thus with the day of the festival (p. 56). To this reviewer these interpretations far surpass in interest the highly conventional and "politically correct" account of the "social function" of the festival, given by the author at the end of his description (pp. 62-68). We are told there that burning incense in the temple in some ways represents a healthy activity for old people, that it may keep them from gambling, and that religious worship, when practiced with moderation, is not at all a bad thing for "old peasants and people living in the new residential quarters". While containing an (apparently harmful) element of "idealism", it clearly has a social-psychological and moral value that can be viewed as useful to society.[12] The most striking example, however, of the urge to find political justification for religious activity is in the afore-mentioned appendix by Hu Zhixin (pp. 81-84). The reconstruction of the temple is referred to here as resulting from the "enlightened leadership of the party", and the advantage of its existence for the inflow of foreign currency is applauded. However, since the author of this appendix is misinformed about the festival to the point of being confused about the date of the Middle Prime (it is performed each year on the eighteenth of the eighth month in the lunar calendar, he claims), one truly wonders what could possibly have made the inclusion of this appendix appear to be called for.

All this said, it should be emphasized that political pressures are of course very far from being irrelevant to religious practice. On the contrary, and as the study of any of the modern religions in China would show, political interference and manipulation stands out as one of the factors which contributes to the change of the form and content of ritual and for this reason should be followed with close attention. The present book gives at least one example of sensitivity to this issue, namely in the account of the ways in which the legends of the gods are transmitted among the Taoists and the other believers in the Shengtang daoyuan (p. 65). We are told that in the public sphere the Taoists will underscore the heroic, humanitarian, and patriotic nature of the gods, that is, their "positive social meaning", in an effort to obtain the support of the gov-

---

12 The book here reflects the ongoing attempts at legitimization of Taoism in the eyes of political authorities, represented by numerous articles in the journal *Zhongguo daojiao* 中國道教, which serves as a central mouthpiece of the National Taoist Association.

ernment and to avoid influencing public opinion unfavorably. The result, however, inevitably, is that the legends are shaped after a single mold, that they loose their freshness and distinctiveness of detail, and that the "weakness of complete uniformity" appears. One is relieved to hear that this political coloring of the legends apparently does not characterize their transmission within the more intimate setting of the confines of the temple, but one is led to wonder, nonetheless, how long this situation will be able to withstand the pressures of a more public and politically structured mass culture.

A related form of political influence (at least in the sense of "academic politics") shows up in the choices of terminology and theoretical concepts applied more or less as "window dressing" in this and other books of the series. It remains a cause of puzzlement to this reviewer whether the subsuming of the practices described in the book as surviving elements of "*nuo* culture," *nuo wenhua* 儺文化, is in the end motivated by anything but the fact that the original project description for the whole series defined it as being concerned essentially with Nuo plays, *Nuoxi* 儺戲. Similarly, it should be said once and for all that the mere occurrence of animals in the context of religious worship is very far from justifying the reference to this worship as "a reflection of the culture of totemism within popular Taoism" (p. 68). As indicated, the mentioned labels are called up only in the beginning and at the very end of the book, and they contribute absolutely nothing to the analysis. If, however, they are to be understood as nothing but polite nods in the direction of acknowledged academic positions, then why not simply do without them?

III.

The second book by Zhu Jianming is co-authored by Tan Jingde, who, according to the postface (pp.246-247), had collaborated with Zhu also on earlier field-work projects, and who presumably is from Taiwan. In any case, the postface presents the book as the result of a joint effort of scholars from both sides of the Taiwan Strait, and indeed it differs from the one reviewed above in comprising a comparative perspective, that is, in including summaries of some ritual practices from Taiwan that serve to place the primary field-work materials of the book in a larger perspective, as well as some references to the related ritual program described in the Song dynasty compendium by Lu Taigu 呂太古, *Daomen tongjiao biyong ji* 道門通教必用集 (DZ 1226) (pp. 32-55).

The ceremony described in the book is the "Ritual for Crossing the Bridge," *Duqiao keyi* 渡橋科儀, and like the ceremony of the book reviewed above it pertains to the Taoism of the Zhengyi school of Shanghai, *Shanghai Zhengyi pai daojiao* 上海正一派道教, though in this case the framework is that of the funeral liturgy. The venues of the ceremony mentioned are in most cases private homes, and in one case the Temple of the Eastern Sacred Mountain, *Dongyue miao* 東嶽廟 in Shanghai, the core event of the book being the performance on July 9, 1994, in the home of the Shen 沈 family in the township of Laogang, Nanhui county, some thirty-five kilometers to the southeast of the city center of Shanghai. The occasion of the ceremony was the completion of the third seven day cycle after the death of the head of the family, Shen Laigen 沈來根, who had died rather suddenly from a liver disease, under circumstances that appeared to have provoked a sense of remorse among the children for having been somewhat negligent, and thus conceivably had created a relatively strong motivation for having a ceremony for the benefit of the deceased in order to alleviate this feeling.

The social and economic background of the family, which represents a rather well-to-do milieu of managers of small industries, is accounted for in great detail, and so are the circumstances of the participating Taoists (pp. 3-5 and 9-10). Once again, these fall into two major categories, namely the local Taoists who live in the township itself and are referred to as *sanju daoshi*, and the Taoists of the *Dongyue miao*, who are designated "temple Taoists," *yuandao* 院道. The division of labor between the two categories is very clear, the local Taoists (as the first to be involved) being responsible for the basic organization of the event, including the preparation of altars, offerings, and other ritual paraphernalia, as well as for contacting and inviting the "temple Taoists". The scope of the event (two days and one night) surpassing the capacity of these local Taoists, the "temple Taoists" clearly are needed for their ritual expertise, and also apparently for the sense of official approval that they lend to the event. The head of the *Dongyue miao*, Chen Xuegeng 陳雪賡, not being available because of illness, the con-

tingent of seven "temple Taoists" was headed by the president of the
Taoist Association of Nanhui, Lu Xiangzhi 陸象之. It included, notably,
the sixty-three year old Taoist, Ji Wangyi 季望一, who clearly is considered a leading expert on the core element of the ceremony, the rite of
"crossing the bridge," *duqiao*, and who is a key informant referred to
throughout the book for his interpretations of the rite (biographical
details on p. 84).

The full ritual program for the event is listed, including the initial
and concluding parts presided over by Lu Xiangzhi (pp. 14-15 and 24-
26), but only the core rite of "crossing the bridge" performed by Ji is
described in detail (pp. 15-24), and almost all of the photographic illustrations are of this rite (pp. 230-245). The interpretations by Ji Wangyi
and the other priests are interspersed not only in this descriptive section,
but also in the initial part of the comparative section, which focuses on
the ritual manuals used by Ji (pp. 32-40). The interpretations are of great
interest, both for the window they open to the understanding of the
Taoist priests themselves of the meaning of their ritual activity, and
especially for the light they throw on the ways in which ritual may be
constructed by an individual priest. Thus we are told that Ji possesses an
essentially complete manual for a rite entitled *Muyu duqiao* 沐浴度橋,
"bathing and crossing the bridge" and that he bases himself on this manual for the performance of the rite, while occasionally supplementing it
with material from the more extensive manual belonging to Chen
Xuegeng, entitled *Wangfang muyu qiaoshi* 王方沐浴橋式. (Both these
manuals are included in the book, in full punctuated editions, along with
the manual of Chen for the initial rite of "entertaining the kings [of
hell]," *Daiwang* 待王, pp. 95-123). His reasons for adding material are
both aesthetic and practical (for instance, serving the purpose of extending the duration of the rite at a larger occasion), but it is interesting to
notice that in organizing the material from these varied sources, Ji takes
great care to analyze the import of the elements of ritual in question, and
that occasionally he will rearrange them in an order that differs from the
sequence found in the manuals, but that appears to him more logical in
relation to the actual content of the texts in question. See especially pp.
23-24 on the addition of the final hymn of "Paying Tribute to the
Ascent," *Chao chaosheng* 朝超升, which extols the merit accrued by
the family through having organized the ceremony, and p. 37 on the

rearrangement of the sequence of the hymns relating to the different bridges crossed by the deceased soul. We are far removed, in other words, from the notion of a mindless repetition of the fixed structures of ritual, viewed by some western scholars as characteristic of the transmission of ritual traditions in Asia.[13]

As mentioned, this book has a section containing a certain amount of comparative material referring to related forms of ritual in Taiwan and in texts found in the *Daozang* (pp. 40-55). Additional comparative material is provided in the section dealing with the deities mentioned in the rite of "crossing the bridge" (pp. 61-72), as well as in a general section on the "culture of bridges," *Qiao wenhua* 橋文化 (pp. 78-94). The latter section contains an interesting discussion of the different Buddhist and Taoist concepts of the all-important *Naihe* bridge 奈河橋, to be crossed by at least some dead souls, and it ends with a discussion of the materials referring to this bridge in Mulian plays of southern Anhui, Jiangxi, and Hunan provinces (the book further includes the text of the printed version of an episode related to the crossing of the Naihe bridge, deriving from a Mulian play of a Jiangxi theatre troupe, pp. 123-133). While undoubtedly all this material contains much information of interest, it also raises the question of relevance to the project at hand. It might be asked, for instance, whether in fact the practices of *hongtou*, "redhead" priests in the *Dongyue miao* in Tainan — though of course in a manner similar to the rituals described in the present book they aim at saving the souls of deceased human beings by leading them across the Naihe bridge — in the end constitute the most appropriate frame of reference for the purposes of comparison. The choice of the *Guoqiao* 過橋, "crossing the bridge" rituals, performed by "redhead" priests in Jinmen, described by Paul Katz (pp. 43-45), certainly seems rather arbitrary, since they are not related to services for the dead, but performed for the benefit of the living. There is an almost endless amount of ritual practices and popular customs in various parts of China that have to do with bridges, and it may be suggested that for the purposes of the present book a far more interesting frame of reference for comparison would have been similar services for the dead, performed by other Zhengyi priests, preferably in neighboring parts of China. It is, unfortunately, an

---

13 See especially Frits Staal, "The Meaninglessness of Ritual," *Numen,* 26 (1979), pp. 2-22.

option that has not been explored by the authors of the present book.

Compared to the earlier book by Zhu Jianming, on the annual festival in the Shengtang daoyuan of the suburb, Pudong, the present book to some extent represents a greater effort to place the ritual described in a larger context. It should be noted also that the fact that the book is based on a collaborative effort has made it possible to achieve greater completeness in the descriptive aspect of the work. Thus the book also includes at the end a very comprehensive analysis of the musical accompaniment of the ritual, contributed by the other author, Tan Jingde, and with notations for all the melodies used (pp. 134-229). All in all, the book appears less contaminated by political considerations than the earlier work, and indeed the fairly long section on the "[social] import of the ritual of crossing the bridge," *Duqiao zhiyi* 渡橋旨意 (pp. 72-78), while taking recent social and political developments into account, is much sounder and more interesting than the corresponding section in the other book. A key notion is that of a growing influence of Taoism in modern China, based on the growing emphasis in modern Taoism on traditional "Confucian" values such as *xiao* 孝, "filial piety," and on the promotion of traditional morality, especially through the performance of ceremonies such as the one described in the present book, for the salvation of dead souls on behalf of members of the ordinary population, who desire in this way to fulfill their final obligations toward their parents. We are told that in this way "clever Taoists" have found a niche for themselves in modern Chinese society, which has little to do with the traditional Taoist pursuit of individual immortality, but which secures them a role in modern society as providers of psychological relief in connection with bereavement, and of a certain social-psychological equilibrium in the families. It may be questioned, of course, whether in truth this function of Taoist liturgies represents a departure from the traditional function of Taoism in Chinese society. What is clear, in any case, is that the implied strong emphasis on morality corresponds very well to the official policies of the Chinese government and of the National Taoist Association, concerning the future role of Taoism in Chinese society. It should be noticed, furthermore, that it is supported in the present book by interviews, both with the Taoist priests and with the family members involved in the ceremony described. The book faithfully reports the variety of attitudes expressed by the people involved

(including those of the family members, who would not commit themselves to participating in the ceremony). It thus provides a precious
insight into the situation on the ground, which is addressed more
abstractly in official statements found in the official mouth-pieces of the
authorities, and often in the form of policies for the repression of the
undesirable activities of Zhengyi priests. It is to be hoped that fieldwork of this kind will continue to be carried out in China, thus making it
possible to get an impression of current developments, and to keep an
eye on the impact of these repressive policies.[14]

---

14 See for instance the "temporary regulations for dealing with *sanju* daoshi of the Zhengyi tradition," in eleven paragraphs, passed by the Sixth Congress of the Chinese Taoist Association on
August 24, 1998, *Zhongguo daojiao,* 1998.4: 22. Carried out to the letter, these regulations
clearly would have had the effect of making a good part of the activities described in the present
book, namely those of the "local Taoists" involved, practically impossible.

D.
NORTH CHINA

16

A "LANTERN FESTIVAL" RITUAL IN SOUTHWEST SHANXI

David Johnson

1. Huang Zhusan 黃竹三 and Wang Fucai 王福才, *Shanxi sheng Quwo xian Renzhuang cun Shanku shenpu diaocha baogao* 山西省曲沃縣任莊村扇鼓神譜調查報告 (*A Report On the "Fan Drum Roster of the Gods" Ritual of Renzhuang Village, Quwo County, Shanxi*), *Min-su ch'ü-i ts'ung-shu* 民俗曲藝叢書 (Studies in Chinese Ritual, Theatre and Folklore Series), No. 14, 1994. 214 pages. Referred to hereafter as *Report*.

"Fan Drum Roster of the Gods" is the name of a ritual, though it sounds like the title of a text. It was traditionally performed in Renzhuang Village, Quwo County at the time of the *yuanxiao* 元宵 festival, the first full moon of the new year, now generally known as the Lantern Festival. Hence it was a seasonal festival, marking a particular point in the cycle of the year, rather than a temple festival, celebrating the birthday of a god. This alone sets it apart from most of the village rituals treated in the volumes of the *Min-su ch'ü-i ts'ung-shu*. The ritual takes its name from two of its characteristic features: the round one-sided drums resembling large fans that were used to accompany most of the dancing, and an invocation to over 500 gods near the start of the ceremony.

The book has 131 pages of main text and an 81-page appendix that includes maps, plans, dance diagrams, seventy-four invaluable black and white photographs, and, most important, a reproduction of a hand-written copy, dated 1909, of the liturgy of the Fan Drum ritual. The text is divided into five chapters and a short conclusion. The first provides a brief sketch of the geography, history, population, communications, products, and pre-modern religious life of Quwo County, together with a somewhat more detailed account of the topography, history, population, temples and temple festivals, and customs of Renzhuang Village, plus some remarks on the Xu lineage, the dominant lineage in the village. The material on the county is drawn largely from a few local histories, that on the village from similar sources supplemented by local infor-mants. As is the case throughout the book, information provided by vil-lage residents is not labelled as such (there are a few exceptions), but instead is simply stated as fact. This can be confusing when it concerns activities that are no longer performed regularly or buildings that are no longer there. The reader must pay close attention or risk the mistaken assumption that a ritual or temple that has been defunct for many years still exists.

The second chapter is a very short discussion (less than five pages) of the provenance and physical characteristics of the manuscript of the Fan Drum ritual liturgy, together with an account of its discovery in 1987 and of the efforts of village leaders and their academic and offical sponsors to reconstruct and film the ritual. To this is added a summary account of the (very sparse) history of performances of the Fan Drum ritual since 1938.

The third chapter is a detailed description of the entire ritual, based on the 1909 liturgical manuscript and the 1989 videotaped performance (of which Huang Zhusan was a sponsor and at which he was present). It contains edited transcriptions of virtually the entire manuscript, together with scripts of three skits that are not in the manuscript but were recon-structed by villagers for the performance. It also contains descriptions of all the non-verbal parts of the ritual, such as dances and music. This is the most important part of the text section of the *Report* and, at sixty-nine pages, is by far the longest. I will pause here to give an account of the *Report*'s description of the Fan Drum ritual, and then resume my summary of the book's contents.

On the eighth day of every twelfth month a meeting was called to decide whether the ritual should be held at the upcoming New Year. The head of the Xu lineage, other respected members of the lineage, and the leader of the gong and drum troupe attended. Also present was the leader of the twelve members of the Xu lineage who held the hereditary position of "godly families" (*shenjia* 神家), the most important performers in the Fan Drum ritual. If the decision was made to proceed, rehearsals began on the 23rd day of the twelfth lunar month under the direction of the leader of the *shenjia*. Other important personnel were the leader of the flower-drum troupe and the stage manager, who had overall responsibility for preparing the courtyard of the Guandi Temple for the ritual and for seeing that all the ritual accessories were ready and that everything else was in good order. Perhaps most important of the ritual accessories were complex constructions as much as six feet tall made by village women of hardened wheat flour dough, which were placed on the temporary altars in the ritual space. Despite their importance in the Fan Drum ritual, and their beauty, the *Report* does not explain the meaning of these objects, tell how they were made, or even describe them (though it provides photographs).

After the performers had been selected and rehearsals were well under way, the Eight Trigrams Altar had to be prepared. It was a temporary construction that was disassembled after the ritual was completed. Eight altars made of ordinary household tables and chairs were erected in a circle about forty feet in diameter. The altar on the north was about twelve feet high, the three at the other cardinal directions about ten feet, and the rest about eight feet. Each was elaborately decorated with, among other things, the towers of hardened dough mentioned above.

The Eight Trigrams Altar was constructed and furnished on the twelfth and thirteenth of the first month. After breakfast on the fourteenth, a small procession composed of the gong and drum troupe, a man holding a large banner with the words "Solemnly Carry Out the *Nuo* Ritual; Expel Disease and Drive Out Illness," the twelve *shenjia*, and the flower-drum troupe made a tour of the village, returned to the courtyard of the Guandi Temple, and commenced chanting the Invitation to the Gods, the list of over 500 deities also known as the Roster of the Gods.

The next important event was an exorcism called Collecting Disasters. The exorcist was a spirit-medium, or rather (in the 1989 performance), a man playing the part of a spirit-medium without actually being possessed.[1] He was called *Mamazi* 馬馬子 and was one of the *shenjia*, not a local spirit-medium. The Collecting of Disasters began with eleven *shenjia* dancing and drumming in a circle around the twelfth, the *Mamazi*, in front of the main (north) altar. The *Mamazi* was stripped to the waist, wore red trousers and a short red apron, and had a plain yellow cloth wrapped around his head. He brandished his "sounding knife" and cracked his whip toward each of the altars, and then left the courtyard of the Guandi Temple and went to the Xu lineage hall, which was in the southeastern corner of the Guandi Temple complex. (These buildings no longer exist.) There he engaged in a dialogue with the lineage elders, speaking in the voice of the goddess Houtu 后土.

After sacrificing a rooster and pouring out three cups of wine, he set off to visit every house in the village. During these visits he received offerings from each family and provided them in return with a charm on which was written in red "Accept the Command to Behead Demons" and in black "Secure the Family — Increase Good Fortune." During the two hours or so that it took for the *Mamazi* to visit every household, the gong and drum troupe and the flower-drum troupe performed at the Eight Trigrams Altar. The report does not indicate how many songs originally were in the repertoire of the flower-drum troupe; only two titles are mentioned, and only one could be reconstructed (there were no written scripts). When the *Mamazi* finished his visits to the village households, he and his entourage returned to the Eight Trigrams Altar. The flower-drum troupe then concluded its performance and the first day's activities came to a close.

On the following day, the night of the full moon and the main day of the festival, the ritual began with a formal welcome to the gods who had arrived the day before, and invitations to any gods who may have been overlooked. The first and second *shenjia* each recited a short verse, the fifth invited any overlooked deities, then the first and second chanted longer verses that each introduced a specific god. Then the pat-

---

1   It would be good to know if the simulation of spirit possession was always a characteristic of this part of the ritual, or whether it is a recent addition.

tern was repeated with the eleventh, twelfth, and sixth *shenjia* taking the place of the first, second, and fifth.[2] This completed the welcoming and settling of the gods. The twelve *shenjia* then began a series of six skits or playlets, of which the first three were performed on the fifteenth and the remaining three on the sixteenth. The skits were all performed at the Eight Trigrams Altar, before an audience of both gods and people. They are short and the language is simple colloquial, but their meaning is by no means obvious.

"The Winds Blow" (*chuifeng* 吹風), the first skit, is composed of brief dialogues between the central wind and the southeast, northwest, northeast, and southwest winds. In the next skit, "Opening the Granaries" (*dacang* 打倉) the characters are the five directions, with the center questioning the other four. Each is asked what storehouse it has opened, and answers with what amounts to a riddle. The final performance of the fifteenth was a comic dialogue, very reminiscent of *xiangsheng* 相聲, that is considerably longer than the previous pieces. It is light-hearted and very colloquial, beginning with a duel of wits about an unpaid debt, moving on to riddles, and ending with a sort of tall tale contest. This is all the *Report* tells us of the ceremonies on the fifteenth, but it seems certain that there was also the usual lantern-viewing, promenading, and other activities associated with the first full moon of the new year.

The first skit on the sixteenth, the third day of the festival, was called "Guessing Riddles" (*caimi* 猜謎), and in it the twelve *shenjia* did just that. The riddles were followed by the only selection with any dramatic character at all, "Picking Mulberries" (*caisang* 採桑). It is set in the Spring and Autumn period, and tells the tale of how an ugly woman bested the King of Qi in both fighting and wisdom, and ended by becoming his wife. Like the previous four skits, this has no discernible religious content. The final skit, "Seating Houtu" (*zuo Houtu* 坐后土), is both simple and somewhat mysterious. Houtu — who was an important deity in the village and the ritual, though by no means its focus — is celebrating her 1,000th birthday, but only four of her five sons have left

---

2   This is the sequence as given in the *Report*; the version in Li Yi's article is somewhat different. Li Yi 李一 "'Shangku shenpu'zhushi" 扇鼓神譜註釋 (Annotated Edition of the 'Fan Drum' Roster of the Gods), *Zhonghua xiqu* 中華戲曲, 6 (1988): 60-87.

their homes on the five sacred mountains to come to the celebration. The fifth, it turns out, is sulking because he does not have a "season" of his own. (Each of his brothers has charge of one of the four seasons.) Houtu comes up with a solution: each brother is to donate eighteen days of his season to the absent one, so that each of the five will have seventy-two. This mollifies the fifth son, who joins the celebration and all ends happily.

At the conclusion of "Seating Houtu" the villagers brought fireworks and firecrackers that would be set off later that evening in the Altar area and placed them on the ground before the northern altar to show the gods. The percussion troupe played a special piece, the twelve *shenjia* made obeisance to all the gods, and then the villagers took the fireworks around the corner of the Guandi Temple and placed them on a small table against the east wall of the Xu lineage hall. Then all the gods except Houtu were sent off by burning their paper spirit tablets, along with the paper banners, flowers, and other altar decorations. As the gods departed, the fan-drums were played, but there was no special prayer or benediction.

That evening, the percussion and flower-drum troupes performed and the fireworks were set off. If snow fell at that time it was an omen of a good harvest. Then Houtu's spirit tablet was taken to the edge of the village and burned, and after she was deemed to have returned to her temple on Dragon Hill, just south of the village, everyone walked home in silence and without looking back, to prevent evil spirits from following them. This brought the ritual to an end.

The fourth chapter describes the costumes and accoutrements of all the main performers, without, however, raising the question of how closely they resembled those that were in use before the war. Indeed, the failure in general to confront the question of how much the tradition of the Fan Drum ritual had been disrupted between the last pre-war performance in 1938 and the filming in 1989 is one of the most serious weaknesses of the book. This chapter also contains detailed scores of the drum accompaniment for every section of the ritual together with information on the melodies used. Since the drummers had frequently been allowed to perform after 1949 it seems likely that their traditions had remained reasonably intact.

In the final chapter the authors depart from simple description to speculate on the origins of various elements in the ritual, such as the twelve *shenjia*, and the sources of the six skits. Nothing solid is established, and the claim of Song or Jin ancestry for some of the skits, while suggestive, is ultimately not persuasive. Just because a particular element in the Renzhuang liturgy also appears in a Song period text is no proof that the former derived from the latter.

All the material in the appendix is useful (though Renzhuang is located incorrectly on the sketch map of Quwo County), but by far the most important part is the reproduction of the 1909 manuscript of the liturgy of the Fan Drum ritual. Originally there had been only one complete copy, which was stored in the lineage hall. From that master copy each *shenjia* family made a part-script with their own lines. But the disasters of the late nineteenth century persuaded the village elders that it would be wise to have multiple copies, and in 1909 three members of the Xu lineage made a total of twelve copies, one for each *shenjia* family. When Japanese troops shelled and burned the village in July, 1938, all but one of those copies were destroyed, along with costumes, instruments, props, and the like. The surviving text was discovered in 1985, and is the one reproduced in the *Report*. It has the date Xuantong 1 (1909) on the cover, along with the name of Renzhuang Village.

The transcription given in chapter Three follows the manuscript closely, with one major exception. In the manuscript the lines spoken by each *shenjia* are placed together, as if simply copied from a part-script, but in Chapter Three the lines are rearranged so that there is an alternation between the twelve voices. However, since many of the speeches are not dialogue but (for example) segments of a long invocation, it is not clear why the present order was adopted. As mentioned earlier, in another transcription of the manuscript a somewhat different order is used. (See note 2.) The version in the *Report* seems better to me, but the reader should be told how it was arrived at. In addition, at least one part of the transcribed text cannot be found in the reproduction, probably because of damage to the manuscript (compare pp. 75 and 176 in the *Report*), and there is a sentence and a dance diagram on the back cover of the manuscript that are not transcribed (see p. 146). (The sentence is also found on the "colored banner" that let the Fan Drum Procession [see p. 30]. It is interesting that even such a small detail had a basis in the manuscript. The writers of the report leave the impression that their information about the words on the banner in based on direct observation, and they may not have realized that they were also in the manuscript.)

Despite these flaws the reproduction and transcription of the Renzhuang liturgy are extremely valuable, since they provide evidence of pre-revolutionary north China village ritual traditions, which is always extremely rare. The publication of such documents is one of the most important contributions of the *Min-su ch'ü-i ts'ung-shu* as a whole. Moreover, precisely because the liturgy is a text, it provides much more information about attitudes and values than the nonverbal matrix in which it was embedded. Words have meanings; gestures can only hint. But of course, the description of the entire ritual program is also indispensable, because it puts the text *into time*. This is why it is important to know how faithfully the 1989 performance reproduced authentic late-nineteenth century practice.

The *Report* tells us that Renzhuang Village had seventeen separate temples or shrines, many of which must have had annual festivals. In addition, the village participated in five large multi-village temple festivals that took place in neighboring villages or on Zijin Mountain, which was not far away (pp. 16-17). Villagers were also free to attend the temple festivals of nearby villages even if Renzhuang was not a formal participant. And of course, as we have seen, *yuanxiao* was also celebrated in Renzhuang with an elaborate ritual program. Thus Renzhuang in late imperial times had an extremely rich ritual life; it was also in many respects unique. The Fan Drum ritual followed no established pattern. It had been created by one or more residents at some time in the past for their own needs, which may well have been the demonstration of the social and ritual superiority of the Xu lineage. Certainly the manuscript and performances do not focus strongly on any specific diety, even Houtu, nor do the invocations, prayers, and skits convey strong religious feeling. There are virtually no Buddhist or Taoist elements, either; instead there is what, for lack of a better word, might be called a "literati" flavor, though much diluted. It is one of the most important contributions of the *Min-su ch'ü-i ts'ung-shu* to demonstrate just this combination of ritual abundance and local uniqueness for villages in all parts of China.

Valuable though this book is, it is not free of flaws. I have already mentioned the failure to confront the issue of the authenticity of the reconstructed performance. It would also have been good to have the texts of the few surviving stone inscriptions from village temples, particularly since the temples themselves have disappeared. At least one inscription is used in the book (p. 12); a transcription would have been very welcome. Most important, there is no clear account of just what the authors' field work consisted in. They say only that they visited the village "many times" between July 1991 and June 1992 (p. 3). Huang Zhusan is a professor of Chinese literature at Shanxi Shifan University in the city of Linfen, and also editor of the journal *Zhonghua xiqu* and director of the Institute for Research on Drama Antiquities at Shifan University. Wang Fucai is deputy director of the Institute and Associate Professor at Shifan University. He trained at the Institute and, earlier, in politics and history at Shifan University. Both are specialists in the history of drama, and it is unlikely that they have had formal training in field research. Their work was guided by the sample questionnaire that was supplied to all authors of the books in this series. It is possible to make a day trip from Linfen to Renzhuang (I have done it), and so it is possible that the authors never spent a night in the village. Certainly we are not given much information about how they conducted their research there. This is the most notable shortcoming of a book that is, nevertheless, a significant addition to our knowledge of village ritual in north China in late imperial times.

17

A REVIEW OF MINXIANG:

CIVIL INCENSE WORSHIP IN LIAONING, CHINA BY REN GUANGWEI

Fan Lizhu

Ren Guangwei's 任光偉 *Minxiang: Civil Incense Worship in Liaoning, China* 遼寧民香的考察與研究 is among the books published in the *Min-su ch'u-i ts'ung-shu* 民俗曲藝叢書 (Studies in Chinese Ritual, Theatre and Folklore Series), edited by Professor Wang Ch'iu-kuei 王秋桂, No. 26, 1994. 526 pages. It is a historical survey of popular ritual in Liaoning Province in Manchuria, China. In this book, the author gives a detailed account of *minxiang* 民香 worship based on very exhaustive field studies. Ren's survey covers a wide range of subjects, e.g. the details of incense worship, drum and dance performances, scores of *minxiang* music, and the various instruments used in the worship. The appendix contains the author's collection of "incense volumes" (*xiang juan* 香卷) used in the ritual in the Shenyang 瀋陽 and Xinbin 新賓 regions of Liaoning. These materials present a general outlook on the tradition of worship and chanting practiced by the local people for the past one hundred years or more, through which we gain access to the spiritual life of Chinese common folk.

I. The Origin and Development of Incense Worship in Liaoning

Civil Incense (*minxiang*) "is a worship that differs from the Eight Flag Incense (*baqi xiang* 八旗香) of the Han soldiers in the Manchu army and the Shaman Incense Burning (*shaman shaoxiang* 薩滿燒香) of the Manchus. The expression "*minxiang*" literally refers to the incense worship practiced by civilians of Han ethnic origin who did not have Manchu citizenship. This kind of worship is based primarily in Liaoning and is popular in Manchuria. It is also the major form of worship in the region."[1]

The target area of Ren's study is Xinbin County. Ren's starting point is Dongjiang Yan Village 東江沿村 in Wangqing Gate 旺清門, where the practice of *minxiang* dates back to the Kangxi 康熙 and Yongzheng 雍正 periods in the Qing Dynasty (1662-1735). The main purpose of the worship is to dispel disasters and drive away evil, and to reinforce the sense of unity through worshiping the ancestors. From the Qianlong 乾隆 period (1736-1795) to the late-Qing, Civil Incense masters providing services in incense worship and chanting have been in great demand. Their major responsibilities include ancestor worship, fulfillment of vows, cleansing the household of bad luck and dispelling evil. In addition to the use of the "elbow drum" incense burning (*zhouzigu shaoxiang* 肘子鼓燒香), these ritualists, also incorporate different kinds of popular entertainment, with restrictions of their forms, into their performance to please both gods and humans. There were very few theatre troupes in the Xinbin area; even the shadow-puppet play, which was popular in northern China, was uncommon in Xinbin. This explains why incense worship remains an important local entertainment among the rural communities in this region. In local terms, incense worship is also called "singing short drama" (*chang xiao xi* 唱小戲).

According to Ren, the practice of Civil Incense worship reached its peak in the Qing Dynasty during the reigns of Daoguang 道光 (1821-

---

1 Ren Guangwei, *A Study of Civil Incense Worship in Liaoning, China* 遼寧民香的考察與研究 (Taipei: Shih Ho-cheng Folk Culture Foundation), p. 1.

1850), Xianfeng 咸豐 (1851-1861), Tongzhi 同治 (1862-1874) and Guangxu 光緒 (1875-1908); then it was restricted during the Republican period. After 1949, the PRC government enforced the policies of "eliminating superstition" and "destroying feudalist secret societies and sects" and consequently *minxiang* worship as well as many other local religious activities were banned. However, in the mountain regions of eastern Liaoning, especially in Xinbin County, a number of performing groups secretly continued their activities. During the Cultural Revolution, a Chang Family Troupe performed incense worship a few times in a well-enclosed place. In 1984, under the incentive to compile the ten collections of popular folk art, the government sent specialists to Manchuria to study the three main types of incense worship activities. Although Civil Incense worship was encouraged once again, a complete revival was impossible because most of the incense masters were dead by that time.

There are two kinds of Civil Incense troupes, one based on inheritance and the other on apprenticeship. In the latter case, a book of certificates (*die shu* 牒書) is maintained to keep track of the development of the troupe.

The tradition of civil incense worship in Liaoning cannot be completely revived, mainly due to the scarcity of incense troupes, and of incense masters who are well trained in both literary and martial skills. As a result, purely anthropological research based on empirical evidence from observations of the ritual process is not possible. As an experienced researcher in popular literature, Ren Guangwei has been studying Civil Incense worship in Lioaning for forty years. Beginning from the literary value of *minxiang* practices, his interest has now shifted to the performance and music of incense worship. Regretfully, due to the constraints mentioned above, Ren had to base his research primarily on hand-written copies of scrolls and therefore could not fully represent the special character of the ritual itself.

According to Ren, five copies of scrolls for incense worship still exist today. The "*minxiang* scroll" by Zhang Mingxue 張明學 in Dongjiang Yan Village, Qingmen 清門 Township, Xinbin County, is the most complete copy. If fighting scenes are added, the performance can last for five days and nights. In Budayuan 步達遠 Township, Kuandian 寬甸 County, an oral script by Tang Yixian 湯義賢 was published by the Ethnicity Affairs Commission of the Manchu Autonomous County of Kuandian 寬甸滿族自治縣; it was originally a hand-written copy by Yang Qingyan 楊青岩. A more accurate copy by Yu Xinyou 于新友 has been found in Jianchang bao 鹼場堡, Benxi County. Because Yu's father was an incense master himself, Yu's copy has a more precise description of the worship. It has been used in Civil Incense worship and by the Han banner registers and Manchus. In Donggou 東溝 County, Dandong 丹東, there is a copy by He Zhonggui 何忠貴, in which the notes regarding body gestures are incorporated into the lyrics for chanting. Finally, there is another copy by Zhang Enbao 張恩寶 in Sujia tun 蘇家屯 Shenyang Province.

As mentioned, these *minxiang* manuscripts are the primary materials on which Ren's study is based. For instance, Ren adopted Yu Xinyou's copy in making a projection of the historical origin of *minxiang*. However, Yu made this copy in 1955 when he was seventy-two. According to Yu, he practiced incense worship with his father at the age of ten. His father, then, was an apprentice of a master Guo in Jianbao. At that time the master was at least fifty. By inference, therefore, the original scroll had been in existence in the Benxi 本溪 region since the first two decades of the eighteenth century.

Owing to his experience in *minxiang* studies, Ren can judge whether a scroll is genuine or fake. For example, the recorder of the oral version of Tang Yiyan in Kuandian County insisted that it was a scroll used by the Han military within the Manchu Banner Registers, and therefore gave it the title "The Incense Hymn of the Han Banner Register in Kuandian" 寬甸漢軍旗香神歌. However, Ren disputes this view, based on the fact that in this scroll both the ritual and the lyrics are compatible with typical *minxiang* worship; there is not a trace of the Han military in this text. In addition, he notices how the recorder deliberately modified the content headings in order to prove his case. Headings like "Hymn of Battle Drums" 戰鼓神歌, "A Song of the Gods of Heaven" 天神歌, "A Song of the Gods of the Earth" 地神歌, "A Song of the Mountain Peaks" 山頭歌, "A Song to Welcome the Gods" 迎神歌, and "Miscellaneous Songs" 散歌, according to Ren, do not reflect the reality of the worship itself.

II. The Organization of Civil Incense Worship

Although it is impossible nowadays to learn the complete details of the *minxiang* ritual in Liaoning through actual observation, Ren has made every effort to record its process and organization.

Incense troupes usually have a crew of five or six, but never fewer than four. These people include a master of the altar, second drummer, a third drummer and a "runner" who can be either part-time or full time. During winter, the runner will bring a notebook to the host family to arrange the date of the worship. They will devise a time schedule for the worship according to the host family's purpose and financial resources. Normally, the host can choose from four categories, namely small incense 小香 (one-night; *yixiu* 一宿), one and a half 節半香 (two-nights, *liangxiu* 二宿), large incense 大香 (three-nights; *sanxiu* 三宿) and full incense 全香 (four-nights; *sixiu* 四宿). Once the commitment is made, it cannot be changed. The incense troupe will then arrive at the host family's home at noon the day before the ritual.

Once they arrive, the troupe will immediately set up the altar. This is an important part of the process because it involves setting up the incense hall and altar, mounting the portraits of the ancestors and the family geneology, as well as preparing the sacred instruments and offerings. In the middle of the courtyard will be placed a *ba xian* table (square-shaped table 八仙桌) in honor of Heaven and the Earth; in front of this table are the offerings of "three livestock" (*sansheng rou* 三牲肉), i.e. a rooster, the head of a pig, and "fire-dragon fish"(*huolong yu* 火龍魚). Finally, water is sprinkled all over the courtyard to cleanse it.

In Civil Incense worship, the altar is made up of an outside altar 外壇 and an inner altar 內壇, also known as "outer road drum" (*wailu gu* 外路鼓) and "inner road drum" (*neilu gu* 內路鼓). The ritual of the inner altar is divided into eight sections called "*ba pu*" 八鋪, indispensable parts of the worship during which incense is burnt. This involves the following procedures: opening the altar 開壇, erecting the opera shed 搭棚, going down to Shandong 下山東, dedication 開光, racing the circle of the Gate of Heaven 闖天門圈子, the circle of summoning the souls of the dead 句亡魂圈子, seating [the gods] 安座, and farewell

to the gods 送神. The outside altar has twenty-four parts (*er'shisi pu* 二
十四鋪, or twenty-four plays). They can be long or short depending on
the host's preferences and financial resources. These mini-plays are
divided into drama scenes and action scenes. The drama scenes are
complete stories that correspond to the ritual itself; for example, "Li
Cuilian Making a Journey" 李翠蓮盤道, "Meng Jiang Looking for her
Husband" 孟姜女尋夫, "Mr. Zhang Divorces his Wife" 張郎休妻, "The
Han Emperor Gaozu Slaying the White Snake" 漢高祖斬白蛇, "Yang
Erlang Breaks Open the Mountain to Save his Mother" 楊二郎破山救
母, "The White Monkey Stealing the Peach" 白猿偷桃, "Generals Sun
and Pang Scheming Against Each Other" 孫龐鬥法, "Miss Huang
Touring the Underworld" 黃氏女遊陰, "Emperor Wu Launching an
Expedition Against Emperor Zhou" 武王伐紂, "The Emperor of Tang
Making an Expedition to the East" 唐王東征, "Liu Ling the Drunkard"
劉伶醉酒 and "The Pearl-sewn Mini-shirt" 珍珠衫. Action scenes, on
the other hand, combine Mini-drama and martial arts; for example,
"Five Daoist Priests Pursuing a Monster" 五道捉妖 and "Summoning
the Stove God" 勾灶王. If it is a full incense worship, the performance
of the outside altar is three to four times longer than that of the inner
altar. However, the eight-part inner altar performance has become much
larger in scale nowadays; as a result not even the master of the altar can
give an accurate description of its original appearance.

In civil incense worship, drums are a very important instrument. In
ritual performances, large drums and small drums are used. The master
of the altar and the second and third drummer will use large drums, and
the remaining member will use a small drum. Drum beats usually
accompany the lyrics of the chanting, and vary according to the kinds of
drums used, for example, free rhythm, slow rhythm, medium rhythm
and quick rhythm. The ritual masters will also perform a "feather step"
(*yubu* 羽步) also known as "pacing on the stars of the Big Dipper"
(*gangbu* 罡步, p. 32). In addition to the different kinds of drumbeats
and dance steps, Ren also provides a detailed depiction of the costumes,
props, and the names and characteristics of the sacred instruments used
in Civil Incense worship. Explanations are also given for the special
qualities of *minxiang* music, which is basically an arrangement of
melodies in series. The songs are sequential in form with titles corresponding to the different parts of the ritual. Nonetheless, *minxiang*

music is also quite spontaneous in nature, for there are no apparent paradigms governing its composition. Although Ren has included a few music scores in his book, an overall understanding of *minxiang* music is still lacking. "Nine tunes and eighteen tones, tuning and toning never really click." As such, the spontaneity of *minxiang* music means that the few works cited by Ren are far from representative of the whole picture.

III. The Legends and Oral History of Civil Incense Worship

An important issue raised in Ren's book is the origin of Civil Incense worship. Since this worship was practiced entirely by common folk, historical sources for it are difficult to find among official records. In this regard, oral history and legends contained in the incense volumes become important clues to an understanding of their origin and historical development. In Ren's view, popular legends regarding the origin of *minxiang* in general concur on one point, i.e. the eastern expedition of the emperor Taizhong in the Tang Dynasty. These legends differ only in certain details in the story. Among the three different versions of this story cited by Ren, one has it that Taizhong returned to the capital after his expedition to the east. He became so immersed in government affairs that he simply ignored the martyred soldiers in eastern Liaoning. The ghosts of these soldiers then clustered in the Underworld without hope of reincarnation. Even the Emperor of the Underworld was helpless. One night, Taizhong had a dream in which the Heavenly Emperor invited him to visit the Underworld. When he reached a place called "Souls of Darkness Gate"(*yinhun guan* 陰魂關), he saw one million ghosts of the dead soldiers and was heart-broken. When he awoke, the emperor immediately issued an order to build temples all over the Guandong Mountain region. Civilians were asked to beat drums and burn incense to relieve the souls of these soldiers from purgatory. This legend is supported by the "Emperor Taizhong of Tang's Tour of the Underworld" 唐二主遊地府 episode in an incense volume.

These oral sources and legends are supported by evidence from official histories. In the historical records and related documents of the Tang Dynasty, there is evidence that emperor Taizhong did make an expedition to the east in 645 AD (the nineteenth year of the Zhenguan 貞觀) period, and that the emperor did order the worship of the soldiers killed during the expedition. Ren repeatedly addresses the issue that *minxiang* legends do not concur with historical reality, and tries to find historical evidence that can verify these legends. One can say that Ren has the inclination of an "orthodox" intellectual eager to find official testimony behind popular legends and oral histories in order that the latter will not be dismissed. Ironically, such proof is by no means easy to find in official histories. In an attempt to resolve this dilemma, Ren puts forward his own point of view: "Legends, as oral history, necessarily differ from historical reality. We can certainly gloss over those episodes about a dream tour to the Underworld or shrimp- and crab-spirits making a bridge as pure fairy tales."[2] Understandably, popular culture has its own way of transmission; the century-old tradition of Civil Incense worship in Liaoning does not depend on whether or to what extent it concurs with official history. What is most important is the kind of consensus and social customs that have been preserved in the popular beliefs of the common people. If we were to limit our scope to official documents and ignore the dynamics of popular culture, our efforts would be in vain, for in such an approach a large quantity of valuable sources on Civil Incense worship would have to be left out.

IV. The Regional Character of Civil Incense Worship

Originating in the Qing Dynasty, the lyrics of Civil Incense worship are rendered in simple language. At the same, since *minxiang* worship always displays a strong local color, its lyrics inevitably bear the imprint of the historical and regional outlook of the ritual itself. In the lyrics for chanting in incense volumes, outdated expressions and colloquialisms of the Manchuria are very common. These lively local expressions, however, may seem puzzling to a non-local audience, who will possibly misinterpret the meaning of the colloquial language. Even a local northerner may have difficulties at certain points. In editing the texts, Ren does

---

2 *Ibid*, p. 66.

not translate these colloquialisms into standard expressions. Instead, explanations are provided alongside the text to facilitate the reader's understanding.

For example, in an incense scroll from Xinbin, the author explains a difficult sentence "turning over the *xian shu* 憲書"[3] in this way: "*Xian shu* is the lunar calendar. In pre-Republican times, it was called 'the calendar of the Emperor.' During the early years of the Republic, it was called *xian shu*, the same as what we call *li shu* 曆書 (lunar calendar) or *nongjia li* 農家曆 (farmer's calendar) nowadays."[4] Another example of this kind can be found in the same section. On the expression "honorable host, don't 'sell your stupidity;' sweep the courtyard and clean up the street," Ren pays special attention to "sell your stupidity" (*mai dai* 賣呆): "*Mai dai*" comes from the northeastern dialect. It means standing on one side watching the fun."[5] Others include: "Put three drops of blood from the crown of the golden chicken on a one dollar coin. Whoever is the ghost of the dead please take this *kou qian* 口錢 (money or allowance)."[6] According to Ren, " '*kou qian*' refers to staple allowances or *kou liang qian* 口糧錢. In the Qing Dynasty, naturalized citizens of the banner registers were given an allowance for each newborn baby. Since ordinary civilians did not have such allowance by birth, it was offered to them by their offspring."[7] Another term is "*yi man* 一滿 (a full one) in a row of six characters, your Highness of ten thousand *sui* is well known Heaven and earth."[8] "*Yi man*" again is a Manchuria colloquialism. According to Ren, "*yi man*" means "in total."[9] Among the more intriguing expressions, we have "Where comes this foolish big chap? How dare you challenge (*zao xing* 糟興) me in the middle of the night?" In the original, the verb "*zao xing*" defies interpretation. Ren adds that " '*zao xing*' originates from Manchuria, meaning rampage or challenge."[10] Examples such as these abound in Ren's

---

3 *Ibid*, p. 181.
4 *Ibid*, p. 192.
5 *Ibid*, p. 193.
6 *Ibid*, p. 229.
7 *Ibid*, p. 232
8 *Ibid*, p. 229.
9 *Ibid*, p. 231.
10 *Ibid*, p. 444.

book.

Ren has put in much effort to compose these footnotes, which greatly enhance the intelligibility of the original texts. This also reflects the author's solid foundation in the historical background of Civil Incense worship and the depth of his knowledge of popular customs. Ren's achievement in this book therefore should be recognized.

V. The Religious Content of Civil Incense Worship

Scholars from around the world have come to realize that popular religious traditions in China are embedded in the daily life of the people, including the family, the clan, the elders of the community and the local temples and deity altars. From what we know of the century-old practice of Civil Incense worship in Liaoning, it is obvious that non-sectarian religions have their own structures and ways of transmission. The local people can lead their religious life and maintain their own principles, rituals, and beliefs.

Minxiang is a religious ritual for ancestor worship, redeeming vows, house cleansing and dispelling evil dating back at least to the early Qing Dynasty. Civil Incense worship was once a very popular practice in Dongjiang Village, Xinbin County. The most influential and ancient troupe was called the Chang family Troupe 張家班; its incense volumes had a wide circulation in the region. Interestingly, Ren Guangwei says that Dongjiang and its nearby villages "do not have any temples. In the past, both Han and Manchu villagers would journey to the Buddhist temple in Yongling 永陵 (originally Hetuala 赫圖阿拉) to participate in festivals offering incense. In times of draught, model dragons made of grass would be used in incense worship to pray for rain. Yet, in the village there were no believers who adhered to a strict vegetarian diet as part of their devotional practice."[11] The Han villagers have primarily practiced incense burning. Every year in the winter months and the first lunar month of the next year, troupes are invited by individual families to set up an altar for incense worship.

Thus we can see that *minxiang* as a local religious practice does not

---

11 *Ibid*, p. 18

have a specialized clergy nor does it have any designated temples or appointed leaders from the local gentry. Nonetheless, it still has a unique tradition of its own. Those who function as the agents or coordinators of Civil Incense worship are mostly local artists. In troupes, these artists will visit individual families and set up altars to invoke the gods, chanting hymns from scrolls, and pay tribute to the dead. This kind of religion may seem very unusual because its activities are based primarily on individual family functions instead of those across families and communities. However, *minxiang* is as effective as any religion in preserving ancient ritualistic traditions. Not only are the form and the procedure of the ritual similar among different families, but the time of worship is also invariably set in winter. In traditional Chinese society, the social status of local artists was very low. They made their living by soliciting business from every household, and it was never easy. According to some artists themselves, "Asking for a living from place to place, earning our daily bread from altar to altar, we would starve if we all looked the same."[12] Apparently, these incense masters regard their work as just a job to make a living from local demands. However, they have a mission that is both secular and sacred; they provide a channel for the people to express their religious feelings. One can say that the most significant factor in this ancient religious tradition is the religious consciousness of the Chinese people in ancestor worship.

Paying tribute to one's ancestors is the core of Civil Incense worship. Every year around New Year's eve, the slack season in agricultural societies, families will invite incense masters to their houses to set up an altar to invoke the gods and honor their ancestors. No matter what kind of service a family can afford, the first and foremost thing to do is to invite the ancestors back home. This is a gesture to pay respect to one's ancestors and to pray for their blessings.

Civil Incense worship in Lioaning, moreover, enables us to see different aspects of popular religions insofar as Civil Incense worship itself is the medium through which the local people express their attitudes toward religion, including their views of afterlife and the relation between the sacred and the secular worlds, as well as the concept of the

---

12 *Ibid*, p. 20.

unity of heaven and humans (*tian ren he yi* 天人合一). Also, both the language and the customs in *minxiang* worship come directly from the people; through them we can gain access to the reality of their spiritual life.

VI. Civil Incense Worship as Sacred and Secular Art

Ren Guangwei's attempt to situate the practice of civil incense worship within a religious-social matrix seems to be paradoxical at some points. First of all, Ren regards Civil Incense worship as a ritual to honor one's ancestors. In addition, he has carefully proven the interrelationship between *minxiang* worship and shamanistic rituals of dispelling evil and epidemics; in his own words, incense masters are "ritual officiants."[13] In reality, the host always actively participates in the ritual, by setting out the offerings, burning incense, bowing, and calling upon the ancestors and gods from all directions to accept the incense. Under the guidance of incense masters, host families enter into a communion with the extra-human realm for various lengths of time. Such practices have been handed down through a long tradition, but still Civil Incense worship is a form of entertainment that is as much secular as it is sacred. However, to regard it as a form of secular entertainment does not necessarily undermine its religious meaning. The elbow drum performance, for example, is a synthesis of popular art forms such as pop songs, local legends, customs, dialects and acrobatics. Thus, the sacred and the secular are not mutually exclusive in this religious tradition.

Due to the presence of these popular art forms in *minxiang* worship and the performative function of the incense master, Ren is much inclined to discover the value of *minxiang* in popular literature and the performing arts. One question he raises is the transition from incense worship to popular opera: "Compared to China Proper and Jiangnan (i.e. the south), the transportation network and culture of Liaoning were relatively underdeveloped. No doubt incense worship as both a sacred and secular activity appealed to the spiritual needs of the middle and lower

---

13 *Ibid*, p. 86.

classes. Once it was accepted as a general way of life, it could develop steadily within these communities."[14] The implication of Ren's argument is that the existence of popular rituals such as *minxiang* is the result of cultural backwardness. We may ask: if this is the case, does it mean that once a culture is more advanced, popular ritual is no longer needed? Does it also mean that the transformation from ritual to opera is the highest end of popular religions? These are questions for serious inquiry, not instant conclusions. Undeniably popular culture is "genetically" related to popular rituals; however, popular religions have their own way of survival and transformation whose meaning is not limited to their contribution to the development of popular literature.

VII. Conclusion

Ren Guangwei's study of *minxiang* worship gives a systematic account of this popular religion in Liaoning as revealed in its existing literature, the incense scrolls. As a result, it sets an excellent example for future research in popular religions in China. In particular, the use of anthropological approaches in this study (and others) is highly commendable. Without the persistent efforts of these scholars, we would have no means to understand Civil Incense worship as an extremely popular religious practice in Lioaning and northeastern China. Nor would we have the chance to even glimpse those incense volumes that so vividly reflect the religious life of the local people. The publication of *Min-su ch'ü-i ts'ung-shu*, therefore, not only contributes tremendously to the preservation of the treasures of popular culture, but also to the possibility of genuine and in-depth knowledge of popular religions in China.

---

14 *Ibid.*

Traditional Hakka
Society Series

18

COMMENTS ON THE FOUNDATIONS OF CHINESE CULTURE IN LATE TRADITIONAL TIMES

Daniel L. Overmyer

1. Fang Xuejia 房學嘉, ed., *Meizhou diqu de miaohui yu zongzu* 梅州地區的廟會與宗族 (*Temple Festivals and Lineages in Meizhou*). John Lagerwey, Traditional Hakka Society Series, No. 1, 1996. Hong Kong: International Hakka Studies Association and the École Française D'Extrême-Orient. 293 pages.
2. Fang Xuejia, ed., *Meizhou Heyuan diqu de cunluo wenhua* 梅州河源地區的村落文化 (*Village Religion and Culture in Northeastern Guangdong*). John Lagerwey, Traditional Hakka Society Series, No. 5, 1997. Hong Kong: International Hakka Studies Association and the École Française D'Extrême-Orient. 503 pages.

I. Introduction

The volumes of Traditional Hakka Society Series, based on reports of their own customs by local people, provide rich and detailed information about the foundations of rural culture on the China mainland, and hence on the roots of late traditional Chinese culture as a whole. Here for one area of southeast China we can understand more clearly than ever before the quantitative mainstream of that culture as it still existed deep into the twentieth century, based on the fieldwork and reports organized and edited by John Lagerwey, Fang Xuejia, Yang Yanjie 楊彥杰 and others. Though there have been many changes and dislocations in Chinese society in the last 160 years, the sheer weight of detail and repetition in accounts in these volumes from different communities supports their reliability. From them we learn that some basic structures of traditional perspective and practice remained alive until they were destroyed by the Chinese government after 1949, though in some areas they have been partially revived in recent years.

The reports included in these books were written by local scholars and retired officials based on their own experience and observations and on interviews with older people in their communities who still remembered traditional activities and practices from the time before the Cultural Revolution in the 1960s and early 1970s. These reports were first presented in conferences in district towns organized by Lagerwey and his colleagues, then edited to make sure all possible details were included. Each report begins with a description of the geographical setting and history of the village or town in question, with some comments on economic activities as well. The result is a new kind of primary source for the study of Chinese local culture that can supplement anthropological reports where they are available. These Chinese reports provide building blocks for a fresh and more detailed understanding of that culture, and deserve inclusion in analytical and comparative studies. Since my own research is concerned primarily with local or popular religion, this review report is focused on that topic, but there is also rich information in this material on the other aspects noted above, geography and history, particularly the history of lineages.

There is evidence in these volumes for the interaction of villagers with local scholars and officials, Daoist priests and Buddhist monks, but fundamentally in the context of the practical needs and values of the people themselves. Their world was shaped by concerns for the survival of family and community, concerns expressed in the slogan "summon blessing and drive away harm"(*zhaofu quxie* 招福驅邪). Scholars and priests of course had their own traditions of expertise and training, but once they entered the realm of village culture they were put to the service of the people's needs. This applies even to cases where ancestors were believed to have become gods through their study at Daoist centers on sacred mountains like Lü-shan and Mao-shan. As gods the whole point of their power was to help resolve the problems people brought to them. In the village context Guanyin was worshipped for family protection, the *Diamond sūtra* was recited to bring good harvests, and Confucian-style "masters of ceremonies(lisheng 禮生)" (Lagerwey's translation) cooperated with spirit-mediums to help make rituals efficacious. All such specialists were valued as bearers of auspicious power in the quest for blessings. Since what we call Confucian moral values began to spread from scholars to the people as early as the Han dynasty, their presence in traditional village life was just an expression of being Chinese. In the material in the volumes at hand there is no problem of the relationship between "elite" and "popular" culture, because for the villagers all was assimilated into their own world-view, shared in part by others all the way up to the emperor. In this context the people sought extrahuman support from wherever it might be available, regardless of its sectarian background, in as many ways as possible. This is the ritual and social basis of what has been called Chinese "syncretism," which was in part a response of more specialized traditions to the practical needs of ordinary folk for multiple sources of divine support and aid. Their logic was that of redundancy in the positive sense of that term.

The material in these books provides a fresh perspective on what one part of traditional Chinese culture was in actual practice, and reveals to us how long we have been led astray by starting from the top down instead of with the common ground, by emphasizing what seems most intellectually compatible and satisfying to scholars in China and the West instead of what has really been doing the cultural work for the majority of the Chinese people. See similar comments in Chapter Nineteen of this volume, by Dong Xiaoping 董曉萍. Of course, there is much beauty and wisdom in more specialized Chinese traditions such as philosophy, poetry and landscape painting, and their study is most rewarding, but such activities engaged only relatively few and had little impact on ordinary people. My point here is simply that to understand Chinese culture as a whole we should begin with those at its demographic foundations, in the villages and towns where by far the most poeple lived. In the 20th century there have been a number of anthropological studies of Chinese local society that have provided information for such a perspective, but relatively few from the mainland, and none at the focused, specific detail of the mainland studies discussed here.

The religious rituals and beliefs described in this material reveal a society concerned at every turn to relate to extra human powers, from the living vital force (*shengqi* 生氣) that wells out of apertures (*xue* 穴) of the earth to the celestial gods (*tianshen* 天神) worshipped in the "celestial wells" (*tianjing* 天井, recessed courtyards) in Hakka houses and lineage shrines. Everything in between heaven and earth could have its own mode of sacred power that required recognition and worship; ancestors, orphan souls, demons, and gods and spirits for every level of being, from the stove, house door, latrine and farm implements to fields, neighborhoods, villages, towns and beyond. All of these powers were addressed by rituals of offerings and invocation that assumed their existence. Beyond such rituals were the powers of spirit-mediums to call the gods down into their own bodies where they could be questioned and supplicated. To determine one's own relationship to extra-human power in a particular time and situation one employed divination, either by oneself or through a specialist. Every significant situation or problem was to be divined. The world of village religion was a world alive with powers for good or ill, powers that could be dealt with either by oneself or with the help of those with special knowledge. In this world what was valued was survival and success through cooperation and harmony with positive powers, beginning with one's own relatives and ancestors and fellow villagers. Such cooperation helped bring life and ward off the powers of harm. This was the bedrock of traditional Chinese values and moral principles, specific and practical throughout. It is these values, expressed in rituals and human relationships, that have kept the society going all these years. It is here that an attempt to understand China should begin.

In this review report, I discuss topics for which information in these volumes is particularly rich, emphasizing what for me is new or at least more detailed than I have seen before. For fine summaries of their contents, see John Lagerwey's introductions. I do not attempt general description of topics such as *fengshui* 風水 , since they are already known to specialists in the field. In all of this I am concerned not to summarize the contents of these books, but to point out the best material in them on topics that may be of interest for teaching and research. Since I already have more than enough to learn about the customs of the Han people, I do not comment here about those of the She, concerning which there are one article on pp. 188-222 of Vol. I and two on pp. 466-496 of Vol. 5. Though in some places the rituals described have been revived in recent years, many have not, so with a sense of regret I use the past tense throughout. Since this is a review and summary rather than a research article per se I do not provide cross-references to studies of the topics discussed.

II. Volume I

There are thirteen reports included in the 293 pages of Volume I, plus a preface and postface in English and Chinese, by John Lagerwey and Fang Xuejia respectively. The most detailed information provided is on temple festivals (*miaohui* 廟會) and rituals of community purification and renewal (*jiaohui* 醮會), ancestor worship at lineage shrines (*citang* 祠堂), and rituals for funerals, burials, *fengshui* and marriages. There is also interesting information here about spirit-mediums, the origins of deities, and rituals through which children were adopted by gods. Throughout this material there is an emphasis on the importance of following traditional rules for the preparation and carrying out of rituals, and sincere （*qiancheng* 虔誠） belief by the participants. (Page number references here are to those following the introductions).

1. Temple Festivals and Rituals of Community Purification

Temple festivals were celebrations by the whole community of the presence and power of a local god, best described here by Zhang Quanqing 張泉清 in his article on festivals in the Wuhua 五華 district of eastern Guangdong on pp.1-36 of this book. In a discussion of rituals carried out on the birthday of Tianfei 天妃 (Tianhou 天后), the "Celestial Empress" (pp. 2-9), he describes three main stages of this ritual, preparation, sending up a memorial to invite the god's participation (*shang biao* 上表), and taking Tianhou's "travelling image" (*xingshen* 行身) on a procession around the community. Preparations by local leaders of the ritual who were selected the previous year included hiring Daoist priests, musicians, an opera troupe, etc., decorating the streets, and building a temporary theatre for opera performances. The memorial sent up includes prayers for divine aid and the names of the leaders of the ritual, offered in the proper way with bows and incense. Zhang describes seven components of the procession, emphasizing the excitement, joy and sense of satisfaction that accompanied it (pp. 8-9).

In this same article Mr. Zhang also describes other temple festivals, and a *jiao* 醮 ritual of community renewal in Hutian 湖田 village that was carried out once in three years (pp. 23-31). Here again careful preparation and procedures are discussed in detail. In such festivals the whole village was reunited, the living, dead and gods, all together, to celebrate the renewal of the forces of life, but their success depended on doing everything in the proper way, according to tradition.

There is another detailed discussion of temple festivals and processions for Tianhou (pp. 111-115), and others for a City God (pp. 116-118), and of two local protector deities (pp. 141-148, 232-239). Descriptions of *jiao* rituals may be found on pages 22-36. The goals of such worship are clearly stated in an offering to the Lord of Ledong 樂洞 settlement in the Wuhua district of eastern Guangdong: "In this auspicious day and good hour, when heaven and earth have opened wide, with the three sacrificial animals all complete, we worship the Lord (Gongwang 公王). Lighting incense and kowtowing, we pray for protection and health. We offer a cock to the Lord that wealth may increase and family enterprise flourish. We offer vegetables and fruit to the Lord that old and young may be submissive and obedient; we offer the three sacrificial animals to the Lord that wealth may approach from all directions" (p. 54). The author of this report, Zhuo Shangji 卓尚基, comments that the Gongwang was both a protector deity and a god of wealth (p. 54).

The processions carried images of the gods on sedan chairs, preceded by red banners, placards instructing bystanders to stand back and be reverent, then lanterns, gongs, drums and flutes, with large dragon banners "to provide protection." Those participating wore their best clothing, some riding on horses. Accompanied by music and a roar of firecrackers, the procession entered the village, and then proceeded to stop in front of each household for worship. Finally the procession returned the image to its temple (pp. 143-144).

Descriptions of similar processions in other villages note that two altar tables were set up in front of each house along the route, one for the travelling image of the god and the other for offerings to it. Offerings included a whole chicken, bowls of meat balls, fish and pieces of pork and *doufu* 豆腐, as well as candles, incense, spirit money and wine. Bearers of the god's image were permitted to go through the whole house "to drive away mosquitoes." The image was then put on an altar table of the main room of the house, with women scattering rice on the floor before it. After the family members worshipped the god, a Daoist priest took the spirit money from the table and burned it, recited an invocation and threw divining blocks [to determine if the offerings had been well-received. Then the procession went on to the next house. After all the houses had been visited the image was taken to the "water exit" of the village, where paper boats and the incense and candles offered by each household were burned on the sand, all of which was intended to "drive away disasters, illness and harm so that they float down the river." Finally, the god's image was taken back to the temple to watch the opera (pp. 236-237). The following pages describe the organization and founding of this festival, while an appendix provides the invocations recited by the Daoist priests (pp. 242-243).

Zhang Quanqing notes that while only the main god of the local temple was invited to participate in a temple festival, in a *jiao* outside deities were invited as well (p. 5, note 1). *Jiao* rituals were similar to *miaohui*, but they were distinguished by being held only once every three, five or ten years, by lasting from three to seven days, and by being more complex, and related to many gods. He describes in detail a village *jiao* held once every ten years that involved months of advance preparation, selection of leaders from prosperous and complete families, and the hiring of priests, opera troupes and musicians. The leaders each contributed five pecks of rice to meet expenses, an amount specified by the proto-Daoist Celestial Master sect in the 2nd century C.E. All had to maintain a vegetarian diet, bathe, and wear formal clothing. A mat shed was constructed to cover a temporary altar. Bamboo poles were erected, decorated with red ropes and lanterns to guide the spirits of the dead to the festival. Rituals for spirits of the dead included floating downstream paper boats with candles inside for the benefit of the spirits of those who had drowned, lighting lanterns in front of each home, and burning paper clothes, all to guide and provide for the dead (pp. 22-30). This care for the dead is not mentioned in discussions of temple festivals. It is clear here and elsewhere that such rituals for the spirits of the uncared for dead functioned also to exorcise them from the community.

2. Worshipping Ancestors at Home, Shrines and Tombs

On this topic Mr. Zhang provides in Volume 5 a fine discussion on pages 18-29 of his Wuhua district article, noting the importance in such rituals of following the strict sequence of the generations (p. 20), and the procedures for venerating ancestors at the New Year festival, marriage and the birth of male children. He describes twenty-four steps for the worship of lineage ancestors, including types of offerings, bowing and prayers (pp. 25-27). Most interesting is Zhang's discussion of the worship in a temple (*miao* 廟) of two Zhang clan ancestors in image form, with red faces and black beards. According to his investigations, one of these deities was posthumously enfeoffed as a "great general who protects the people" after he suppressed disorder during the Ming period. He and other deities in the temple came to be served by spirit-mediums who could exorcise and heal illness (pp. 59-60).

There is also a discussion of ancestor worship in Volume 1 in the chapter by Lin Qingshui 林清水, pp. 72-76, which provides a detailed description of a lineage shrine (*citang*) and rituals carried out there at the lunar new year festival. On the morning of New Year's eve the principal wife (*zhufu* 主婦) made offerings to Heaven (Tianshen) at the ancestral shrine gate or in the open air. That afternoon the men of every family bathed, while their wives prepared flesh sacrifices, paper clothing and other offering items, which they then carried to the lineage shrine. Later in the afternoon large candles and incense sticks were offered there by the oldest people in the community. Then each family laid out their offering food on tables they themselves provided, after which the men offered incense and candles before the ancestral tablets, bowed and kowtowed. Then in proper sequence they offered tea to the ancestors, the Locality Earth God, Lord Yang (patron of *fengshui*), Guanyin, Lord Stone and the "Immortal Ancestress" (Xianren shu potai 仙人叔婆太). Then each family took back home the burned incense and stuck it in their gate frames. Wine was also offered, as well as spirit-money, all accompanied by firecrackers, gongs and drums. Mr.Lin also describes annual offerings at ancestral tombs, noting that unmarried daughters could also participate, and that the spirits of later ancestors could be ritually led to the tombs of the earlier for joint worship (pp. 76-79).

The title *zhufu* indicates the woman responsible in the household for offerings to ancestors. The role of women in shrine rituals is also worthy of note here.

3. Funeral and Burial Rituals

Funeral and burial rituals are discussed in most detail here by Lin Qingshui (pp. 83-86) and Xie Meixing 謝梅興 (pp. 165-170). The material on funeral rituals is a useful supplement to that provided by J.J.M. De Groot in Vol. I of his *The Religious System of China* (Leiden, preface date 1892). However, on burials there is some information that was new at least to me. Mr. Lin describes the following sequence:

1. Select the grave site aided by an almanac and a *fengshui* master to determine the most auspicious orientation of the tomb.
2. After the tomb was dug, the daughters and daughters-in-law of the deceased jumped into it, wiping away their footprints as they left, reciting an invocation of good fortune for the family. The point of this was to inspect the grave, which was the *yin* 陰 dwelling of the dead, to make sure they would be comfortable.
3. After the coffin was lowered into the grave, monks or nuns were asked to recite scriptures and scatter rice. Sons and grandsons held up the hems of their garments to catch as much of the rice as they could, to take home and put in the granary, to "drive away harm and seek for blessings."
4. Cover the tomb with earth.
5. Cap the tomb mound with a stone, accompanied by offerings of meat and incense.

Second burial was carried out three or four years later, with the tomb opened by a hired laborer. If the flesh was not entirely gone, the tomb was covered to wait until the following year. If only the bones remained, the worker removed them, beginning with the feet, and gave them to relatives to wipe clean with paper. Afterwards they were wiped with tea oil until they had a golden color. In some cases relatives would try to pull out the teeth, in the belief that only those the deceased loved the most would succeed. Finally, the workmen put the bones feet first in a "golden urn"(*jinying* 金罌), with the kneecaps and thigh bones pointing up. When covering the urn, care had to be taken that no one's shadow was caught inside. The bone urn could either be left buried at the spot, or a formal second burial provided with the help of a *fengshui* master, who was to select an auspicious spot with a shape like a writing pen, elephant, bird, etc. The tomb was built with bricks and cement, with the bone urn placed inside. Flesh sacrifices, incense, music and firecrackers accompanied the burial, which was followed by a feast at home (pp. 83-85).

4. Fengshui

On pages 9-18 of his Wuhua district article in Volume 5, Mr. Zhang discusses the four basic criteria for the placing of a grave or house at an auspicious site, describing how the shapes in the whole landscape had meaning, noting the importance for local people to "sincerely believe in *fengshui*, and maintain many *fengshui* rules" (p. 13). The rules for selecting and dedicating a proper site "were very strict" (p. 14). It is clear from this discussion that the *fengshui* master functioned as a priest who with offerings and petitions invited "several hundred gods" (p. 15) to protect the new home or tomb to be built. So the gods supported the patterns of order and power that the *fengshui* master discerned in the landscape. I note below more material on this theme.

5. Rituals of Marriage and the Adoption of Children by Guanyin

Zhang Quanqing also provides a beautifully detailed description of marriage ritual on pp. 29-47 of Volume 5. On p. 32 he distinguishes eight basic steps in such a ritual, all of which are expressions of *li* 禮, the proper forms of ritual and social behaviour. Xie Meixing describes marriage rituals in his home area on pages 159-165 of Volume 1. I comment below on more material concerning this theme. Rituals for adoption of a child by Guanyin are discussed by Mr. Zhang on pages 15-16.

These rituals were carried out by nuns in a convent in which all the worshippers were women. They prayed primarily for the security and health of their children. The adoption ritual was called *xufu* 許福 "vowing for blessings," a process the author describes as follows:

> If a child were ill, or the eight characters [of its horoscope] conflicted with those of its parents, then its mother or grandmother took a slip of red paper with the year, month, day and hour of the child's birth written on it, together with offerings of vegetarian food, fruit, incense and paper items to the convent to pray. The red paper, called a *niangeng* 年庚, was left on the altar of the convent, to indicate that the child was being sold (*maigei* 賣給) to Guanyin. Then, Guanyin (through a nun) selected a new given name for the child including such characters as "miao" (temple), "Guan 觀" and "Fo 佛" (Buddha) ... In this way the child became a child of Guanyin. This relationship continued until the child was sixteen *sui* 歲 old. Until that time every year on a day between the sixth and fifteenth of the first lunar month the mother or grandmother took the child and offerings to the convent to worship Guanyin. This was done in the same way when the child reached sixteen *sui*, in a ritual called *choufu* 酬福 "thanking for blessings." At this time the child stated before Guanyin that it had become an adult. Because of this special function this convent was consistently full of worshippers even though it did not carry out temple festivals. (pp. 15-16)

6. Spirit-Mediums

The best information about spirit-mediums in this volume is also provided by Zhang Quanqing on pages 17-22, including the writing of charms with the medium's blood, climbing knife ladders (lit. "mountains," *shan* 山) made with thirty-six butcher knives, by mediums from the whole surrounding area, carrying mediums in sedan chairs behind those of the god in processions, etc., all of which is similar to descriptions in Volume 6 of De Groot's *Religious System* and Alan J.A. Elliott's *Chinese Spirit-Mediums in Singapore* (London: The London School of Economics and Political Science, 1955).

The new information for me here is discussions of spirit-mediums for deified ancestors in lineage shrines (pp. 19-20).

III. Volume 5

In addition to its introduction and concluding chapter, Volume 5 includes twenty-one chapters in 503 pages. The material in it of most interest to scholars of local religious traditions, some notes above, can be discussed under the topics of *fengshui*, funeral rituals, ancestor worship, the use of written prayers and invocations by villagers themselves, the implicit religious symbolism of weddings, the roles and importance of auspicious people (see the disussion below), spirit-mediums, the purposes of worship, and local definitions and roles of Daoist priests and Buddhist monks. Other interesting themes are noted in the "Concluding Comments" of this review. For good examples of these essays, read those by Zhang Quanqing, pp. 1-76, and Ling Shuangkuang 凌雙匡, pp. 364-369.

To provide an impression of the detailed information available here I begin this review with an account of young women going into trance to visit the spirits of dead family members in the underworld. With this story we are plunged into the heart of village religion. It is in Zhang Quanqing's article on the Zhang lineage and god worship in his home village of Hutian in Wuhua county, pp. 61-62.

1. A Case in Point: on the Worship of the Bamboo Leaf God （Zhuye *shen* 竹葉神） during the Mid-Autumn Festival

Mr. Zhang writes:

It is said that the Bamboo Leaf God is particularly efficacious on the 15th of the 8th month, when it leads people to enter the Yin realm (*Yin jian* 陰間)... According to the report of several Hutian women of the Zhang lineage over 70 *sui* old , they had all personally observed this ritual. Every year on the evening of the Mid-Autumn Festival three or four young women who wanted to enter the Yin realm would sit around a low table, with their folded hands placed

on top of it, with heads bowed on their hands. Then a woman standing beside the table lighted a single stick of incense and placed it in
the middle of the table. Beside the incense she put a bowl of clean
water, and then burned paper money while reciting the invocation,
"Bamboo Leaf God, Bamboo Leaf God, you are divinely efficacious
on the 15th of the 8th month. Bamboo Leaf God, Bamboo Leaf God,
lead us disciples down to the Yin realm. If you want to go, just go,
go with one mind and will; by no means allow yourselves to be dis-
tracted." [I take the latter part of this invocation to be addressed to
the young women]. While reciting this invocation the reciter continually sprinkled incense ashes on the heads of those bowed at the
table, and with a small bamboo branch sprinkled water from the
bowl on their bodies. In general, the whole bodies of those able to
succeed in going down to the Yin realm would begin to shake by the
time the incense was burned half-way down, continually slapping
the top of the table and stamping their feet. (At this point those who
were not able [to become possessed] would immediately leave the
table). In a little while those who did succeed would shout in alarm
"Ai-ya; it's really dark; it's really dark!" At this time, the reciter,
continually burning paper money, would tell them "I am giving you
a lantern." After they had gone a bit further, the women would say,
"Ai-ya; evil dogs are blocking the road." Still burning paper money,
the invocator said, "Look for sticks to chase them away." Then they
would call out, "Oxherds are blocking the way and won't let us
pass," to which the reciter, burning paper money, responded, "Sing
antiphonal folk songs with them (*dui shan ge* 對山歌); when you
have defeated them, you can pass." Soon the women would begin to
sing, "All you young oxherds, we will kick you to both sides (of the
road); we will beat you with our fists and leap over you."

When they reached the underworld, the women were believed to
first seek out their relatives there to talk with them, and then were
"driven" (*gan* 趕) back to the Yang realm by those relatives. Once they
arrived they awoke from trance, though some had to be pulled away
from the table by their living relatives, who might also sprinkle cold
water on their foreheads and the backs of their necks. If they still didn't
wake up, they might be beaten with *su-mao* 蘇茅 grass. Only a few

could succeed in going to the underworld, and those who did would be confused for several days thereafter. Those who succeeded once could do so more easily a second time.

This description of the Bamboo Leaf God ritual ends with a poignant story of the young mother of a dearly loved boy who died at only eight, after which she herself did not want to live, and unfortunately could not bear any more children. She thought of her dead child all the time, and so every year at the Mid-autumn Festival she went down to the Yin realm. "Once she reached it, she looked for her beloved and precious son, weeping ceaselessly. She did not want to return to the world of the living, and so each time she went down her relatives had to pull her back, and beat her with the grass before she could return" (p. 62).

2. Fengshui (pp. 9-18, 111-117)

In the descriptions of the practice of *fengshui* in these volumes there is almost no discussion of its relationship to *yin/yang*, the five phases, etc., rather, the emphasis is on auspicious shapes in the land-scape, and the relationship of *fengshui* apertures (*xue*) to them. Every house, temple and tomb is to be built at such a *xue*, which is where the dragon veins (*longmai* 龍脈) of the surrounding hills are exposed at that location, where it is marked with a "dragon god tablet," (*Longshen wei* 龍神位) under the main altar or beside the tomb. In a discussion of *feng-shui* on pp. 9-15 of Vol. 5, Zhang Quanqing notes that since it was believed that tombs control the prosperity of the lineage "the people all sincerely believed *fengshui*... If the dead are not in a suitable [location], the living will not be at peace." (p. 9) He describes the four basic characteristics of a good site as 1. The "coming dragon" should come slow-ly. 2. The areas on both sides of the site (i.e., the hills around it) (*sha* 砂) should be full and complete. 3. The peaks in the distance should be like writing pens. 4. There should be a stream winding about the site. (p. 9) He then goes on to discuss auspicious shapes such as a feeding pig, a dragon, tiger, crescent moon and an old pagoda. The latter represents a writing brush that can presage the production of scholars by the clan (pp. 10-11), of which Mr. Zhang discusses several examples, including a county magistrate, township head, military officer, *juren* 舉人 scholar, and two professors! (pp. 11-13).

Mr. Zhang then discusses the ritual for selecting the *xue* for constructing a new house (*dianxue* 點穴), beginning with the selection of a good day by the *dilixiansheng* 地理先生. One first bought new clothing, cap and shoes to give to this "Master of the patterns of the earth" (*fengshui* master), who then selected the house site and facing direction according to the "eight characters" of the date and time of birth of the owner. Then the "dragon aperture" of the site was selected with the help of a compass (*luopan* 羅盤). After the *xue* had been fixed, one set up a spirit tablet there for Lord Yang 楊公, described here as the patriarch of *fengshui*. This is a piece of wood six *chi* high wrapped with red cloth and thread, with Lord Yang's name written in the center, and those of Jiutian xuannü 九天玄女 and Patriarch Liao (Liao gong xian shi 廖公先師) (the god of measuring implements) on each side. It was put in a pottery crock full of sand, and then the Master recited an invocation before it, inviting gods to descend and bless the site, including the above-mentioned three, Lu Ban 魯班, gods of all streams, dragons, and the ancestors of the family. Then firecrackers were set off. With the *xue* ritually established, the owner feasted the Master and the workers, and construction could begin. The spirit tablet became a protective charm for the house, where it was put in the main room. The Master was paid with money in a big red envelope (pp. 15-16). Mr. Zhang comments that "hundreds of gods" were invited by the Master, including those of mountains and local *shuikou* 水口 (where the stream left the village). The *fengshui* master was asked to return later to bless the roof beam, main entrance and drainage ditches when they were raised or constructed.

The Master similarly presided over the construction of tombs in rituals to select the *xue*, thank the earth (*xie tu* 謝土) , and worship the earth god at his tombside altar. The Master was taken to the site in a sedan chair, recited invocations for the blessing of the family, and sat in the place of honor in a concluding feast (p. 18). In other words, in all of this the *fengshui* master functioned as a priest, a ritualist, invoking gods at every stage, from beginning to end.

There is an equally detailed discussion of *fengshui* practice by Xue Fansheng 薛凡昇 on pp. 111-117 of this volume, also emphasizing shapes in the landscape, and for house building, the invocation of protective gods, the names of forty-three of which are provided on pages

114-115, including Lu Ban, Guanyin, all the locality and kitchen gods from the area, door gods, "all the gods." Mr. Xue's discussion is supported by quotes from a *fengshui* handbook, including a chant for properly siting the kitchen stove. He also discusses rituals for digging wells, the "eye of the *fengshui* dragon" of the site. All must be done carefully, otherwise water from the Yellow Springs [an old term for the place of the dead] will gush out! A verse for siting the privy (toilet) is also provided (p.117). In the chapter by Xie Liyan 謝立言, there is also a discussion of the *fengshui* master functioning as an exorcist on the occasion of moving into a new house, wearing a red turban while holding a big red cock in his left hand and a seven star sword in his right (pp. 91-92). All this discussion of the *fengshui* master as priest and exorcist, inviting the protection of the gods, was new to me.

3. Funeral Rituals (pp. 123-130, 160-164)

There is not a lot of information on funerals in the materials consulted for this review and much of what there is quite similar to the descriptions by J.J.M. de Groot in the first volume of his *Religious System of China*. The two items new to me in the material at hand are a list of posthumous titles (*shihao* 諡號) for both men and women (p. 126), and an invocation directed to the dead soul reminiscent of Han "tomb quelling texts" (*zhenmu wen* 鎮墓文) (pp. 163-164). The forty-five titles for men all refer positively to their personal or moral characteristics, or to their accomplishments. Definitions are provided for each, as "One whose essays are well known is called *wen*, 'literary,' and 'one who has made himself and his family famous is called *xiao* 孝, 'filial'." The twelve posthumous titles for women all refer to their obedience, devotion and purity. For them, *xiao* is defined as "good at serving father and mother." These lists are a good source of information about ideal values.

The invocation to the dead, to be recited in a period of seven days and seven nights after the funeral, provides many similes for the lost soul (*wanghun* 亡魂); it is like "incense smoke that floats up to the sky, never to return," like an arrow shot from a bow that disappears, so "once the lost soul leaves it does not return home." The soul is also reminded that everyone dies, even the most famous like King Wen, Zengzi and

Mengzi (Mencius), with the concluding line reading, "For humans there are life and death, for flowers blooming and withering, for the sun bright and dark, for the moon full and partial, for humans to lack birth and death, or the moon to lack constant roundness; how could there be two kinds of order (Tian) in the world?" Given the prescriptive nature of much Chinese religious language, this invocation sounds to me like Han texts telling the dead to stay where they are and not return. (On which see Poo Mu-chou 蒲慕州, *In Search of Personal Welfare: A View of Ancient Chinese Religion* (NY, Albany: State University of New York Press, 1998, pp. 165-177). The generally conservative view of the dead this implies is supported by a prayer that, "they will sleep peacefully under the Nine Springs [another term for a place of the dead]" (p.161), by ideas of tombs as "*yin* dwellings," and by the absence of much imagery here concerning Buddhist ideas of purgatory. As we can see in the account of the "Bamboo Leaf God" ritual above, the dead live in an underworld, but how they get there and what happens to them are unclear. (On p. 118 there is a brief discussion of burial practices for children who die between three to five years of age, on which see pp. 13-14 of Lagerwey's introduction to this volume).

4. Ancestor Worship (pp. 18-29, 171-175)

Though ancestor worship has been discussed in detail by China anthropologists, there are still some points in the material at hand that are worth noting, particularly in the chapter by Zhang Quanqing. Mr. Zhang begins by distinguishing between *baizu* 拜祖 and *jizu* 祭祖, worshipping and sacrificing to ancestors. *Baizu* is worship offered to the tablets of one's father, mother and direct ancestors. It was normally done frequently and at home. *Jizu* is a more formal affair involving more elaborate offerings at the lineage shrine or the tomb. Its performance must be guided by a "master of ceremonies" From this definition, Mr. Zhang moves to a discussion of the preparation of a spirit-tablet after a funeral, a ritual that also involved putting ashes from the incense burner at the altar in small, red, tricornered bags with the generation and posthumous name of the deceased written on them. These bags were hung on the walls on both sides of the main room of the house, and were taken by sons and grandsons to be worshipped in their homes. Mr Zhang then describes ancestor worship at the New Year festival (pp. 20-22), during weddings, (pp. 23-24), twenty-days after the birth of a baby boy (p. 24), and before a daughter marries (p. 24). The only significant point I had not read about before is unison group worship of early ancestors on the second day of the new year, led by the lineage leader (*zuzhang* 族長). Here all together offered incense and wine, bowed and kowtowed, then burned paper money and set off firecrackers (p. 22). *Jizu* rituals are described in detail on pages 25-27, but with no significant differences from earlier discussions by anthropologists. For family New Year ancestor worship Yang Zuwu 楊祖武 adds that before the cooked food is offered to ancestors it is put beside the "celestial well" of the home and offered to the "celestial gods" (pp. 171-173). Other authors here note the worship of deities in image form at lineage shrines (pp.303,409,444), and that women could worship in shrines, but only with shallow bows with hands folded (*yi* 揖), not the deep bows (*gui* 跪) of men.

5. The use of written prayers and invocations

The evidence of this volume indicates that most collective rituals in villages were accompanied by the recitation of written invocations and lists of the names of deities. Some of these ritual texts were recited by Buddhist monks or Daoist priests, but others seem to have been read by villagers themselves. In his article here Xiao Wenping 蕭文評 provides a "sacrificial text" (*jiwen* 祭文) from a manuscript entitled the *Shu shi shu* 庶世書 (Book on the common world) dated 1939. This text was read by the leader of a temple festival in honor of a local protector deity, the Gongwang 公王. The leader, called a *shentou* 神頭, was chosen by divination at the end of the previous year's festival. The text appeals to the god for limitless mercy, good fortune, prosperity and good health (pp. 296-297). Another passage recited invites local ancestors and deities to the ritual; no particularly Daoist deities are mentioned (pp. 298-299). Another passage from this same manuscript prays for the protection and aid of those in different occupations; scholars that they may succeed in the examinations, farmers that their crops and animals may flourish, merchants that they obtain wealth, travellers that they become rich, and "when they return buy fields and build big houses." There are also passages here about driving away harmful forces, such as bandits, that their plans may not succeed and that they be "spontaneously decapitated and burned," and that diseases and wild animals be dispersed (pp. 299-301). Mr. Xiao also provides two "memorial texts" that he says were" written by the *shentou*" (pp. 306-307). Another article provides a text that invites gods to assist in divination. Again, no priests or monks are mentioned. This evidence appears to indicate that the use of written texts in local rituals in some cases did not depend on the presence of clergy, but how widespread this may have been is not clear. Of course, the use of texts in local rituals is common in modern Taiwan.

6. The Implicit Religious Symbolism of Weddings (pp. 29-47, 83-89, 119-123, 158)

Before I read from the books in the Hakka Studies series I had the impression that the traditional Chinese wedding was basically a social affair related to religious activities only by worship of the groom's ancestors, but I now see that in fact it was pervaded with rituals and symbols similar to those in temple festivals. I do not know how intentional this was, but it seems to me worth discussing. The parallels that I see begin with consulting a diviner to check on the compatibility of the horoscopes of the intended groom and bride, thus to ensure that the marriage was in accord with the order of things. A diviner was also asked to select an auspicious day for the wedding, just as for a festival (though in the latter case a spirit-medium might also be involved). The *meiren* 媒人 (go-between) served as an intermediary between the families and rode in a sedan chair at the head of the bridal procession, again in a way structurally parallel to a medium. Before the ceremony both the groom and bride paid their respects to their lineage ancestors, in each case aided by an elder. On the second day of the wedding bride and groom together worshipped heaven, earth and the groom's ancestors. In the procession the bride, dressed in a fine red gown, rode in a sedan chair, as did a god in a festival. When she reached the home of the groom's family, firecrackers were set off, and she was met and led out of the chair by an auspicious woman, in good health, with a stable marriage and many children. All spoke of only good things (*haohua* 好話). Here we see parallels to the roles of auspicious people in the organization of festivals, and to the New Year tradition of avoiding all inauspicious topics and actions. Firecrackers are also used frequently in god rituals. Even more interesting is the custom in Meizhou of the new bride stepping over a cooking pot full of burning charcoal as she entered the groom's house, "to destroy bad influences." Here a form of firewalking was a part of wedding ritual (p. 41). All of these actions in a temple context have ritual significance; no doubt participants in weddings were aware of these parallels. Paul Katz informs me that most of the religious symbolism in weddings described here can be found in Taiwan (personal communication, Sept. 26, 2000).

7. Auspicious People (pp. 24-25, 40, 92-97, 158, 189)

In its constant quest to bring in blessings and avoid harm, Chinese popular religion depended not only on gods, ancestors and ritual specialists, but also on living people who by their accomplishments and status demonstrated that they were fortunate, blessed by destiny and the gods, and who hence could have a beneficial influence on others. They could be women or men, gentry or commoners; what counted was their representation of beneficent presence and power, independent of particular ritual skills. Thus, it was an older woman with a "good destiny" who helped prepare a fifteen-year old bride-to-be to worship her ancestors (p. 25). We have seen that a woman similarly described led the new bride from her sedan chair into the groom's home (pp. 40, 158). At the dedication of a new house, it is a fortunate older married couple with lots of children, well-known in the village, who were invited to come and open the main door. First they worshipped the door gods, then the man opened the left side of the door, and the woman the right. While doing so he said, "may wealth and sons come," while his wife said, "may prosperity and honored position come." Then people took lanterns and torches into the house [to drive away harmful influences], and the family could move in (p. 92). At funerals a local wealthy person or gentry member could be invited to officiate, wearing a ritual robe and saying auspicious things (pp. 95-96), while in times of drought a member of the gentry (*shenshi* 紳士) might be invited to make offerings to the local *Shegong* 社公 (locality god) instead of a peasant family head (p. 189). The main leader of a *jiao* ritual also had to be of high moral and social status, and of a successful family. This could be a local scholar, such as a *xiucai* 秀才, or a retired county magistrate (p. 189). But here gentry members were selected as bearers of local prestige and power, parallel to commoners with the same characteristics. This is an excellent example of how representatives of more specialized traditions were incorporated into village culture and put to work for the interests of the people.

8. Spirit-Mediums (pp. 136-139, 196, 277-282)

Xiao Wenping says of spirit-mediums (*tongshen* 童身/*shentong* 神童 / *tiaotong* 跳童) that,

> They were chosen by the gods themselves. According to the report of [an 83 year old male villager] spirit-mediums were all very loyal, good and honest people with exceptionally sincere beliefs, under forty *sui* of age. Why? Because when a medium brought down a god (*luo shen* 落神; was possessed) his actions were very energetic and abrupt, and required great strength. His speech was loud; only the very strong could handle this responsibility. If one were too old, it could influence the results. Mediums could marry and have children, no different from others; they were not full-time specialists but only transmitted the instructions of the god, at the god's service [the gods here being the Wuxian dadi 五顯大帝, five long-established deities believed to be able to subdue harmful forces, rescue from difficulties and aid the people]. They were not mediums their whole lives, but retired after forty, at which time the god would select a new medium from among the people (p. 277).

Mr. Xiao continues with a discussion of the role of mediums in *jiao* rituals, beginning with their selecting the time of the ritual, usually in response to some difficulty like an epidemic. In the ritual procession mediums would sit in sedan chairs with sharp nails pointing up from their seats. They would also climb sword-ladders and fire walk, assisted by a Confucian-style "master of ceremonies," bowing, kowtowing and burning memorials. The medium had to prepare for all this by maintaining a vegetarian diet for three days. He was not to be watched by pregnant or menstruating women — if they did so the medium could be harmed by evil force (*shaqi* 煞氣), and their babies would die in their wombs. As the procession proceeded, offerings were made at each village beside the road. The medium would descend from his chair, possessed by the god, and question people about their situation. If there were no special problems, he would leave. In one case, when a medium spoke the people could not understand the god's language, thinking perhaps it was Hunanese, so they asked the god to ask another local deity to transmit his instructions in their own dialect (pp. 278-282).

Xue Fansheng discusses female mediums called *shenpo* 神婆 who abstained from food and drink for three or four days before a procession ritual. When asked why, they replied that the god, Zhengu dadi 真姑大帝, (Perfected Maiden Great Emperor) had confused (possessed) (*mile* 迷了) them because she wanted to go on a procession. While participating in a procession such female mediums were called *shentong*. Before the procession began it was necessary to go to the god's altar to invite her to descend into the medium. The medium's sedan chair had three sharp, upturned knife blades on its seat and three on its footrest. While seated in it the medium held two sharp swords. The procession visited five villages over a thirty kilometer route. At each an offering was prepare, where people asked the medium to order "wild spirits and orphan ghosts" to mind their own business (*anfen shouji* 安份守己). While so ordering the medium constantly waved the swords. If a family had a problem they would ask the medium to drive away the *gui* 鬼 ghosts / demons, for which the medium would cut her tongue and spit the blood into a bowl of water; which would then be called "*fashui*"法水 (ritual water). This in turn would be spat about to drive away the *gui* (pp. 136-137). (It is interesting to note that this was all done by a female medium possessed by a goddess).

Yang Zuwu's 楊祖武 essay also has a brief discussion of spirit-medium rituals intended to heal illness. After the medium was possessed he would say that the god had descended into him, adding, "what do you ask?" The people would respond by saying that so and so was ill, asking the god to reveal to them the cause of the illness. In a question and answer session they would tell the god the eight characters of the sick person's horoscope. Eventually the god would decide that the person had angered some spirit or *gui*, and gave instructions for offerings to see it off (*songgui* 送鬼). The medium performed a similar role in cases where it was believed a child had lost its *hun* 魂 soul due to fright (pp.

196-197).

9. Purposes of Worship and Local Definitions of Daoists and Buddhists

Xiao Wenping lists eight purposes and functions of god worship in his village:

1. To protect the village, particularly in times of warfare and disorder. He provides a story of how the Gongwang drove off Taiping rebels by turning grain into hornets that bit them. (The Taipings here are called "long hairs" *changmao* 長毛).

2. To drive away disease by taking the god in a procession in which disease demons were gathered into ritual boats that were set afloat.

3. To support justice and fairness by treating all worshippers equally; "all who are interested can participate."

4. Calm disputes between lineages. There were thirteen lineages in the village with over forty shrines, so competition could be intense. However, in temple rituals and processions all were required to participate and eat together, which "softened their contradictions."

5. Improve culture through the performance of operas and puppet plays, and inviting monks to read scriptures, "Praying for good fortune, responding to, celebrating and thanking for blessings, weddings, daily worship and divination all greatly enriched the cultural activities of the villagers."

6. To unite people by the gathering of friends and relatives at festivals, including those from other places.

7. Give support to people in difficult economic circumstances; "the people are many but fields are few." Prayers to the gods also help those who must work outside the village or migrate to Southeast Asia.

8. Stimulate economic activity through the purchase of goods used in offerings (pp. 309-313).

On definitions of local religion and of the Daoists and Buddhists who might be invited to assist in it we read, "The people of [this village] very rarely believe in or support Buddhism and Daoism, while those who maintain vegetarian diets and recite scriptures have almost disappeared. The deities they worship are those they have selected [themselves], they don't just worship any god they see. They worship only those gods with which they recognize they have a beneficial relationship, such as those who protect the locality, grains and hunting, the literary deity Lord Wenchang 文昌, etc., toward whom they are all sincere and pious" (p. 411).

Daoist priests are defined as those who "drive away demons and perverse forces, install dragons (*anlong* 安龍) and *fengchao* 奉朝 (lit. "to worship and have an audience with"). They only pray to the gods for blessings; they do not perform rituals to save the souls of the dead" (p. 346). Elsewhere we are told that while Buddhist monks recite scriptures, Daoist priests *fengchao*, install dragons and summon spirit troops" (p. 457).

John Lagerwey says that *anlong* refers to inviting the local *fengshui* dragon to dwell in new houses and temples. Of *fengchao* he suggests that it is "really just another term for *jiao*" (personal communication, April 6, 1999).

10. Daoism and Daoist Priests

(This section is taken by permission from the review of part of Vol. 5 presented at the May, 1998 Ethnography conference by Dr. Stephen Eskildsen, now at the University of Tennessee at Chattanooga. I have modified it slightly).

The Daoist priests mentioned in these essays are almost invariably non-monastic ritual specialists of the Sannai 三奶 (Three Ladies) variety. References to the Longhu Shan Heavenly Masters School (the most well known variety of priestly Daoism) and the monastic Quanzhen 全眞 School are conspicuous by their absence. Wang Jiebu 王捷步, on p. 341 of his article mentions a temple called Zanhuagong 贊化宮 that belonged to "the Quanzhen faction of Daoism." This may indeed have been a monastery, but I rather suspect that it belonged to the non-monastic variety of Quanzhen Daoism commonly found in Guangdong and Hong Kong.

Sannai priests ascribe the origins of their ritual methods (*fashu* 法術) to the Sannai Niang (the Three Ladies); three priestesses of 10th century Fujian named Chen Jinggu 陳靖姑 Lin Jiunang 林九娘 and Li Sanniang 李三娘, who are said to have protected the populace by slaying demons and monsters with their thaumaturgic powers. Sannai priests are acclaimed for their great demonifugic talents, and are particularly notable for the highly entertaining and dramatic nature of their rituals. In administering their rites they frequestly dress in costumes (often in female garb to represent the Sannai), and perform musical skits depicting the career and demonifugic exploits of the Sannai Niang. They also perform daredevil acts such as climbing up a ladder of knives, scooping coins out of hot boiling oil and walking on hot coals (for which there is also audience participation).

In regard to how Daoists came to pursue such activities, it would seem that one must be mindful of the interflowing and cooperative nature of the relationship between Daoism and local spirit-medium traditions. The daredevil stunts of the Sannai priests resemble the feats of male mediums (*tongshen*). In fact, as is mentioned in the first of the two articles in this volume by Xiao Wenping (p. 280), at some community festivals, mediums perform all the standard stunts of the Sannai priests, while the priests perform all the other Sannai ritual procedures including the musical skits. It would seem that local spirit-medium traditions have left their impact on Sannai Daoism. While the Sannai priests and the mediums maintain distinct identities, their relationship appears intimate. It would be interesting to know the process by which Daoism and spirit medium traditions came to blend and cooperate. Again, it would be worthwhile to search out parallels and precedents to this phenomenon in other regions and historical periods.

Ultimately, however, the difference between a Daoist ritual master and a medium would seem to lie in the fact that the former does not become possessed or lose consciousness. The Sannai priest can walk on sharp blades and hot coals because he invokes divine power and protection through his knowledge and mastery of ritual methods (*fashu*). The medium is impervious to pain because a god has taken control of his body, while his own consciousness (which would feel the pain) has become dormant. In our essays, I did not find information that would serve to contradict this view. However, despite this important distinction between the two categories, it should be noted that sometimes the persona and function taken on by male mediums in possession is similar to that of the Daoist Demonifuge. Xiao Wenping describes mediums who go out and fight demons by drawing talismans and wielding divine seals and weapons (p. 278, 281). Such a medium resembles a Daoist priest in his mighty persona and exorcistic function. He is something more than just a passive mouth-piece that channels divine advice. On the other hand, many of the mediums described in our essays essentially seem to be such passive mouthpieces, and do not assume the mighty, demonifugic persona. Female mediums appear to usually be of the passive, benign variety. If one is to conjecture that Sannai rituals (if not Daoist rituals in general) somehow developed out of or drew influence from spirit medium cults, one should perhaps look into the history of the "mighty" variety of medium, and its parallels in other parts of China.

11. Folk Buddhism (pp. 57-59, 189-195, 210-212, 239-246)

I first used the term "folk Buddhism" years ago in my studies of Chinese popular religious sects, but my reading of the reports edited by John Lagerwey and his Chinese colleagues has given new meaning to this term. In these reports, Buddhist ideas and symbols are almost totally subsumed by the concerns of village religion: women employ divination to decide whether or not to worship Guanyin (pp. 57-58), and the Duanwu 端午 mid-summer festival is treated as a vegetarian festival for Guanyin, in which she is petitioned for protection and prosperity (p. 58). Monks carry out *jiao* rituals in which they firewalk and recite the *Diamond sūtra* for material blessings (pp. 191-193), and sickly children are adopted out to Guanyin for her protection, after which they are given new "divine names" (*shenming* 神名) including such characters as Fo "Buddha", and *Guan* (for Guanyin). These names were formally given to the child after it was a month old, *while worshipping the ancestors* (p. 59). Yang Zuwu describes ritual activities in a village by monks living at a nearby monastery. When there was a funeral or *jiao*, the monks were invited to "worship the Buddha and recite scriptures." Every third day of the third month they would go into the village for ritual begging (*huayuan* 化緣), carrying an image of Guanyin into every household. There in front of the ancestral tablets they would recite scriptures while sounding their cymbals. The family would then put a pint of white rice on the table, hoping to gain the bodhisattva's protection and aid for family peace and good harvests. When the recitation was finished the monks put the rice in a begging bag and went on to the next place (p. 187).

Mr. Yang then provides a detailed description of a *jiao* ritual employing Buddhist monks which focussed on praying to Guanyin and other deities for protection and peace. Preparations for a large-scale ritual sequence called a Taiping qingjiao 太平清醮 began five months in advance, and involved the usual hiring of an opera troupe, setting up temporary buildings and altars, raising five-metre high bamboo poles with banners and lanterns at the top, sending up a memorial, and a procession around the village. He also describes firewalking by barefoot monks wearing their robes. In addition to the deities worshipped and the sūtras recited, Buddhist aspects of this ritual involved releasing living creatures (*fang sheng* 放生) and setting up a special Guanyin altar to save orphan souls (*dugu* 渡孤). This included lighting bright candles to attract the souls and then reciting scriptures, offering food and burning paper money and clothing to aid them (pp. 189-195).

Wen Yanyuan 文衍源 describes a similar Buddhist-style *jiao* carried out by monks from a temple first built in 1092. The ritual, called *zuofu* 作福 "creating blessing," culminated at 11:00 p.m. in a big bonfire for lost souls (pp. 210-212). However, the most detailed description of such a *zuofu* ritual is provided by Lin Qingshui 林清水 (pp. 243-246), carried out again by monks who lived in a local monastery. There they practiced their own daily scripture recitation, while on the first and fifteenth of the month people came to the temple to worship and divine. The biggest blessing ritual was carried out for three days and nights between the Lantern and Qingming 清明 festivals. It involved raising funds, selecting ritual leaders, sending up a memorial with the names of *all* the villagers on it, making a three-meter high "Great Being" (*Dashi* 大士) image on a platform, with a small Guanyin image on the top of its head, building a shed for puppet plays, and making lanterns with the character *fu* 福 on them. In addition, a *dugu* platform/altar was built. The *Dashi* is a transformation body of Guanyin.

The most interesting aspect of this festival was its three-night ritual for saving orphan souls. On the first and second nights rice and vegetables were offered and scriptures recited at the *dugu* altar, with food given to beggars as well. On the third day the *Dashi* image was taken on a procession, carried by family heads, with monks sounding their cymbals. The procession passed through twenty-three villages; at each the Great Being was worshipped, the monks recited scriptures and people recited invocations to bring blessings and avoid harm. At each village as well a man carrying a "mandate pennant" (*lingqi* 令旗) walked around calling out "those who want food and clothing come," to inform orphan souls of the final *dugu* ritual that night. For that ritual huge candles four meters high were put at road intersections around the monastery and in each village, so that the way to the offering platform was illuminated for the orphan souls. There were two ferry boat crossings along a river beside the village. On the last night of the *dugu* ritual "from evening until midnight, whether or not there were human passengers, [ferries at these two crossings] continuously crossed back and forth to carry the orphan souls from the other side of the river to the *dugu*." At the end of the ritual the Guanyin image on the head of the "Great Being" was invited to return to its altar, the pennants were taken down, and then pennants, the *Dashi* and paper clothing were all burned (p. 246).

In addition to the detailed descriptions of the rituals, what interests me most in these accounts is their evidence that until deep in the twentieth century Buddhist monks were still going out into villages and homes to perform rituals. There is no evidence here about what the monks themselves intended by this, but for the people they were another means of "summoning blessing and driving away harm," in part by placating uncared for spirits of the dead so that they would not cause trouble for the living. The poignant account of the empty ferry boats rowing back and forth at night also reminds us of the sincere belief of the people in the objects of their worship. As one ferry boat man is reported to have said, "In the first part of the night the boat was heavy coming and light going, while in the latter part it was heavy going and light coming" (p. 246).

IV. Concluding Comments

There is scattered information in Volume 5 about many other interesting topics, including discussions of celebrations of birth and birthdays (pp. 117-118, 181), the relationship between martial arts and Lion-dance troupes (pp. 49-54), divination (pp. 195, 253-254), and the worship of a god of hunting (Shelie gongwang 射獵公王) (pp. 247-249). The emphasis in the latter is the protection of crops from wild animals. There are also interesting discussions of the destruction of temples and images in 1958 and during the "Cultural Revolution," noting that people hid some images, "the older people still remembered," and that there was a black-market in ritual goods (pp. 228-232, 266). Yang Zuwu discusses a case of what Yang Yanjie has called an "ancestor god," *zushen* 祖神, an ancestor who has come to be worshipped as a protective deity by people from different lineages. It involved a deity named Sibo gong 四伯公 who was a seventeenth-generation ancestor of the local Yang lineage, of whom we read that he "was a well-known Daoist." After he died people set up an altar where he had lived and worshipped him as a god. At marriages and funerals people offered incense to him to seek his aid, while at festivals he was worshipped by those from ten villages and eight townships. Three thousand people of six surnames prayed to him, and small children were adopted out to him for their protection (p. 188). Here an ancestor became a fully-developed local patron god.

There is also an interesting discussion on pp. 354-363 of the worship of the ancient diety Pangu 盤古, the Chinese Purusha, in a village in northern Guangdong deep into the twentieth century. The first records of this deity are in sources from the third century C.E., where he is described as splitting open creative chaos and separating heaven and earth, with the parts of his body transforming into the sun, moon, mountains and rivers — the whole created world. In Volume 5, we learn that in Shijiao 石角 village he has been worshipped as a local protector diety whose whole traditional mythology is known to the people. We are told that "the people, in gratitude for Pangu's opening up of heaven and earth have venerated him down through the generations and look on him as the ancestor of humanity" (p. 357). For other useful information here see pages 447-449 for worship at the tomb of a spirit medium, with rubbings of his tomb inscription used as charms, pp. 452-453 for divination with coins shaken in a turtle shell, and pp. 458-460 for a detailed description of redeeming the lost souls of children in a ritual employing a length of bamboo as a temporary substitute for the child.

Material on a traditional Chinese form of civil society appears here in connection with local Buddhist temples, though other temples had similar social roles. Lin Qingshui notes that in his area every surname had a lineage organization, and that lineage feuds were frequent. However, during a *zuofu* ritual all the lineage leaders sat together and formed good relationships. Each year at the first meeting to prepare for the ritual the leaders of each lineage and village met to discuss plans, all of which concerned good things. [The temple] was located on an important road, so that people [from different] clans had to pass by it on their way to the market. During the war against Japan, the temple arranged a "guest meeting room" where newspapers were available, so older people from all the villages came there to talk and rest their feet. This led to communication of news, increased mutual understanding, and furthered friendship between lineages (p. 241).

Mr. Lin also notes that after the *zuofu* ritual people broke their four-day vegetarian fast and arranged a big feast to which everyone was invited, without regard to social status or lineage. At this feast people talked about everything, including matters of mutual benefit to their villages, such as repairing irrigation ditches (p. 246). Clearly, a search for a Chinese civil society should begin with its presence in village temples and rituals.

In sum, there is much rich and interesting material in these volumes that deserves to be widely known and discussed. It is a contribution to providing a new foundation for our understanding of traditional China and for comparison with popular religious traditions elsewhere.

19

THE DUAL CHARACTER OF CHINESE FOLK IDEAS ABOUT RESOURCES:

ON THREE WESTERN FUJIAN VOLUMES IN THE TRADITIONAL HAKKA SOCIETY SERIES

Dong Xiaoping

1. Yang Yanjie 楊彦杰, *Minxi Kejia zongzu shehui yanjiu* 閩西客家宗族社會研究 (*Hakka Lineage Society in West Fujian*). Traditional Hakka Society Series, No. 2, 1996. 305 pages. Hong Kong: International Hakka Studies Association, Overseas Chinese Archives, and École Française d'Extrême Orient.
2. Yang Yanjie ed., *Minxi de chengxiang miaohui cunluo wenhua* 閩西的城鄉廟會村落文化 (*Temple Festivals and Village Culture in Rural and Urban West Fujian*). Traditional Hakka Society Series, No. 4, 1997. 419 pages. Hong Kong: International Hakka Studies Association, Overseas Chinese Archives, and École Française d'Extrême Orient.
3. Yang Yanjie ed., *Tingchou fu de zongzu miaohui yu jingji* 汀州府的宗族廟會與經濟 (*Lineages, Temple Festivals, and the Economy in Tingzhou Prefecture*). Traditional Hakka Society Series, No. 6, 1998. 525 pages. Hong Kong: International Hakka Studies Association, Overseas Chinese Archives, and École Française d'Extrême Orient.

Chinese rural society has three prominent characteristics: large population, scarcity of arable land, and a culture with a long history. Chinese and Western scholars have studied these since the beginning of this century, but most have focused on only one of the three. A few have discussed the relationship of two, such as the function of the peasant population in economic ups and downs,[1] or the connection between peasant mentalities with land use. In 1985, Philip Huang used the concepts of "economic involution" and "peasant self-exploitation" to explore more deeply the changing relationship between population and land resources. He pointed out the harmful effects of peasant population growth on land resources, but did not pay attention to how cultural traditions might limit this harmful process.[2] Since then further progress has been made by scholars in anthropology, political science, religion, folklore, and other fields,[3] who, approaching Chinese peasant society from various angles, have discovered the special function of traditional culture in energizing hundreds of millions of farmers. However, they have tended to exaggerate the power of traditional culture while ignoring the ways in which diversity of population and land resources can lead to cultural variation. In fact, at times even peasants' activities in developing the land can create cultural variants and weaken peasant cultural values.

Are these three factors in Chinese rural society mutually interdependent, and if so to what extent are they reappearing? Apart from that, how can ethnography be written free of biases from informants, memories and researchers' interests?[4] What sort of terminology should be used for ethnographies of China that will be accepted by both Chinese

---

1　Ramon Myers, *The Chinese Peasant Economy: Agricultural Development in Hopei and Shantung, 1890-1949* (Mass., Cambridge: Harvard University Press, 1970).

2　Philip Huang, *The Peasant Economy and Social Change in North China* (Stanford: Stanford University Press, 1985).

3　For some examples of relevant research since the 1980s in political science, anthropology, and history, see Prasenjit Duara, *Culture, Power, and the State: Rural North China, 1900-1949* (Stanford: Stanford University Press, 1988); David Arkush, "The Moral World of Hebei Village Opera," in Paul A. Cohen and Merle Goldman eds, *Ideas Across Cultures: Essays on Chinese Thought in Honor of Benjamin I. Schwartz* (Mass., Cambridge: Harvard University Press, 1990); and Odoric Wou, *Mobilizing the Masses: Building Revolution in Henan* (Stanford: Stanford University Press, 1994).

4　James Clifford, *Writing Culture: The Poetics and Politics of Ethnography* (Berkeley and Los Angeles: University of California Press, 1986), p. 32.

and foreigners? As we move beyond the 1990s the need to resolve such questions, it must be said is all too evident. The recently published volumes on western Fujian in the "Traditional Hakka Society Series" under the direction of John Lagerwey are important works which begin to answer these questions. They attracted the attention of China studies scholars overseas as soon as they were published, and they have been regarded enthusiastically by Chinese scholars as well. Especially in China, these recent ethnographies of China written or edited by Western scholars have stimulated in readers an ardent interest seldom seen before.[5]

While the success of this series has involved the cooperation of French and Chinese scholars, the contributions of local people have been primary, and inside information from local cultural groups has been fully respected and utilized in compiling the ethnographies. Only after that did Professor Lagerwey carefully give the ethnographic materials an appropriate theoretical cast. Compared with earlier Sino-Western cooperative efforts, this process better resolves the methodological problems encountered by the two sides in fieldwork. It has been able to uncover interactions of the three elements mentioned in the opening paragraph of this review by approaching them from the Chinese situation. Its theoretical explanations are original and enlightening for both Chinese and Western scholarship.

I. Overview of the Minxi Series

The Minxi 閩西 (West Fujian) volumes are based on local materials gathered by Professor Lagerwey and Yang Yanjie of the Fujian Academy of Social Science. Yang organized these materials into three volumes, to each of which Lagerwey contributed a succinct introduction.

---

5 Speaking from personal knowledge, I know for example that Beijing Normal University folklore specialist Liu Xiaochun 劉曉春 used this work in writing a Ph.D. dissertation on "Contemporary Social Change in a South Jiangxi Hakka Mountain Village," and Kim Ho-jeol 金鎬杰 used it in an M.A. thesis on "Western Fujian Hakka Earth Mound Residences and Daily Life" (1997, typescript).

Minxi kejia zongzu shehui yanjiu (*Hakka Lineage Society in West Fujian*) edited by Yang Yanjie (referred to hereafter as *Yang A*) was published in 1996 as Volume 2 in the "Traditional Hakka Society Series." It has four chapters: "Lineage Society and Culture," "A Comparison of Two Neighboring Communities," "Examination of a River Valley Region," and "Hakkas and the She 畬 People." As the chapter titles suggest, Yang's investigation of Minxi Hakkas is intensive, multi-layered, and rich.

Minxi de chengxiang miaohui cunluo wenhua (*Temple Festivals and Village Culture in Rural and Urban Minxi*), Volume 4 in the same series, was published in 1997 with Yang Yanjie as chief editor and an introduction by John Lagerwey (*Yang B*). This volume contains sixteen field reports by local people from a 1996 conference convened by Lagerwey and Yang after four years of village studies. They are arranged under three categories: "County-Seat Temple Fairs," "Village Temple Fairs," and "Lineages and Village Culture." The area of research extended into several counties of northern Minxi. The contents emphasize description of the area's traditional town and village festivals, the annual ritual cycle, and other folk customs, including such popular communal activities as *fengshui* 風水, worship of Mazu, dragon dancing, and lantern parades, all of which are rich in ritual and legends.

Tingzhou fu de zongzu miaohui yu jingji (*Lineages, Temple Festivals, and the Economy in Tingzhou Prefecture*), Volume 6 in the series, was published in 1998 with Yang as chief editor and an introduction by Lagerwey (*Yang C*). This volume contains twenty field reports by local people which were revised following another conference convened by Lagerwey and Yang. The reports are divided into five sections, on "Township-Level Temple Fairs," "Village-Level Temple Fairs," "Lineage Traditions," "Popular Taoism," and "The Traditional Economy." Geographically, the investigations extend into several counties of southern Minxi. The contents are more wide-ranging, adding descriptions of the important areas of folk Taoism and the traditional economy. A biographical sketch of the author is appended to each report in this volume, unlike the previous one, and some reports also list the names of their village informants. These effort provide additional background for the authors' fieldwork, clarify the origins of the research data and lines of transmission of local culture, increase confidence in the fieldwork data, and make it easier for readers to grasp Professor Lagerwey's methodology and theoretical ideas.

II. The Overall Research Methodology of the Series

Altogether the three volumes contain 1360 pages and over one million characters. More than 160 people were interviewed, mostly old people from different communities and villages in Minxi. The categories are consistent, and the contents are thorough. This constitutes a major study. The methods the researchers used to compile it can be understood as follows:

1. Research Sites Based on the Distribution of Traditional Culture, Combined with Deep and Comprehensive Ethnographic Investigation

Perhaps it would have been enough for the Minxi study to sample a single village or township. That has been the customary standard in anthropological fieldwork, and most earlier Western ethnographies of China did that. But Professor Lagerwey and Yang Yanjie "traveled throughout the mountains and rivers of Minxi" (*Yang A*, 305), and the scope of the places they selected for research is several times, several tens of times, greater than the implicit standard of earlier scholars. Is this method appropriate? After reading the three Minxi volumes I am convinced that Lagerwey is right.

There has been a contradiction in recent anthropological fieldwork in China. Everyone says China's territory is huge, its population enormous, and dialect differences so great that fieldwork must concentrate on one comparatively small area to study it in depth, and that it is also important to pull back and consider general questions about Chinese society. But China historically has had a centralized administration and mobile population. Its local societies, although varied, have differing degrees of cultural connections, and are part of a shared national culture. Unless it cannot be helped, local culture generally adopts similar approaches to the shared national culture. The dates for many temple festival rites, for instance, are the same for all ethnic groups and regions.

If the official national culture needs the cooperation of local cultures, it also has the influence to make the area of shared culture expand. Therefore, anthropologists must not be too rigid in selecting sites for fieldwork in China. While it may seem empirically sound to study a single village or place, under certain conditions this can lead to vacuous theories.

For example, in past ethnographies of China some Western anthropologists have used broad terms like "state," "society," and "power" while drawing their evidence from just one village or spot. This seems very open to objections in the eyes of Chinese colleagues: how can one know that a single village represents the whole of Chinese society? Since the 1980s, ethnographies by Western scholars have emphasized local variation, correcting their earlier one-sided view of a single Chinese culture, and so increasing our understanding of certain aspects of Chinese society. But variation must not be made into an absolute. Such research neglects at least two factors mediating difference and similarity. First, it neglects the points of identity among local cultures and between local culture and national culture, which makes the study of local difference lapse into over-simplification. Second, it neglects the common people's lore about representations of local society. Is there not a danger when we listen only to scholars debating and not to the voices of ordinary people? As a result, applying Western theories to Chinese society often fragments the wholeness of local cultures and their identity with other non-autonomous cultures that have similar forms. We know that if the local popular culture loses this integral structure its meanings and functions change.

To improve the quality of ethnographic fieldwork in China, I think scholars need to get a hold on the scope of the area of shared culture in the local society they want to study, and they need to soak up the knowledge of the common people. At the same time they should, according to the needs of different research agendas, break out of the single-village model and revise the way anthropological sites are selected, using multiple criteria. All this, of course, should be based on concrete practice, not dogmatism. Lagerwey selected his sites according to the shared area of the Minxi Hakka traditional culture he wanted to study, which required having accurate knowledge of the of area folk culture. If a one-point or one-village study could cover this area, he could have done his work in one point or village, but he had a better idea of the shared cultural area and so determined to make a number of investigations in a multipoint field. That he had spent many years going to the Minxi mountain cultural region, speaks beautiful Chinese, and had a companion like Yang Yanjie with whom to discuss and exchange ideas gave him additional advantages in selecting sites.

The problem is where to start and how to combine investigation indepth with a broad overview. This is not easy, but to judge from these three volumes, Lagerwey found a way.

Previous studies of western Fujian concentrated on Changting 長汀 and Yongding 永定 counties. Changting was the political, economic, and cultural center of Minxi Hakka society and had been a prefectural capital. Yongding has attracted much outside interest for its many circular walled villages, visible cultural markers. But apart from these two sites, relatively little attention has been paid to the villages and people of Minxi. Besides Changting and Yongding, Lagerwey and Yang also went to neglected counties like Shanghang 上杭, Liancheng 連城, Ninghua 寧化, Wuping 武平, and Qingliu 清流, in effect establishing investigation sites spread over the central, northern, and southern parts of Minxi. Apart from the old prefectural capital, Changting, in each of three other areas they established two county-level sites — seven counties in all, basically covering the whole Minxi region. In these seven counties relatively concentrated investigations were made of nineteen towns and fifty villages. There are plains villages, mountain villages, riverside settlements, flourishing market towns, multi-county folk territories for religious rituals, territories of customary rural regional alliances, and so on. Each place, because of differences in kinship, population, water patterns, mountains and forests, gods, communities, feelings, interests, ideals, values, oral traditions, and ethnic customs, has over the course of centuries formed a certain cultural distinctiveness, but at the same time in many important folk matters each also reflects a common Hakka style. As a whole, the region's traditional culture also revolves directly around limiting the use of resources — which reveals a general characteristic of the dynamic behind the development of Chinese rural society.

What is important is that in finding these rural locations, Lagerwey and Yang did not use the earlier ethnographic method of distinguishing so-called central places from peripheral areas, much less the method of taking the village as unit. Doing their best above all not to rely on pre-conceptions, they pursued multiple lines of inquiry, discussed matters in depth, compared neighboring sites, organized data in a matrix, and from all this teased out the logical pattern of the ecological distribution of the region's culture. Only then did they finally decide on the research map of many mutually reinforcing sites. The interpretive framework of the Minxi series is also drawn precisely from this distribution pattern of the cultural ecology, and is thus full of local flavor. The authors' analyses do not lack cool rationality and historical depth, and so have been able to resolve the contradiction between in-depth research and an overall perspective in recent Chinese and western scholars' fieldwork in China. The theoretical style of the books also opens up new ground, such that even a reader who has never been there can feel that this is Minxi and nowhere else.

2. Full Revelation of Local Inside Materials, to Achieve Identity between Indigenous Culture and Western Interpretations

The series contributors are all insiders from villages Lagerwey went to, the majority old people in their 60s or 70s, born in the late Qing or early Republican period and still alive, from whose mouths came a storehouse of data. When visiting them Lagerwey was sincere about learning from them, and afterwards they were happy to accept his suggestions and write down things they had heard and experienced. They revealed in detail family histories handed down from ancestors, the composition of the village population, agricultural and sideline products and trade, the ups and downs of folk society, the village's network of relations with the outside, and their opinions about the changes in village life — without restrictions of form or length. These are pure insider cultural records, of inestimable historical value, which must be read.

There are two other important points about the writing of this series that are worth noting. One is the inclusion of two research reports from Yang Yanjie and another Fujian scholar, Zhou Lifang 周立方. Unlike Lagerwey, Yang and Zhou are locals who have a natural affinity with the native culture in which they were raised. But they are also urban scholars, for whom Minxi mountain villages are to a certain extent a "foreign world." They too could experience a sense of unfamiliarity when visiting the countryside. Yang especially has been going with Lagerwey to Minxi villages to gather volumes of original data since 1992, and they have become good friends. Lagerwey has been completely respectful toward Yang ever since starting this research. Yang modestly writes that Lagerwey gathered the majority of the materials, and "gave them to me to arrange and publish. I particularly thank Mr. Lagerwey for his help and sincere friendship" (*Yang A*, 2-3). Thus, how can these two local scholars, Yang and Zhou, look at indigenous culture with insiders' eyes today? What are the differences between their explanations and the views of old villagers? And what are the connections? These are matters one wonders about. Needless to say, Lagerwey was quite correct to include their reports in the internal documents. Theirs is a level of local knowledge which should not be ignored in compiling new ethnographies of China.

The other special thing is John Lagerwey's introductions. His style is to let local informants speak fully. He waits for them to finish before offering his brief analyses. Lagerwey's introductions clearly report questions about Minxi Hakka society and traditional culture which need further explanation, including classification, nomenclature, connotations, habits of thought etc., At the same time he preserves his outsider's distance and places the insiders' descriptions of a particular district's culture against the background of Chinese rural society in order to move toward theoretical generalizations. The concepts he uses, based on knowledge of all the local data he has been able to gather, are not obvious. How as the director of the Franco-Chinese cooperative project, he planned the research, organized local ethnographic materials, and made anthropological theoretical explanations-all these seep into his introductions without leaving traces. Lagerwey's greatest quality is that he strives for dual approval from both local culture and Western scholarly interpretation. The reader can discover in wording that naturally slips into every report that local Hakkas cooperated with him and praised his work. The elucidation of this culture he gives in the introductions also reveals remarkably well the integration of different cultures. What he sought was close harmony between outsider interpretation and local culture, and on this basis he gives Western readers theoretical explanations of Chinese Hakka words, acts, and ideas. His discussions are informed by fondness for the Chinese people he studies and for the Western theories he carefully constructs. The reader can discern similarities and differences between Lagerwey and Yang Yanjie et al. Looking at the three volumes and two introductions from the perspective of Franco-Chinese cooperation, it is clear this is a big program worth careful consideration. Having the introductions in Chinese and in English enables both Chinese and Western scholars to read them with ease.

3. Xiang-level Discourse, and Comprehensive Ethnographic Research Including People, Resources, and Culture

From a theoretical standpoint the biggest breakthrough of this series is to replace the vocabulary such "state," "society," "power" used by earlier anthropologists writing on China with one based on traditional Hakka society's ample lexicon and the ways its words are used. A mode of expression for communicating local culture has been taken directly from local ethnographic data, and a *xiang* 鄉 (a township divided into villages) —level research terminology established for use by scholars in collecting, arranging, and writing up fieldwork data. This is not macro-level research like early work on Chinese lineages and national politics, nor is it micro-level like some early twentieth-century Western eyewitness accounts of single Chinese villages. It is in-between, mid-level.

Mid-level research has three advantages. First, it can encompass the cultural memory of local elders. The books' elder authors, who can generally remember things going back three generations from the mid-Qing to 1949, talk about an area that on the whole does not go beyond the *xiang*. If they touch on national society, it is just in expressions about refugees such as "fleeing disaster" or "escaping social disorder." This shows their distance from national politics and their reliance on anonymous orally transmitted history. Thus *xiang* is a concept used by Hakkas themselves in their self-construction. Second, mid-level research can uncover the workings of Hakka society's politics and economics. Traditional Minxi society is in a geographically poor area: surrounded by mountain ranges, river systems, and basins, its arable land was scarce, food insufficient, and settlements scattered. In such an environment it proved difficult to form large economic or political centers, and in people's minds the central area of administration is nothing other than the *xiang*. *Xiang* is thus a geographic concept which is in circulation. Third, it can make clear the points of attachment among the Hakka's multiple peoples, multiple origins, and customs involving multiple gods. Minxi Hakka folk culture is a mixture of many elements; as Lagerwey says, "nothing can be taken for granted" (*Yang C*, 63). But in any case, ordinary people all share knowledge of the *xiang*. In the collective life of the *xiang* can be found general characteristics of kinship relations, social organization, and folk religion which are shared throughout local society. As to differences — between Han and minority customs, of worshipping different founding ancestors, and so on — these appear at levels below the *xiang*: village, ward, lineage, *she* 社. Thus *xiang* is still a concept of shared culture.

As Lagerwey discovered, Minxi local societies' patterns of "irreducible localization" and their ties with "subcultures" can be found in the oral traditions of *xiang*-level ethnographies. His introductory analysis says:

> Some of the recurrent themes are more random, or more local, than others: that both the immortals Ouyang 歐陽 and Lai 賴 are said to have left home in their teens and are worshipped in temples at the foot, halfway up, and on top of their mountains would seem to be a case of "local contagion." Tales of powerful bones, whether those of immortals or of an ancestress, tales involving Song Renzong 宋仁宗, black-faced gods, cliff caves, fox spirits, and one-legged despoilers of women — all have the ring of the familiar. As here presented, these "travelling motifs" fully belong to local culture, even though they clearly come from "elsewhere." Some themes of this kind belong to specific "subcultures" such as that of Taoist magic. Examples of this are the tales told by Hua Qinjin 華欽進 of a Taoist's hubris leading him to inadvertently rape his own daughter, or of the Nammu 南無 sending hornets to attack a rival, and Lai Jian 賴建's stories of why Taoists ascend sword ladders and dance on bamboo strip mats. As much as the recurrence of such tales gives the ethnographer a sense of "patterns of local culture," so also do their seemingly limitless transformations give the impression of "irreducible localization" and vitality. [*Yang C*, 61]

I agree with Lagerwey's analysis. The shared culture of the Chinese people is formed by many subcultures dispersed over a broad geographical area. Shared national culture is a political, elite, and systematic construction dependent on the machinery of state. Subcultures are regional cultural forms which have taken shape in the course of Chinese history. Local societies' cultures are the day-to-day culture of common people. Both of the latter are non-official cultures. The development of local cultures has drawn on the power of oral tradition and customary folk law to invent national administrative forms and establish local authority. It also used subcultures' cultural patterns to protect the influence of local authority, a combination of divine justice (shen-pan 神判) and rule by men, to control the growth rate of goods and people, and so guarantee that local society could continue to develop. Only a Minxi local society which formed a relatively independent "irreducible localization" and maintained ties with subculture groups, can be regarded as a local society and a relatively satisfactory object of research for understanding Chinese rural society.

Yang Yanjie, intimately knowledgeable about the region's culture, also thinks that starting research from the *xiang* level is a methodology that corresponds to real life. He writes:

> Our investigations concentrated on the level of the rural town (*xiangzhen* 鄉鎮). This is due to the following considerations. Rural towns are often where market fairs are located. Historically the bureaucrats of successive dynasties were stationed only at the county level, below which were no administrative organs, and so rural market towns, today's township centers, are particularly important. Because past historians have concentrated mostly on the county, prefecture, and up, and anthropologists on the natural village, the rural town in between has been neglected [Yang cites John Lagerwey, "The Structure and Dynamics of Chinese Rural Society" (paper presented at the Fourth International Conference on Hakkaology, November 4, 1998, unpublished)]. We tried to get a grasp of the full picture by gathering information in the field on all aspects of rural towns, including their natural environment, products and resources, people's conditions and customs, markets and trade, marriage networks, and so on. [*Yang A*, 3]

In my opinion, mid-level research is appropriate for Minxi and also other local societies in China. Its advantage lies in discovering an intermediary level between the "village" and the "nation" which locates the most basic and most vibrant growing points in rural Chinese society's traditional culture. When the folk use this mid-level, it forms the embryo of the nation and conserves the traits of democratic village life.

Chinese and Western scholars have discussed the *xiang* to some extent in the past, but for the most part they have engaged in a theoretical critique from the point of view of official political control. No one has tried to investigate Chinese folk concepts of *xiang*. Lagerwey discovered this void. He and his Chinese collaborators in their fieldwork continue to use the *xiang* in their discussions, writing new ethnographies, and explaining local forms of Chinese folk life and rural society. Opening up this new territory is even more of an innovation and a happy surprise.

III. Dual Chinese Peasant Approaches to Resources: Some Important Points of Inspiration from the Minxi Series

The three Minxi volumes have solid fieldwork, rich data, and outstanding scholarly results. Their contents raise a series of questions worth pondering.

1. Affirming the Dual Nature of Resources: the Chinese Folk Notion of "Xiang"

The abundant materials in these ethnographies allow us to see that the *xiang* of Minxi Hakka's traditional vocabulary is not today's administrative township *xiang*. The geographic boundaries and human connotations of the two are different. A *xiang* is a natural village in Baisha 白砂 in Shanghang county, in Zhuotian 濯田 in Changting county, and in the Pingyuan mountain 平原山 region (*Yang A*, 9; *Yang C*, 218). But in another part of Shanghang, in Gufang 古坊 village in Zhongdu zhen 中都鎮, it follows the divisions, also called sectors (*jia* 甲), used by the older generation when carrying the images of the dieties

Wuxianwanggong 五顯王公; each sector was a voluntary territorial and lineage association. Or, it follows the boundaries for dragon or lantern processions (*Yang B*, 127, 151). On both sides of the Dongliu River 東流溪 in the western part of Wuping county, common people used *xiang* to refer to sections of the river, as in "traveling four *xiang*", or "nine and a half *xiang*", expressions which have come down from the past and are still in use today (*Yang A*, 157). In Mapu 馬埔 village in Pengkou zhen 朋口鎮, Liancheng, the custom is for 13 wards (*fang* 坊) of the valley to rotate in sacrificing to great grandfather (*Taigong* 太公). The thirteen wards cross county lines and each ward's situation is differant; some refer to lineages' places of origin, some are natural villages, and one takes its name because "there are mountains on two sides and fields in between". Old people today can still recall the history of moving from Pengkou to Shanghang in the Song dynasty, since which time the lineage has gone through twenty-five generations (*Yang A*, 49). The scale of what Minxi Hakkas mean by *xiang* is today roughly comparable to an administrative village but not altogether the same (*Yang B*, 162-63). In Qingliu and Ninghua counties, people from an alliance of eighteen villages on the edge of the urban district never enter the city. According to an informant named Huang Zizhen 黃子珍, northeast of Changting county in the "ten *xiang* under Tongfang 童坊" the concept of "*xiang*" was formed originally to sacrifice to Fuhu 伏虎, who came from the city; this *xiang* is also the same as a village (*Yang B*, 79, 233). Nonetheless, in all cases, the common people can explain where the *xiang*'s borders are.

A *xiang* in Minxi can be big or small but it is a mental entity. Its ancient boundaries are generally revealed once each year during Chinese New Year's in the folk activity of patrolling the borders (*xunjing* 巡境), whose atmosphere of mysteriousness and lively actions especially cultivate feelings of love for the locality in local people. The limits of the *xiang* are constituted by boundary gate towers, settlement peripheries, ancestral shrines, *fengshui* groves, water outlets (*shuikou* 水口), and mountain dragon mouths (*shanlongkou* 山龍口), which may not have changed for centuries (*Yang A*, 68, 258; *Yang B*, 221; *Yang C*, 211). An interesting example informs us how the route of lantern processions (*youhuadeng* 游花燈, a kind of local patrolling the borders) has been passed down unchanged to today. "The lantern procession does not go by certain places that are densely settled today because in the past they were lakes and sand dunes, while it still must pass behind shops, [official pits] (*guankenglong* 官坑隴), and behind the highway, places no longer populated today" (*Yang B*, 157-58). The upriver thirteen wards' rotating sacrifice to Taigong, which is also called "approaching the *xiang*" (*linxiang* 臨鄉), has its own circuit which has been handed down for thirty generations (*Yang A*, 249). Clearly *xiang* are stable.

Compared with common people's dull everyday life, making a circuit of the *xiang* borders is a grand folk holiday in which male and female, young and old all participate, observing the *xiang*'s boundaries with their own eyes. When the locals use the word *xiang* what they understand is a permanent sacred boundary and an actual lived space, and also the concrete route of a multi-clan, multi-village, self-managed activity. It is an independent term which the people, combining cultural and natural resources, use for understanding society: a self-made dual concept.

Equally important is that by adopting folk usages of *xiang*, anthropologists doing fieldwork can analyze these two elements of the locality's culture to recover traditional social structure. To take Guzhu 古竹 *xiang* in Yongding as an example, according to Yang's analysis, a big lineage prospered and formed a *xiang*; the family's gentry and officials were powerful and numerous in the *xiang*. The *xiang* also had various popular and religious associations — an association of merchants, one of literary men, a Tianhou society, a womanhood (Potaihui 婆太會), a Guanyin society, a Guandi society, a brotherhood (Xiongdihui 兄弟會) and a burial society (Yizhonghui 義塚會) — a network of ties extending to all levels of that place's society (*Yang A*, 14, 217, 314). Since 1949, many religious sacrifices are no longer carried out, but the network of interpersonal relations remains. This network, using or creating gods, preserving the basic system of gods, establishing alliances between people and the gods, is able to operate religious associations and control the development of land and people. In sum, scholars, by uncovering the *xiang*, this "both outward- and inward-pointing, both expanding and condensing" flexible mechanism (*Yang A*, 116), can explain the mutual correlations of a particular *xiang*'s conditions with the common national Chinese culture and subcultures.

2. Fengshui: A Romantic Illusion and Rectifying Custom for Continuing to Utilize Limited Resources

That southerners attach great importance to geomancy (*fengshui*) is well known, but Professor Lagerwey's formulation "geomancy [involves] making the best of limited available resources" (*Yang B*, 44 / 26) seems beyond the ordinary. This generalization, to judge from the three Minxi volumes, touches on the conceptual heart of the area's social development, which is using the cohesive force of a culture based on human sentiment to alleviate the problem of many people on limited land, and cooperatively build an egalitarian rural society.

In studies on the Hakkas from the late Qing to the first half of the twentieth century, many scholars judged them particularly good at struggle[6] and also highly imaginative.[7] In other words, a capable, story-telling, migrant group. These foci are reflected in the concept of *fengshui*. In their oral narratives, the key to discovering *fengshui* is 8 or 9 times out of 10 a dream or mythical legend. A *fengshui* treasure is just the special form of a bit of land and a *fengshui* master's explanation of it, full of metaphors predicting the future, such as saying a ridge shaped like a brush rack will produce a scholar in the family, or a line of hills like a sleeping dragon, a soldier, or a well like crab's eyes, a wealthy person. *Fengshui* involves synonyms for people, wealth, and good fortune.

---

6 For the main points see Luo Xianglin 羅香林, *Kejia yanjiu daolun* 客家研究導論(*Introduction to Hakka Studies*, Xishan shucang 希山書藏, 1933; reprint Shanghai wenyi chubanshe, 1992).

7. For material on this one can consult: Huang Zunxian 黃遵憲, *Ren jing lu shi cao* 人境廬詩草 (1891), *juan* 1 "Mountain songs," which includes nine of fifteen folk songs Huang gathered in his native Meixian, and Zhong Jingwen 鍾敬文, *Ke yin qingge* 客音情歌 (*Hakka Love Songs*, Beixin shuju, 1927). In addition, among the new local histories and collections of folk literature being developed in China since 1984, many concerning Fujian contain materials on traditional Hakka society. For instance: *Yongding xianzhi* 永定縣志(*The Yongding County Gazetteer*; Zhonghua shuju, 1992) and county gazetteers for Wuping county (Zhongguo dabaikequanshu chubanshe, 1993), Liancheng county (Qunzhong chubanshe, 1993), Qingliu county (Zhonghua shuju, 1994), Changting county (Sanlian shudian, 1993), and Ninghua county (Fujian renmin chubanshe, 1992). "Zhongguo minjian wenxue san tao jicheng" 中國民間文學三套集成 (*Materials Collected from Fujian for the Three Collections of Chinese Folk Literature*) are in the general office for the project.

The question is whether in recounting these symbols, Hakkas can convice and inspire themselves. In the face of impoverished natural endowment, they do not complain, lose hope, or give up, but put all their efforts into realizing *fengshui*'s metaphors, like "literary peak", "dragon ridge," or "water exit" (*Yang A*, 211; *Yang B*, 203). On the basis of the *fengshui* of a tiny bit of land, they make big plans, involving family, wealth, human life, and all of society's kinds of good fortune. This is nothing but a romantic dream. But romanticism has its strong point, which is that people do not argue about whether the opportunities of *fengshui* are fair. Based on the folk authority of dreams and myth, they believe this is a matchless piece of land and that their hopes are not extravagant.

The capability of the Hakkas is seen in what thay can achieve in human relations: everyone strives hard, generation after generation. For this striving to keep developing in an agricultural environment, the ideal situation is popular society's vision of equality, characterized by farmers equally creating gods to protect their *fengshui*. Yang says that in Nanfang 南坊 village on the Dongliu river "every village's water exit has several altars and shrines, and they are arranged according to a regular pattern as though stamped from the same mold" (*Yang B*, 44). Equality is preserving the security of home; equity involves the equal sharing of the benefits of natural resources. Here the human element is stressed; it hints that every individual in the group who shares the folk culture, should maintain a balanced posture toward the limits of natural resources in his psychological desires and material production, Anyone who breaks this constraint will be punished by folk society. Farmers in Hucunzhen 胡村鎮, Ninghua, discovered too many people were pouring in from other provinces and buying too much. Afraid their good fortune (resources) were flowing out, they blocked up one of two wells that represented crab eyes. The collective sanction of Mao 帽 village in Shuiping xiang 水平鄉, Wuping, is in oral literature. A village legend says that to reduce wasting resources they negotiated with the God of the Soil (*Shegong* 社公). He demanded a whole pig and whole sheep, which they "thought too expensive" and refused. Only when he bargained down to everyday family food, which they could afford, did they "make a sacrifice" to Shegong (*Yang B*, 203; *Yang A*, 209). This is in fact the villagers' folk argument for restricting themselves; the goal is by means of belief in folk gods, to live industriously and frugally in the *xiang* and village, to grow in the midst of limited resources, and to transform the limited resources into changeable resources. This example illustrates what Lagerwey's "irreducible localization" is, as well as its function.

On the side of doing all that can be done, the chief solution for the Hakkas to increase their variable resources is to produce more males, and give birth to male children to supplement the labor pool. Their mode of acting is generally symbolic, such as regarding as "men" the dragons and lanterns processing around the periphery of the *xiang*. Dragon and other lanterns please both gods and people. Because *deng* 燈 (lantern) sounds like *ding* 丁 (man) the folk think of lanterns as representing men and call the head of a lineage "lantern head" (*dengzhu* 燈主) (Lagerwey in *Yang B*, 43-44). But if a family reaches more than five generations in one place, the population has surpassed the limit, and the family must be divided, and beginning with the sixth generation, move away to avoid exhausting the resources of that place. This is known in Minxi as "5 together, 6 splits," or "12 together, 13 splits" or "16 together, 17 splits" (*Yang A*, 43, 98; *Yang B*, 209; *Yang C*, 149).

The Minxi ethnographies described here are exceptionally interesting. They use a large quantity of data to prove how Minxi society uses temple festivals, sacrifices, marriage, trade, splitting kin groups, and building earth fortresses, to tie together population, resources, and culture.

Judging from the data, people's calculations that the fixed quantity of *fengshui* of an area of land can nurture five generations of blood relatives is for us an indication that in a rural society's territory the same surname is not equivalent to the same lineage (*jiazu* 家族) but is perhaps the same as the clan group (*qinzu* 親族, *xingzu* 姓族). Therefore, it is not enough to study just lineage culture when looking at *xiang* society. Especially in the Minxi Hakka mountainous areas with their resource shortages, changes in the history of lineage life are normal, and internal variations manifold. The people in this region have lived together for generations in the same *xiang*, and they have had many instances of cooperation between multiple generations of people of the same surname but different families, between people of different surnames, and even with ethnic minorities. In the case of the people from thirteen valley wards sacrificing to Taigong for thirty generations cited above, these thirty generations are not all descended from the same lineage, for there is a history of She and Han cultural blending in this area (*Yang A*, 266). In this sense, *fengshui* is a classificatory concept within the concept of *xiang* society; after combining lineage population, agricultural resources, and local folk culture, it adds a narrower independent term to use in strictly regulating society.

3. Ritual: For Inventing State Authority and Constructing Democratic Village Society

Lineage, after all, is a basic unit in constructing *xiang* society. Another unit is the area where people of the same surname or same *xiang* live. After reading the Minxi volumes we can see that a lineage, the influence of which has grown for about five generations, is often limited to its historical area. So, to increase the prestige of the lineage and solidify its position, the locals construct genealogies. The more they are migrants, the more they make genealogies and invent a long and broad line of descendants (*Yang A*, 6, 87, 120, 167).[8] On the other hand, people with the same surname or from the same *xiang* establish groups and associations and invent kinship forms to construct mutual-aid networks. The two kinds of relationships sometimes help each other, as when lineages and associations become entwined together, but in any case the influence of the two cannot go beyond the *xiang*. *Xiang* society can, to the greatest extent permitted by territorial resources, invoke national authority, arouse lineage and *xiang* [*xiangshe* 鄉社] energies, spark competition, reveal the strengths of each side, and then, relying on folk customs, re-adjust power to divide resources, balance interpersonal relations, soften the contradiction between rich and poor, and arouse local society's energy for developing.

In the pages above, I mentioned function of marching around the *xiang* periphery in order to confirm the "*xiang* borders". Now I want to discuss such processions in more detail.

First the images of the local gods are cleaned, dressed, and decorat-

---

8 Xie Chongguang 謝重光, *Kejia yuanliu xintan* 客家源流新探 (*New Explorations of Hakka Origins and Development*. Fuzhou: Fujian jiaoyu chubanshe, 1995), pp. 14-40.

ed, there is *sūtra*-chanting and a *jiao* sacrifice, and legends are spoken. This is locally called *"kaiguang"* 開光 or *"shangguang"* 上光 (*Yang B*, 7, 218), and serves to reaffirm the high authority of the gods among the local people. At this time some elders, rural gentry, and association heads appear and make contributions.

Next is the procession ritual, during which *xiang* people imitate government actions. They act out stories about deities descending to earth, emperors or historical battles, immortals exorcizing demons, county magistrates judging court cases, bringing peace and prosperity to people and nation, and so on; emotions run high, as they express their similarity with the shared national culture. An ethnographic account of a procession ceremony in Mapu village, Liancheng, describes this vividly:

> Eight point horses lead the circus troupe. Particularly robust horses are chosen for point horses, and the people riding them are specially selected too, generally seven men and one woman. In the old days everyone wore court dress and insignia, dignified and solemn. Others dressed as the "eight immortals" or famous people. All rode horses and carried in their hands or on their backs a ritual object from in front of Taigong's shrine such as a *wansui* 萬歲 tablet, royal seal, portrait, box of *qian* 簽 divination sticks, brush stand, pennant, command box (*lingtong* 令筒), and so on. The *wansui* tablet used to read "Long live his imperial majesty" but now has been changed to "Long live the People's Republic of China." (*Yang B*, 168)

This account also informs us that during this period conflicts that lineages and associations normally cannot resolve dissolve on the spot. The most important themes are the locality's annual needs: setting up a ferry, cattle fairs, temple products, warding off epidemics, disaster relief, seeking children, prayers for blessings, pig raising competitions, scholarships, and similar matters of common interest for the people (*Yang A*, 33, 76-77; *Yang B*, 200, 225; *Yang C*, 62, 70). This is uncoerced voluntary behavior, but it has great mobilizing power because it is founded on the basis of lineage obedience and associations' ties of allegiance, and also can express courageous loyalty to the nation.

Based on local ties, common-interest organizations mostly take the form of mutual aid between villagers or alliances between villages. Most rest on oral contracts, but because oral commitments are honored they have great power to consolidate rural society. This reflects the Hakkas' ardent spirit of enterprise, a kind of internally-chosen traditional democratic control. The annual procession around the bounderies also controls and encourages the implementation of this village democratic systems, another function of ritual.

4. Internal Consumption in Rural Society: Traditional Economic Views

The three Minxi volumes also discuss economic aspects of that society, especially production quantities. To reflect rural society's internal economic life, the authors of the series gathered various economic data on agriculture, boat transport, fishing, sericulture, forestry, and paper making. In this discussion, I was most interested in people's customs regarding expenditures, which can be divided into four categories.

1) Expenses for ancestral rites, mostly placed in land called "*zheng chang tian*" 蒸嘗田 or "*ji tian*" 祭田 (ritual fields). In the mountainous regions of western and northern Fujian such fields are considerable, amounting, according to a 1950 survey by the Fujian Peasants Association, to over 50 percent of total agricultural land and in some areas as much as 60 percent. In the richer coastal areas, however, ritual land comprises only 20 to 30 percent (*Yang A*, p. 9), which shows that the poorer natural resources are the more importance people attach to ancestral rituals. This item of expense amounts to an expropriation of excess family wealth to be used for common lineage purposes.

2) Expenses for the rural community's collective seasonal rituals like temple fairs, Buddhist festivals or *jiao* activities. According to estimates in the report on rotating sacrifices to Taigong in thirteen upriver settlements, "when they occur, in one year peasant households basically spend all they have saved over ten to twenty years. Each household spends at least 1000 yuan, and in a whole settlement of 100 or 200 families the total expended is 100,000 or 200,000 yuan. Such enormous extravagance leaves one speechless with astonishment" (*Yang A*, p. 259).

3) Expenses for communal village construction, such as roads and bridges. These are often organized by families coming together. Some villagers are "always willing to participate" and "happy to help" if they have any money (*Yang A*, pp. 109, 188); they use up their hard-earned savings on good works for others.

4) Basic living expenses. In a very interesting item about boat transport, Wubei 武北 raft workers "form village-based work gangs, whose heads contract work for them without taking a commission. Between them are a sense of duty, sympathy, helpfulness, and no basic conflicts" (*Yang C*, 506). In Minxi's Yongding 永定 area, the history of people's lives is typically expressed in the history of building "earth towers (fortified villages)." Putting one up requires expending an average year's savings of a whole family, or two brothers' families, or a lineage, but from a small parcel of land one can acquire a large living space and save water, wood, and fuel, and so solve rather effectively the problems of people, earth, and capital" (*Yang A*, 40-41), and also increase the traditional cultural atmosphere.

These four kinds of expenses show that the economic views of Minxi Hakkas emphasize internal cohesion and villagers' common interests.

While we may not esteem the technical capabilities of Chinese peasants, we must not underestimate their ability to form human ties with which to resist poverty. Building a society of human feeling (*renqing* 人情) became a spiritual pillar of the Chinese peasantry for just this reason. This spirit is particularly clear in the Minxi Hakkas, with their decidedly meager natural endowment. The data cited above make clear they particularly value feelings of cooperation, and have created romantic illusions of equal division of resources and a life style of frugally conserving them. They ward off the crisis of diminishing resources by means of pious ties between people and gods and between people and people, and the internal costs of what Philip Huang calls "peasant self-exploitation" they hold to a minimum with multifarious folk customs. Because of this, in Minxi Hakka society ideas of regulating the behavior of those who use resources, opposing the waste of resources, and advocating patience and restraint constitute a kind of motivating energy. They tend toward balance and coexistence with fixed natural resources. Nourished precisely by these two kinds of attitudes to resources, the Hakkas became a people with "a special spirit, rich in dynamism and extremely energetic and capable."[9] The pressure of what Philip Huang calls the "economic involution" of Chinese peasant society is alleviated in this south Chinese rural culture featuring tight natural resources but developed human feelings.

From fieldwork to ethnological writing, the "Traditional Hakka Society Series" volumes on Minxi are full of breakthroughs. In advancing the study of "*xiang*" society, in analyzing the combined functions of population, resources, and culture in controlling people's ideas and behavior, in uncovering two kinds of Chinese folk ideas about resources, and in deepening research on the motive power underlying the growth of Chinese rural society, these achievements of these volumes are inspiring.

But the *xiang* can not be isolated from the shared Chinese national culture or subcultures. The tie between *xiang* society and subcultures is particularly close. This point needs to be carefully considered. The "*xiang*" in Minxi are not the same size, but vary with the richness or poverty of natural resources; under these conditions the *xiang* has especially rich connections with subcultures. The Minxi series books in several places refer to Hakkas adding to genealogies, passing down folk-tales of ancestors coming from the central plain (Yellow River basin). This shows that people from these *xiang* have a persistent notion of relationship with the distant North China subculture. This notion is also revealed in these volumes in the words "*lang*" 郎 and "*xiexi*" 寫戲 they use in their myths and boundary-circling rites, which are exactly the same expressions found in North China today.[10] We cannot exclude the possibility of elements of coincidence here, but at least we can say that when a local society's internal resources are unevenly distributed, this can create stronger popular hopes for democracy and equality in the spiritual world. People also find ways to satisfy these hopes by even more happily reciting subculture folktales about bad fortune turning to good or suddenly becoming rich. Lagerwey is conscious of this and says there really exists a "recurrent theme" which wanders between this

---

9 Luo Xianglin, *Kejia yanjiu daolun*.

10 See Dong Xiaoping, *Xiangcun xiqu biaoyan yu Zhongguo nongmin shehui* 鄉村戲曲表演與中
   國農民社會(*Village dramatic performance and Chinese peasant society*. Beijing: Beijing
   Normal University Press, forthcoming).

local society and other subcultures. This is exactly parallel to what I and Professor David Arkush have found in North China in recent years.

I think this is a characteristic of Chinese rural society. The cultures of small local societies and subcultures echo each other. They can build a strong mass opinion calling on the many to aid the few. Areas rich in food help poorer ones, people of high social status lend a hand to the lowly, democratic redistribution is mobilized inside folk society, urging that everyone have a share and everyone be equal. Not too far from Hakka realities, during the enormous changes in modern Chinese society since the Opium War, were not the peasant troops who first shouted "equal land" and "cooperation is the key," two slogans about resources, precisely the army of the Taiping uprising, which was primarily Hakka? When I said before that it was not altogether appropriate for Chinese and Western scholars in the past to use sweeping terms like "state" and "society" to generalize on the basis of one village, what I meant was this: they ignored a middle level, and it is this middle level which is a special feature of Chinese rural society. It explains how in thousands of Chinese rural small societies, under historical conditions of sharp competition for resources which comes from too many people on too little land, Chinese peasants, relying on folk resources, nonetheless increase in self-confidence, love and guardianship of their localities, qualities which continue to exist and develop generation after generation.

Unfortunately, researchers have still not dug up enough information about this. The methodology used in these volumes of having local people write about local cultures is certainly good, and one admires the two collaborators for finding so many old Hakkas who can write, but I suspect even more villagers are unable to write or know few too characters, and depend on mouth and ear to pass on and preserve folk culture. It cannot but be regretted that very little material in these volumes comes directly from them. They have surely been a major force in the historical processes connecting rural society with subcultures. They know most about the value of each inch of land, the capacity of each ounce of human feeling, and the magical effect of each item of folk culture. If their data could be used to supplement the present Minxi ethnographies, I believe it would better reveal the connections between local small society and subcultures, and would perfect the researchers' mid-level study of rural society. Otherwise, I worry that the dialogue which has now been established about the Hakka *xiang* and the motive power of Chinese rural society is in danger of lacking an important level of information.

(Translated by R. David Arkush, University of Iowa)

20

LOCAL RELIGION IN SOUTHERN JIANGXI PROVINCE:

A REVIEW OF THE GANNAN VOLUMES IN LAGERWEY'S TRADITIONAL HAKKA SOCIETY SERIES[1]

Tam Wai-lun

Both volumes 3 and 7 of John Lagerwey's Traditional Hakka Society series are collections of ethnographic essays on temple festivals, lineages and customs in southern Jiangxi (Gannan 贛南). To these two volumes, one should add three more essays in Volume 1 of the same series, which are also about the Gannan area.[2] The overall emphasis of

---

1 The Gannan volumes of Lagerwey's series are Volume 3: Luo Yong 羅勇 and John Lagerwey eds., *Gannan diqu di miaohui yu zongzu* 贛南地區的廟會與宗教(*Temple Festivals & Lineages in Gannan*. Hong Kong: International Hakka Studies Association, Overseas Chinese Archives & École Française d'Extr ême-orient, 1997); Volume 7: Luo Yong and Lin Xiaoping 林曉平, eds., *Gannan miaohui yu minsu* 贛南廟會與民俗(*Temple Festivals and Customs in Gannan*. Hong Kong: International Hakka Studies Association, Overseas Chinese Archives & École Française d'Extrême-orient, 1998.) Hereafter, we will refer to Lagerwey's series by volume number only.

2 See the three essays on the township of Luokou 洛口 in Ningdu 寧都 county by 1) Lin Xiaoping, "Gannan Ningdu xian Luokou xiang Nanling cun di Lushi yuanliu yu huolong jie"贛南寧都縣洛口鄉南嶺村的盧氏源流與火龍節, 2) Luo Yong, "Gannan Ningdu xian Luokou xiang Luokou cun di Zhugong miaohui,"贛南寧都縣洛口鄉洛口村的"朱公廟會," and 3) Liu Jingfeng 劉勁峰, "Gannan Ningdu xian Luokou xiang Guxia cun di minsu wenhua"贛南寧都縣洛口鄉古夏村的民俗文化, collected in vol.1 of Lagerwey's series, pp. 223-285.

all these essays is on local religious traditions: more than two third of the essays are about temple festivals. The title the series notwithstanding, these volumes and essays can also be used as a good source for the study of Chinese local religion. Lagerwey's series is the result of a project entitled Structure and Dynamics of Chinese Rural Society, funded by the Chiang Ching-kuo 蔣經國 Foundation. This project covers three provinces in South China: Fujian, Guangdong and Jiangxi. As in the other volumes in the series, the objective of Volumes 3 and 7 is to preserve local cultural traditions by recording them in as much detail as possible. These traditions are disappearing and now survive mainly in the memories of the old. Those memories are the most important source of information collected in the series.

I. Methodological Issues

To understand more about the nature of the two volumes under review, we have to go into details about how the essays collected in the two volumes were written. The preface in volume of the series provides us with some clues.[3] Lagerwey, the general editor of the series, first gave instructions and on-site training to a team of academics on how to conduct fieldwork and produce ethnographic reports in the area. In the case of Gannan, the team was made up of professors from the Department of History in Gannan Normal University.[4] At the same time, Lagerwey in cooperation with his Chinese collaborators, actively sought the participation of retired teachers and government cadres from the offices of cultural affairs, the local monograph, and the political consultative committee. These local participants were given either on-site training or oral instructions and continuous guidance from the academic collaborators of Lagerwey, on producing ethnographic reports about their areas. They usually chose to write about their own native areas where they them-

---

3 See also Lagerwey's prefixs in Fang Xuejia 房學嘉, ed, *Meizhou diqu de miaohui yu zongzu* 梅州地區的廟會與宗族 (*Temple Festivals and Lineages in Meizhou*. Traditional Hakka Society Series, Volume 1. Hong Kong: International Hakka Studies Association, 1996), pp. 1-14.

4 They are professors Luo Yong and Lin Xiaoping, whose essays are collected both in Volumes 1 and 7 of Lagerwey's Traditional Hakka Society Series.

selves had grown up and had plenty of informants to interview. These local authors are the keys to the whole operation. A majority of the essays collected in Lagerwey's series come from these amateur local ethnographers. The question of the quality and reliability of the essays produced by them has been addressed in Lagerwey's introduction to Volume 5 of his series.[5] Besides suggesting that a native son can do a better job than a participant observer, Lagerwey raises one convincing point to help us to value these amateur products. Chinese rural society is now undergoing rapid changes that are being further speeded up by the *Ben xiaokang* 奔小康 (rush to low-level prosperity) movement. This fairly recent government initiative aims at replacing traditional village buildings with multi-floor concrete houses. Even more serious than the change in the appearance of rural China is the aging of informants. A main source of information for the reconstruction of traditional rural China comes from interviews with old people in towns and villages who can still remember how local traditions were practiced before the destructive years of the cultural revolution (1966-1976). Most of these people are now in their 70's. When they die, many local traditions will die with them. In other words, what is at stake here is the rescue of whatever information is still available. By making use of this added pool of non-academic local ethnographers, in the case of Gannan, twenty-four people altogether, Lagerwey was able to cover a large area in a relatively short period of time.

Another issue is the way in which these essays by local ethnographers were written. As stated clearly in the introduction, their tasks were simply to describe the most important temple festivals in their county and village (Volume 3, p. 19). The result is a collection of raw data concerning local traditions. The nature of the essays produced resembles that of a source book, as the main purpose of the essays in these volumes is not to argue a case but simply to record painstakingly the local traditions. If the reader is unfamiliar with the area, he or she will be overwhelmed by the variety and diversity of the raw data recorded in these volumes. To appreciate and understand the significance of the data recorded, as well as to see the patterns they reveal, the reader definitely has to rely heavily on the introduction written by Lagerwey himself

---

5 Vol. 5 of Lagerwey's series, 1997, pp. 1-7.

in the beginning of each volume. Perhaps the advantage in having the raw material of the essays is that one can appreciate oneself the richness and vitality of local culture in Gannan.

II. The Cult of Xu Zhenjun

As indicated in the introduction to each volume, among the diversity and variety of the data presented, some patterns can be detected. For instance, essays in Volume 3 and 7 show that the cult of Xu Zhenjun 許眞君 (239-374 C.E.) to be a dominant cult in Gannan. There are five detailed reports on the worship of Xu, covering the area of western (Shangyou 上猶, Chongyi 崇義), southwest (Xinfeng 信豐), eastern (Ruijin 瑞金) and central (Yudu 于都) Gannan. References to temples dedicated to Xu are also found in northeast (Ningdu) and southern (Anyuan 安遠) Gannan. According to the report on Yudu, pilgrimage groups worshipping Xu Zhenjun in Yudu came from as far away as the north (Xingguo 興國) and northeast (Shicheng 石城 and Ningdu) of Gannan. The author of the report on Xinfeng states that there are temples to Xu Zhenjun in almost every village and township (vol. 7, p. 28). In the report on Ruijin, we are told that the temple festival of Xu Zhenjun in that area was basically sponsored by the merchant guild from Fengcheng 豐城 in central Jiangxi, indicating that worship of Xu is also carried out beyond Gannan area. The cult of Xu Zhenjun is clearly one of the most popular in Jiangxi Province.

Li Feng-mao's 李豐楙 study of Xu Zhenjun shows that his cult started in Xishan 西山 (near Nanchang 南昌) as Jingming 淨明 Taoism — a Taoist sect emphasizing filial piety.[6] The cult later incorporated the myth of Xu defeating a dragon, and Xu became a water deity in the Tang dynasty. Although there are various versions of Xu's myth collected in Volumes 3 and 7, the basic thrust is that Xu learned magic on Maoshan or Lüshan in order to defeat a dragon that had caused floods in Jiangxi. The dragon was transformed from his friend who came from

6 See Li Feng-mao, *Xu Xun yu Sa Shoujian: Deng Zhimo daojiao xiaoshuo yanjiu* 許遜與薩守堅：鄧志謨道教小說研究 (*Xu Xun and Sa Shoujian: A Study of the Taoist Novels of Deng Zhimo*. Taipei: Xuesheng shuju, 1997), p. 11.

Guangdong Province. Xu's temple is usually situated in marketplaces (Xinfeng, Shangyou and Chongyi), where Xu supports the federating function of local gods. In Xu's temple at Xingcun 星村 Market in Xinfeng, for instance, four dominant lineages take turns organizing the temple festivals for Xu Zhenjun. According to the report on Xinfeng, the organizing of Xu Zhenjun's temple festivals, which bring all the lineages together, helped to solve a lineage feud in the early 19th century which arose because of an outbreak of drought (Vol. 7, p. 28).

III. Unifying Function of Local Religion

There are numerous examples in Lagerwey's series of lineage alliances built around joint worship of local gods. In the case of Gannan, the temple festival for Xu Zhenjun in Shizao 石灶 village of Yudu, which lasts for twelve days, is co-organized by representatives from nine lineages. Another example is the cult of the Three Grandpas found in Guyan 固院 Village of Zishan 梓山 township in Yudu county. The village consists of fifteen houses (*wuchang* 屋場) each of which is inhabited by members of the same lineage. There are altogether eight different lineages because the Zeng 曾 lineage occupies seven of the fifteen *wuchang* while the Li 李 lineage occupies two. The Three Grandpas or *sangong* 三公 are Zhanggong 張公, Gaogong 高公 and Laigong 賴公. Little is known about Gaogong and Laigong but many stories are circulated about Zhanggong. He was a Taoist trained on Mt. Qi 祁山. There are stories of his magic warfare (*doufa* 鬥法) with another local Taoist named Han Yigong 韓一公. Zhang won the sympathy and approval of the old mother of Mt. Qi, a divine instructress, by drinking the water used to wash her wounded leg. She eventually taught Zhang how to become an immortal.

The temple festival for the Three Grandpas takes place in the fifth month and lasts for half a month. The fifteen *wuchang* take turns receiving the gods in sedan chairs in their lineage halls, where they stay for one night. By rotation each year a different *wuchang* is first to receive the gods. The date on which the gods arrive is so important that the traditional Dragon Boat festival (*Duanwu* 端午) will be celebrated at the same time. This means that the festival of each *wuchang* is different and changes every year because of the system of rotation.

The most exciting part of the temple festival of the Three Grandpas is the ritual that takes place right before the gods are passed on to the neighbours. It is called *lian pusa* 煉菩薩 (refining the gods or practising with the gods) or *zaying* 紮營 (to set up a base camp). Five flags with different colors are set up in the four directions. The sedan chairs on which the gods are seated are carried by youths who zigzag between the flags. The youths wear no upper clothing so as to show off their muscles. They only hold one handle of the sedan chair in order to allow maximum shaking. Running ahead of them is another youth carrying a command flag. Should he not run fast enough, the youths carrying the sedan chairs will run into him. The running is accompanied by loud shouting, which shows the strength and power of the gods and the people carrying them. It is very interesting to read about this ritual in the context of the many conflicts between the *wuchang*, especially between the two biggest lineages, Zheng and Li.[7] The noise and display of strength in the ritual can be understood as the channelling and symbolizing of the conflicts and clashes between neighboring lineages.

Temple festivals act as the social glue of an area by bringing people together regularly.[8] Like military exercises of modern countries, the purpose of the parade of gods, a major activity of temple festivals in all areas, is to show to neighbors the power of both the gods and the people (represented by the youths carrying the gods). The power is shown through the muscles of the youths and the noise created by regular shouting and beating of drums.[9] Potential conflicts and violence are

---

7   The author mentions that there were many conflicts between the Zheng and the Li, and he records an incident that happened in the forties: the Zheng family had built a grain-drying area that the Li family believed destroyed the geomancy of their home. Fighting was about to develop but was stopped by negotiations initiated by a Peking University graduate of the Li family. (Vol. 3, p. 106.)

8   For the role of religion in China as an underlying structuring framework for communal organization, see also Kenneth Dean, *Taoist Ritual and Popular Cults of South-East China* (Princeton: Princeton University Press, 1995), p. 175.

9   See also the essay on the Dong 董 family in Fenggang 鳳岡 town of Nankang 南康 city. We are told in this essay that the other big lineages always took advantage of a branch of the Dong lineage that lived in Tankou 潭口 Jiangba 江壩 because of their small number. To solve the problem, one year, the Dongs organized a big procession of dragon lanterns. The noise of the drums

channelled and sublimated through the violent procession of gods, and sometimes through blood sacrifice. Demonstration of the unifying function of local religion and local gods as the foci of local identity is one of the major contributions of the ethnographic essays collected in Lagerwey's series.[10]

IV. Pilgrimage

As mentioned above, pilgrimage groups from five counties (Ningdu, Shicheng, Ruijin, Xingguo and Yudu) in the form of flowery assemblies (*huahui* 花會) come to participate in the temple festival of Xu Zhenjun in Shizao village of Yudu county. Each pilgrimage starts in the home village, and the faithful bring along a statue of Xu Zhenjun in a box called *huaxiang* 花箱. Besides lanterns, drums, and flags, each assembly will bring along one to three parasols with colourful tassels for their procession to the temple. The tassels are for the expression of the gratitude of the faithful to Xu Zhenjun for fulfilling their wishes. Each assembly, upon arriving at the temple, carries out group worship. A Taoist is invited to present a memorial to Xu Zhenjun that includes the names of all the assembly members. Representatives are sent to the temple to light big candles that will burn for three days. Meats may not be sold in the market during the festival. Fruits sold near the temple, however, are considered immortals fruits, and toys are thought to possess the power of driving away evil. These beliefs produce enormous commercial activities around the temple. This report on the worship of Xu Zhenjun in Shizao is an important piece of information regarding pilgrimage activities in South China.[11]

---

was so loud that it reached the sky. After that no one dared to take advantage of the Dong family in Tankou again. Vol. 3, pp. 160-161.

10 See Lagerwey's discussion in Vol. 1, p. 5; Vol. 4, p. 18 and Vol. 5, p. 24. Cf. John Brim, "Village Alliance Temples in Hong Kong," in Arthur P. Wolf, ed., *Religion and Ritual in Chinese Society* (Stanford: Stanford University Press, 1974), pp. 93-103.

11 For a study of pilgrimage in China, see Susan Naquin and Yü Chün-fang eds., *Pilgrims and Sacred Sites in China* (Berkeley: University of California Press, 1992).

V. Spirit Writing

The most striking variation of the Xu Zhenjun cult in Gannan is found in the Shangyou county seat, where the worship of Xu is related to spirit writing. Xu is described as a deity of spirit-writing (*jixian* 乩仙). Spirit-writing became popular in the second half of the 19th century as a movement to reform the morality of society by means of public preaching of morality books produced by spirit-writing.[12] There are four reports about spirit-writing in Volume 7, covering the areas of western and central Gannan (Chongyi, Shangyou, Xinfeng and Yudu). The report on Ganzhou 贛州 tells us that spirit-writing became popular in the middle of the Qing dynasty (1644-1912) (Vol. 7, p. 126). According to the same report, spirit-writing in Ganzhou was related to a smallpox goddess called Xianniang 仙娘. The practice declined after 1949 but came back in the 1990s. That is to say, spirit-writing is still practised nowadays in Ganzhou. According to the report on Xinfeng, spirit-writing in this area was an unorganized divinatory practice that took place during the Mid-autum festival, when the gods all came out to enjoy the full moon (Vol. 7, p. 21). Spirit-writing in the Shangbao 上堡 market-place of Chongyi County was practised in a highly organized temple established in 1918 with Wenchang 文昌, Fuyou 孚佑 and Huangdi 黃帝 as main deities. Every four years, there was a temple festival. The temple was instrumental in saving the people of the area during an epidemic initiated by Xu Zhenjun, who wished to punish those who had offered him meat instead of vegetarian food. The temple made a successful petition to heaven to drive away the spirits of pestilence (*wenshen* 瘟神). The temple, which had a membership of 120, was burnt down in 1928 by the government.

---

12 See David K. Jordan and Daniel L. Overmyer, *The Flying Phoenix: Aspects of Chinese Sectarianism in Taiwan* (Princeton: Princeton University Press, 1986).

VI. City Gods and Earth Gods

Other frequently mentioned deities in the Gannan volumes are Chenghuang 城煌 (the city god) and Shegong 社公 (the earth god). There are four reports on Chenghuang, two from the south (Dingnan 定南, Anyuan 安遠), one from the northeast (Shicheng), and one from central (Yudu) Gannan. Almost all of them had elaborate temple festivals in which the image of Chenghuang was taken out on processions. Only the report on Yudu does not mention a temple festival for Chenghuang. Conceived as the other-world equivalent of the administrator of this world, Chenghuang was in charge of all the spirits of the local area.[13] Chenghuang was usually worshipped side by side with other local deities.

The Gongwang 公王 (earth gods) cult central in the Hakka area of Minxi and Yuedong 粵東 is absent in Gannan. Earth gods in Gannan are known as Shegong. There are also four reports about Shegong: one from Shicheng and Ningdu (northeast), one from Shangyou (west) and one from Xinfeng (Southwest). Reports from both Ningdu and Xinfeng tell the story of how the image of Shegong was later replaced either by a brick or a tablet. As noted by Lagerwey, the use of tablets as opposed to statues to represent the earth god in Gannan requires further research (Vol. 7, introduction, p. 37). Shegong seem to play a relatively small role in the life of villagers: They help recover lost items, bless small children before they starts school, and heal some illnesses.

VII. Guanyin and Buddhism

Many of the reports in Lagerwey's series give more information about the Taoist dimension of local religion than the Buddhist dimension. The report on Yingqian 營前 in Shangyou county, however, points out that many families have a statue of Guanyin 觀音 in their houses (Vol. 7, p. 289). Guanyin is also found in many local temples such as the temple

---

13 See David Johnson, "The City God Cults of Tang and Song China", *HJAS*, 45.2(1985): 428-431.

of Xu Zhenjun in Xincun market of Xinfeng County. According to the report on Dingnan County, in 1948 more than fifty-six nunneries were dedicated to Guanyin. There were so many children adopted out to Guanyin that Guanyin was locally referred to as *Qiai* 契娭 (adoption). Although there are three temple festivals for Guanyin, most temples do not organize parades. The major activity of the temple festival consists of presenting a memorial to gods (*shangbiao* 上表) and scripture reciting by nuns, followed by a vegetarian meal. Because of its relatively simple program, people of Dingnan describe anything fake by saying even the temple festival for Guanyin is not as fake. The only temple that organizes a parade for Guanyin is the Sanshui 三水 temple in Yuezi Gang 月子崗 Market. After the recitation of scripture, Taoists are invited to perform charcoal-walking and river lamp release. The worship of Guanyin in Dingnan explains to us the Taoist orientation of popular religion in China. A Taoist provides the military (*wu* 武) part of the ritual — the charcoal-walking or the climbing of sword ladders — which are both exciting and entertaining. When a Taoist has not been invited to supplement the civil (*wen* 文) ritual of Buddhism, a Buddhist monk from a temple in town will do somersaults in addition to prostration and scripture reciting, as in the case of the Hua feng xian an 華峰仙庵 at Shangbao 上堡 in Chongyi county. According to the report on Chongyi, the acrobatics performed by the monk are to help the burning of maple branches — a ritual to show the power of the gods. At the same time, it also adds entertaining elements to a solemn religious ritual.

VIII.Women and Religion

The report on Shicheng shows that Buddhism flourished in both Shicheng and its adjacent county of Ninghua 寧化 in Fujian Province. According to this report, not only was there a Buddhist temple every five or ten miles in Shicheng, but all women after they turned fifty would start their *nianfo* 唸佛 (Buddha s name recitation) practices. These practices required an elaborate ritual of initiation (*dianfo* 點佛) in which either Buddhist monks or nuns or Taoists were to be invited to perform rites of repentance (*baichan* 拜懺). Every year all the initiated women would join together for *nianfo* practice. Every three years, they would gather and invite a Taoist to perform a ritual in which their records of *nianfo* practice would be burnt. After performing six such rituals, a woman was eligible for a *dianfo* ritual. This ritual required a Taoist or Zhaigong 齋公 to perform rites of repentance for five to seven days, ending with a *Fang yankou* 放焰口 ritual. Only one *dianfo* ritual was required in a lifetime (Vol. 3, p. 147). This short report on the practice of Buddhism on the village level is precious. Not only does it give us information about a popular religious practice which is clearly Buddhist in orientation, in contrast to the Taoist emphasis of most essays in the series, it also provides a glimpse of the religious life of women in Chinese villages, an aspect which is basically lacking in the series.[14]

IX. Local Deities: Kangwang, Handi and Xiangyu

If blood sacrifice is a defining feature of popular religion in China,[15] the worship of Kangwang 康王 in Ganzhou exemplifies this aspect of popular religious practice. Kangwang has two brothers. The three of them are known as the three Kangwangs but only the third is carried out in a parade.[16] Two swordsmen, who are responsible for the killing of ducks offered by the faithful and the pouring of blood on the god, accompany Kangwang. The porters carrying his sedan chair have to stop frequently at ponds to bathe the god because of the abundance of the blood offerings.

---

14 Lagerwey is aware of this masculine bias in the essays of his series; see his introduction to Vol. 5 of the series, p. 7, where he suggests that the only solution to this problem would be for more women to do fieldwork.

15 See Terry F. Kleeman, "Licentious Cults and Bloody Victuals: Sacrifice, Reciprocity and Violence in Traditional China," *Asia Minor*, Third Series, VII.1(1994): 185-211.

16 Triads of gods are common in Gannan. Other examples are: the Sanxian 三仙 (Liang 梁, Xiao 蕭, Yen 顏) in Shangbao, Chongyi county(Vol. 7, p. 367), and the Sandai zhenjen 三大眞人 (Zhang 張, Ge 葛, Xu 許) in Shangyou county (Vol. 7, p. 303), both in western Gannan; the San xiantai 三仙太 (Ling xiao 凌霄, Bixiao 碧霄, Qiongxiao 瓊霄) in Ruijin county of eastern Gannan (Vol. 7, p. 250), also mentioned in Ganzhou (Vol. 7, p. 117); the San nainiang 三奶娘 (Chen 陳, Lin 林, Li 李) in Xingguo of northern Gannan (Vol. 7, p. 142); the Sangong (Zhang, Gao, Lai) in Yudu of central Gannan (Vol. 3, p. 97); and the three *Fenghou*, also three brothers, in Ruijin of eastern Gannan (Vol. 3, p. 57).

Other interesting local deities worshipped in Gannan area are the historical figures Handi 漢帝, Liu Bang 劉備 (R. 206-193 B.C.E.), the founder of the Han dynasty, and Xiang Yu 項羽, the competitor of Handi and the founder of Chu 楚, better known as the hegemon of Chu (Chu Bahuang 楚霸王). The worship of both Handi and Xiang Yu is mostly found in northeast Gannan (Shicheng and Ningdu). The grave for Handi is said to be in Ningdu, where there was an important local Liu lineage. In Qiuxi 秋溪 of Shicheng, Handi was worshipped together with another famous local deity, Huaguang 華光, by the local Lai lineage. During the temple festival of Handi, when his statue and that of Huaguang were carried out on a parade, Handi and Huaguang had first to go pay homage to Xiang Yu. This is because it was Liu Bang had attacked Xiang Yu, from whom he had to beg forgiveness. As for Huaguang, he is the patron of the Lai lineage, and the Lai took the land of Qiuxi from earlier inhabitants. Hence the Lai, represented by Huaguang, have to pay homage to the local deity of Qiuxi, Xiang Yu.

X. Ancestor Gods

A striking report about ancestor worship is found in the report on the Xiao 蕭 lineage of Shahekou 沙河口 in Ganzhou. The members of the Xiao lineage were fishermen along the Gan river. They lived on boats in Gan, Xinfeng, and Wan'an 萬安 counties. On every fifteenth day of the first lunar month, all Xiao family members would gather at their lineage hall at Shahekou in Ganzhou City for a two-day ancestor worship ritual. There are four special features of the Xiao's ancestor worship: 1) they made statues of their ancestors and worshipped them together with Buddhist and Taoist deities. Eleven ancestors were chosen along with seven other deities to form a group of eighteen. 2) Non-family members also worshipped their ancestors as gods. 3) Ancestors would possess designated descendants who acted as their mediums or *fama* 發馬. 4) Ancestors demanded blood sacrifice. The author is, therefore, correct in describing the ancestors of the Xiao family as ancestor gods (*laozu shenming* 老祖神明). As noted by Lagerwey, the classic distinction made by Wolf is blurred here.[17]

XI. Concluding Remarks

We have shown in this review how the Gannan volumes may be used as a source for the study of local religion in China. Essays collected in these volumes deepen our understanding not only of local cultures in China but also of religion and Chinese society at large. As such, they are a good resource for teaching. Examples are the detailed reports on the Taoist *Jiao* 醮 rituals as well as reports on funeral and marriage practices.[18] A helpful sourcebook on Chinese popular religion could be created from Lagerwey's series, although a thorough analysis of the information presented in the volumes is not found in the book themselves, and is very much needed.

Bibliography

Brim, John. 1974. "Village Alliance Temples in Hong Kong," in Authur P. Wolf, ed., *Religion and Ritual in Chinese Society*. Stanford: Stanford University Press.

Dean, Kenneth. 1995. *Taoist Ritual and Popular Cults of Southeast China*. Princeton: Princeton University Press.

Li, Feng-mao. 1997. *Xu Xun yu Sa Shoujian: Deng Zhimo Daojiao xiaoshuo yanjiu*. Taipei: Xuesheng shuju.

Johnson, David. 1985. "The City God Cults of Tang and Song China," in *Harvard Journal of Asiatic Studies,* 45.2: 428-431.

Jordan, David K. & Overmyer, Daniel L. 1986 *The Flying Phoenix: Aspects of Chinese Sectarianism in Taiwan*. Princeton: Princeton University Press.

---

17 See Arthur P. Wolf, "Gods, Ghosts, and Ancestors," in Arthur P. Wolf, ed., *Religion and Ritual in Chinese Society*, pp. 131-182.

18 See, for instance, the essays Popular Religion in Yingqian Shangyou by Zhang Shengjun 張升俊 and Zhang Shenghong 張聲宏, where they give a detailed description of a Taoist *jiao* ritual (vol. 7, pp. 301-308), and their essay on Marriage and Funeral Customs in Shangyou collected in the same volume, pp. 347-365.

Kleeman, Terry F. 1994. "Licentious Cults and Bloody Victuals: Sacrifice, Reciprocity and Violence in Traditional China," in *Asia Minor,* VII.1 (Third Series): 185-211.

Naquin, Susan & Yü, Chün-fang. 1992. *Pilgrims and Sacred Sites in China.* Berkeley: University of California Press.